LEE'S CHIEF OF ARTILLERY:
WILLIAM NELSON PENDLETON

By Thomas Rittenburg

Also by the author: *At the Mercy of Passion and Madness: The Secession Crisis in Rockbridge County, Virginia* (originally published as *Compelled to Fight*); and *The Brilliance of a Meteor: The Life and Times of Robert M. T. Hunter of Virginia.*

Dedicated to my children Andrew, Lauren, and Jennifer

"It may be suggested that a sympathetic note in the scale of sentiment is struck by the heroes of defeat."

Jennings C. Wise

Gen. W. N. Pendleton 1864

TABLE OF CONTENTS

PREFACE

While researching and writing this book I used as my computer screen picture a photograph of General Pendleton taken in late 1864. Many of his contemporaries thought that William Nelson Pendleton strongly resembled his good friend and fellow eastern Virginia scion Robert E. Lee. Consequently, most books display the photograph of Pendleton in which he most resembles Lee. But my favorite photograph reveals a different Pendleton, one who does not look like his famous chief. It is a Pendleton grieving for the death of his only son in battle, angry at the situation in which he and the South find themselves, but still haughty and proud. His icy blue eyes stare back at you full of life and reflective of experience. For me this is the true Pendleton.

Pendleton's reputation has suffered at the hands of historians. The only previous biography of Pendleton was written by his devoted daughter Susan Pendleton Lee late in the 19th Century. Since then historians have enjoyed attacking his reputation as a cleric and as a military officer, usually by ignoring the command structure or how Civil War field artillery operated. Pendleton certainly opened the door for criticism with his pompous attitudes, needlessly verbose reports, preaching, and lack of independent tactical initiative. Each recent history relies on the errors made by its predecessors in their assessment of Pendleton.

It is time for a fresh appraisal of William Nelson Pendleton, one taking into consideration his unheralded contributions as well as his flaws and limitations. It is forgotten that he created the army field artillery organization, perfected it through multiple reorganizations, and ensured it was adequately supplied with equipment, shells, and provender. Until the day of the surrender at Appomattox Pendleton provided General Robert E. Lee with an equipped and effective fighting force. He also provided an extra set of eyes and ears for Lee in reconnaissance and preparing battlefield positions while at the same time administering a corps of artillery larger than most divisions. Although many ridiculed his preaching, many others found solace and comfort in his worship services. Finally, but not unimportantly, he provided the ever more self-isolating Lee with companionship. As a scholar he authored a book advanced for its time urging the religious to accept geologic science.

Pendleton warmly praised those who were critical of him and held no grudges against those he felt merited promotion. He understood his own limitations and recommended over time that he hold no tactical command. It is a shame he never left a memoir behind for Pendleton acknowledged his strengths and weaknesses, and recognized his own essential human qualities. Unlike many of his contemporaries Pendleton would not trumpet everything he achieved. In fact, Pendleton left a solid legacy as an educator, priest, soldier, and author. Not only was he the heart and soul of the field artillery of the Army of Northern Virginia, he alone kept it well organized, equipped, and fed until the end of the war. It is time we look back at his life with a new assessment of his challenges, flaws, and accomplishments.

It should be noted that this book is not a history of the evils of slavery, the rights of secession, the Army of Northern Virginia, or the Civil War. Readers interested in those topics must look elsewhere.

I wish to thank my former law partner Lance Selfridge, Esq. for his assistance in reading and editing portions of the book. I also wish to thank my old friend and classmate from East Cleveland, Ohio; novelist, songwriter, and singer Gair Linhart, who was of great assistance in suggesting revisions clarifying the language of the text. Finally, and as always, I thank my wife Mary Ann for her patience and tolerance for my love of the Civil War period.

Thomas Rittenburg
Genoa, Nevada
February 24, 2023

Boteler's Ford 1862

SHEPHERDSTOWN, SEPTEMBER 19, 1862

[SHEPHERDSTOWN, VIRGINIA]

Cast thy burden upon the Lord and he shall sustain thee: he shall never suffer the righteous to be moved.

Psalms 55:22, King James Version

He worked through the night, just as he had the night before. All night long and into the early morning hours the Army of Northern Virginia re-crossed the Potomac River under the light of torches and bonfires. Robert E. Lee and his weakened army moved south to safety in Virginia after an overnight departure from the bloody battlefield along Antietam Creek at Sharpsburg, Maryland. As the sun rose the morning mist still hovered above the river. The tail end of the retreating army, consisting of some cavalry, a field artillery battery, and wounded soldiers, completed the crossing. In the early dawn others still close to the ford were waking up and preparing to march, leaving the more seriously wounded or apathetic in their wake.

By mid-morning he was alarmed by the sound of a different army arriving on the opposite bank. No sooner had he completed his defenses when Federal cavalry and horse artillery fanned across the hills overlooking the Potomac. A brief exchange of artillery fire struck panic into the retreating Confederate columns, speeding them on their way. Soon after, the vanguard of a Federal army corps appeared on the hills north of the river. Enemy field artillery set up

9

70 guns in positions for more than a mile along the riverfront. Perhaps better than any other Confederate officer, Brigadier General William Nelson Pendleton knew that the Federal army's artillery far outclassed his own. The Federal guns were modern 12-pounder smoothbores or long range rifled guns. Pendleton's artillery of forty-four guns consisted of a handful of the rifled guns and 12-pounder smoothbores, and a lot of the now obsolete 6-pounder smoothbore guns of the past. The Yankees, with nearly a two-to-one superiority in the number of guns and with superior quality guns could shoot more shells at a longer range more effectively than Pendleton's command.

Pendleton's reputation in the Confederate Army was not the best. Despite being an excellent organizer and administrator some saw him as a useless administrative officer, others as incompetent to hold a field command in battle. More ridiculed him for practicing his Episcopal ministry among the troops. His own haughty and at times bombastic appearance did not help. Even worse, there were whispers of cowardice on the field of battle.

As Pendleton later wrote, the day of his "great responsibility" had arrived. With only forty-four inferior reserve artillery guns in place protected from assault by a mere handful of infantry and cavalry, Pendleton was ordered by General Lee to hold the fords, if pressed, until dark that evening. Pendleton had never handled combined arms in combat, his only battlefield experiences being as a small unit artillery officer. Yet, if he failed, the vanguard of McClellan's Army of the Potomac would cross the Potomac free to wreak havoc on the scattered, exhausted, and demoralized brigades of Lee's army.

West Point 1820

1. LEARNING A TRADE

[VIRGINIA, NEW YORK, 1809-1830]

And all thy children shall be taught of the LORD; and great shall be the peace of thy children.

Isaiah 54:13, King James Version

The first English settlers in Virginia in 1607 were driven by a spirit of adventure and a desire for wealth. They heard the stories of the Spanish conquistadors and hoped that if they travelled to the New World there would be large quantities of gold there for the taking. Instead, they found starvation, fever, and death. The native communities, unhappy with their treatment by the English, sought to drive them off the continent. The colony was saved by the European discovery of tobacco, which the settlers cultivated on large lots of lands by exploiting the labor of enslaved Africans or indentured whites. This gave rise to a privileged elite consisting of the large tobacco plantation owners and some others involved in shipping.

The Virginia plantation class believed it was special. The discovery and colonization of a new land allowed many without title or wealth to establish a new aristocracy free of the restraints of English society. The families later described as the First Families of Virginia were descended from early settlers who succeeded in creating wealth that endured for generations. They were socially prominent, wealthy, and politically powerful. Most of the colony's

11

leadership up to and through the Revolution were members of this class, including George Washington. Among the prominent families were the Lees, Randolphs, Harrisons, Carters, Pages, Nelsons, Ballards, Wythes, Byrds, Taliaferros, and Pendletons. They settled in the lands accessible to the navigable waters of the James, York, and Rappahannock Rivers, and in the Northern Neck. For the most part they intermarried and relied on the rule of primogeniture, inheritance only by the eldest surviving son, to preserve their wealth and power, and to avoid the fragmentation of their estates.

By the mid-18th Century, these prominent landowners aped the traditions and style of the British aristocracy while preaching liberty and democracy. Their culture was sophisticated, and filled with educated men raised to be gentlemen. "It was a very beautiful and enjoyable life that the Virginians led," George Cary Eggleston later recalled. It was a "picturesque commonwealth" with a "soft dreamy, deliciously quiet life, a life of repose, an old life, with all its sharp corners and rough surfaces long ago worn round and smooth. Everything fitted everything else. Virginians were satisfied with things as they were…. Their way of living was … a very agreeable one to share and to contemplate, the more because there was nothing else like it anywhere in the land." It was a pleasant way to live with the best quality of life the times could offer.

The younger sons and the daughters who failed to marry an eldest son probably disagreed. The sons usually moved west and started their own plantations. Or, they sought a socially acceptable profession, such as the law, the Church, or the military. The daughters remained at home with their parents. Even though not being the first born and denied the superiority of social rank these extra sons and daughters retained their patrician view of the world. After a few generations those descended from the younger siblings descended into the laboring classes, including the author's Ballard ancestors.

The first Pendleton arrived in Virginia in 1674. He was a schoolmaster from Norwich, England named Philip Pendleton. At eighteen his eldest son Henry married a bride just thirteen years old. When Henry died in 1721 he left his youngest son Edmund without family connections or a classical education. But Edmund refused to accept his lot. At age fourteen Edmund Pendleton was apprenticed to the Clerk of the Court for Caroline County. He studied law, and by age sixteen Pendleton was the Clerk of the Vestry. By age twenty he passed the bar and commenced the practice of law. Edmund married a young local beauty but she survived only two years. Edmund re-married in his mid-twenties to Sarah Pollard but the couple had no children. Edmund Pendleton established his family seat in Caroline County, Virginia. Edmund Pendleton's estate grew along with his practice and fame. He built a rural family seat at "Edmundsbury" several miles southeast of the county seat at Bowling Green, and just east of the main post road. This was the plantation where William Nelson Pendleton was raised.

Caroline County lies in Eastern Virginia, north of Richmond, east of Fredericksburg, and south of the Rappahannock River. British settlers first arrived in the area in the mid to late 17th Century. The county was created in 1728 by cessions from the neighboring counties and named in the honor of the wife of King George II. It is best known as the birthplace of thoroughbred racing in America. During Pendleton's time and well into the 21st Century the county was primarily agricultural and lacked any large towns. At the time the subject of this biography was born there were about 18,000 residents in the county. The county seat at Bowling Green was established in 1803, and by 1850 had fewer than 400 residents. As of 2020 Caroline County could boast no more than 31,000 residents. The main post road between the Virginia state capital at Richmond and all points north ran through the western part of the county. This was also the road used by the major stagecoach lines of the day, and later by the railroads and the interstate highway.

Edmund Pendleton's peers successively elected him to the Virginia House of Delegates from 1752 until 1776. As a Burgess, Edmund was a member of the committee drafting petitions to the British Crown and Parliament protesting the treatment of the colonies and in 1773 joined the revolutionary Committee of Correspondence, a voluntary group of revolutionaries across the seaboard in every colony. The Committees were an early form of a united effort to combat British intransigence, although as a moderate Pendleton first sought to reconcile the differences between the colonies and Great Britain. When efforts to compromise failed Pendleton became a patriot and supported independence. He served one term in the Continental Congress of 1774 along with George Washington and Patrick Henry, but declined another term because of illness. Pendleton chaired the Virginia Convention declaring independence in 1776, and served on several elected bodies during the Revolution. His most prominent position was as head of the executive Committee of Safety for Virginia. The committee was revolutionary in nature and without precedence. It remained in session at all times and exercised discretionary powers which were seemingly unlimited.

Pendleton was permanently lamed in a fall from his horse in 1777, but he did not permit this accident to limit his service. Along with Thomas Jefferson and George Wythe, Edmund revised the legal codes of Virginia after independence. After the new Commonwealth of Virginia organized its legal system in 1779, Pendleton was appointed the presiding judge of the Virginia Court of Appeals, now the Virginia Supreme Court, and a position which he held until his death in 1803. He also served as the president of the Virginia Convention of 1788 which conditionally ratified the United States Constitution by reserving the right to secede.

The elder Edmund was close to his nephew Edmund, the son of his brother John. The affection between the two Edmunds was strengthened when the younger Edmund married Millie Pollard, the younger sister of Sarah Pollard Pendleton, the second wife of the senior Edmund. The younger couple settled at White Plains near the "Edmundsbury" plantation and had two sons and several daughters. The second son was also named Edmund. In his will, the senior Edmund named his grand-nephew Edmund as his heir and adopted son. The heir, now Edmund Pendleton, Jr., married Jane Byrd Page, who died shortly after giving birth to a daughter Elizabeth. Edmund, Jr. re-married, this time to Lucy Nelson, of the Nelson family of Virginia.

Lucy's ancestor Thomas Nelson arrived in Yorktown in 1705 from Penrith, England. Taking advantage of the location of the booming seaport he built a successful merchant shipping company. Two of his sons, Thomas and William, served on the King's Council. The eldest, Thomas, was educated in England and on his return was elected to the House of Burgess before the age of twenty-one. During the Revolution he served on a number of conventions and as a member of the Continental Congress. He signed the Declaration of Independence and served as a General and Governor of Virginia. During the Revolution Thomas Nelson contributed his wealth as well as his influence, and when he died in 1789 he left behind an impoverished family.

A third Nelson brother stayed away from the hurly burly of revolutionary politics and war. Instead, Hugh Nelson acted as a lay preacher in the Episcopal Church reading services and sermons since the church in York was often without a minister. This more passive Nelson was the father of Edmund Jr.'s bride Lucy. Some of Edmund's and Lucy's children died in infancy, but by 1809 there were two sons and two daughters born to the couple.

Edmund Jr. and Lucy Pendleton spent the greater part of every year on their plantation in Caroline County. However, each winter they stayed with Edmund's widowed mother in Richmond on Grace Street. It was here, on the day after Christmas, December 26, 1809, that their third son William Nelson Pendleton was born.

*   *   *   *

William grew up in a crowded household. His parents ultimately had six sons and two daughters. Hugh Nelson was the first born and was nearly ten years older than William. Two daughters, Mildred and Judith, were older as well. The next surviving son was Francis Walker, born the year before William. Robert, James Lawrence, and Gurdon Huntingdon were the three sons younger than William. The children were raised in rural Caroline County on an isolated plantation where there were few close contemporaries of their social class. There were few schools in the area, and the use of private tutors was as yet uncommon. Instead, the Pendleton children were taught at home by their parents when other chores permitted.

The family felt that children were best taught by following the examples of their parents. The Pendleton children learned truth and honor from their father and faith in God from their mother. The upper classes of Virginia historically attended services offered by the Episcopal Church. From the founding of the colony the Episcopal Church was the Establishment Church of the Colony of Virginia, and as such was supported by taxes paid by all citizens. The other classes usually attended services with the Methodist, Presbyterians, or Baptists. Following the disestablishment of the Episcopal Church in Virginia during the Revolution the largely rural areas were left without any Episcopal churches owing to a lack of funding. In the Pendleton family's part of Caroline County there was no Episcopal church for them to attend. Thus, it was Lucy Nelson Pendleton who ensured that her children received a rigorous religious training in the proper faith of the Episcopal Church.

She provided the family with a large Episcopalian Book of Common Prayer with large, clear print the children could easily read. In fact, the book was used to teach the children *how* to read. When they were old enough each child would daily read the Psalter with appropriate responses with their mother. They were also tasked with memorizing psalms, hymns, and Bible verses on a daily basis. The family worshipped together. Every morning a prayer was read by one of the parents, and on Sunday morning the whole household (including enslaved African servants) assembled at 11:00 a.m. to have the morning service and a sermon read by Edmund Pendleton, Jr. On Sunday afternoons all the children were examined by repeating their Episcopalian catechism.

According to his daughter Susan, William grew up "tall and well formed." He was "full of animal spirits and activity, always busy at work or at play, noisy, [and] mischievous." One time William rather maliciously pulled the chair out from under his old nurse as she was sitting down with another baby in her arms. The old nurse dragged William to his mother's chambers for punishment. Lucy demurred, and passed the duty of punishing William on to her husband who gave William a few "sharp cuts" with a peach switch.

William also had a pugnacious streak. His brothers and cousins relied on him to ensure that any younger boy kept their place. Despite his willingness to administer such beatings, William afterwards accepted his adversary as a companion. On one occasion when William fought one of his brothers their father came unexpectedly on the scene and laid his riding whip on the shoulders of both boys. After that they never fought each other again. In spite of this aggressive behavior, according to his daughter, William was of such "bright good humor and universal kindliness" that he was a "great favorite" among the boys in the community.

The greatest family tragedy during Pendleton's childhood occurred during the family's seasonal stay in Richmond in December 1811. Other members of the Nelson family joined them for the Christmas season. On the evening of December 26th some of the family proposed a trip to the theater. Lucy Pendleton was in mourning and beginning to question whether the theater was appropriate for a Christian to attend. She was persuaded by Edmund to tag along in order to celebrate William's second birthday (without William), and to chaperone her step-daughter, sister, and cousin.

The theater was a newly built multi-story brick building resembling a barn more than a theater. It was crowded that evening, the audience was eager to see the star Alexander Placide in a new pantomime, *The Father; or Family Feud.* Among the crowd were scions of the best families, including Pages, Henrys, Botts, Tuckers, and Braxtons. There were almost 600 people in the audience, including eighty children. Early in the second act a lamp became entangled in the cords used to raise the chandelier. Flames rose up the scenery and spread into the fly gallery where separate scenery hangings were suspended. As the hangings burned small bits of burning cloth dropped down onto the stage. Panic struck the crowd and everyone raced at once for the exits. For the audience in the pit and boxes the only way out was down a narrow passage and then up a steep staircase. It was soon blocked by a frightened mob of people. The surge of the crowd separated Edmund, Lucy, their daughter, and their companions from each other. Lucy was forced upwards and carried across the heads of those in front. Edmund and their daughter climbed up to a window and jumped. They were saved but the daughter suffered a severely broken leg. Every other member of the party was presumed dead.

Lucy Nelson Pendleton lost consciousness. When she awoke she was in utter darkness and wondered if she had been buried alive or was already dead, but then she felt a cool breeze blowing over her face. Frightened that she might have been buried alive she raised her hand and felt nothing above her, but discovered that a large beam lay all along her back, pinning down parts of her dress. She tore her clothes apart to escape, and crept over the charred and burning ruins in the direction of the wind on her face. The sun was just rising. She found herself half naked and bruised on the street, and walked alone to her mother's house. The servant opening the door screamed with fright at what she thought must be a ghost. Her sister and cousin were not as fortunate. Their remains were identified by "the diamonds lying among them." Seventy-six people died from the fire, including the sitting Governor of Virginia. All of the victims were buried together on the spot of the old theater, and a memorial church was built over the mass grave. No one in the Nelson family ever again entered a theater.

The Pendletons maintained a lifestyle appropriate to their social status. Gentlemen farmers owning large estates were expected to live well and provide lavish hospitality. The gentlemen spent their leisure hours hunting, playing cards, and engaging in convivial drinking. Both men and women enjoyed a continual round of dinners, dances, parties, and balls. Edmund Pendleton enjoyed fox hunting and was proud of his pack of hounds, but he did not drink or gamble as the rest did. The Pendletons did not enjoy all the social reveries and did their best to keep their children from attending. This did not mean they did not join their neighbors in entertainments, dinner, and riding. Edmund particularly enjoyed dancing. A graceful dancer in his youth, he "set young people dancing" when he picked up his fiddle and bow.

Around 1820 Edmund Pendleton, Jr. received a political appointment requiring his presence on a constant basis in Richmond. His sons Walker and William came with him and were placed in a school for two years. William discovered that no matter how hard he studied, or how much his older brother Walker goofed off, William could never do better than Walker. Nor were either of them ever caned for infractions as were the other boys. Many years later William was told by the schoolmaster that Edmund demanded that the younger son never be permitted to score better than the older, and that neither of them was to suffer the indignity to their class of a whipping. As Susan Pendleton Lee wrote in the 1890's "the right of primogeniture could scarcely have been pushed further."

Soon after, the first born son Hugh graduated from William & Mary College and returned home to study the law. While Hugh was an excellent classicist, his mathematical skills were wanting. Nevertheless, Edmund entrusted to Hugh the education of his younger brothers without any restrictions as to discipline or grades among them. Under his brother's tutelage William excelled at Latin, Greek, and elementary mathematics. But the moment was not to last. Hugh needed to find a place more urban in which to commence his practice and departed the plantation. William's education came to a halt. The absence of a teacher did not stop William's hunger for knowledge. In his evenings and spare time William read Rollin's "Ancient History," Goldsmith's "Greece and Rome," Plutarch's "Lives," Hume's "History of England," Waverley novels, Scott's "Metrical Romances," and poetry by Byron, Milton, Dryden, and Pope.

To keep the boys busy they were given truck garden patches on which to grow vegetables. This was a skill which William put to great use after the Civil War in order to feed his family. The boys competed in growing the best corn, sweet potatoes, and watermelons. They also assumed some of the duties of the plantation overseers. As of 1820 the plantation kept twenty-nine male Africans and seventeen female Africans enslaved. There were twenty male Africans and nine female Africans old enough to work. In all, the plantation was home for sixty people. Every morning the younger Pendleton sons were up early, collected the keys for the sheds and pantries, and saw to the feeding of livestock and the preparation of the agricultural teams for their daily tasks.

Once this was done, the boys were expected to appear clean and dressed neatly for morning prayers and breakfast. After breakfast they re-visited the fields to ensure their assignments had been properly completed. At noon the livestock was fed again and all the enslaved workers were provided dinner. In the evening the boys made sure that the animals were again cared for and fed, and evening supper rations distributed for use in the slave cabins. Walker and William also made sure the farming equipment was in good repair. Finally, they furnished provisions for the cooks to use the next day, and returned the keys to their father with a full accounting of their day. Their father would then give them the orders for the next morning. This regulated and careful maintenance of the slaves and the livestock proved of great value to Pendleton during the Civil War. This work lasted through all four seasons. In the spring they planted and hoed corn, harvested and threshed wheat in the summer, and pulled fodder and cut corn in the autumn.

As his younger sons grew into manhood, it was time for Edmund Pendleton, Jr. to find them a career inasmuch as Hugh was destined to inherit the entire plantation. In the 1820's nominations for the United States Military Academy at West Point were made by the Secretary of War, not by the local congressmen. Nor were the appointments restricted in any way by the state from which the cadet was chosen. For example, as many Virginians as there were openings could be appointed. In 1826 the Secretary of War was James Barbour, a prominent Virginian and friend of Edmund's. Edmund asked Barbour for a warrant naming one of his sons to the Academy as a cadet. However, Edmund was uncertain whether the elder Walker or the younger William should get the appointment. He asked that the name on the warrant be left blank.

Walker had first choice as the older son but he did not want the appointment. He was a quiet boy, and unwilling to leave home. Instead, Walker eventually became a medical doctor. William anxiously awaited Walker's decision. He wanted the education offered by the Academy, and he yearned for the adventurous nature of military service and an honorable military career. In the end it was William's name that filled in the blank space on the warrant. The Academy required candidates to be between the ages of fourteen and twenty-five, able to read, write, and have a fundamental basis of knowledge in mathematics. Candidates were to be free of physical defect, and would be required to pass an oral examination on arrival. Pendleton met all these requirements. He was going on seventeen years old, well educated, handsome, graceful, six feet tall, broad shouldered, with clear blue eyes and curly brown hair. William's appointment was completed on February 25, 1826, naming the Honorable R. Taylor as his Preceptor. Ordered to report before July 1, 1826, he was ready for an adventure.

      *   *   *   *

The United States Military Academy sits on the hills overlooking the curve of the Hudson River at West Point, New York. All around are the mountains of the Catskills and across the river were the highlands settled by the patrician class of New York. The scene is absolutely beautiful and puts the Rhine River gorge in Germany to shame. The Academy was established in 1802 but was not considered a serious academic education until after 1817 when Sylvanus Thayer was named as Superintendent. A native of Massachusetts, Thayer grew up in New Hampshire and graduated from Dartmouth College in 1807 as the valedictorian of his class. However, Thayer was unable to attend graduation as he accepted an appointment to West Point from President Thomas Jefferson. He graduated a year later and was commissioned a Second Lieutenant in 1808. After active service in the War of 1812, Thayer was sent to the French Ecole Polytechnique by the Army where he spent two years studying engineering and mathematics. In 1817 he was appointed Superintendent at West Point.

Thayer created the academic program making the Academy the nation's first engineering school. He also instituted many policies, now traditions still maintained at West Point, including the honor system, mental and physical discipline, the demerit system, and the summer encampment. Thayer instituted the four year class curriculum, requiring the completion by the cadets of each year's curriculum before advancement with graduation following the fourth and final year. Thayer remained the Superintendent during Pendleton's time at West Point. Because of Thayer's contributions before the Civil War, West Point provided American industry and transportation with its trained engineers. They built most of the nation's roads, railroads, bridges, ports, and canals in the antebellum era.

In 1826 it was still far easier to travel by water than by land. Young William Nelson Pendleton took a stagecoach to the Potomac River, presumably near Port Royal, boarded a steamboat headed up the Potomac River to Washington, and there boarded another stagecoach for Baltimore. He crossed Chesapeake Bay on another boat to Frenchtown, and boarded a stage for New Castle, Delaware. Another steamboat carried him to Trenton, New Jersey on the Delaware River where stagecoaches and a canal boat took him to Amboy, New Jersey. There he boarded yet another steamboat to reach New York City. From the city he took a Hudson River steamboat up to West Point. A skiff picked him up at the boat and deposited him on the landing for the Academy. The journey encompassed an entire week.

On his arrival at the Plain above the river Pendleton saw the old Revolutionary War fortifications and a series of otherwise unimpressive stone buildings. Two stone dormitories, the North and South Barracks, met at a right angle on the edge of the parade grounds. Behind them were a two story high academic building and a long mess hall. Before he was accepted as a cadet Pendleton took an oral examination by professors, possibly including Sylvanus Thayer. Once he passed, Pendleton was sworn into the military service of the United States, and sold kits and uniforms of dress gray and blue fatigue uniforms.

During the summer the Corps of Cadets, then consisting of up to 250 cadets, lived in tents at the summer encampment until the start of September. Here they were taught the basic principles of military drill and discipline. Many of the instructors were upperclassmen, including many later prominent Confederate leaders, including Jefferson Davis, Robert E. Lee, and Joseph E. Johnston. John Banks Magruder, another Confederate general also from Caroline County, was one of Pendleton's classmates.

The academic program commenced in September when the Corps moved into the barracks. Pendleton's roommates were Magruder, Lloyd J. Beall of Maryland, and William C. Heywood of South Carolina. Magruder enjoyed playing the flute. Pendleton, a bit of a musician himself, enjoyed playing music with Magruder during the study hours, Cadet Beall, unable to escape the punishment brought on by his roommates, began to join in on his fiddle. On occasion the men would strew the floor with sand and dance to the music to polish the boards. The roommates were all given demerits for "music in the study hours."

For the first six months new cadets were on probation and were required to pass an additional examination in January. The course of instruction focused on chemistry, engineering, mathematics, history, physics (then called natural philosophy), French, military science, drawing, rhetoric, geography, and ethics. Mirroring most of the constitutional theorists of the time, the textbook on Constitutional Law by Rawles taught that states had the right to secede from the Union under extreme circumstances.

The plebes, as new cadets were called, were initially sorted alphabetically for their sections in instruction. Such an arrangement initially placed Pendleton in the third section. His academic performance was so impressive that only a month later he was transferred into the first section, and was never absent from the "merit roll" during his time as a cadet. His specialty was applied mathematics and engineering, in which a fellow cadet described him as "brilliant." He joined a debating society and learned to become an effective public speaker. By the end of his first year Pendleton was seventh in a class of 63 cadets. At that time the cadets were separately rated on their conduct and Cadet Pendleton did not perform as well as in his studies. After his first year he ranked 72nd out of the entire Corps. This ranking continued to slip and he completed West Point ranked 107th out of 215 cadets, just barely in the top half.

The daily routine rarely varied. Cadets awakened at dawn with reveille followed by a roll call. There was a period of time for cleaning, and then study before a thirty minute breakfast at 7:00 a.m. at the mess hall. Guard mount was held at 7:30 a.m. and then another roll call. Course instruction followed until 11:00 a.m. when the cadets went back to their barracks for another study period. Dinner was served from noon to 1:00 p.m. The food was described as being unpalatable. One cadet reported that the soup was "uneatable," the pudding "untouchable," and the molasses "inedible." After dinner the cadets had an hour of free time but at 2:00 p.m. appeared at another formation. They were then given instruction in French and additional study time. At 4:00 p.m., the cadets engaged in various military exercises until sunset. A dress parade was given and supper served. The cadets then went to their quarters where they studied until the 9:30 p.m. tattoo and roll call. Lights out came at 10:00 p.m.

Chapel with an Episcopalian service was mandatory for all cadets. Even so, many of the cadets looked forward to the services because of the minister. The Reverend Charles P. McIlvaine was still under 30 years of age, and served not only as chaplain but also as an instructor in geography, history, and ethics. He carried himself with a majestic bearing matched by his rich voice and tall frame. His sermons were so eloquent that they captured the attention of the cadets, even if they ran on to two hours. McIlvaine awakened a religious revival at the Academy, one which deeply affected Lee, and the later Episcopal Bishop of Louisiana, and Confederate General, Leonidas Polk. Halfway through Pendleton's second year McIlvaine answered the call to serve at St. Ann's Church in Brooklyn. Later in life he became the Episcopal Bishop of Ohio.

Ironically, William Pendleton was not among those affected by McIlvaine. As often occurs among educated young men the expansion of their knowledge and intellectual horizons cause them to seriously question the simple and inexplicable faith of childhood. Some conclude that religion lacks any basis in reality or nature, others discover the question can never really be answered to any degree of satisfaction and leave it unresolved through life. While others find that the simple religious faith of childhood may no longer apply, and find instead a deeper and more abiding understanding of the teachings of Christianity. Pendleton's intellectual curiosity and his special interest in science caused him to abandon the unquestioning faith drilled into him as a child. His readings led him to doubt religious teachings and he became skeptical of Christianity and its doctrines. His sister later referred to Pendleton having infidel beliefs as a cadet. It was important to Pendleton that he investigated the great question as to the existence and nature of any deity on his own. This process continued after his graduation from West Point.

Pendleton was well served over the years by the friendships made at the Academy. The upperclassmen remained cadet leaders throughout the year, and Pendleton befriended many of them. Among these were his relationships with Robert E. Lee and Jefferson Davis. Pendleton was well liked. One cadet described him as "loved by all for his amiability, kindness of heart, disinterestedness, sprightliness, being always full of fun, with a bright, laughing face, —and of intelligence, for he was decidedly the most talented of the class, always ready to assist the dull or indolent ones with their lessons." His roommate Lloyd Beall wrote that Pendleton "was noted for his manliness, his strict observance of regulations, and his studious habits. He was the soul of honor, and bore himself with such an air of dignity as to command the respect and esteem of all his fellow students…. [T]here was nothing haughty or overbearing in his disposition; on the contrary, he was genial and affable, and an agreeable companion at all times." Beall also noted that Pendleton was free "from the follies of youth, few pursued the path of moral rectitude more strictly…"

When his second year as a cadet commenced Pendleton was no longer a plebe, and became one of the upperclassmen at the summer encampment. Two of the new plebes he helped to instruct were Lucius Northrop, later the notoriously incompetent Confederate Commissary General, and Andrew A. Humphreys, later a Union General and Corps commander in the Army of the Potomac. When his second year ended Pendleton ranked 3rd in his class academically and was mentioned in the Richmond newspapers as one of the Virginia cadets who had distinguished themselves.

In July 1828, Pendleton turned down the opportunity to hold a higher cadet rank so that he could go home on an extended leave. The family celebrated his return with a large ball at the plantation. One day while out riding he encountered another party. He dismounted and spoke with them, and became enchanted with a lovely blonde girl named Anzelotte Page who was in the group. When he returned to the Academy Pendleton diligently applied himself to his studies and by his last year was one of the four cadet captains.

But then he got into trouble with Superintendent Sylvanus Thayer. One day John Magruder, as a cadet captain issued an order to a cadet Allen to "close up" the ranks. Allen chose to treat it as a personal affront requiring an apology or satisfactory explanation.

Failing to receive such, Allen sought gentlemanly satisfaction by issuing a challenge to a duel which Magruder accepted. Pendleton agreed to act as Magruder's second. The parties gathered for the duel, after the preliminary rituals were performed Pendleton stepped in between the duelers and stated that matters had gone far enough, and protested against any further proceedings. Allen replied that it was too late to smooth things over and demanded that Pendleton step aside. Pendleton refused, instead asking Allen to listen to reason. Allen agreed but asked that "if you have anything to say, say it quickly." A discussion followed, explanations provided, and the matter resolved, except that Pendleton lost his rank for his involvement. Allen ended up, as karma demands, killed in a duel some years later.

On July 1, 1830, Pendleton graduated from West Point ranked 5th in a class of 42 despite his run in with the Superintendent. He was commissioned as a Brevet Second Lieutenant and was recommended to the President because of is academic brilliance for a commission as a full Second Lieutenant in the Artillery Corps. Two months later he received his orders to join the 2nd U.S. Artillery Regiment in South Carolina. In his four years at the Academy William Nelson Pendleton learned a trade as an Army officer, excelled in mathematics and engineering, questioned Christianity, made useful and influential friends, and met the girl he was going to marry. There was a bright future ahead for the young Virginian.

Fort Hamilton & Verrazano Straits

2. "TOSSED ABOUT ON THE SEA OF DOUBT"

[SOUTH CAROLINA, NEW YORK, 1830-1833]

The night is far spent, the day is at hand: let us therefore cast off the works of darkness and let us put on the armour of light.

Romans 13:12, King James Version

The Army is generous with time for furlough, especially for newly minted officers recently graduated from West Point. Pendleton received a furlough of three to four months before reporting for duty and he spent it at home in Virginia. During his absence his two sisters married but did not live far away from the plantation. His brother Walker graduated from a medical school in Baltimore and settled down to practice his craft in Richmond. The elder brother Hugh married a cousin Lucy Nelson, who was also a cousin and companion of Anzelotte Page, the young blonde who charmed Cadet Pendleton two summers before. Hugh and his new wife lived at the "Edmundsbury" plantation giving William plenty of opportunity to court Miss Anzelotte. Anzelotte was slender, with delicate features, and a fair complexion. She had golden blonde hair, soft blue eyes, and perfect teeth. However, as befit the times, her only education was what her mother taught her. Nevertheless, she displayed a quick intellect, a thirst for knowledge, and a retentive memory. Over time a strong devotion emerged between the couple and Second Lieutenant Pendleton and Anzelotte Page became engaged to marry subject to approval by her parents according to the custom of the time.

Anzelotte was the eldest daughter of Captain Francis Page, the third son of a Revolutionary era hero and Governor of Virginia John Page of "Rosswell" plantation. As a later son Francis Page did not inherit the family wealth. He was well educated in the classics and the law, but despite his education Page opted to be a gentleman farmer instead. Naturally lazy, Page spent his later years reading, travelling about the state by coach to visit family, and fulfilling his role as a magistrate. Anzelotte's mother was a great aunt of Pendleton's on the Nelson side, and is reported to have been a woman of great intellect, beauty, charm, and a strong personality.

Francis Page had no objections provided his wife agreed. She did not. Lucy Nelson Page questioned Pendleton's income, the living quarters provided by the Army, and the constant changes in station required by military service. On top of it all, Anzelotte had "poor health," and her mother worried about how she might be affected by living in forts among the sand dunes and swamps of the coast. She refused the offer. However, when Lucy Nelson Page realized how miserable her daughter became after the rejection, she changed her mind and allowed the engagement to proceed.

Once Pendleton's leave expired in September 1830, he was ordered to report for duty at Fort Moultrie with the 2nd U.S. Artillery Regiment. The post sat at the mouth of the harbor at Charleston, South Carolina. Fort Moultrie dated back to the Revolution and was where South Carolinians successfully beat off an initial British amphibious attack in 1776. Later, the British occupied the fort from 1780 until their departure in 1782. When war tensions grew between France and Great Britain during the first of the Napoleonic Era wars in 1793, the War Department began an ambitious program to strengthen coastal fortifications later called the First System of fortifications. By then the palmetto log walls of old Fort Moultrie were rotting away and in 1798 the Army constructed a new brick fort on top of the ruins. A hurricane in 1804 wrecked the fort, and a new brick fort was completed as part of the Second System of forts in 1808. This fort had a battery of large fixed coastal guns on three sides facing the sea mounting 40 cannon, and enclosed with ramparts and parapets. There was also a brick barracks for 500 soldiers.

The Army which Pendleton now joined reflected, as most armies do, the needs of the most recent war. In this case, that was the War of 1812 with Britain. In that war the most common cannon used by the field artillery was the 6-pounder smoothbore, an iron tube used to shoot a 6 pound iron sphere at the enemy. The gun weighed a ton and had recoil of up to six feet. The recoil required the use of a large team of men to manhandle the gun back into position each time it was fired. The howitzer was the other common cannon of the War of 1812, a shorter and wider gun used to launch projectiles at a high angle towards the enemy. The round could be a large iron ball or a shell designed to explode into shrapnel when over the battlefield. Such was the state of technology for field artillery when Pendleton was an active officer.

However, after the War of 1812 changes were made in the organization of the artillery. In 1821, an Artillery Corps was formed by combining twelve battalions of coastal and heavy artillery with the light (or field) artillery (6 to 24-pounder guns) and the Ordnance Department. There were four regiments of nine companies each, and each regiment had just one company of field artillery. In other words, nearly all of the artillery officers spent their time working the big coastal defense cannons. In addition, while at West Point Pendleton received training in artillery tactics using the most current manuals and concepts. Given the use of advanced mathematics and physics in artillery, it was the branch most desired by officers other than that of the Engineers. In 1824 the Army created its first post-graduate training school for officers in artillery at Fort Monroe, Virginia. Every artillery officer was expected to attend for one year, but there is no record that Pendleton did so.

Pendleton arrived in Charleston about noon on October 28, 1830. He deposited his trunk and hired a row-boat to reach Sullivan Island and Fort Moultrie. His new commanding officer invited him to his quarters for dinner. Knowing of her family's concern for his fiancée's comfort, he described the commander's quarters as "a handsome apartment, comfortably arranged. This was the dining- and sitting-room, the only one I saw. But he has one or two others, all comfortable. The table was plentifully yet frugally spread, and I cannot say when I have been more taken with the appearance of comfort and contentment than in this small domestic circle." He also wrote Anzelotte that the commander was not very busy and "wants excitement and amusement, and consequently must have his wine and his whist-parties." It is difficult to say whether this was a caution or an enticement for the young girl.

During his trip from Virginia to South Carolina by stage through hundreds of miles of pine-barrens and sand dunes, and while recuperating later in Georgia, Pendleton investigated the nature of his religious beliefs. By the time he left West Point Pendleton discarded his infidel beliefs and concluded that there was a deity ruling over the universe. Now he struggled over the nature of that deity, asking himself whether the Deism of some of the Founding Fathers was correct, or whether the Bible was the revealed truth of God and his nature. The staunch Christian faith of his fiancée probably influenced his ruminations.

Lieutenant Pendleton did not remain at swampy Fort Moultrie for long. Exposure to insect bites caused him to contract malaria and possibly yellow fever. By November Pendleton was confined to bed for ten days with a sharp attack of violent ague and a burning fever. He was able to tell Anzelotte that the absence of a severe illness was "another proof of the Divine mercy to me…" Initially the doctor thought he had yellow fever but later changed his mind. Instead, the doctor concluded that the medicine provided to Pendleton allegedly prevented him from coming down with the disease. By the end of November the Army transferred him to the Arsenal at Augusta, Georgia where he was responsible for artillery ordnance, the manufacture and storage of cannons, shots and shells for the artillery, as its higher elevation at Augusta was considered to be healthier. Once again, this experience enabled him to cope with ordnance issues arising after secession. He would remain there until new orders arrived from Army headquarters in New York.

Throughout his illness Pendleton struggled with depression caused by his separation from Anzelotte and by his indecision about his religious belief, although he appeared willing to consider a life as a clergyman:

> Do what I will, I cannot overcome the oppression of heart and depression of spirits under which I have been laboring; …. The wish has more than once occurred to me that I were prepared and might dare to join the Christian Church of which you are a

member, and might turn whatever abilities God has given me to the highest use of which they are capable in studying and proclaiming the holy truths of Christianity. The more I reflect upon it the more I am convinced that such a life of useful tendency would contribute more to my own peace of mind than any other could. Indeed, I do at times feel that I ought to devote myself to this life, and that I shall be happy in no other. ...

Pendleton enjoyed the military life but for his absence from his fiancée. He preferred to read books from the post library and was reprimanded by his commander for not wishing to attend the regular balls given in Augusta. Every morning he dressed, made a fire, and studied his prayer book and Bible. After breakfast he attended to his duties, which Pendleton described as being very light. He then read Greek and Latin until dinner. Until supper he studied history, and in the evenings visited with the family with whom he boarded. On returning to his room he wrote letters and read the Bible. On some occasions he hiked out "some miles into the desert, pine forests, where the solemn silence of nature makes me feel wondrous sad and sentimental, and often gives rise to emotions more rational and beneficial." Pendleton made friends during his stay in Georgia and greatly enjoyed his time there.

But his religious doubts continued. He wrote to Anzelotte that:

I feel that I have undergone no sudden operation of the Holy Spirit; I feel that I am still liable to the charge of an unstable faith, that I am still under the dominion of sin and worldly thoughts, and that my heart, though sincerely turned towards the great and good God, and endeavoring to yield itself in gratitude and love to Him, is still unchanged. All that I can in strict truth say is that, in obedience to the instructions of the Gospel, I feel bound to change the habits of my life, and this I can only do in a measure; that is, I find evil thoughts will enter my mind and render that act which might appear good frequently wicked, as being a species of hypocrisy.

And does not this prove that a change of heart has not been wrought in me?

Pendleton painfully explained that while he accepted that when a person converts to the teachings of Christianity it would bring "regeneration," but he could go no further. He wanted to believe, but he refused to be the hypocrite claiming faith in something he actually doubted. In the spring of 1831, Pendleton wrote:

> Sometimes I am so tossed about on the sea of doubt and error that I am almost compelled to believe that the devil has immediate hold on me. At times I have had a kind of despair lest I should be given over to the dominion of doubt and sin, at others I have looked darkly on the fair face of nature, and turned, not in love, from the contemplation of the Deity. And always when I remember my precarious state I am seized with dread…. I hardly hope for a sudden conversion, but that God will one day give me a fuller and a surer faith.

At some point that spring Pendleton finally felt that his belief in Christianity was pure and solid, and that his doubts were all resolved. In all probability Pendleton finally understood that even with the use of all known science and logic he could not answer the unanswerable. Rather, he learned to accept belief based on blind faith in something he could not prove. Yet his struggles over his faith had not ended.

        *   *   *   *

Pendleton took leave that summer and married Anzelotte on July 15, 1831, at the bride's home at "Rugswamp" plantation using the Episcopal service. Family and friends came from as far away as fifteen miles, so the ceremony was held at 4:00 in the afternoon to permit them all time to return home. The wedding dinner was prepared by the servant chef "Cook Billy," who had long presided in the Nelson plantation kitchen. He made a special trip to "Rugswamp" to oversee the preparation of this important meal. The chef was perturbed by the bride's mother's instruction to include only thirteen meats, and not the usual fourteen, in the menu.

He fumed, "Never hear tell of wedding dinner without fourteen dishes of meat. Can't cook no decent dinner excepting you has fourteen dishes." The chef won the argument and was given authority for the full and proper menu.

The Pendletons enjoyed a strong and enduring marriage. Looking back forty six years later, Pendleton wrote that "In all that I am, and have been enabled to do, my heaven favored wife has been incalculably instrumental....And by her counsel and influence has been determined, in great measure, any good the All-gracious Disposer of lots has enabled me to do."

$$* \qquad * \qquad * \qquad *$$

In September 1831 Pendleton received orders from Army headquarters in New York. He was to report for duty as an assistant professor of mathematics at West Point, from which he had graduated only little more than a year before. Once there he and his new bride found a better quality of life for Army officers than they would have had in rural Georgia. They made good friends among the faculty and enjoyed the beauty of nature that surrounds West Point. The couple took long walks around the post and up into the mountains overlooking the Hudson River to enjoy the scenery and for Anzelotte to collect flowers. Pendleton's position as a teacher opened new doors of opportunity to him. He found that he was an excellent teacher, and even more, that he enjoyed teaching. It was even possible in his free time to pursue his intellectual interests.

By the spring of 1832 Anzelotte was expecting their first child. As was common then, she went home to be cared for by her mother and family mid-wives. Pendleton corresponded with her regularly. What is so odd for this devoted couple is that he signed his letters formally as "your husband, William Nelson Pendleton." On his return to West Point Pendleton stopped in Washington, D.C. to see his government in action. He toured the Capitol and visited both houses, although only in the Senate was anything of interest happening. Pendleton watched as the Henry Clay and Robert Hayne debated the tariff law that spawned the Nullification Crisis. He described Hayne as having "captivated" him and Clay as having "charmed" him.

From Washington he took boats and coaches to reach New York. Low tides and water levels in the rivers slowed his progress, and he complained of the time required to reach New York from

Philadelphia, "fifteen hours and a half between Philadelphia and New York! In these days of rapid transit we marvel at the patience which could endure such delays." Pendleton took time in New York to visit religious publishing houses and charities. He thought that, "it would do your heart good, and your mamma would be delighted to see the air of Christian benevolence about everything…." The expenses of the trip troubled him, having cost $26.00, or approximately $843.00 in today's currency.

On his arrival home Pendleton returned to his routine. He awoke at sunrise, prayed and studied his Bible, ate breakfast at 7:00 a.m., and at 8:00 a.m. commenced teaching classes. At 11:00 a.m. he devoted an hour to tutoring a few students, ate dinner at 1:00 p.m., then spent two hours of studying Greek, followed by two more hours of reading. In the evening he studied mathematics. Life at the Academy involved a great many parades and drills, and he enjoyed the musical accompaniment of an Army band. He wrote to his wife of "how sweet the Point is looking now, with the grass, flowers, and trees. Everything is beautiful at this season. The clouds about sunset are the most splendid you ever saw."

Too much indolent reading led to a more slothful existence, and his anxieties from being separated from his wife and his lack of exercise put him into a deep depression. On top of it all his malaria returned. He wrote to Anzelotte, "… Do not let my saying that my spirits are not very good marr [sic] your happiness. What I feel of depression is in a good degree owing to the want of regular exercise." His religious doubts returned as well. Pendleton had yet to make a public confession of faith. He wrote his wife that, "I do not feel fit for the sacrament at this time." Yet, ever in the back of his mind he considered the possibility of becoming a clergyman. Toward this end he studied Hebrew, Greek, and Latin.

He discussed religious faith with some of the other faculty members. He noted the prevalence of infidel belief among the Corps of Cadets and viewed it as being natural among young men to question the religious faith of their childhood. He expressed his belief that pressing religion on the cadets at this stage might be counter-productive. During his re-consideration of faith, Pendleton found that he was not persuaded by the arguments of others that Christianity was wrong. In fact, he recognized that those without faith were also naturally without hope of eternal life. When confronted with the apostasy of another instructor, Pendleton concluded that he had studied the issue more deeply than others, and wondered at how "melancholy it is that a man should thus try happiness, the confidence we have in the death and resurrection of our Saviour being taken away? Thanks to a merciful God, no earthly power can destroy the ground on which that confidence rests; and how delightful it is to the heart, when distressed, to trust in the sure promises of a religion whose evidences have stood the test of eighteen centuries, and still convince every fair mind!"

An inner peace returned to Pendleton. He wrote, "last evening, while the battalion was at parade, I was standing near the corner of the south barrack gazing at the glory spread around the sun as he sank behind the mountain, ... I pointed out the object of my attention, and he characteristically alluded therefrom to the glory of the scene continually beheld in heaven by those who have been faithful to the end."

Pendleton was anxious to get away to Virginia as the school year wound down. A visit by General Macomb and the President of Colombia postponed the final exams for the cadets. This was followed by a visit from the Board of Visitors. However, he wrote, "the examinations begin to-morrow, and to-morrow week I leave for Virginia, if it be the will of heaven." Before he was able to depart West Point the news came from Virginia of the birth of his daughter Susan. After he arrived in Virginia, Pendleton was confirmed as a professing Christian in the Trinity Episcopal Church of Hanover County by Bishop William Meade.

On his way back to West Point from his furlough in Virginia, Pendleton became violently ill with nausea and vomiting. He took a stagecoach from Philadelphia to New York City. Half way across New Jersey he ate a little ginger cake. It did not sit well, and he immediately vomited. Pendleton's limbs seem paralyzed while his hands and feet muscles contracted. One of his fellow passengers offered a sugar cube soaked in camphor and Pendleton felt immediate relief from the abdominal distress, but the fever continued. On the boat trip from Brunswick, New Jersey, people crowded around to see the man with "the cholera." He disembarked at New York City where he was cared for overnight. The next morning he made his way up the Hudson to West Point. After a short visit with Superintendent Thayer, Pendleton returned to his hotel room and summoned the doctor. The doctor took one look at him and sent Pendleton to the post infirmary for treatment. He wrote Anzelotte that he was sick but not desperately so, but his handwriting was shaky and nearly illegible. For many years after Pendleton was subjected to recurrent bouts of "sudden and violent attacks of bilious fever."

That summer Pendleton received orders transferring him to the 4th U.S. Artillery Regiment at Fort Hamilton, New York to exchange positions with his classmate Lieutenant James Allen. All in all, it should have been a desirable assignment. The fort is located on the western tip of Long Island across the Verrazano Straits from Staten Island. The Verrazano Straits Bridge now bisects the fort. From the fort there is a panoramic view of New York City and its harbor. The city, with all of its attractions and amusements, was only a short boat ride away. As with Fort Moultrie, the post began as a Revolutionary War battery guarding the harbor. Following the War of 1812 construction of a new fort as part of the Third System of fortifications was authorized. The cornerstone was laid in 1825, and the fort occupied in 1831. The brick fort faced the Narrows but also provided defenses on the landward side. The post was not yet completed, and the officers were compelled to live in the battery casemates. Pendleton's assignment was to mount 60-pounder coastal defense cannon on the parapet.

When the Pendleton family arrived they were greeted by the officer corps stationed at the fort. Since the life of an Army officer involves a great many moves, the Army culture makes it easy for a newcomer to assimilate into the local Army social life. One of the officers, a Captain Gardner and his wife, became close friends, sharing a common interest in the Episcopal Church. Pendleton also found the Rev. McIlvaine, the former West Point chaplain, as the rector of St. Ann's Episcopal Church in nearby Brooklyn. If the officers could not attend to service at St. Ann's Pendleton and Gardner provided a service and acted as lay readers.

Despite the warmth of their welcome and the joy of living close to one of the busiest ports in the nation, living in the damp and windy casemates during the cold winter proved too much for Anzelotte. When Gardner's company was ordered to Fort Monroe on a packet schooner Pendleton took the opportunity to send Anzelotte and Susan with them so they could continue on to the Page plantation while he remained at Fort Hamilton. At that time, and largely because of the Commanding General Winfield Scott's personal preference, the Army headquarters were located in New

York City. During an overnight visit to headquarters and the city, Pendleton obtained a twenty day furlough, and on May 1, 1833 Pendleton followed his family in the packet "Portsmouth" bound for Norfolk. The family returned to Fort Hamilton at the end of the furlough. Their stay in Virginia was lightened by visits from Pendleton's older brother Hugh and his family, Anzelotte's sister, and Bishop Meade.

The winter of 1832-1833 brought with it the Nullification Crisis during which South Carolina dared to defy President Andrew Jackson by "nullifying" the Federal tariff law. Pendleton was raised as Southerner, and held Southern political views. He disagreed with Jackson, and felt that South Carolina acted in self-defense in refusing to enforce a tariff which penalized the Southern markets and provided a benefit only to the New England manufacturers. Jackson threatened to send troops to force South Carolina into submission. An allegedly authentic rumor circulated that Pendleton and his unit would be included in that Federal army. True to his upbringing and his understanding of the Constitutional right of a state to protect its interests, Pendleton seriously considered resigning his commission. His friends and Anzelotte tearfully begged him to wait until the truth could be ascertained. However, South Carolina backed down in the face of Jackson's credible threat, and Pendleton set aside his thoughts of resignation.

But not for long. After the crisis passed Pendleton reconsidered his choice of profession. He found garrison duty in coastal defense to be narrow in scope and lacking in challenges. He was bored in his work as it was not as challenging or rewarding as his time teaching at West Point. He looked for something new to pursue. When an invitation arrived from Bristol College in Pennsylvania to become a teacher, Pendleton did not hesitate. On October 31, 1833, he resigned his commission and started a new career as an educator.

During his three years of active service Pendleton never handled field artillery, but was constantly assigned to the larger coastal defense guns. Nor had he spent time with troops in the field. For the next twenty-eight years Pendleton acquired no new knowledge or training in artillery usage or tactics. The world was at the brink of the beginning of the industrial revolution. Technology was evolving faster than ever before, including in military science. After Pendleton left the service to pursue education and the ministry significant changes occurred in the field of artillery science and equipment. In 1841, a new ordnance manual laid down an entirely different system of artillery usage ranging from weapons and organization to field tactics.

During the Mexican War (1846-1848) the field artillery transitioned to using bronze tubes, which were sturdier, more reliable, and less likely to burst when fired. Field artillery batteries in the war used the 6-pounder bronze cannon as the primary weapon. Each gun weighed 880 pounds, less than half the weight of the iron guns of Pendleton's time. The range of these guns was also longer than the ones Pendleton used; each gun could fire its projectile as far as 1,500 feet, although most gunners preferred a range of less than 1,000 feet. Some of the field artillery batteries were outfitted with 12-pounder cannon and 12-pounder howitzers. The 12-pounder bronze smoothbore weighed 1,800 pounds and fired at a maximum range of 1,600 feet. The 12 -pounder bronze howitzers weighed 785 pounds and fired at a maximum range of 1,000 feet.

By1861 and the onset of the Civil War, the science and equipment of field artillery advanced even further than in the Mexican War, including the development and use of rifled and breech loading guns with ranges of effective fire unimagined in 1833. By then Pendleton's training was obsolete, and his military training at the beginning of the war qualified him to be just a commander of a small 6-pounder smoothbore cannon battery.

Old College, Newark, Delaware

3. "TO SECURE A COMPETENCY WITH NO DIMINUTION OF USEFULNESS"

[PENNSYLVANIA, VIRGINIA, MARYLAND, 1833-1853]

Behold, we beseech thee, the afflictions of thy people; increase the fruits of the earth by thy heavenly benediction; and grant that the scarcity and dearth, which we now most justly suffer for our sins, may, through thy goodness, be mercifully turned into plenty…

1789 Episcopalian Book of Common Prayer

In the early days of the nation most goods and people traveled from one state to another by boat. One could load cargo and passengers comfortably in one port and usually carry them without any problems to any port on the seaboard. On the other hand, travel by land was tedious and time consuming. Goods were carried in slow moving wagons. Stage coaches were crowded and uncomfortable. At times the passengers had to sit on top of the coach out in the weather. For meals and lodging the passengers were at the mercy of the small inns along the way, most of which produced poor food and filthy and crowded sleeping quarters. This explains why most of the desirable places to live lay along the main rivers and bays of the American eastern seaboard.

Twenty-three miles up the broad Delaware River from Philadelphia sits the town of Bristol, Pennsylvania. Founded in 1681, by the early 19th Century the town was a center for textile production and boat building. At the time that Pendleton resided in Bristol the town had not yet experienced the industrial boom resulting from the completion of canals running from the Delaware River through New Jersey to New York City. In 1830 the population was only 1,262 people. Sad to say, until 1847 the Commonwealth of Pennsylvania permitted slavery, although only a handful of slaves still existed in the state at the time. This allowed the Pendletons to bring their enslaved black servants to Bristol. Pendleton never had any qualms about holding slaves; after all he firmly believed that God and the Bible sanctioned slavery. Rather oddly though, he also thought that a slaveholder should never treat his slaves as though the owner was in any way influenced by self-interest even though self-interest was at the heart of slave ownership.

Pendleton was hired as a professor of mathematics and physics (then known as natural philosophy) at the new Bristol College. The College was created by the Episcopal Education Society of Philadelphia in the autumn of 1833. The founders hoped to educate young men with a combination of manual labor and intellectual development. A grammar school was attached to the program as well. With the support of the Episcopal Church and the enthusiastic approval by the Bishops the school had a fair promise of success. It received its charter from the state in January 1834 and was in business. But from the outset the College faced financial problems. The destruction of the United States Bank by Andrew Jackson expanded easy credit from unreliable sources. This was followed by the subsequent Species Circular order issued by Jackson which rapidly contracted the useful money supply causing no end of misery for all. By 1837 the resulting economic depression held the country in its grip, and the Episcopal establishment in Pennsylvania soon forgot about its commitment to the school.

The College was established on the banks of the Delaware River two miles from Bristol, and opposite the town of Burlington, New Jersey. An old mansion on the river was purchased and converted into the college building. The ball room was used as a chapel, and the bedrooms either set aside for the professors, or used as dormitories for the students. The main rooms were converted into classrooms. From the outset the college planned to expand.

From 1834 to 1835 the college constructed the White Hall for use as a main building. The structure was designed by Andrew Jackson Davis, the same architect who designed the Virginia Military Institute and some state capitol buildings. The main block of the building stood nearly four stories high with five bays wide and two rooms deep.

During his first year at Bristol Pendleton lived in the original College building and made new friends among the faculty. Given the cramped living conditions, at some point he sent his family home to Virginia. Pendleton's involvement with the College, and his reputation as an instructor at West Point, encouraged a number of students from Virginia to enroll. Among these were Pendleton's younger brother Gurdon, later an Episcopal minister, his cousin Robert Nelson Pendleton, who later became a missionary in China, and Anzelotte's cousin John Page. A fellow professor later described Pendleton when he taught at Bristol:

> I was struck with his military bearing, his firmness and decision of purpose combined with gentleness. He always showed great ability in the discussion of any debatable point, and a willingness to be set right if in error. I have never met with anyone so far removed from anything like guile; so generous was he that his generosity was taken advantage of by those who were so disposed.
>
> As a professor I need say nothing as to his competency and ability as a teacher. … He introduced something of a military discipline, which was much needed…. In his social relations he was loved and esteemed by us all. He was gentle and courteous to all men.

Pendleton's daily routine started at 5:00 a.m. when he awoke and dressed. From 6:00 a.m. to 7:00 a.m. he taught class, then ate breakfast, and cleaned his room until 9:00 a.m. with the help of his brother Gurdon. He spent the next hour teaching followed by two hours of study. After a mid-day dinner at 3:00 p.m. he read, wrote, and studied. He then taught Greek for an hour and studied an analytical geometry text to help him prepare for class the next day. Pendleton strived to make his reading time provide intellectual progress and value. He was especially interested in books recommended by the recent General Convention of the Episcopal Church.

With his wife absent and his mind enthralled with intellectual study rather than daily exercise it is not surprising to hear that Pendleton relapsed into a state of deep depression and anxiety. In February 1834 he wrote, "I am much harassed by a sort of sinking of hope, calling upon me for vigorous effort in every way, by prayer and self-examination, and a wielding of the sword of the spirit and active exercise." He prayed for gifts of grace and strength and explained away his moodiness by writing, "as to being happy, there is at all times the delightful reflection that I can pray, happy or not, and, provided I am still left to do my duties aright, it matters little in the great account whether I was or was not allowed a tranquil course." Rather, he sought solace in Dr. Johnson's maxim, "when solitary be not idle, and when idle be not solitary."

In late spring 1834, Pendleton traveled to Virginia to retrieve his family. During the return trip he suffered a recurrent "bilious fever" which detained them for several weeks. When he felt better the family left for Bristol. During the stay in Philadelphia one of the enslaved African servants left to "get a cradle for the baby," and never returned. On investigation it was learned that she carefully planned her escape. She left with all her belongings and was never heard from again. When Pendleton concluded that the servant had deliberately left he refused to make any effort to find her.

The next autumn the family moved out of the College and into nearby "Long Cottage" a few hundred yards away. The family enjoyed long walks and drives in the adjacent countryside to enjoy nature. Anzelotte became an amateur botanist, and the family collected specimens for her during these trips. During the winter sleighing and skating on the frozen Delaware replaced the ramblings about the countryside. Evenings were spent entertaining fiends in the cozy parlor of the cottage. A second daughter Lucy was born, and Pendleton made sure he spent quality time with both of his daughters. The next summer the Pendletons traveled from Bristol to Virginia in a small one-horse carriage. The mode of travel was spurred by the need for economy as well as Pendleton's desire for adventure. The experiment was abandoned on reaching the Chesapeake Bay port of Elk Point, Maryland. Anzelotte, the girls, and the horse were all worn out. The family boarded a steamboat there to continue their journey.

During their residence in Bristol tragedy stalked the extended family. William's brother Robert died suddenly during a business trip in western Pennsylvania. He had suddenly became desperately ill with a fever in a country inn, and died without adequate medical care. No one notified the family of his illness until after he died. His sister Judith passed away in Virginia at about the same time. With two of his remaining brothers busy with their professional lives, and the youngest under his care as a student, William felt it fell upon him to take care of his elderly parents. His father Edmund, Jr., was blinded by cataracts and any hope of restoring his sight abandoned when the doctors found that his optic nerves were both damaged. Surgery merely gave Edmund the ability to differentiate between light and dark, allowing him at least to move about his home.

In 1834 Bristol College embarked on an ambitious project of constructing Penn Hall to accommodate the growing number of students. But the College was begun with no endowments in the expectation of support from the Episcopal Church. When the support proved to be insufficient, the College needed to charge the students tuition adequate to keep the college financially sound. However, in the expectation of financial support the college made the decision early on not to charge a high tuition in order to be able to provide an education for as many eligible students as possible. The ordinary tuition for a term was $116 for forty weeks, but many of the students were charged only $75, and many others who had no means, especially those interested in the ministry, were taught tuition free and given what we today would call a work study program. Consequently, the annual salaries for professors at $800 were comparatively low, and in many cases delinquent.

In order to make ends meet Pendleton agreed to work as an engineer over the summer of 1836 laying out the path of a railroad. For a salary of $150 a month Pendleton led a surveying party through the mountains and hills of Southwestern Virginia and down into North Carolina. He took along some "pills… and some calomel, magnesia, and rhubarb, in case of sickness among our party…" Along the way he stayed in the homes of people along the surveying route, and totally enjoyed himself in being out of doors and away from any other stress. Some days the team could complete a sixteen mile trip. The team stayed at public houses, enjoyed mineral springs, and hunted deer. He wrote home, "If you were with me, how I could enjoy the noble character of the country! ...The climate is fine, but it has rained every day since our arrival. The mineral water which attracts people here has not been analyzed, but it has a twang of iron, Sulphur, and salts, and has a most beneficial effect on me."

They reached Christiansburg, Virginia after a ten mile moonlight survey:

> I wish you and others of my dear friends could witness the scene through which we passed. I cannot pretend to give you the slightest idea of its mingled grandeur and beauty. Imagine us, after nightfall, traversing the mountain defiles. On either hand the tall hills frowning darkly upon us below, the little mountain stream dashing in its wildness, and making an incessant sound to break away the solemn stillness of the road, while here and there the prevailing darkness was relieved by the moonbeams finding their way through openings in the trees, now illuminating the road and hill-sides, now glittering on the foaming cascades. I never saw anything like it.

Despite the outdoor travel and the pressing nature of his work Pendleton remained anxious about his faith and service to the church. More and more he felt the need to do more as a Christian than simply teach. In order to feel fulfilled Pendleton felt the need to become a minister but doubted his faith was sufficiently pure enough to do so:

> What distresses me often is a heavy sense of my unfitness, through a depraved and unsanctified heart, for the sacred and responsible office of the ministry. I have come to the conclusion, years ago, that God required of me to preach the Gospel, and I think myself unfit for it. You cannot conceive how I suffer at times from this.

By the end of the trip Pendleton felt healthier, although he had doubts about his liver when staying in Danville. Pendleton returned to Bristol for another year of teaching with his health restored and some more cash in his pocket. The session started with an even larger number of students but an insufficient amount of money. By January 1837 it was obvious that the College's funding could no longer sustain its expenditures. The seniors were advanced in order to have them graduate, but it was a different story for the faculty. Being laid off was difficult in the middle of a school year as all other school positions were filled for the academic year. On top of it, their salaries, as inadequate as they were, had not been paid, and it was becoming obvious that they never would be. In February 1837 the decision was made to permanently close the College.

This left the staff with the nearly hopeless task of finding another position but Pendleton saw it as an opportunity. He wrote his father-in-law that the family would return to Virginia. He planned on their arrival to be ordained as an Episcopal minister. Pendleton explained to his wife's family that he understood this could mean a life of poverty, but:

> I am principled against allowing my family to be so ill provided for as to make them uncomfortable. And I am morally certain that I can use the means I have in such a way as to secure a competency with no diminution of usefulness and with comparatively little inconvenience. My plan to this end is simply this: to employ one or, if required, two well-qualified teachers, who shall have the immediate conduct of such a school as I think would be useful and acceptable in Virginia, I myself having the direction and moral influence over the same. This will provide me an income sufficient, and will allow me to perform fully and faithfully all the duties of a parish minister, and will occupy to a good purpose the scientific acquirements which circumstances have secured to me, and which otherwise would be scarcely better than thrown away for any useful purpose.

Pendleton understood his decision meant abandoning the well paid life of an engineer, but that he was fulfilling his duty to God. In March 1837 Pendleton was ordained a deacon at the Episcopal Convention in Petersburg by his great uncle by marriage Bishop William Meade of Virginia.

*　　　　*　　　　*　　　　*

Pendleton's next stop was Newark (pronounced "New Ark"), Delaware where he accepted a professorship of mathematics and chemistry at Newark College, now known as the University of Delaware. The Pendletons enjoyed Newark as it was still a small village and was located in a slave state. The town was settled in 1694 and a school called Newark Academy begun there in 1765. In 1833 the state issued a charter to a new school called the Newark College, and a year later the two schools merged.

In October 1837, Pendleton left his family behind in the comfort of family on a Virginia plantation and arrived in Newark along with several of his former students from Bristol College, including his young relatives. The College paid a salary of $1,000 a year and provided a comfortable home for the professors. Before he could settle into his new position word arrived from Virginia that his infant son Robin had died from measles and that his daughter Lucy was desperately ill. The loss of Robin grieved Pendleton and desolated him, but he turned to his faith in God to assuage his grief. He learned to submit to God's will and the lessons of submission to trials and consolation. In turn, he consoled the family members with sympathizing tenderness and assure them of the life to come after death.

When the family joined him in Newark they filled up the house. Pendleton's brother Gurdon, his brother-in-law John and a number of cousins boarded with the family, earning Pendleton the sum of almost $2.00 a week. Other students came to him for tutoring in mathematics and engineering for $5.00 a week. In this way Pendleton managed to raise enough money to provide for his family. The house had an attached garden large enough for Pendleton to cultivate for food. However, Pendleton did not forget his commitment to the church. Under the auspices of Bishop Onderdonk of Pennsylvania and Delaware he ministered as a deacon in two poor churches several miles from town for which he initially received no compensation. He worked hard as their minister and after some time was paid a salary of between $100 and $200 a year.

In March 1838 he was issued Priest's orders by Bishop Onderdonk in Wilmington, Delaware.

Nevertheless, his recurrent liver and digestive problems returned in 1838 accompanied by bouts of depression. His new doctors treated him aggressively with their tools of the era, including cupping and using leeches for a period of months. Pendleton's daughter Susan later attributed her father's poor health to his indecision about an offer made to become the principal at a new Episcopalian high school in Alexandria, Virginia. Pendleton was very happy teaching in Delaware, serving as a pastor for two churches, and for the first time since he was in the Army he felt financially secure. He shook off his illness and depression after he decided to accept the offer.

＊   ＊   ＊   ＊

Bishop William Meade of Virginia long planned to open a high school for teenage boys near his home in Alexandria, Virginia. Unfortunately, the plan for the school echoed that of the failed Bristol College. The tuition would be low so as to admit needy students eager to pursue an education; even so all of the school's needs were expected to be met through the tuition payments alone. Pendleton's experience at Bristol College should have warned him not to become involved in the new school. Instead, he agreed to be the Principal of the school in order to use "his talents to the glory of God and the good of [mankind]." Pendleton sought a quiet life of practicing his ministry in the light hearted but serious education of young men.

Bishop Meade and his friends put up the funds to acquire a large old residence called "The Howard," and the adjacent 100 acres of land. The house was large enough to accommodate thirty students, and the expectation was that more buildings would be constructed as needed. The site was three miles outside of Alexandria and within a day's ride of Bishop Meade's residence at "Mountain View." In 1839, Episcopal High School opened its doors with thirty five students. The school was intended to be a first rate program. Pendleton envisioned that the school would provide "for boys during the critical period of middle youth and incipient manhood the safest and best superintendence, the soundest and most healthful moral influences and the most faithful Christian guidance, associated with the most useful and extensive course of learning practicable." Pendleton was joined by three new teachers in

1840 and enrollment quickly increased to 101 students. A new building was erected to accommodate the students but Pendleton found he intensely disapproved of it, finding it to be ugly and inconvenient.

Otherwise, initially Pendleton thoroughly enjoyed himself. He conducted the religious services and taught advanced classes in mathematics, chemistry, astronomy, and engineering. He led the students and faculty with "spirited fun, gentleness, and most importantly, a sense of humor." When some students played hooky to go fishing he punished them by having them dangle hooks all day out of the upper stories. When a couple of students challenged each other to a duel they were forced to fight it out, with their seconds, using water shot from large tin cans. Pendleton set the school on a firm academic basis, offering courses in philosophy, Latin, Greek, physics, geometry, algebra, arithmetic, engineering, and geography.

The family settled in and enjoyed life in northern Virginia. They grew vegetables and fruit for the table in their adjacent garden. Pendleton taught his daughters Greek and conducted their religious training in much the way his mother had done. He was able to spend time in nearby Alexandria. In September 1840 Anzelotte gave birth to Alexander ("Sandie") Swift Pendleton, their only son to reach adulthood.

However, the constant stress of managing the school with insufficient funds caused a return of his liver and digestive ailments. In the summer of 1841 he sought relief by vacationing up the Shenandoah Valley, and then to the health spas of Greenbrier and White Sulphur Springs. He and Anzelotte spent six weeks ranging about the mountains of Virginia. Anzelotte was fascinated by the flowers, but William took a serious interest in the new science of geology and collected rocks. This adventure came close to tragedy when he and Anzelotte visited the Natural Bridge, just south of Lexington, Virginia. They were walking below the bridge along Cedar Creek when a storm in the nearby hills caused the water to suddenly rise. The couple narrowly escaped drowning in the creek. Pendleton enjoyed the trip so much that he did not have a return of his "bilious complaints" for many years.

The student population at the Episcopal School continued to rise to over 300 boys. In October 1843, when the front of the school building caught fire from a defective chimney flue, strong winds threatened to carry the fire into the adjacent buildings.

Anzelotte took the family to safety while Pendleton led the boys fighting the fire with blankets and buckets of water. Everyone was saved but there was nothing left but brick walls when the fire subsided. The Pendletons lost nearly all of their personal belongings and had to crowd themselves into small two rooms in a smaller building on the campus.

Insurance on the building adequately enabled the school to re-build an even more commodious building, and to that extent the fire turned out as a benefit to the school. But it was not enough to end the school's financial problems. By the end of the fifth year the school carried a debt of $5,000.00 to cover its expenditures. There were sixty-eight students on a reduced tuition and twenty-two more who paid no tuition at all. In addition, Pendleton had incurred a personal debt of $3,000.00. In the meantime Pendleton had to support his family of six. The debts grew larger in 1844, with a total shortfall of $14,950.00 in school expenses. The debt proved to be an ongoing burden which Pendleton could not be shed, and to a large extent he struggled with some form of debt for the remainder of his life.

By the end of the spring term in 1844 Pendleton lost patience with the school's and his own financial difficulties. He resigned his position and the school closed its doors. The school re-opened in 1866 and still honors the memory of its first Principal. For Pendleton it was another failure, this time saddling him with large debts. Once again he took his family back home to Hanover County to live while he searched for a new opportunity.

       *   *   *   *

The city in which Pendleton sought to re-kindle his career as an educator and priest was one of the fastest growing and most prosperous in the nation. Baltimore's harbor thrived with shipping and it streets with commerce. Before the Civil War it was one of the few major cities in the nation. It was encouraging for him that he was received warmly by the Episcopal clergy there and urged to pursue his dream of opening an Episcopalian school. Thus, in October 1844, the St. Luke's Hall opened its doors as a classical school for boys and Pendleton accepted the position as the school President.

At first Pendleton could not find a home to accommodate both his school and his family. He was not planning to accept boarders either, but at the urgent requests of some of the parents he ended up doing so anyway. But Pendleton could not afford to rent two homes, one for the school and one for his family and lodgers, so one evening he decided to send his wife back home to Virginia where their children remained while he got settled. However, that same night a clergyman dropped by asking Pendleton to accept the ministry of two small rural churches, Sherwood Chapel near Cockeysville and St. John's in the Valley in Baltimore County. It was understood that Pendleton would be an absent rector for which the two churches could offer only a small but steady income. The offer could not have come at a better time. Pendleton was now able to rent two homes; one on Fayette Street near Charles for the school, and one on Lexington Street near Liberty for his home. The school prospered, enabling the family to move at the end of the first year into a house on Courtland Street large enough to accommodate both the school and the family.

But his past mistakes still hounded him. His old creditors pressed for payment as his notes became due. Twice in Baltimore Pendleton was forced to pawn his valuable scientific instruments to buy food. One morning there was neither cash nor food in the house. Pendleton concluded he had to sell his invaluable theodolite, a precision instrument used in surveying, in order to feed his family. A reprieve came to him after the morning service at the school when an elderly lodger permitted to reside in the house pressed an envelope with rent money into his hands. Now there was enough money to buy food for the home.

Pendleton was thrilled to be the rector of the two small rural churches. He worked during the week on his sermons and took the train out to the parishes over the weekend to deliver them. He held a morning service in one and gave a sermon in the other. When he was finished Pendleton remained each Sunday night at Sherwood to wait for the morning train back into town to be present when the school opened on Monday. Occasionally, he was called upon to ride out to Cockeysville to officiate, and he was routinely asked to assist at other churches in Baltimore. His parishioners grew fond of him, sending him provisions for his family, and inviting the family to stay with them over weekends. These visits were heavenly for the family, providing them with rest, recreation, and good cheer.

While the Pendletons lived in Baltimore the war with Mexico erupted along the disputed territory north of the Rio Grande River. There is no record of Pendleton showing any interest in returning to the Army at any time throughout the war although he retained his many friends in the service. By the time he left Baltimore the war in Mexico was winding to a close with Winfield Scott's conquest of Mexico City.

During his stay in Baltimore Pendleton's many friends tried to help him find a more lucrative position. He was proposed for the vacant post as Chaplain for West Point but President Polk preferred a Presbyterian minister. When a large academy in Alabama offered him a full time position as head of a school Pendleton turned down the offer by affirming his primary interest to be "my ministerial duties as those to which I am first pledged, and as those for which I resigned my commission in the army." He added, "I have no expectation or intention of engaging in any situation where full prominence is not at once allowed to clerical duties...." William Nelson Pendleton was set on making the ministry his primary profession.

    *   *   *   *

Pendleton chose to focus on a religious profession just when the Episcopal Church faced a doctrinal crisis. Ever since the 17th Century there had been an ongoing battle over the liturgical texts of the protestant Church of England. Known as the Book of Common Prayer, the text set out the beliefs and the services to be offered to the congregations. The calendar provided with the Book stated which Biblical texts and liturgy would be used on each Sunday and for each of the sacraments and services. For the next two to three centuries a struggle ensued as to whether the liturgy would be more apostolic or more Roman Catholic in nature. It was critical for each sect of the Church to have their preferred texts chosen for use. The struggle was strongly influenced by the faith of the sitting monarch, the Stuarts being Catholic and the Tudors and Hanoverians being Protestant.

The Episcopal Church in America was founded in 1607 with the settling of Jamestown, Virginia, where it later became the Establishment Church of Virginia. In 1789 after America gained her independence the Church produced a new Book of Common Prayer. This text relied heavily on the 1764 Book of Common Prayer but also included text from the more ritualistic Scottish Liturgy. The Book also included liturgical text derived from the older liturgies of the Eastern Orthodox churches and the Liturgy of St. James. The 1789 Book stated that "this Church is far from intending to depart from the Church of England in any essential point of doctrine, discipline, or worship...further than local circumstances require," but there were significant differences. The most important was the re-introduction of the Eucharist as a sacrificial offering similar to that by which Christ was sacrificed. This put the Church's tenets closer to that of the Roman Catholic Church.

By the 1830's there was a strong movement to reform the Episcopal Church that began in Oxford, England came to be known as the Oxford Movement. The group was also called the Tractarians because of their multiple religious tracts espousing a move closer to the Roman Catholic Church and away from the Protestant liturgies of Western Europe. They supported what was called "ritualism," the use of candles, incense, vestments, and other elements of the Roman Catholic liturgy and rites. However, Bishop Meade and a majority of the clergy in the Diocese of Virginia opposed the Oxford movement. While the movement was popular among most seminarians and younger priests, it was opposed by Pendleton.

Pendleton spent a significant time studying the Oxford tracts and related articles, and concluded that the movement and its teachings were contrary to the historical standards of the American and English Episcopal Churches. He considered himself a "Low Churchman," preferring a doctrine closer to the apostolic and Anglican traditions. Thoroughly convinced of his position he eagerly entered into the discussions on the issue trying to persuade the younger clergy of the errors of the Oxford Movement. He preferred a simpler and freer religious tradition.

*   *   *   *

In the autumn of 1847 Pendleton finally committed himself solely to the pulpit, abandoning the schoolroom for the moment. He was accepted as the rector of All Saints Church in Frederick, Maryland, located at the foot of the Blue Ridge Mountain range not far from Washington, D.C. and Virginia. The position provided Pendleton with an annual salary of $1,000 supplemented by other fees for services. The manse was comfortable and allowed Pendleton to take in boarders as well as house his family. The social life in town was sophisticated and town society welcomed its new minister with open arms.

The family settled into a regular routine for the next several years. They arose between five and six in the morning when

Pendleton lit the fires. On dressing he went to his study and spent some time in his devotions. After breakfast the routine varied depending on the seasons. In the summertime, Pendleton worked the kitchen garden turning it into a paradise. There were pear trees, grapevines, strawberries, roses, and beautiful flowers everywhere. In the winter he chopped wood. Then while Anzelotte taught the girls their lessons and work, Pendleton took his son Sandie into his study for lessons in mathematics, Greek and Latin. Because he was a boy Sandie was also sent for lessons at an excellent boys' school in town. Occasionally, Pendleton also spent time teaching his daughters the same subjects.

Before lunch Pendleton was in his study reading and writing, except on Mondays when he rested from his labors on Sunday. After lunch he paid a pastoral visit on the ill, infirm, and poor, and later took a walk with his wife. After tea, Pendleton either worked or had his children read their lessons to him. Following dinner the family held prayers and retired for the evening, usually by ten o'clock, leaving him and Anzelotte with an opportunity to read or write. In addition to the two Sunday and two weekly services at All Saints, Pendleton also ministered to those incarcerated in the Frederick jail and almshouse, and held occasional services in the parishes around Frederick. All in all the routine was leisurely compared to his work the years prior, and it provided time for reflection and study.

During the war with Mexico the highly partisan President Polk promoted the interests of his Democratic Party and his best friends. He appointed his law partner Gideon Pillow, a man bereft of military knowledge, experience, or skill but full of self-importance and inflated ego, as the second in command to the Whig Party's General Winfield Scott in the campaign to conquer Mexico City. Inevitably, Pillow not only ignored military rules, regulations and orders, but also published criticism of General Scott in the press. For this Scott ordered him court-martialed. Polk used his command influence to convert the process to a court of inquiry on Scott's conduct, and to ensure that the court would rule in favor of his friend Pillow. The trial was set to be heard in Frederick, Maryland. In the spring of 1848 a series of witnesses, consisting mostly of high ranking and distinguished officers from the campaign. Pendleton knew many of these men from his time at West Point, and he spent many evenings at his home providing relaxation and comfort for his old companions. The court exonerated Pillow as expected, and soon after Pillow and two of the officers sitting on the court received promotions.

As was common before 20th Century medicine conquered most childhood disease children often failed to live until adulthood. The Pendleton family was not immune. In August 1849 their daughter Lucy, by now a teenager, was visiting her uncle Hugh Pendleton in nearby Jefferson County, Virginia, in the Shenandoah Valley just across the Potomac River from Maryland. She became violently ill. Her parents were summoned but despite the best care available at the time Lucy passed away. A family favorite, her loss was crushing to the family. A couple of months later Anzelotte's eccentric father Captain Page died, with her mother following only two months later during a visit to the Pendletons in Frederick.

By 1850 the Pendletons were well established in Frederick, and Pendleton was becoming known for his religious work outside the community. The family consisted of four daughters, one son, and three boarders, including a Nelson relative. The Diocese of Maryland selected Pendleton to attend the General Convention of the Episcopal Church in Cincinnati that year. He presented a memorial from the rectors and vestries of the "Low Church" parishes in Maryland setting forth their views on the "nature and extent of the claims of episcopal authority." It appears that only one item, the authorization for a bishop to administer the Sacrament of the Lord's Supper, or Communion, during his visitations, met with the convention's approval.

Pendleton wrote home of his travels, including a stay in Uniontown, Pennsylvania, where his brother died some years before. He travelled by coach to Wheeling, [West] Virginia, and then took the steamboat *Buckeye State* "down the Ohio River to Cincinnati, which he described as a "novel thing" and a "western steamboat." Rains at the start of the trip made the ride down to Maysville, Kentucky pleasant, but from there to Cincinnati the boat constantly grounded on sand bars.

One spring the Monocacy River flooded Frederick carrying away the Patrick Street Bridge. The town turned to Pendleton to apply his engineering skills to survey the riverbanks and plan a new bridge that could resist flood waters and the debris it carried. He did so without compensation, and the bridge remained in place for many years.

As he entered the early 1850's Pendleton's nomadic nature returned. In 1852 he was tempted by an offer of a pulpit from a church in Iowa to strengthen the Episcopal Church in the Northwest until a West Point friend cautioned him that the severe winters would be a hardship for Anzelotte, and that he would have to hire rather than own his servants. A year later a dispute arose between Pendleton and the vestry of the All Saints Church. It seems that clergymen are always eager to build new and bigger churches and Pendleton was no exception. He saw All Saints Church as poorly designed, more resembling a barn than a church, poorly built, and inconvenient to use. It needed repair and was no longer appropriate for the congregation. A similar dispute led to the resignation of his predecessor.

An offer by two gentlemen of land and cash to build a new church raised the issue anew. Pendleton worked hard to persuade the vestry to commit to building the new church but was unpersuasive. In late January 1853 in an effort to resolve the dispute in his favor he sermonized one Sunday morning on King David's address to the prophet Nathan; "I dwell in a house of cedar, but the ark of God dwelleth within curtains." The sermon consisted of two parts; one emphasizing "the leading principles which should regulate the character of a Christian sanctuary," and the other "the state of facts connected with this present edifice." (II Samuel vii: 2). Pendleton had the sermon printed and circulated among the congregation but it changed nothing. The original church still stands.

The stress of the dispute caused Pendleton to fall ill with the same old complaints again. He started applying for teaching positions in Virginia, or in the alternative, in a parsonage. He was ready to go back home. When he recovered from his illness in July 1853 Pendleton resigned the pulpit at All Saints and departed Frederick. This time William Nelson Pendleton was going home to Virginia, and to a location he found a place so beautiful and tranquil he made his home there for the rest of his life.

54

Rev. Dr. Pendleton

Lexington, Virginia

4. IN THE MIDST OF THE GARDEN OF EDEN

[LEXINGTON, 1853-1861]

And the Lord planted a garden eastward in Eden, ...And out of the ground made the Lord to grow every tree that is pleasant to the sight, and good for food; the tree of life also in the midst of the garden, and the tree of knowledge of good and evil.

Genesis 2:7-8, King James Version

The Pendletons arrived by stage in Lexington Virginia in October 1853, and found themselves in one of the most scenic areas in America. Henry Kyd Douglas, Stonewall Jackson's aide during the Civil War, in describing the Shenandoah Valley wrote: "The sun from its rising to its setting does not shine upon a more blessed spot than the Valley of Virginia. From the beautiful banks of the ...historic Potomac, to where the ...solemn mountains ...send their streamlets to form the Shenandoah and the James, are countless evidences of the generosity with which Providence has dealt with this royal region. The Blue Ridge on the east, the Alleghenies on the west... enclose this favorite Valley in a magnificent frame....From ...Harpers Ferry to the Natural Bridge the traveler may wander over picturesque mountains, by splendid rivers and clear rivulets, through stately groves and broad green fields, each richest of its kind and unsurpassed in this ...continent."

Rockbridge County, Virginia is located at the southern end of the Shenandoah Valley. It is bordered on the east by the Blue Ridge and on the west by the North Mountain of the Appalachian Mountain chain. The valley itself consists of rolling hills, woods, and fields dotted with farms and brick mansions. Throughout the 1850's Rockbridge County was a quiet rural community, isolated by the mountains from easy access to the outside world, the perfect image of a Jeffersonian paradise. The soil was rich and supported bounteous crop productions. The area was a "bread basket" for Virginia, and indeed, later for the Confederacy, as the land was covered with apple orchards and fields of corn, rye, oats, and wheat.

In the center of Rockbridge County is Lexington, the county seat. The town was laid out in 1778 on the banks of the North River where it was crossed by the Borden Trail, and named after the Massachusetts town where the Revolutionary War began. Before the Civil War various travelers referred to Lexington as being "beautifully situated on an eminence in the midst of a great valley... its horizon bounded on all sides by blue mountains, whose outlines are uncommonly diversified and pleasing,....the most beautiful [ever seen]," and "few finer subjects can be found for the artist's pencil than the well-built village - long, graceful crescent of hills topped with handsome private residences, a fine female academy, the colonnade of Washington College, and the castle like Military Institute, with the Jump, North, and House Mountains as a background, and in the intervening forests the ivy covered ruins of Liberty Hall Academy."

The town's Main Street of two story brick stores and homes rose from the North River at Jordan's Point and climbed a ridgeline to the south. Along the peak of the ridge sat the center of town providing an unparalleled vista of the surrounding hills, glens, and mountains. The sidewalks were made of red brick. Running parallel to Main Street were tree-shaded roads of homes, most of average size, but some quite large and beautiful. Law firms, wood working shops, groceries, banks, pharmacies, two bookstores, an oyster house, cigar store, clothing store, and two hotels made up the center of town. On a ridge to the north running parallel to Main Street sat the red brick and white columned colonnade of Washington College and nearer to the North River sits the Virginia Military Institute.

Washington College began as Augusta Academy near Staunton in 1749. After several moves the school was located just before the Revolution near Fairfield in Rockbridge County. In 1776 the school moved to Timber Ridge, just north of Lexington, and changed its name to Liberty Hall Academy in support of the Revolution. In 1789 the school adopted the name Washington Academy, and in 1797 it received a gift of Potomac Canal stock from George Washington. The gift remains a part of the endowment to this day and contributes a small amount towards every student's tuition. In 1813, the school became Washington College. In the 1820s the College built a series of two story brick buildings fronted with white columns stretched out along the crest of the ridge. But by 1853, when the artist and writer David Hunter Strother praised the beauty of the scenery and buildings of Washington College he also noted, "this institution, like the name and principles of its great namesake, seems to be drifting out of public notice and esteem."

The Virginia Military Institute was an institution modeled on West Point to train young men for the military and civilian life. The Virginia legislature established arsenals to care for the state's accumulation of arms and munitions for the militia, one of which was located in Lexington. In 1839 the state created the Virginia Military Institute at the Arsenal to train cadets to serve the state as teachers and militia officers. The VMI barracks were designed by Andrew Jackson Davis, the architect of Bristol College, and built on a high promontory one half mile from the center of town. The barracks consisted of a U-shaped limestone structure with crenellated parapets and octagonal towers built in a gothic style.

The people of the County differed from those living east of the Blue Ridge. The Blue Ridge had blocked most of the migration from the heart of Virginia into the valley. Instead, the settlers coming up the Shenandoah Valley from the north were Scots-Irish and strongly Presbyterian. Their imprint was on everything. One VMI cadet reminisced later that: "The blue limestone streets looked hard. The red brick houses, with severe stone trimmings and plain white pillars and finishings were stiff and formal. The grim portals of the Presbyterian church looked cold as a dog's nose. The cedar hedges in the yards, trimmed hard and close along straight brick pathways were as unsentimental as mathematics. The dress of the citizens, male and female, was of single-breasted simplicity; and to spend an evening among strictly reared young female Presbyterians…is like sitting upon icebergs, cracking hailstones with one's teeth…."

This was a land filled with Presbyterians and with only a sprinkling of Baptists and Methodists, but hardly any Episcopalians. Before 1843 the Episcopalians were scattered about the county, and only at Walker Creek was there an authorized reader for any congregation. A vestry was organized only by combining with a congregation in Buchanan some twenty-five miles away to the south, creating the Woodville Parish. In 1846 the Latimer Parish was separated from the Woodville Parish and became the rectory for Rockbridge County.

In the 21st Century it is difficult to conceive of the intensity of the dislike and mistrust between the various Christian sects. But for the people of the 18th and 19th Centuries these differences were very pronounced. Individual social and family life centered on the church. For the Low Church Presbyterians memories of the Episcopal Church reminded them of their grandparents' horror stories of the English religious terrorism against the Presbyterians in Scotland. The Episcopalians, being mostly of the educated and higher social class, tended to look down on the Presbyterians as ignorant Low Church. The Presbyterians believed in pre-destination, that their fate as Christians was determined for them at birth, while the Episcopalians were too ritualistic in their services using some of the same rites and liturgies as the Roman Catholic Church, and were feared as the old state establishment church they were once required to support and attend. Each felt that the other violated key principles of Christ's teachings. Such mistrust continued in some areas well into the 20th Century. As a Low Church Episcopalian, Pendleton did not reflect these fears and prejudices.

At first the local Presbyterians in Lexington blocked the construction of an Episcopalian church by denying them a lot on which to build. However, by purchasing the property through an intermediary the first Episcopal Church in the county was erected in 1843 at the base of the hill below Washington College and named Grace Episcopal Church. By the time of the Civil War many of the leading men in the county were members.

It seemed an unlikely place for an ambitious and needy clergyman to choose to pursue his ministry. The congregation was small and poor, and could only offer a salary of six hundred dollars, to which the Diocesan Missionary Society added one hundred dollars. But despite the small income, there were other advantages which appealed to Pendleton. He would be in a position to influence the students at both colleges, and could find a local education for his son Sandie. In addition, a large rectory house would be placed at his disposal.

The Rectory was recently acquired by the parish and required extensive repair before the family could move in. For a couple of months they lived in the Lexington Hotel in the heart of town. The Rectory was to be William Nelson Pendleton's home for the rest of his life. Located at what is now 107 Lee Avenue, the Rectory was originally built for the prominent lawyer Charles Dorman. It sat on the western edge of the ridge north of town, with a lawn stretching all the way down to where Jefferson Avenue now runs. Built by John Jordan and Samuel Darst, its design probably came from next door neighbor, lawyer, farmer, and politician Samuel McDowell Reid.

The house incorporated classical revival and Federalist designs. The large brick house is set back behind iron fence and tall old trees. The entrance hall has a lovely stairway above the fanlight of the doorway. The two story house had a one story Doric columned porch and balustrade. Above the fanlight is a carved hand, the meaning of which is unknown. Inside there is wainscoting along the walls, wide moldings around the windows, mantelpieces above the fireplaces with free standing columns and fanned oval medallions as decorations. Pendleton took advantage of the size of the house by installing a top story to accommodate a dormitory and a classroom. In this way he supplemented his income by teaching and boarding boys at a small academy in the rectory. After a while he relied on his older daughters and son to teach so that he could focus on other matters.

*　　　　　*　　　　　*　　　　　*

The day after arriving in town Pendleton sent his son Sandie to Washington College to enroll him as a student. That afternoon, Sandie, only thirteen years old at the time, was examined by the faculty to see if he was qualified. To the amazement of the professors, Sandie handled the examination with aplomb, easily passing the tests in Greek, Latin, and mathematics. When one of the professors asked Pendleton why he had sent Sandie off for the examination on his own, Pendleton replied, "I knew that he was well prepared, and my son must learn to depend upon himself and not on me. I wish him to be a good scholar, but still more a strong, self-reliant man." Sandie joined with twelve other pupils in the class, most from the locality or adjacent counties.

Pendleton immediately found friends in town. VMI Superintendent Colonel Francis H. Smith, and Major Thomas Williamson, one of the VMI professors, knew Pendleton through West Point and were also staunch Episcopalians. This enabled him to give a public discourse at VMI in November 1853 soon after his arrival. Later, Pendleton provided a testimonial in promotion of Colonel Smith's text on mathematics, and joined the town's prestigious debating club called the Franklin Society. Nevertheless, an abyss existed in the relations between VMI and Washington College. VMI, as an established state school, favored the Episcopal faith while Washington College, founded as a Presbyterian school, remained rock ribbed Presbyterian. The split was furthered by a tragic incident in which Pendleton became collaterally involved.

On December 23, 1853 the Pendletons staged a holiday fair which was one of the most eagerly awaited social occasions of the Christmas season. As one cadet recalled, "All the beauty and fashion of Lexington" was to attend, and the VMI cadets were given permission to come as well. The cadets shined their boots and brass, brushed their wool uniforms, and got their hair properly trimmed. Many of the cadets went to the barber shop located at the Lexington Hotel, home to the Pendletons at the time, as well as to the students of the Brockenbrough Law School (later the Washington & Lee University Law School). One of the law students was the notorious lover Charles B. Christian. Christian's current amorous target was Mary Evelyn Anderson, a cousin of VMI Cadet Thomas Blackburn. Blackburn was no innocent. Known for drinking and violence, he was court martialed and convicted for a prank pulled on Thomas J. Jackson, later to earn the nickname "Stonewall", one of the VMI faculty members. The conviction was reversed on appeal by Superintendent Smith. Blackburn was also known to be overly sensitive about smears on his honor.

The morning of the party Blackburn arrived at the barber shop to find Christian sitting in the barber's chair in front of him. Another cadet commented on the "ladykiller" looks of Christian in front of Blackburn, to which Christian tauntingly claimed that he could seduce any woman in Lexington. The term seduction was not to be tolerated by a family member of the young lady involved, and Blackburn brooded over the remarks. He continued to brood when he arrived later at Grace Episcopal Church and the Pendleton party. There he saw Christian and Anderson arm in arm promenading about the fair. Later there was a dispute as to whether Christian's attentions were welcomed by the young lady. She claimed that Christian was boorish, ungentlemanly, and very disagreeable. One of Christian's friends said that he could not say if Mary Anderson was pleased or not by the attentions. At some point she agreed to "walk out," or date, with Christian, but later on her carriage ride home from the fair announced to friends that she had decided not to allow Christian to escort her. However, Mary's cousin Blackburn was incensed, complaining about Christian's behavior, Anderson's "promenade" with Christian, and Christian's remarks about "seduction." He complained enough about Christian for the comments to reach Christian, and Christian decided that his honor had been impugned.

For the next few weeks rumors flew and confrontations between the two men escalated. Christian wrote Mary Anderson that he needed to know who had besmirched his honor with such accusations. In a confrontation at the hotel Blackburn told Christian he was the man who questioned his character. Both men became increasingly angry, Blackburn stalked Christian with some VMI cadet friends to which Christian took exception to as a threat of physical violence. Christian armed himself with a bowie knife and cane for protection.

Blackburn may not have been religious but was attending Superintendent Smith's Episcopal services at VMI. However, he had developed an interest in Julia Junkin, the daughter of Washington College's President and Presbyterian minister George Junkin. They had recently agreed to "walk out" together. Christian regularly attended services at the Presbyterian Church on Main and Nelson streets at the heart of downtown Lexington.

The morning service on January 14, 1854 at the Presbyterian Church passed peacefully although both Christian and Blackburn attended. The evening service began after sunset, and the lights of the church shone on the adjacent streets leaving pockets of darkness nearby. Blackburn escorted Miss Junkin to the church that evening. As they passed through the front door Christian was standing there. He asked Blackburn to step outside to talk. Blackburn took Julia to her pew, excused himself, and went outside. Blackburn and Christian turned the corner and walked down Nelson to the end of the church lot where it was dark. Bystanders heard the sound of someone being whipped by a cane, which was probably Christian thumping the much larger Blackburn. There was a further struggle during which Christian lunged at Blackburn and stabbed him. The wound was fatal.

What at first blush appears to be an open and shut murder case became a complicated and expensive legal battle dividing the VMI and Episcopalian community from that of the College, town, and the Presbyterians. Junkin was an opinionated man of strong beliefs and a hard core Presbyterian. Previously he had refused to hire William Nelson Pendleton as a mathematics professor because he was an Episcopalian priest and since Lexington already had an Episcopalian school in VMI. These comments so angered Superintendent Smith that he demanded that Junkin appear before the VMI Board of Visitors to explain himself.

The murder case similarly divided the community. VMI rallied behind its murdered cadet Blackburn while Junkin, the Presbyterians, and the town establishment defended Christian's honor. A large, expensive, and well trained team of lawyers defending Christian spent the preliminary hearing attacking Blackburn's reputation for violence. Hugh Pendleton, William's oldest brother, attended the hearing and took notes to share with his friend Superintendent Smith. Hugh Pendleton concluded that the Commonwealth's Attorney needed help, and that since Blackburn's family was not wealthy, funds needed to be raised. The famous lawyer Thomas Michie was hired to assist in the prosecution.

The case came to trial in Lexington where intense peer pressure on the jurors resulted in a hung jury. Another trial was held in Liberty, now Bedford, Virginia, near Christian's hometown leading to his acquittal. After the verdict crowds burned effigies of Superintendent Smith. The strain between the ruling class Episcopalians and the mainstream Presbyterians in Lexington was palpable, and made Pendleton's ministry much more difficult. Later the same year the Presbyterian Thomas Jackson resigned from the Rockbridge County Bible Society due to a rift with the Episcopalian Superintendent Smith and Pendleton. The rift was buried during the war and Reconstruction periods but re-emerged in a new form afterwards.

A month after the murder Jackson and Pendleton both applied for a position as a mathematics professor at the University of Virginia. Pendleton had complained to his brother Hugh that it was the "need of salary which most affects me. Here I can hardly live, and must have a school which is a great drawback. Besides, I have never been able to get out of debt." Hugh actively promoted his brother's appointment and a series of testimonials on his behalf were presented to the University's Board of Visitors. However, when Pendleton heard that his West Point classmate and good friend Albert Bledsoe had also applied for the job he withdrew his candidacy, and in doing so highly recommended Bledsoe. Bledsoe received the appointment.

*   *   *   *

Pendleton focused on his ministry. Not only did he preach at Grace Episcopal he traveled about the county when weather permitted and preached wherever he could find a handful of Episcopalians. In May 1854 he attended the Virginia Diocese Convention in Lynchburg and proposed the next convention be held in Lexington. The idea was initially ridiculed, but Superintendent Smith and Pendleton persuaded a majority to approve the proposal, and prevailed. The next May the convention was held in very Presbyterian Lexington.

Pendleton also travelled extensively on church projects, serving as a general delegate to the national convention of the church in Philadelphia and at Sabbath school conventions in Virginia. In 1854 he travelled to Philadelphia, Cape May, Wheeling, Cincinnati, Chicago, Milwaukee, Cleveland, Rochester, and other Northern cities to present the needs of the American Sunday-School Union on behalf of the church. During this long trip his old liver ailment returned. He was told to be regular in his rest, take tepid baths, rub himself vigorously, and not to engage in too much exercise.

In Massachusetts he encountered active abolitionism. One acquaintance urged him to read Adams's "South Side View of Slavery" which Pendleton found to be more just than Harriett Beecher Stowe's "Uncle Tom's Cabin." On the whole he viewed the abolitionists in New England as "the most lawless radicals,— ignorant and undisciplined, but self-reliant, bold, and active,—ready to push abolitionism to the very death." As a counterpoint to the abolitionists' complaints about slavery Pendleton pondered on the exploitation of young women working in the woolen mills of New England:

> I could but think of them to-day at Lowell. Those girls—with their three dollars a week—steaming the livelong day amid the din of machinery that deadens every sense, standing forever over the clattering looms or spindles, and inhaling an atmosphere charged with the mingled fragrance of fish oil and fetid exhalations, and with common dust interspersed with cotton or woolen fiber, seemed to me doomed to a harder lot than thousands of slave girls.

On the whole he saw the people of New England as suffering from their greed and ambition, "The very sharpening of the wits by continual effort to make their way so cultivates selfishness that you can see it in every lineament and motion."

*   *   *   *

All of the turmoil in town did not affect young Sandie Pendleton. He excelled at his studies and in his third and fourth year assisted in teaching Latin and mathematics. As a student Sandie was asked to join the Graham Society debating and lecture club along with his father and Thomas Jackson. Over the years he heard debates on black equality, the Kansas Nebraska bill, slavery, seduction, and the Revolutionary War. He also misbehaved on occasion with his various reported infractions including disorder, sleeping, laughing, indecent language and rudeness to President Junkin. The penalties usually ran between a nickel and a quarter of a dollar. Sandie, as well as Junkin, were also reported for failing to promptly return overdue library books.

When his class held their graduation ceremony at the Presbyterian Church in 1857 Sandie delivered the oration for the Society of the Cincinnati on the character of the State of Virginia. Only seventeen years old at the time Pendleton felt that his son was too young to start studies at the University of Virginia. Instead, he opened up the attic school and had Sandie and his older sisters teach the young men. This relieved Pendleton of an obligation while also bringing needed income into the family. Sandie, who had a warm and harmonious relationship with his father, was pleased to comply.

In 1859 Sandie entered the University of Virginia at the same time his oldest sister Susan married Edwin "Ned" Lee of Shepherdstown, [West] Virginia, a cousin of Robert E. Lee. The marriage confused the senior Pendleton as he did not know whether he should refer to Ned Lee by his Christian name or by Mister. When Sandie matriculated at the University of Virginia he was described as not necessarily handsome as he had an elongated face and lantern jaw. His hair was light, complexion fair, and he bore a "kindly, benevolent expression." Once in Charlottesville, Sandie embarked on a Master of Arts program in liberal arts studies with the purpose of entering the clergy, and he greatly enjoyed engaging in various sports.

As news filtered back home about Sandie's excessive love of sports his parents expressed concern. Pendleton wrote Sandie that he should not permit pursuit of "secular study and over indulgent recreation" to the neglect of his soul:

> Of course there is urgent need in each of these directions. You must study a great deal, and you ought to enjoy vigorous and mirthful recreation, suitable to your age, disposition and association. But it requires care to avoid the spirit of selfish worldliness under such circumstances, and to cherish the life of God in the soul. The great work of life…. to which you are looking forward, can neither be rightfully prepared nor discharged without a very close intimacy with heaven, and this cannot be cherished without much prayer, watchfulness, and self-denial.

Of course, Sandie replied that he was grateful for the advice and would be more cautious. But this was not the only concern of his parents. They also were aware that Sandie was a very poor money manager. He lent money he did not have and had to borrow money in return to meet his expenses. His father scolded him, "In all pecuniary matters …if you are obligated to raise a sum, & [the borrower] has made his arrangements in view of this understanding, you must carry it on to the extent that it may be necessary, but limit the amount to the smallest scale…." Pendleton reminded his son in the autumn of 1860 that in the aftermath of Lincoln's election there would be a "season of disorders in all the relations of society such as has not been known in out part of the continent since our Union was established." Therefore, Sandie was urged not to "incur needless pecuniary liability." Pendleton urged Sandie to ask his uncle Hugh for reasonable terms on a small loan in order to pay off his debts.

       *   *   *   *

      The work as a minister and tutor permitted Pendleton enough spare time to pursue his intellectual interests. He studied geology, archaeology, biology, and of course, religion. He submitted articles for publication in magazines such as the Southern Literary Messenger on such topics as the need for a dress code based on "dignity, moderation, neatness, and above all of true penitence and celestial faith." On a more serious note Pendleton immersed himself in the study of ethnology and geology and their impact on religious faith. He joined other Southern thinkers asserting that all the races shared a common intellectual and moral nature and that all races were capable of improvement to a point and capable of adopting Christianity. The clergy of the South also dominated the debate on the application of the expanding fields of science to the Bible. Many, including Pendleton, urged others to accept the fact that the earth was far older than previously thought. For his works Kenyon College in Ohio conferred on Pendleton the degree of Doctor of Divinity in 1857 claiming that "seldom in these latter days has the title been so justly merited."

      Pendleton gathered his thoughts on science and faith in a published seminal work on the subject. The book, "Science a Witness for the Bible," consisted of five previously published articles re-written for the book. When published by Lippincott & Company of Philadelphia in June 1860 the book was well received by reviewers despite the pomposity of the writing style. As elementary as some of the conclusions appear to be today, for mid-19th Century America the argument for the geologic interpretation of the age of the world was *avant garde* for its time and place.

      The first chapter is on "Science and Revelation." In it Pendleton reviews the necessity of religious leaders to address the recent discoveries by science. Science was becoming the controlling field of intellectual and social development, and it was now competing with the moral element of culture produced by religion. But Pendleton did not see that the two fields had to conflict:

That there is, in truth, an entire harmony between the moral and the material agencies that have been mentioned, between the triumphs of Science and the teachings of Scripture, nay more, that they are so thoroughly intertwined and blended in their relations to the human mind, as to prove their common origin in the Source of all wisdom....

Pendleton saw mankind as being torn through "the complexity and disordered condition of his faculties" into becoming fitful, wayward, impatient, turbulent, passionate, as well being conscientious, affectionate, and aspiring to lofty ideals. This "want of harmony" causes "actual warfare, between the moral sense and the selfish purpose" leading then to a "false philosophy." This is to be countered by allaying "the strife in man's breast and to quiet the turmoil of society, to loosen the iron bands of unlawful authority" so as to permit mankind to engage in a reasonable and truer inquiry. For the faithful the Bible is the best means to accomplish this task. After all, in Psalm 104 the Bible includes a description of the entire universe, "Who coverest thyself with light as with a garment: who stretchest out the heavens like a curtain." It was the Bible that educated the barbarians who destroyed the Roman Empire, and their Church preserved civilization. Since then "great advances in religion, such as Luther came about with great advances to science, religion helping science. In return, science validates the record of revelation in the Bible. "

The then up and coming field of geology, which Pendleton first studied during his trip to the Shenandoah in the 1830's, presented a history of an age before the Garden of Eden which required a "more candid and comprehensive reading of the entire Scriptures ... in all the astonishing precision and fullness of its meaning..." For Pendleton the primeval beasts and worlds described in the Bible demonstrate God's awful power to destroy and create whole worlds.

In the second chapter, "The Human Family," Pendleton begins with the observation that the "whole range of ethnology" has proven what the Scripture teaches, that "man is one." Despite all of its variations all of mankind came from one stock; that the human race came from a common ancestry. He disagreed with those claiming that some races are absolutely "inferior," and not only "born to be ruled," but "destined to live and prosper," merely, "till a superior destroying race shall come to exterminate and supplant them, and that no philanthropy, no legislation, no missionary labors, can change this law." Such thoughts conflicted with the moral tone of the Scriptures.

Pendleton then commented on how Christianity supported the enslavement of others. Christianity dictated that there is a duty of those responsible for the enslaved. Those who claim that slavery is a sin fail to understand that the Bible approved of slavery and sets forth the proper duties of slave and master. God issued "reiterated injunctions to masters to treat their slaves considerately and kindly and to servants religiously to obey, even under the severest species of bondage." This "sacred code" guiding the faithful is the "surest directory to duty… And so long as we abide by the sanctions of this code, whatever deluded enthusiasts and corrupt agitators may pretend, we have with us not only the decisive voice of constitutional law, but the disturbing acquiescence, if not the full approval, of the enlightened Christian mind…"

Pendleton attacked the then current theory of "diversity," that every region of the earth had its own original species of human. The theory was based on how flora varies from region to region. Pendleton cited the geologist Sir Charles Lyell that if a man started in one spot in the world his race would spread due to the tendency of populations to increase beyond the means of subsistence and by the drifting of boats to distant shores. Pendleton also questioned those relying on the variations in physique and color among mankind, noting that the Native American tribes differed from each other but were in the same locale, and the same could be said of Europeans. He again relied on Lyell in stating that the human race can evolve since "modifications occur and are transmittable to offspring." But then he concluded erroneously that "there is a point beyond which they cannot deviate." Again citing Lyell, he posited that "a short period of time is generally sufficient to effect nearly the whole change which an alteration of external circumstances can bring about in the habits of a species."

Pendleton sidesteps for a moment to let the reader know he is not questioning the time line of the Bible, rather that the genealogical lists in the Old Testament were incomplete. This allows for the passage of vast amounts of time between the creation and the present as is reflected in the ancient bones dug up in very ancient rocks.

He disagreed with the proposition that black slaves were incapable of improvement. After all, he contended, they were undergoing a generation or two of social improvement by their introduction to Christianity and western civilization, and with a mixture of blood [thanks to the rapacious nature of some of the slaveholders] their blood line was improving. Thus is God's purpose in promoting slavery fulfilled. Nevertheless, the "pollution of blackness" means that they will never become restored to European status. In fact, hybrid races are only a transitory stage since they have difficulty reproducing.

Pendleton observed that a comparative study of languages around the globe showed that all languages are related. He cited U.S. Navy officer, oceanographer, and VMI professor Matthew Fontaine Maury for the relationship between the Micmac language of Mexico and that of the Inuit in the Aleutians. Thus, he concluded, "all the languages of the earth however at first view apparently dissociated and incongruous, traceable to one source; and, by consequence, all human tribes have proceeded from one center and descended from one parentage."

The third chapter is entitled "The Chronology of Creation," and reconciles the Book of Genesis with the new science of geology. Pendleton felt this was necessary since those who adhere strictly to the timelines set for the Creation only alienate the men of science by their ignorance. The simple answer, Pendleton noted, is that the six periods of time in Genesis are not meant to be literally read as a twenty four hour day but as an age.

Those who claim that God simply created what appear to be old rocks and fauna or that they are merely antediluvian in nature contradict the Scriptures. After all, Genesis mentions the two rivers of Eden which still exist today. Both Psalm 90 and Proverbs chapter 8 mention the ancient age of the world. Those claiming that geology is an unproved science would have to ignore the evidence before their own eyes:

> ...so facts, the most striking and convincing, in the structure of our earth's crust, are so commonly noticeable, as not only to claim the attention of all reasonable men, but to furnish a secure basis for

70

proper reliance upon the achievements of able and faithful investigations in this department of research....The truth is, almost every man may discover for himself, alike in great utterances of the Bible, and in strange tokens everywhere presented by the earth's strata, much more than enough to discredit every form of the six-thousand-year hypothesis.

Look at Niagara Falls, he noted. There you find very hard rock, hundreds of feet deep, with a slowly receding wall, "when the agency and its observed results are compared with the total achievement, the period for such wear and tear is found really to baffle calculation." When you add the fossils embedded in the rock, the pressure turning sediment into hard stone, it tells of a story of "ancient vicissitude and unregistered ages." Then in discussing the nature of earthquakes Pendleton unconsciously hints at the as yet undiscovered movements of tectonic plates by referring to the lifting of the Norwegian coast and the sinking of Greenland. Layer upon layer of rock and earth disclose older and older species. Each period of time cannot be assigned a definite age, they are "unmeasured and immeasurable antiquity....:

> We find ourselves on a road, where the lapse of duration is marked not by the succession of seasons and years, but by the slow excavation, by water, of deep valleys in rock-marble; by the return of a continent to the bosom of an ocean in which ages before it had been slowly formed; or by the departure of one world and the formation of another....The mountain masses of stone which now surround us, extending for miles in length and breadth, were once sentient existences; and coralline; living at the bottom of ancient seas and lakes. How countless [are] the ages necessary for their accumulation.

This slow kind of geologic process furnishes "one, consistent, unequivocal testimony, to the occurrence of successive orders of beings, in periodic course, with marked diversities gradually introduced, one after another, through prolonged intervals and ages."

Pendleton believed that the use of the term "day" in Genesis is imprecise. They could not be real days as the sun was not created until the fourth day. The ancient Hebrew word used was "yom," a term not meant to describe any particular duration. It is found in the description of eras as well, such as in "Yom of Jerusalem" or the "Yom of justice, or mercy." Pendleton believed the word was used in four distinct senses: "(1) To specify the light-time … as we speak of daylight or daytime. (2) To denote the phenomenal days, which, with seasons and years, the sun was to mark off…. (3) To characterize … the sum-total of the whole series of creative periods. And (4) to express those strange, phenomenal intervals, of whatever extent and however divided … as not marked off by rising or setting sun."

For Pendleton the Bible was not meant to be a scientific text but to provide enlightenment. After all there are three great periods of time in geology. The first era was dominated by corals, crustaceans, and fish; the second with dwarf mammals and large birds, and great sea monsters; and the third with the mammals. Creatures from all three eras can be found everywhere in the world today, so one cannot say that there is a great gulf of time between the first and second verse of Genesis. He then concluded that man is the end point of creation, and that no further evolution of the species may be feared. God intended instead that by preparing an imperfect man that his work of creation culminated in a final day of redemption of mankind by man.

The fourth chapter is on "The Age of Mankind," and repeats much of what Pendleton noted earlier about the passage of time. He ridiculed those believing the world could not be older than 6,000 years. Fossils found throughout the world show layers of extinct cypress forests going back 150,000 years. But then Pendleton backtracks, questioning the accuracy of the determination of age by geologists of the time and the evolution process as described by Darwin.

There is a difference, he observed, between the evolution of lower species and the creation of man. The former are lower species and lack an immortal soul, nor did God "breathe immortality" into the process. In Pendleton's mind mankind did not evolve by chance because the record is imperfect. "Geology assuredly does not reveal

72

any such finely graduated organic chain…. The explanation lies, I believe, in the extreme imperfection of the geological record." Archaeology proves that no civilization existed more than 6,000 years ago, and that the created man would not have existed for thousands of years "in darkness, feebleness, and stagnation." Therefore, mankind came into existence by creation relatively recently. Exactitude in this is inessential for the purpose of religious faith since the "Bible is essentially and intrinsically wholly independent of all learned confirmation."

His final chapter is entitled "The Monuments of Lost Races," and addresses the criticism of the Bible by those relying on archaeology. Pendleton reviewed the ancient civilizations of the world and pointed out their similarities in calendars and worship. Yet, he noted, all of these civilizations failed due to their pursuit of false religions. He concluded:

> But this suggests a final thought, arising also from the old monuments: the end that comes to human things. It may be that Divine Providence sees best to order change for nations as for individuals, even irrespective of their vice or virtue. It may be that in its best condition, yet to be expected, the great moral atmosphere of the world, like its physical, demands the ventilating energy of storm and tempest, though in the rush many a valuable structure fall. But however this be, one thing is certain: the lost races tell it, as history tells it, as the Bible declares, nations, like individuals, suffer for their sins….. Yes, this entire planet shall one day be the funeral pile of all that is consumable in whatsoever has had part with humanity,—or it shall be the purified, renovated scene of a different existence, the enduring memorial of all generations of men.

Pendleton's reading of the great geologists, archaeologists, and Hebrew scholars of his time only confirmed his deep faith in the truth of the Christian religion.

*   *   *   *

Whenever he was home Pendleton continued his usual routine. He preached twice at Grace Episcopal on Sundays with a carefully prepared sermon. He also held two weekly Episcopal services for the cadets at VMI. But his mind was clouded by the upcoming tempest caused John Brown's attempt during his raid on the Harpers Ferry arsenal in Virginia to create a slave uprising throughout the South, and the North's reception of the news. He asked his Northern friends to "do what you can towards such expression and action in your section of the country as may restore to our people the friendly spirit which mad abolitionism has so sorely revolutionized." He saw Virginia's "fountains of popular sentiment so thoroughly stirred," and feared a disunion he was convinced would bring with it a "dread train of strife, animosity, blood, sorrow, retardation to piety and all happy influences…" unless the North disavowed Brown's conduct. Pendleton feared that the process of abolitionism would eventually cause a break because of Northern attitudes. He was appalled at a Northern clergyman attacking John Brown's radicalism while at the same time demanding the abolition of slavery. "It really seems to me amazing that a good man, with the Bible in his hand, can thus outrage the claims of peace in the pulpit itself….Depend upon it, without something adequate at the North, we shall have disunion and civil war before another year finishes its course."

At the end of 1859 smallpox broke out in three places in Rockbridge County. Deaths were numerous and the streets of the town were desolate. Fear closed the houses of worship, that is, all but one. Pendleton kept Grace Episcopal open for worship and held regular services. By doing so he hoped to calm people and assure them of God's care of them. He also went to the homes of the sick to provide ministry. He stood outside their doors, greeting them and inquiring after their condition and needs. He would then obtain whatever they needed, such as groceries or medicines, and leave them outside their door with words of good cheer. By January 5, 1860 the town paper reported that no new cases had appeared, and that the population was "pretty thoroughly inoculated." The epidemic lasted until the end of January 1860, shutting the country folk out of town and keeping the townspeople from venturing into the countryside.

By 1860 Pendleton had put the military well into his past. Twenty seven years had rolled by since his resignation, and he was content not to study military science. The years after his arrival in Lexington and the outbreak of the Civil War were in all probability the happiest of Pendleton's life. In the mornings he could stand on his front porch and look out at the beautiful scenery before him; the town of Lexington across the way and the Blue Ridge rising in the distance. Behind him there was a bustle in the house as the Pendleton women and their enslaved black servants tidied up the home, and up above his eldest daughter and son were getting their young men into the classroom for a day of instruction. Off to the left a short distance away was his church, Grace Episcopal, on the same ridge below Washington College. Just beyond the castle like structure of VMI could be seen. His various ailments were gone. His ministry broke through many of the barriers of religious prejudice and he was well liked and respected in town. He thoroughly enjoyed teaching young men to use their minds in Latin, science, and higher mathematics. His family was happy and well settled in a beautiful and large home. Apart from the debts still plaguing him, Pendleton must have felt the countenance of Almighty God shine upon him. As the New Year began Pendleton focused on publishing his book and travelling out of state raising funds for the Sabbath Schools, but the year was to end on a different note.

Colonel W. N. Pendleton

Harpers Ferry, Virginia

5. BUCKLING ON THE SWORD LIKE
GOD'S SERVANTS OF OLD

[FALLING WATERS AND FIRST MANASSAS, 1861]

O LORD, our heavenly Father, by whose Almighty power we have been preserved this day; By thy great mercy defend us from all perils and dangers of this night; for the love of thy only Son, our Saviour, Jesus Christ. Amen.

1789 Episcopal Book of Common Prayer

While Pendleton worked on his book and otherwise occupied his time preaching in the churches or teaching the young the nation moved closer to a cataclysmic division. Pendleton was aware of what was happening. During his travels he spoke with people with many different opinions. Yet, although he was an experienced and confident public speaker given his position as a minister for all people, regardless of religion, he was reluctant to take part in a partisan debate. Publicly he made few comments on the political issues facing Virginia, but we know from his letters that he was deeply concerned about the direction in which the country was moving. He loved the Union, but he respected states' rights more, and he sensed the tragedy approaching in the near future. Having spent a great deal of time in the Northern states

Pendleton was well aware of the economic power of the North and the strength of the anti-slavery movement.

In May 1860 the Republicans nominated the relatively unknown Abraham Lincoln of Illinois for President. As a dark horse candidate the Republicans hoped that without the political baggage the other Republican candidates carried the nomination of Lincoln could be used to bring in otherwise uncertain supporters. The party also felt that based on Fremont's successes in the North in the 1856 election they had a good chance of winning the election by relying on a purely Northern vote. The Southern wing of the old Whig Party still existed in some form, and it banded together as the Constitutional Union Party and nominated John Bell of Tennessee on a platform of preserving the Union as it existed.

On the other hand, the Democratic Party, ostensibly the nation's majority political party, was coming apart at the seams. Northern Democrats promoted the "Little Giant," the short, rotund, and hyperactive Stephen A. Douglas, also of Illinois. Douglas had stepped aside and allowed the party to nominate Pierce and Buchanan in 1852 and 1856 and felt that it was his turn in 1860 to be the candidate of the party. However, the Southern wing of the Democratic Party was repulsed by Douglas' position that a territory or new state could vote to abolish slavery. He further disappointed Southerners with his promotion of a homestead act for free land for settlers and immigrants, and his support of a transcontinental railroad connecting in the North, both of which were seen as benefitting the North at the South's expense. Additionally, the Harpers Ferry raid seriously alienated Southern Democrats, some of whom felt that the South and its slave institution would never be safe within the Union. Their goal was to force a division of the party to promote secession.

The Democrats met in Charleston, South Carolina, a hotbed of secessionist fever. The party doomed itself in opting first to choose a platform, and then a candidate. The secessionists walked out when the pro-Douglas platform on slavery in the territories was adopted, even though they approved identical language just four years before. The convention Chair, Caleb Cushing of Massachusetts, ruled that the nomination still needed a two-thirds vote of the entire convention, including the delegates who walked out. While Douglas had two-thirds of the votes of those still voting, he could not reach the magic number of two-thirds of all the delegates and failed to win the nomination. The party agreed to meet later in Baltimore and ended splitting into two sections. The Northern Democrats nominated Douglas and the Southern Democrats nominated John C. Breckinridge of Kentucky. Despite efforts to compromise between the two wings of the party during the election campaign the writing was on the wall. Lincoln was going to win, and did so in November 1860.

The people in Rockbridge County faced the election with deep concern. They shared a sense of uncertainty and dread, and a growing realization that the division in the Democratic Party guaranteed not only the election of "Black Republican" Abraham Lincoln in November but the subsequent secession of the Cotton South. They dreaded what they could foresee but could not control, hoping against hope that others would come to their senses to avert the coming national tragedy, yet knowing in their hearts that nothing could stop it. Their fears came true. Lincoln's election caused the Cotton South to act on their long asserted threat to secede. President Buchanan did nothing to discourage them, and the first state, South Carolina, left the Union on December 17, 1860.

Pendleton did not wish to see troubles. Finally, by 1860 Pendleton was prospering although he still carried some of his old debt. He owned empty lots near town valued at $4,000, and personal property worth $3,000, probably his enslaved blacks consisting of one man and two women. At fifty years of age Pendleton was content and looking forward to gracefully growing into old age. His wife Anzelotte was also fifty, and they had five children living at home with them; Mary, Rose, Sandie, Nancy, and Hughella. There were twelve male students living in the Rectory, all between fourteen and seventeen years of age. During the summer of 1860, while the election debates raged, Pendleton was on a working vacation preaching in the western counties of Virginia, now the state of West Virginia. He was also away from home a great deal on behalf of the church. As such he played little part in the gathering storm back home.

During the campaign the followers of the three political parties in the South met frequently in Lexington and out in the county. Public meetings at the Courthouse discussed the dangers of a Republican victory. The greatly outnumbered Breckinridge Democrats, including Superintendent Smith and Thomas J. Jackson spoke of protecting Southern interests and their fear that the South would exercise its right of secession. Jackson, who mirrored the way Pendleton felt, endorsed Breckinridge since he believed in the right of secession, but he also believed that it was better for Virginia to fight for its rights in the Union than outside of it. The evening before the election he attended a Breckinridge rally at the courthouse. Jackson spoke for fifteen minutes about the dangers to "our common country" and the need for every citizen to make a stand for what they believe was right.

While the County debated, Pendleton generally remained quiet. Since childhood he was strongly in favor of State's-Rights, but like Thomas Jackson he saw these rights threatened by the "fanaticism and mad abolitionism" in the North. He had apocalyptic expectations of what would happen in the aftermath of the election, and spoke of "the likelihood of Lincoln's being elected and the revolution to follow." When the votes were counted Bell carried every district in the County, and also carried Virginia by defeating Breckinridge by a thin margin. Douglas trailed far behind. Underscoring the national division, Lincoln received no votes in Rockbridge County, and only a handful in Virginia. Despite this Lincoln carried the North and West, winning 173 electoral votes to Breckinridge's seventy-two, Bell's thirty-nine, and Douglas' twelve.

*   *   *   *

It took a while for the outcome of the election to sink into the minds of Virginians. Early efforts in November to hold town meetings were stymied by shock or apathy. By late November the people of Rockbridge County began to stir. A town meeting was called for December 3, 1860 at the county courthouse in Lexington. Under the circumstances Pendleton set aside his refusal to discuss politics in public. At the well-attended meeting Pendleton spoke, and because he was non-partisan the people listened carefully to what he had to say. He asked for calmness and deliberation. Speaker after speaker, including Jackson and Pendleton, denounced South Carolina for calling a secession convention to divide the Union. A series of resolutions condemning South Carolina was discussed and a committee appointed to report back on a unified resolution to be discussed on December 15th. The subsequent meeting was delayed by an early snowstorm dropping nine inches of snow across the county the night before preventing those outside of town from attending. We know what Pendleton was thinking though, because he expressed his fears and anxieties in a letter to Sandie in Charlottesville.

On the 15th he wrote Sandie of his fear that extremists on both sides would reject "any accommodation." Pendleton believed that if the people knew what was at stake they would preserve the Union, but "in a country so extensive and so exposed to the arts of demagoguism," the politicians motivated by "personal aims, prejudices, and passions," would control the outcome of events. While he favored slavery, Pendleton ironically favored a slave republic only if it forbade the slave trade. He warned Sandie not to "commit himself to any untenable view or rash course." As a minister, he put his faith in "God's ability" to control the forces confronting the nation, and reminded Sandie that "commerce is not only peaceful but organizing in its nature" and that "disunion is its destruction." He concluded that "we may be destined to terrible disturbances." Pendleton foresaw that with the establishment of a "Cotton Confederacy" the Border States had only undesirable options. They could join the Confederacy, stay with the Union, combine with other Border States, or go on their own. For Pendleton the first choice was the only feasible one, provided that the Cotton South would not re-open the slave trade. He admonished his son to "look to God and stand by the Old Dominion." Sandie felt that despite his fervent prayers the "issue of affairs is doubtful." However, he agreed that Virginia needed to avoid both slave trading states and the extreme abolitionist states. Nevertheless, Sandie associated with the secessionists at the University of Virginia. A group of Sandie's close friends placed the Confederate flag on the Rotunda and joined others in secessionist speeches.

The unrest spread to Lexington. On December 6th, the local newspaper printed a letter from "Vox Populorum" urging the students to rise up and put their belief in secession into action. This probably inspired some Washington College students to raise a flag with a red star and the word "DISUNION" over the statue of George Washington atop Washington Hall. Some of the students wanted to remove the flag but were prevented by the secessionist students, the secessionists threatening "if they tried it there would be a war." President Junkin ordered the flag removed but the conspirators spirited away all of the ladders. Junkin sent to town for some more ladders but high winds prevented the flag's removal. During the night the secessionists guarded the flag. The next morning janitors removed the flag and peace returned temporarily to the campus.

Through December the tension increased between the mostly Unionist town residents and the growing number of secessionist students and cadets. The town meeting held on December 21, 1860 was attended by a largely pro-Union crowd as the secessionist students and cadets had gone home. The advent of the Christmas season helped to deflect the attention of the people from the crisis. Pendleton made an effort by eloquently decorating the sanctuary at the church. In a small and sedate town it meant a lot when one resident credited the rector with having "gained quite a hold upon the affections of the people of the village," since he was still viewed as an outsider after living there for seven years.

The Christmas season turned out to be "gay and frivolous." Just down Lee Avenue from the Rectory one of the most prosperous residents threw a Christmas party at his home. The festivity was "closing, guests gone, lights being extinguished," and there was the sound of an impromptu amateur orchestra composed in part of violins, flutes, and a bass viola coming from the front porch. One of the daughters, "an accomplished pianist," joined in the music. The hostess brought in refreshments to the musicians, and as they were leaving, one of the musicians invited the whole party to gather at his house the next night to repeat the performance. This began a series of entertainments, each night at a different house, and each night gathering a larger group, as the merriment continued. Many of the partiers were home from college or elsewhere for the holidays, and these charming, impromptu parties came to an end at the end of the holidays. The final gathering (of the season) took place again where the first party was held. Even so, the festivities were marked by constant talk of secession, especially among the students and cadets.

Down in Charleston harbor the commanding officer of the United States Army garrison in old Fort Moultrie realized that his post was not safe in the aftermath of the secession of South Carolina. He moved the garrison to the newly built brick fortress of Fort Sumter in the middle of the channel connecting Charleston to the sea, thereby threatening to shut down commerce passing in and out of the harbor. For the fledgling Confederacy this was a challenge to its national identity which could not be allowed. Meanwhile, in correspondence to his supporters Abraham Lincoln made his position clear: "Let there be no compromise on the question of extending slavery in the territories. If there is, all our labor is lost... The tug has to come, & better now than at any time hereafter." This decision by Lincoln not to accept a compromise committed the nation to a civil war.

On January 7, 1861, the County-wide public meeting delayed until then by snow was held at the Courthouse. The meeting lasted several hours but never reached a consensus. The meeting suddenly dissolved in disorder when someone called for three cheers for South Carolina. Seventy people present, primarily VMI cadets, responded. The riotous conclusion signaled the end to efforts at reconciliation and compromise within the County. From then on the different factions held separate meetings. Pendleton continued to consult with the community leaders. He and James Dorman asked James D. Davidson to tell his friend Governor Letcher that a secession convention was needed so that the people of Virginia could speak for themselves and to hopefully buy some time for the crisis to blow over.

The state legislature authorized the election of a secession convention to meet on February 13th in Richmond. Pendleton endorsed James Dorman, the son of the former owner of the Rectory and a Unionist, as a delegate to the convention. Dorman and Samuel McDowell Reid were selected. At first the pro-Union moderates controlled the convention and overruled any early secession. However, they stayed in session to await and attempt to control coming events. The legislature also invited all the states to send delegates to a peace conference in Washington on February 4th "to unite with Virginia in an earnest effort to adjust the present unhappy controversies in the spirit in which the Constitution was originally formed and consistently with its principles." From the start the peacemakers faced hurdles when states from the Confederacy and from the Pacific Coast failed to appear. Even worse, Michigan, Minnesota, and Wisconsin refused to send delegates to what they viewed as useless talk. In the Senate the belated Crittenden Compromise reached the floor of the Congress. It was defeated in the Senate by one vote with all the Republicans voting against it. In the House the compromise plan again lost with the Republicans voting against it.

As the New Year progressed the Cotton South states seceded one by one and the new Confederate government was inaugurated in Alabama. The political tensions in Lexington intensified. During celebrations for Washington's Birthday at VMI the cadets raised a secessionist flag atop one of the barrack's towers. It was removed after some difficulty. Later, the Corps of Cadets formally marched under arms to the Presbyterian Church to listen to speeches on the character of George Washington given by VMI and Washington College professors. Students from Washington College read strong Southern rights speeches during the service. Afterwards, there was a sumptuous feast and a dance into the dark when the day closed with fireworks.

Lincoln's Inaugural speech on March 4th caused a sensation. His failure to disavow force in solving the crisis and accept secession as an accomplished fact discouraged the Unionists and elated the secessionists. When the convention did nothing former Governor Henry Wise promoted a new election for a Spontaneous People's secession convention to convene on April 16th in Richmond. Following the unofficial and unauthorized voting the secessionists held the majority in the new but unlawful convention.

On March 25, 1861, thirty students of Washington College petitioned the faculty to allow a military class of students to be drilled by a cadet from VMI, but only if the faculty assumed responsibility for the muskets. The faculty rejected the petition stating that it did not wish to be responsible for the muskets. Then a week later the faculty reversed the decision and voted approval provided no muskets were brought on campus, no drilling occurred during study hours, and the commander of the company met their approval. The faculty reserved the right to terminate the program if it interfered with the proper discharge of college duties. The group was originally called the "Southern Blues" but changed their name to the "Liberty Hall Volunteers" in honor of the College's Revolutionary War volunteers. The Washington College professor drilling the young men became too ill to continue, and the group asked Pendleton to replace him as drillmaster. It was his first involvement with military affairs in twenty eight years.

At about the same time another secessionist flag rose atop "Old George" at Washington College. Junkin went over to Washington Hall in his bathrobe and slippers and asked for a volunteer to remove it. One student volunteered but before he descended with the flag, he called for three cheers for the Confederacy. Junkin locked the flag in his bedroom but a couple of enterprising students used ladders to sneak in and retrieve it. The next morning it was back on top of "Old George." This time the janitors removed the flag and Junkin personally burned it.

On April 7th Sandie Pendleton wrote his sister from Charlottesville that he was "trying to study assiduously and had given up thinking altogether as there is nothing to think about; I have tried to fall in love & can't. The country will not minister to my thirst for excitement by a war….." His father replied, telling his son to not even think about "leaving your studies. I am clear, as things are, that your duty to God, to the country, & to us, requires you – if the University continues in operation – to take your A.M. before breaking off for anything. You may say you cannot study, then pray, for such views of God's will & of your privilege in his service, as may effectually calm your mind…..[S]uccess is imperatively demanded of you."

Pendleton then addressed the turmoil in the nation, "We shall probably have much troubles, and have need for steady faith…. By & by, if the safety of the country requires, and it be clearly the duty of Godly people to meet the issue until death, I will commit you to God in any service. Nay, in such event I may, like God's servants of old, do my appropriate work while buckling on the sword myself. There is, however, time enough. Lincoln may well be frustrated before he gets much blood flowing. God has many ways of overruling the plans of the wicked."

The bitterness of the dispute between secessionists and unionist reached a fever pitch when Fort Sumter was fired on by Confederate forces on April 12th. The news of the attack led Unionists and secessionists to raise competing flags in front of the Courthouse on Saturday, April 13th, a market day. A large number of farmers and country people came to town, most of whom came armed for drill, with the number of Unionists more than four times greater than the number of secessionists. The Unionists brought an unusually long flagpole and left it overnight on Friday. While raising the pole the next day it broke and fell. VMI cadets, or some other secessionists, had bored holes into the flagpole during the night. When the pole fell the cadets loudly cheered and returned to barracks, but left some three or four cadets behind in town. The unhappy Unionists spliced the pole and prepared to raise it again. When a number of VMI cadets began to ridicule the worker's efforts to raise the pole Unionists assaulted the cadets and a general melee ensued ending with the cadets being badly beaten.

Towards the end of the supper a cadet rushed in to the VMI dining hall and raised the alarm about the beatings in town. Without a word being spoken the cadets rushed to their rooms, seized their muskets, cartridge boxes, bayonets and scabbards, and ran down the stoops to the front of the barracks firing their muskets in the air. In less than ten minutes every cadet was ready to fight to "achieve satisfaction by the force of arms." The advanced squads moved down the road into the hollow at the foot of Main Street where they halted waiting for the arrival of the rest of the corps before ascending the slope of Main Street into the center of Lexington. When he heard of the trouble Superintendent Smith rushed to where the cadets assembled and made unsuccessful appeals that did not dissuade the cadets.

Up Main Street town residents gathered armed with pistols and rifles as the report spread that armed cadets were coming. The Rockbridge Rifles, then parading downtown, were asked to defend the city. Seventy-five men, mostly experienced hunters, were posted in windows with orders to fire on the cadets if they approached. Down in the hollow of Main Street the cadets prepared for the attack. But then they encountered Thomas Jackson. Jackson told them that their desire for revenge was inappropriate, but that he would make sure justice followed. He then led them back to VMI where he followed up with a stirring speech concluding, "The time may come when your state will need your services and if that time does come, then draw your swords and throw away the scabbards." A bloodbath was barely avoided.

Pendleton's focus appeared to have been elsewhere. He had been invited to teach a course in science to the students of the Theological Seminary, near Alexandria, Virginia, and had spent the winter preparing for it. On the 16th of April he left home. Before departing he wrote Sandie to focus on his studies and ignore the military preparations for now, "Serious as is the state of things in the country, and imperative as may be the call of duty to brave everything in repelling wrong, — at a day not far distant,—I am very clear that your duty now is to quiet your mind to the utmost, and to finish your course at the University. … Possess your soul in patience yet awhile. If we have real war, your time will come soon enough. Considerable delay will be unavoidable, and I still trust God may frustrate Lincoln's schemes….If it becomes clearly duty by and by, I will bid you go with my blessing, and looking up for heaven's grace to attend you. But now—if you come home—return immediately, and stand firmly in your lot at the University."

By the time Pendleton reached Alexandria the Commonwealth of Virginia had seceded. Being so close to the seat of government Pendleton decided to venture across the Potomac into Washington, D.C. to see what he could do to talk sense into the new government. From Alexandria he wrote to his wife: " Lincoln is so strange and so misguided that he has himself no idea what he means….Things are very quiet here, but it is the hush of alarm and astonishment. In Washington you would not suppose yourself in a land of liberty,—soldiers marching everywhere and everybody seeming suspicious. Dr. Sparrow approved so much of my suggestion about going to talk with Lincoln that I resolved to do it, if possible. I accordingly proceeded to call on General Scott, to get an introduction….Near General Scott's quarters, however, I met Cassius Lee and Mr. McKenzie, who assured me that it was impossible to see General Scott, he being overwhelmed with business, and that, as to going to see Lincoln, I had as well reason with an Egyptian mummy. . . . Whether there is any possibility now of avoiding a dreadful conflict I cannot tell. I fear not."

*   *   *   *

On his return to Lexington Pendleton spent many hours drilling the Liberty Hall Volunteers. When Virginia seceded they were ordered to Harpers Ferry where they joined the 4th Virginia Infantry Regiment. Pendleton remained behind. John McCausland, a mathematics professor at VMI put two 6-pounder cannons used by Jackson at VMI for training to good use by organizing the Rockbridge Battery. Initially, Pendleton assisted with the training but when McCausland was sent to Harpers Ferry to assist with training there the men of the battery elected Pendleton as their Captain in his stead. Pendleton's reputation as a West Point graduate and as a former artillery officer attracted the attention of many who wished to join the battery. The new recruits were of the best caliber, consisting of farmers, students, mechanics, laborers, lawyers, and theological students. Forty-seven Washington College students, twenty eight college graduates, seven graduates holding master's degrees, eight lawyers, and six teachers enlisted. In all, seventy eight men signed up. One enlistee private was Robert E. Lee, Jr.; two were sons of Union Admiral David Dixon Porter.

The battery trained intensively for two weeks. It was readily apparent that Pendleton had lost none of his military training or skill as an artilleryman. But given his age and his obligations as minister and teacher, Pendleton had no intention of marching off to war. Doubts grew in his mind as to where his real duty lay. When he awoke on the first of May he spent an unusually long time at his early morning private prayers and devotions. Afterwards he told his wife he asked for divine guidance as to what he should do. After breakfast two men from the battery came to the door and asked Pendleton to become their Captain. His first response was to decline and he offered the name of another qualified man but when they persisted he agreed. Later that day he wrote in his private papers an explanation for his decision:

> I think it right to record the considerations which influence me to accept as duty the command of the artillery company at this place, tendered me this morning. In the first place, defensive war cannot on Gospel grounds, it seems to me, be condemned. Because, government for the protection of right having God's emphatic sanction,—indeed, being His own ordinance,—it must, to the extent of its ability, after fair and full trials for peace, resist aggression.

Pendleton observed that for the past forty years the South had tried to persuade the North to leave it alone. Instead, the North opted to violate the Constitution and in reaction the South created its own government. As for Virginia, "my beloved native State abstained from all hasty action of that kind and continued, under wrongs of the most serious character, to plead for justice, equality, and peace,—even, indeed, as long as such course seemed at all to consist with her honor or independence as a State,—the astounding call by the hostile representative of the aggressive section for a force of seventy-five thousand men on her immediate borders compelled Virginia to arm for her own defense and that of her sisters, if she would in any measure meet her obligations for the cause of justice on earth and the welfare of mankind. I cannot doubt, therefore, that defensive warfare on her part is requisite and most righteous."

Virginia and the South were now faced with "wholesale murder and universal desolation by the myriads of the North, whose passions have been inflamed by governmental proclamations, a furious press, and a most unchristian pulpit, no man, in my judgment, whatever his calling and his love of peace, has a right to shelter himself from the common danger behind the bravely-exposed breasts of his fellow-citizens." It was therefore his "sacred duty, in some capacity, fairly to share the peril, as well as work for the welfare of my countrymen." When the men of the battery he trained asked him to lead, "and there being no other available to command it who had, like myself, received a military education and seen some service, I was urged to accept the command, and could not decline without discouraging the men and the community…."

The town of Lexington supplied the battery with the needed personal and military equipment, and the town ladies prepared their uniforms and a unit flag. The Governor gave the battery permission to take two of the VMI 6-pounder smoothbore guns. Since a proper battery carries four guns, Pendleton travelled to Richmond in May to ask for two more. He also provided unsolicited military advice to Jefferson Davis, cautioning him as to the dangers of a federal movement up the York River towards Richmond. Given Davis' aversion to being given advice the suggestion was probably ignored.

On May 11, 1861 everything was set for the battery's departure for Harpers Ferry. Pendleton kissed his wife good bye and joined the men gathering in front of the brick Courthouse. Before departing the battery sent a letter to the local paper thanking the women and the town for their assistance. Attorney James D. Davidson formally presented the battery with a flag also sewn by the ladies. Pendleton received it with appropriate thanks. Sergeant James Davis added a formal acknowledgement and a desire that they should "never suffer this banner to be lowered in disgrace, or trail in dishonor before the minions of a tyrant." Town residents, both white and black, wept at their departure.

Since most of the railroads in that part of Virginia travelled east and west it was necessary for the battery to march to Staunton, some forty miles away, to catch an eastbound train in order to take a westbound train back into the Valley. The battery still lacked the caissons used to haul ammunition and were forced to use farm wagons to carry their chests and boxes. The battery left Staunton and travelled by rail to Strasburg, and then marched eighteen miles to Winchester. When they reached Winchester they were greeted with a large feast hosted by other soldiers from Rockbridge County. The guns were stored in a warehouse and the men scattered into individual homes for the night. The next day they boarded another train and arrived in Harpers Ferry in the evening of May 14, 1861. The battery personnel were quartered in an old church with a unit that had been there some time. They put the battery up by the pulpit in recognition of Pendleton's profession.

The battery was attached to the First Virginia Brigade commanded by Jackson along with some other Rockbridge County units, including the 4th Virginia. Jackson also provided Pendleton with two additional guns so that now he had three 6-pounder smoothbore cannons and one 12-pounder smoothbore gun. The overall army commander was Joseph E. Johnston, West Point Class of 1829, whom Pendleton knew well. Pendleton, with a Christian flair, named the cannon after the four Gospels of the New Testament, "Matthew," "Mark," "Luke," and "John." The battery was split into two sections for service on picket duty along the Potomac River in Shepherdstown and Williamsport but it was still unprepared for the field. Even though the army inspector general felt that the battery was well trained in the manual use of the guns, it still had no horses to pull the guns and caissons. The battery needed eighty horses to pull the four small guns assigned to the battery, but they were expected to arrive soon.

The war was still just an adventure for the soldiers then. The days were spent drilling, parading, attending picnics and entertaining visitors. Pendleton even found time to preach to the troops. Pendleton wrote home that "I have prayers at reveille roll-call every morning, and in my quarters every night for such officers and men as may choose to attend, and on Sunday I shall regularly preach." His battery was ready for duty except for the lack of horses. In the meantime he slept in a framed shed with an old tablecloth tossed over the top as a roof for protection from the elements. He reported home that it kept him warm and dry.

In the meantime the Pendletons tried to help Sandie. He asked for another loan of $200 and if necessary would ask his uncle again. Anzelotte, without telling her husband, sent Sandie $70 from their bank account instead. She told him to settle his boarding house bill and thereafter be "economical with the rest as is consistent with your honor." When Sandie made it clear he wanted to sign up for the Army the parents asked their fellow Lexingtonian Governor Letcher to give him a commission. It was not an easy thing to do. Mrs. Letcher was a parishioner but the Governor was not. In fact, Letcher took an exception to "military parsons" and held a low opinion of Pendleton throughout the war. On May 10th Sandie was offered a lieutenancy in the Corps of Engineers because of his expertise in physics and mathematics. Sandie dropped out of school, packed his things and headed towards Harpers Ferry. On the way he borrowed a horse from a relative in Clarke County. Since no engineering troops were in Harpers Ferry Sandie was temporarily attached to the Rockbridge Battery until Jackson asked him to join his staff.

   *   *   *   *

  General Johnston, who spent most of the war epically retreating, ordered a withdrawal from the Potomac and Harpers Ferry as he deemed those positions to be indefensible. The Confederates blew up the railroad bridges over the Potomac and Shenandoah Rivers and then burned the lower part of Harpers Ferry containing the arsenal, depot, and telegraph offices, and the little army pulled back to Martinsburg. Federal troops filled the vacuum left by Johnston, "plundering horses, stealing negroes and stock of all kinds." Meanwhile, the more aggressive Jackson grew tired of being idle and burned the bridge across the Potomac at Shepherdstown.

  On July 2nd the men of Jackson's brigade awoke to wet fields from an overnight thunderstorm. They broke out their cooking gear in the damp and fixed breakfast over smoldering fires. While they were eating messengers arrived announcing that Federal troops had crossed the Potomac and were advancing towards Martinsburg. Johnston ordered Jackson to respond but to neither to cross the Potomac River nor bring about a general engagement. In turn, Jackson ordered the men to pack up and be ready to move in ten minutes; and asked the 5th Virginia and Pendleton's battery to make a reconnaissance in force towards the Federal advance. They were to be followed by the remainder of the brigade in support.

  Pendleton had just finished writing a letter home when Jackson arrived at Pendleton's "quasi shelter" and asked him to have the battery move out immediately in the advance. The Shenandoah Valley near the Potomac River is a land of farms, pastures, and orchards spread out over fields and tree lined brooks. Small dirt roads provided the only means of movement in the area. Jackson's force moved the three miles from their camp on a country dirt lane towards Falling Waters, a small village located at a bend in the Potomac. As they came up on the Federals near the Porterfield farm at Hoke Run Jackson deployed the 5th Virginia to the right of the road and sent out a skirmish line towards the approaching enemy.

This was the first time the raw Virginia troops ever saw any Federal soldiers, and they broke ranks like school children to climb fences and trees to get a better look. They finally heeded Jackson's commands to return to their ranks when bullets started flying past them. Since this was just a scouting expedition toward an enemy force of an unknown size Pendleton was concerned about pushing his guns out in front of the advance in fear of losing them if the Federals appeared in strength. He left three of the guns in a defensive position two miles from the camp and took just one gun another mile to the battlefield. There he set the gun up to fire directly down the road the Federals were using for their advance. Jackson felt it was too far forward and had Pendleton take the cannon a short distance back down the road.

The 5th Virginia probed through the Porterfield farm moving too far forward to be supported by the rest of the brigade. Union forces overlapped the regiment's flanks while Federal cavalry was searching for the flanks of the Confederate line. By this time the Federal field artillery had opened up and dropped shells around Pendleton and the defensive line. Initially, the Federal line halted with the first volley of fire from the 5th Virginia. They advanced again and withdrew three times before additional Federal troops came up in support. The Confederate line fell back. After an hour or so of fighting Jackson ordered the brigade to retire in order to avoid a general engagement.

The Federals, thinking they had won, started chasing the Confederate troops off the field. Pendleton saw what he thought was "a squadron of cavalry about to charge" riding quickly up the road towards his position. He placed his gun in a spot concealed from the road, and gave orders to the gun crew to load solid shot, and how to aim the gun. As the enemy cavalry approached he gave the order to fire. "The effect was obvious and decided. Not a man or a horse remained standing in the road, nor did we see them again. . . . Our next shot was aimed with equal care at one of their cannon in a field on the left of the road. The effect was scarcely less. The gunners scattered, and I am sure that gun fired no more. Meanwhile the balls whizzed by us with tremendous force and startling music."

Pendleton became famous throughout the Confederacy that day for something he may not even have done. Pendleton later recalled that just before firing the first shot he prayed silently, "May the Lord have mercy on their souls." But there were those who reported he said it out loud, although his deputy Lieutenant Poague claimed he never said it at all. Pendleton's handling of the gun was superb. Federal reports spoke of the effective fire by a full battery of rifled cannon when Pendleton only used the single 6-pounder smoothbore gun. Pendleton was hailed throughout the South. "He fights with the sword in one hand and the Bible in the other," one newspaper reporter observed.

Jackson used the 3rd and 4th Virginia regiments to protect the three guns in reserve and the force fell back towards camp. There he prepared to defend the camp from the Federal Army but it had retreated back across the Potomac shaken by the encounter. By 10:30 a.m. the entire affair was over. Jackson lost ten men, two killed, and eight wounded. The brigade had performed well under fire, and actually became rather cocky about their enemies. The Federals, they believed, could not shoot.

Jackson's reward was to be promoted to Brigadier General. The story about Pendleton and the efficiency and skill of his performance reached Richmond. His old friend Jefferson Davis wrote Johnston on July 13th that "I recollect Captain Pendleton well, and when we were all younger esteemed him highly as a soldier and a gentleman. I some days since directed that he should have rank as a colonel and be put in command of the batteries of your army..." Pendleton was now a full Colonel and Chief of Artillery in Johnston's little army. His promotion came from a small skirmish, some overly hyped press, and an old friendship with the Confederate President. At the time no one questioned his qualifications. He was now in command of five batteries of twenty eight guns, nearly all of which were the obsolete 6-pounder smoothbore cannons of his youth. He had only a few days to settle into the position.

       *   *   *   *

Well downstream and across the Blue Ridge from the Shenandoah Valley the Potomac River passes by Washington, D.C., and it was there that Lincoln gathered his great army of volunteers with which to invade the South. General Irvin McDowell was told by Lincoln to advance his untrained army and attack before the enlistments of many of the volunteers expired. When told the men were not prepared, Lincoln suggested the Confederate troops were just as badly trained. In this he was mistaken. After the John Brown raided Harpers Ferry many of the Southern states awoke to their danger and re-organized, trained, and equipped a militia ready for battle, especially in Virginia.

About twenty five miles away from McDowell the Confederate Army of the Potomac under General Pierre G. Beauregard waited along the slowly meandering Bull Run as it sluggishly flowed northward towards the Potomac. The Federal Army of 37,000 men outnumbered the smaller army of 22,000 men under Beauregard. Alerted to the Federal Army's departure from Washington on July 16, 1861, Beauregard requested help from General Johnston's Army of the Shenandoah and its compliment of 12,000 men, including Jackson's brigade and Pendleton's artillery. Two days later the larger Federal Army reached the opposite banks of Bull Run and began to feel out the Confederate positions.

In Winchester Jackson cancelled all leaves on July 17th. The next morning he ordered the officers to pack up camp and march towards the Blue Ridge. A few miles out of Winchester it was announced that the men were urgently needed at Manassas to assist in repelling the Federal invasion. The news was received with loud cheering by the troops. When the brigade reached Millwood they were greeted by a corps of women bearing fried chicken, cakes, and pies, as well as lemonade to quench their thirst. It was to be the final hurrah of the adventure of war.

That evening they reached the Shenandoah River at the western base of the Blue Ridge. The infantry took off their boots and stockings, rolled up their pants, and waded across. The sick were able to use some of the few boats which could be found. The artillery crossed over perched atop their caissons and limber boxes. It took the little army six hours to cross the river, after which it marched in the dark up the Blue Ridge towards Ashby Gap. By 1:00 a.m. the exhausted army reached the little town of Paris at the eastern base of the Blue Ridge. There they stopped for what was left of the night. With the long uphill pull the artillery and its wagons fell behind the infantry. Jackson tried to remain awake until Pendleton and the artillery arrived but fell asleep leaning up against a fence on the side of the road. The next morning Jackson moved out so early that many men were left behind and forced to catch up. Unfed for over a day, footsore, and exhausted the Army marched into the Piedmont Station (now Delaplane) on the Manassas Gap Railroad. A couple of hours later the infantry boarded the trains and rode the thirty miles to Manassas Junction. On arrival they detrained and marched the remaining few miles towards the battlefield.

Pendleton accompanied the Rockbridge Battery on the march as he was still the nominal commander. He took the battery a mile past the rail station and waited nearly the entire day for the rest of the artillery to arrive. Since the cannons and wagons could not be easily placed on a train, General Johnston ordered the batteries to report to Pendleton at the station so they could march together towards Beauregard's army. By the time the sun set on the 19th only three of the five batteries had arrived. While he waited for the slower units Pendleton received orders to hasten to Manassas with the guns at hand at Beauregard's urgent request.

The night was dark, the road was poor, and the weather was bad. Supplied with guides obtained by Pendleton the artillery made their way through the dark. Along the way additional messengers arrived with requests to hurry. When they reached The Plains the column rested for two hours before pressing on. When they were a few miles away from Manassas Pendleton encountered Captain J. J. White of the Washington College Liberty Hall Volunteers of the 4th Virginia. Pendleton shared with White his confidence but also expressed concern that the Union forces back in the Shenandoah Valley were advancing and it might become necessary for them to fight their way back. By two p.m. on July 20th the three batteries reached Manassas and were assigned positions under the shelter of some woods near the center of the line.

The morning of July 21, 1861 broke bright, sultry, and clear. Birds greeted the rising sun with their songs, and some of the men turned their thoughts towards home on this Sunday morning. The day would be a beautiful but hot Northern Virginia summer day; temperatures would be in the 80's with a slight breeze and a few clouds in the sky. Both opposing commanders adopted the same basic battle plan, hold with the left and flank the enemy with the right. The Federal Army under General McDowell moved first and obtained the advantage. When the Federal troops crossed Sudley

Springs Ford early in the morning on the Confederate left the main Confederate army was moving away to its own right. The flanking columns of Federal troops turned down the road paralleling the Confederate positions behind Bull Run and headed south over Matthews Hill towards the critical junction with the Warrenton Pike.

Beyond this junction stood Henry House Hill, a large rolling hill dominating the surrounding terrain. Its top was relatively flat and consisted of farmland, making the main battlefield a tableau for others to watch. The retreating Confederate left rallied on Matthews Hill, supported by fresh troops coming up from the rear including General Barnard Bee's South Carolina brigade. When the Federal attack pushed over Matthews Hill the Confederates fell back onto the rear slope of Henry House Hill. The hill had gentle slopes leading to a plateau 200 yards across. The slope just below the crest of the plateau was covered with trees and provided the best defensive position. It was there that Jackson deployed his brigade in the protected defilade created by the slope of the hill. When Bee tried to rally his shattered brigade he famously called out, "See Jackson standing like a stone wall. Rally behind the Virginians." At the moment only Jackson and a handful of other troops stood in the way of a complete and smashing Union victory.

Pendleton's artillery was initially ordered to provide support behind Longstreet's brigade on the right of the line. Since his replacement as commander of the Rockbridge Battery had not been named, Pendleton assumed command of the battery as well as the other four batteries of the small Army of the Shenandoah. Johnston and Beauregard were on the right of the Confederate Army when they heard the loud noise of battle coming from their collapsing left. As Johnston rode to his endangered flank he stopped and ordered Pendleton to bring his batteries with him. On the way to the left Pendleton received another order from Beauregard urging him to move all of the artillery to the left. When Pendleton brought the eight guns with him up the slope of Henry House Hill through the trees he emerged just to the rear of Jackson. Jackson saw Pendleton and the guns and enthusiastically rode over to greet them and assign them their positions at the crest of the slope opposite the Henry House.

It was obvious to the experienced officers that the Federal artillery was far superior. Their guns were larger, could shoot further and faster, and used better ammunition. While the Federal guns were hitting anything they could see, the Confederate shells tended to tumble or whirl through the air and not land near their targets. One officer blamed this on the experience and training of the regular Federal Army's artillery officer corps and noted that the Confederates had but one trained artillerist and that was Pendleton. However, the Federal superiority disappeared when the guns were firing at targets at close range, and such was the case on Henry House Hill.

Pendleton wheeled his guns into place alongside other batteries already present. Due to a lack of space the guns were spread out across the defensive line. Behind them on the slope lay the Jackson Brigade. For two and a half hours Pendleton's batteries fired on the Federal guns and troops on the Henry House Hill plateau. The three Confederate batteries faced three regular and two volunteer batteries with twenty four 12-pounder rifled guns against their own thirteen 6-pounder smoothbores. The closeness of the opposing guns helped the weaker Confederate batteries. The Confederate round solid shot bounced and ricocheted among the Federal columns while the shells from the rifled cannon, when they missed their targets, flew harmlessly off or buried deep into the ground.

Both Pendleton and Captain Imboden dismounted their horses, tied them in the rear, and then ranged up and down the line helping to aim each gun. As Pendleton went from piece to piece he shrugged his shoulders when a shell came too close. Occasionally, he stopped to chat with the men to build up their courage. While on horseback Pendleton could be seen bobbing up and down on his old roan horse and whirling his saber over his head. One bullet nicked his horse and gave him a slight wound in his ear and grazed his back. The rumor spread he was killed causing Sandie Pendleton to ride over to see if his father was all right.

The firing of muskets and cannon was intense and the warm sun left men parched. When a limber carriage blew up on a direct hit the gun's wheel horses dropped as though struck by lightning. Jackson stayed on horseback near the batteries until wounded in the hand. One eccentric in the battery was the "old major" William Nelson. He wore half military and half civilian dress into battle. One soldier of the 33rd Virginia saw him wearing a stovepipe hat and smoking a pipe on his horse and cried out, "Lord what have I done that the devil should come after me!"

Smoke from the musket and cannon fire covered the hill. The Confederate batteries directed a well-aimed and sustained fire at the Union troops causing immense damage. Federal batteries were abandoned or withdrawn. The heavy smoke on the battlefield added to the confusion caused by the variety of uniforms worn by both sides. Some Northern state militias wore gray, some Southern units wore blue. In the limp humid air both national flags appeared to be alike. One Federal unit came up unnoticed on the batteries' flank but was assaulted by Confederate troops and thrown back. During the melee some of the Confederate guns were withdrawn and re-positioned. The Virginians under Jackson charged and pushed the Federals back further. When they launched a counterattack Johnston ordered another charge and the Union Army collapsed and fled. By the time the batteries were re-positioned and unlimbered the Federal Army was in retreat. All the men could do was fire a few more rounds at the fleeing Yankees to encourage them on their way. As the sound of gunfire faded away it began to rain.

Once again Pendleton enhanced his reputation. Numerous reports touted "Pendleton of the artillery" and the excellent work performed by the field artillery. General Johnston referred to him as the army's only "well educated artillerist, and model of a Christian soldier." General Beauregard wrote that "great praise is due Colonel Pendleton and the officers and men." The newspapers sang his praises, quoting one Federal prisoner of war asking who it was who led the batteries that killed so many of the Federals. The Richmond *Whig*, among others, said that "Colonel Pendleton's guns were handled with a skill and effect which extorted admiration from all beholders."

During the Civil War the absence of the noise now generated by an industrial society and curious atmospheric conditions allowed the sounds of battle to be heard at great distances. All day long on July 21st the people of Lexington heard the thunder of cannon 150 miles away at Manassas. That evening news of the battle and the list of local casualties arrived by stagecoach.

A week after the battle Pendleton was riding through the woods on his way to preach when he came across four black slaves working in the Confederate camp playing cards. Pendleton came up to them quietly and asked them, "Boys, do you think that is a good way for you to be spending Sunday?" Looking up one retorted,

"Master, 'tain't half so bad as what you done last Sunday." After the battle Pendleton wrote reverentially, "I am thankful indeed to be able to state that under the shield of a guardian Providence we were nearly all mercifully preserved." Appeals to a higher being did not sit well with everyone. A senior field artillery officer later wrote, "It was a serious incubus upon us during the whole war that our president and many of our generals really & actually believed that there was this mysterious Providence always hovering over the field & ready to interfere on one side or the other, & that prayers & piety might win its favor from day to day." Pendleton would discover that those in the army who were not religious looked with disfavor on his splitting his time between the altar and the sword.

An ugly rumor started after the battle as well. One of the artillery officers spread the story that Pendleton showed cowardice at the battle by hiding amongst the trees in the rear. Even though the story had no basis in fact the rumor nevertheless damaged his reputation among those already unhappy with his conduct.

Field Artillery

6. GIRDED WITH STRENGTH UNTO THE BATTLE

[BUILDING THE CONFEDERATE FIELD ARTILLERY]

It is God that girdeth me with strength, and maketh my way perfect. He teacheth my hands to war so that a bow of steel is broken by mine arms. …For thou hast girded with strength unto the battle; that thou hath subdued under me those that rose up against me.

Psalms 18:34 & 39 King James Version

The victory at First Manassas convinced many in the South that the war was over and they had won. There was no further need to build up the Confederate armies. Far from it, the North was just beginning to get organized. The battle left a Confederate army needing supplies, men, and artillery. The problem was where to find artillery pieces for use in a modern war.

The South started the war with an inadequate industrial base with which to conduct a modern war and a field artillery force that was largely obsolete. By comparison the North had numerous factories churning out war materiel, including cannons, and started with the entire field artillery corps of the Regular Army as it existed in 1861. Most of the needs of the Confederate field artillery for modern guns were satisfied through capturing Northern cannon in victorious battles. This provided the South with two thirds of all the cannon the Confederate Army used in the war. The remaining third were purchased overseas or made at home. At the time of the Battle

100

of First Manassas the Confederate Army of the Potomac's field artillery force consisted primarily of old 6-pounder smoothbore guns. The Army had gathered the cannons where they could be found in the South, mostly from state militias using old cast off weaponry of the Regular Army.

General Johnston assumed command of the Confederate Army of the Potomac, which absorbed the much smaller Army of the Shenandoah. One of the first things he did was appoint Pendleton as the Chief of Artillery of the new Army. Pendleton was tasked with categorizing and distributing the guns captured from the fleeing Federal Army at Manassas. These included one 30-pounder Parrott rifled gun, nine 10-pounder Parrott rifled guns, nine 12-pounder brass rifled guns, three 12-pounder brass howitzers, two 12-pounder boat howitzers, three 6-pounder brass smoothbore guns, thirty four caissons, more or less complete with spare parts, four battery wagons, six battery forges, twenty four draft horses, thirty four sets of harness and spare pieces. There was severe competition among the batteries and brigade commanders for the captured guns and equipment. The Rockbridge Battery was given some of the rifled guns taken and was able to return the old 6-pounder cannons to VMI. Still, the shortages of proper artillery and the required equipment to man a battery continued after the prizes won in the battle were distributed. General Johnston complained often and loudly that he lacked the necessary artillery ammunition to fight and Pendleton agreed. He advised the War Department and President Davis that the amount of supplies for the field artillery had to be doubled.

On July 31, 1861 Pendleton was chosen for the task of producing the needed equipment and guns, and was appointed as Chief of Ordnance for the Army of the Potomac. He was asked to create a manufacturing and supply base for all types of equipment, horses, personnel, and guns necessary to create a modern field artillery corps. It was an unpleasant and seemingly impossible task. His previous duties as Chief of Artillery were given to Edward Porter Alexander, an up and coming young artillery officer and West Point graduate from Georgia. Pendleton wrote home that summer that:

> Several difficulties obstruct the way. Want of tin to make brass; only one good foundry here, deficiency

of hands, etc.; and not least of all, no suitable head in the War Department. Still, by hook or by crook, we get along. And, I trust our force, artillery and all, will be strong for the work to be done. …My duties about harness, etc., may take me to Staunton and Lynchburg….I long to be back in the brigade again. All this equipping work is the plague of my life, but it must be done, however disagreeable.

Pendleton made his headquarters in Richmond but spent most of the time travelling throughout the South creating a reliable chain of supply so that the field artillery could properly function. He was given complete control of the means to make it happen, and consulted directly with his old friend Jefferson Davis on his mission. Initially, he had to beg and borrow in order to make shipments of parts and ammunition to Johnston, but then the supplies began to come in more regularly.

The U.S. Army in 1861 had, per manual, 6 and 12-pounder field guns, 12-pounder mountain howitzers, and 12, 24, and 34-pounder field howitzers. These guns were all smoothbore since rifling was little known. The ignorance shown by higher levels of the Confederate command as to the impact of rifling and its improvement of the accuracy and range of cannon fire was astounding. As late as August 1861 Johnston was calling not for rifled guns but for more 12-pounder smoothbore guns. He wrote Pendleton, "Do not fail to urge the making of 12 pounder howitzers. I have faith in them. Let them send guns and equipment and leave us to organize. I enclose a requisition for equipment of a battery of rifles, which cannot be filled here (Manassas). Will you see if the authorities in Richmond can do it? Do not, however, let them prefer it to the fitting out of field batteries of smooth-bore guns."

In the Union armies the cannon were placed in batteries so that each battery had uniform cannon and matching ammunition. In this way the supplying of each battery was made simpler. On the other hand, each Confederate battery had whatever guns the unit could get when the war started; creating a potpourri of cannons with various calibers and types requiring a potpourri of ammunition for supply. Three different calibers in a battery of four guns, requiring three different sets of ammunition, were not unusual. Ammunition for the artillery was also in short supply. A month after the First

Battle of Manassas Johnston concluded he had only enough artillery shells for half a battle. Johnston constantly begged for more howitzers, shrapnel, shell and cartridges for the artillery. Alexander wired Pendleton in Richmond that only 6-pounder smoothbore shells were readily available:

> The want of ammunition for the artillery was even more pressing than that of larger and better guns…. Most of the very small stock of ammunition on hand when you left has been issued, and, in fact, I may say that the stock is entirely exhausted. … We are unable to fill requisitions for fixed twelve-pounder howitzers, shrapnel and shell, or cartridges for James's or Archer's projectiles…. We are in very urgent straits for powder.

Throughout the war the artillery shells manufactured in the South were unreliable. Their quality was in "really dreadful shape." Shells and shrapnel in smoothbores exploded prematurely or not at all. Rifle shot and shells tumbled or failed to go point first. Shells exploded fifty to seventy-five feet short of a target and were more likely to kill Confederates than Yankees. The guns had poor ranges and some were worse than useless. Alexander tried fixing the problem in the field but it originated back in Richmond and the factories. After a while Confederate infantry would not tolerate Confederate artillery firing shells over their heads.

It was Pendleton's job to cure these problems but he needed someone permanently in Richmond to help. He wrote on August 11th to the War Department:

> In view of the fact and of the difficulties in the way of having carriages, & etc., gotten ready in sufficient quantity and with requisite speed, I am more than ever satisfied that one of the first desiderata now for our success is a fit man in Richmond to preside over this definite work and give it his whole time.

The War Department appointed Captain Josiah Gorgas, who managed the supply of ordnance through the war in the most efficient and effective manner. Over the next few months Gorgas ordered that any materiel seize or purchased by the Confederacy or any of its states should be carefully maintained and all waste halted. He arranged for the construction of new factories for small arms, cannons, ammunition, and gun carriages.

When the war started the South had but one experienced cannon foundry at Tredegar's in Richmond. All the others learned on the job. Using unskilled workers or more primitive methods the cannons to forge was dangerous because the improper smelting and casting of metal could cause the barrels to explode on firing. In spite of every effort the number of quality guns available to the Confederates did not reach anywhere near the numbers used by the formidable Federal artillery corps.

In addition to the lack of skilled foundry men there was a lack of skilled labor to produce virtually all the necessary war materiel. Most of the skilled workman had joined the army and were no longer available for hire. The businesses manufacturing cannons and shells were too small and either unable or unwilling to take on a large army contract. Instead of one contractor it was necessary to hire dozens or even more, wherever blacksmiths, wheelwrights, harness-makers, and tinners could be found. Country blacksmiths, wheelwrights and carriage builders were later generally exempted from the draft and subsidized to make horseshoes, gun carriages, and transport wagons, among other types of equipment.

The availability of raw materials with which to manufacture military equipment decreased as production fell and the areas of the Confederacy providing the sources of raw material were occupied by the Federal armies. The Confederacy lacked tin to manufacture shell cases. Problems also arose in obtaining leather for artillery saddles, harness, and other equipment, including bronze to manufacture guns. Pendleton had to create a supply system where none existed before.

Pendleton travelled throughout Virginia contracting with a variety of providers. He met with foundry men in Lynchburg, harness makers in Staunton, and businesses in Lexington that made harness, canteen and other small items. By August 17th, less than three weeks after he started, Pendleton reported twenty contracts with companies in Richmond, Petersburg, Lynchburg, Staunton, Charlottesville, Chesterfield County, Florence, Alabama, and Rome Georgia. Those contractors were to construct 159 6-pounder carriages and caissons, seventy 12-pounder carriages and caissons, sixty-five 24-pounder howitzer carriages and caissons; 114 12-pounder howitzers, thirty 6-pounder brass guns, 177 3-inch iron rifled guns, twenty-four 6-pounder iron guns, forty 24-pounder howitzers, and an unlimited amount of harness and horse leather. Most of the manufacturers had never even seen the items they now agreed to make. By 1862 Southern foundries turned out 3-inch rifled guns, 12-pounder Napoleon smoothbore guns, 12-pounder iron howitzers, and a 2.25 inch bronze mountain rifle not used by the Army of Northern Virginia.

Pendleton also contracted for an unlimited supply of horses needed to pull the guns, caissons, and limbers. He was so effective at procuring horses that the Army requested he arrange for the ongoing supply of cavalry horses as well.

Pendleton put a great deal of energy, focus, and organization into his efforts. On the bright side his travels enabled him to visit home in Lexington where he had the chance to preach to his congregation. By October Pendleton felt he had accomplished his mission and requested to return to the field. Johnston demurred, "The duty to which you have been attending is, I think, the most important to which you can attend. I beg you, therefore, to devote yourself to it until we have reason to believe another action imminent when, of course, you will be necessary in the field." Pendleton persisted and he returned to the army as the Chief of Artillery having accomplished what had been the nearly impossible. It was the first time where Pendleton's administrative and organizational skills were displayed, but by no means was it to be the last.

Now in complete charge of the army's artillery, Pendleton put into practice his theory on artillery organization. Before, most armies had their artillery spread out in small batteries across the chain of command. This prevented using artillery in one focused spot on the battlefield, a tactic created by Napoleon to break enemy formations before an assault. In fact, this is how the Confederate armies were organized. Instead, Pendleton sought to maintain a reserve of artillery subject to the needs of the commander and available for any use. The success which had attended Pendleton in handling the five batteries in the movement from Winchester to Bull Run, and the ability he had displayed to direct and control the massed fire of at least three of these batteries in action, called attention to the idea that an artillery reserve should be formed.

Pendleton was joined in this project by E. P. Alexander who had independently reached the same conclusion.

By the end of November Pendleton re-organized the artillery into fifteen batteries of four to six guns each assigned to the infantry brigades for command purposes, and additional batteries were placed in the reserve artillery under the tactical command of Pendleton. More guns were expected to be delivered. What this meant was that Pendleton surrendered tactical control of the batteries assigned to the infantry brigades, but retained field command of the reserve artillery. Still, he maintained responsibility for provisioning and supplying for all the field batteries where-ever they were located. By December 1861 the field artillery corps of the Confederate Army of the Potomac consisted of 129 officers and 2,416 men, the size of an infantry brigade at the time. Pendleton bragged to Anzelotte that, "Success nothing short of remarkable has attended these efforts. Every brigade of this army has its own battery,—often of six pieces, occasionally of four,—besides the reserve corps under Major Walton. And in addition to these I have under my immediate charge, for drill and for action, the large reserve force of nine batteries, numbering forty-four guns, with several other batteries expected."

*   *   *   *

But commanding and providing for an artillery unit involved much more than commanding and providing for an infantry brigade. It was Pendleton's job to provide all of the men, equipment, food, forage, harness, wagons, limbers, guns, caissons, and horses for all of these units. Since Pendleton was later ridiculed because of his large staff and seemingly small amount of responsibility it is necessary to discuss at some length what was involved in managing a field artillery corps.

The gun carriages, caissons, and limbers were constructed of oak. Each cannon was attached to a limber, a two-wheeled carriage with an ammunition chest. The limber was placed between the horse team and the cannon and towed either a cannon or a caisson. The combination of a 12-pounder Napoleon smoothbore cannon and a packed limber weighed 3,865 pounds. This limber was pulled by six horses. Sponges, screws for unloading guns, and buckets were also on the limber and gun. Each cannon also had a caisson, a two-wheeled carriage carrying two ammunition chests and a spare wheel. A fully loaded limber and caisson combination without a gun weighed 3,811 pounds. It, too, was pulled by six horses. Axes, shovels, and extra poles were also on board. Two cannons created a section of artillery commanded by a Lieutenant.

Two sections created a battery commanded by a Captain. Each battery of four guns also had a traveling forge on wheels and wagons for supplies and tents. Extra wagons carried fodder for the horses. Extra caissons carried additional supplies of ammunition. Each ammunition chest carried about 500 pounds of ammunition. All of these were pulled by horses. A Lieutenant was given charge of these wagons. A total of more than sixty horses were required for each battery. The men either walked or rode the caissons. Other pieces of equipment found in every battery included small arms, harness, traces, chains, toggles, straps, yokes, bits, bridles, thumb stalls, grease buckets, sponge buckets, sponges, worms, muzzle sights, friction primers, lanyards, and pendulum sights.

The six gun 6-pounder batteries consisted of four cannon and two howitzers requiring fourteen six horse teams and seven spares for a total of ninety-one horses. The 12-pounder batteries used twenty teams of six horses with ten spare horses for a total of 130 horses. The large number of horses required for the artillery created a nightmare for supply. Each horse had to be fed, maintained, and replaced when worn out or injured. Horses for the artillery were generally selected after the cavalry made their choices and were second best. Their life expectancy, due to overuse and battle injury, was only an average of eight months. They also tended to panic when shells exploded nearby and movement of the horses in the field was made more difficult as they were harnessed together when in the field.

When one battery commander was questioned about the size of his battery he responded:

> Does this begin to explain how 100 men can be of use with 4guns? Add that each gun is drawn by six horses, driven by three drivers postilion fashion & is followed by its caisson or carriage for ammunition with three more drivers, then there are several wagoners for the Battery, a forge driver, two or three mechanics as harness makers, smiths &c, then add for each gun a sergeant & a corporal (a bugler & a flag bearer for the battery), thrown in the chances of

10 per cent being always wounded or sick & you find that 25 to a gun does not more than furnish 10 to 13 actual cannoneers, of which class one brings ammunition from the chest to the gun, one sponges & rams, one keeps the vent or touchhole closed when sponged, one primes, one fires, one aims & all assist to run the piece back when it recoils from the place of fire &c &c.

It was not an accident that both Jackson and Pendleton taught physics and higher mathematics in the civilian world. They were both field artillery officers who required knowledge of those subjects in order to perform their duties efficiently and effectively. It is no surprise to find that most of the battery commanders in the Army of Northern Virginia were alumni of VMI and former students of Jackson. The goal in firing cannon is to send a projectile a specific distance to arrive at a certain time and place. The amount of powder, weight of the shell, length of the gun tube, and angle of the tube when fired all had to be correctly adjusted to hit the target. Throughout the war many complained of Pendleton's incompetence but in doing so revealed more of their ignorance of the requirements of the artillery branch. In order to understand the limitations of the use of artillery in the field it will be necessary to review the specifications for the use of the guns.

Smoothbore guns were just hollow tubes. Their range was shorter and their aim less accurate. However, they were more useful at close range because they could be loaded and fire quickly. They were also of more use in the woods given the limitations on their range. Their shells tended to bounce and ricochet along the ground, and thus times were more effective against massed troops. The most common smoothbore used in the war was the 12-pounder Napoleon, the gun most people associate with pictures of the war. Lee tended to favor fighting in wooded terrain such as the Wilderness to prevent the longer range and more effective Federal artillery from exploiting its advantages. It also rendered the Army of Northern Virginia's large number of smoothbore guns more effective.

Rifled cannons had rifling grooves cut into their barrels in the manufacturing process. They fire further and more accurately but their shells were too fast to bounce, and at times buried themselves into the ground exploding harmlessly. The most common rifled guns were the Northern made 3-inch Parrott and the 10 pounder 3-inch-Parrott. The Whitworth rifled guns were made in England and highly prized in both armies, but rare. The most commonly used rifled gun was the Griffen 3-inch rifled cannon. The iron tube was durable and rarely burst, and it had exceptional accuracy. The Confederacy tried to imitate it but failed to do so. Instead, the South relied on capturing Federal 3-inch rifled guns on the battlefield.

Howitzers are not technically considered "cannons." They tend to be shorter and are used for plunging fire, shooting higher in the air and landing behind obstacles such as walls or hills. They were commonly used in hilly or mountainous terrain.

The most versatile gun was the 12-pounder Napoleon smoothbore. One Confederate gunner recalled that "Our guns were 12 pound brass Napoleons, smooth bore, but accounted the best gun for all round field service then made. They fired solid shot, shell, grape and canister, and were accurate at a mile. We would not have exchanged them for Parrott Rifles, or any other style of guns. They were beautiful, perfectly plain, tapering gracefully from muzzle to 'reinforce; or ;butt,' without rings, or ornaments of any kind. We are proud of them and felt towards them almost as if they were human..." Confederate Napoleons were produced in at least six variations due to resources and casting skills, and were made mostly of bronze but occasionally out of iron. Starting in 1863 Lee sent nearly all of the Army of Northern Virginia's bronze 6-pounder guns to Richmond to be melted down and recast as Napoleons. When the copper mines near Chattanooga fell to the Federal armies in late 1863 bronze production stopped, and Tredegar was limited to casting iron Napoleons for the remainder of the war.

The graph below sets out some of the specifications of the more commonly used and some of the specialty artillery pieces in use in the war. There were many other guns used:

Gun	Tube Weight & Carriage	Make	Caliber	Rounds	Range at 5° elevation
6-pounder smoothbore	1,784 lbs.	Bronze	3.67 inches	6 pound shot	1,523 yards
12-pounder	2,932 lbs.	Bronze	4.62	12 pound	1,663

smoothbore			inches	shot	yards
12-pounder howitzer	1,688 lbs.	Bronze	4.62 inches	9 pound shot	1,072 yards
10-pounder rifled Parrott	1,900 lbs.	Iron	3 inches	9.5 pound shell	1,850 yards.
3 inch-Parrott Rifle	1,820 lbs.	Wrought Iron	3.0 inches	9.5 pound shell	1,830 yards.
6-pounder Whitworth Rifle	1,700 lbs.	Iron	1.5 inches	6 pound shell	2,750 yards.
12-pounder Whitworth Rifle muzzle load	2,000 lbs.	Iron	2,75 inches	12-pound shell	3,000 yards
12-pounder Whitworth Rifle breech load	2,100 lbs.	Iron	2.75 inches	12 pound shell	2,800 yards
24-pounder howitzer	2,446 lbs.	Bronze	5.82 inches	18.4 pound shot	1,322 yards

The ranges varied by elevation of the cannon, the amount of powder used, and the type of ammunition used. In order to understand the complexity of supplying each battery we must review the types of ammunition used.

A solid shot was used for battering walls, trenches, and against masses of troops. It was more accurate than a shell and travelled further. The solid shot used in the smoothbore guns was just a round iron ball. The rifled guns used what was called a "bolt" which had a spherical or cylindrical shape. Both were used to impart kinetic energy for a battering effect. It shattered guns, wagons, caissons, and limbers, and could be used to mow down columns of infantry or cavalry. Accuracy was the key to successfully using solid shot.

There were a wide variety of shells used. They could explode on contact with the target, although they sometimes buried themselves into the ground first. At times the shells relied on timed fuses to set off the charge while in flight. These contained a bursting charge that would explode near the target, if all went well. There were a variety of fuses as well. Shells were used against wooden buildings, earthworks, and troops under cover. For rifled guns there were approximately fifteen different types of shells available.

Shrapnel was similar to a shell but was made for anti-personnel purposes. It was intended to explode well above the target and rain down hot sharp pieces of metal and lead bullets to kill and maim the enemy. The explosions were controlled by timed fuses that were lit when the gun was fired. They were used against enemy troops located 500 to 1,500 yards away. To be effective the goal was to explode the shell about fifty to seventy-five yards before the target allowing the contents to rain down on the targets below. Shrapnel for 12-pounder ammunition contained seventy-eight lead bullets within the metal jacket. The 6-pounder shell contained only thirty-eight bullets. However, the shrapnel was unreliable. It was difficult to properly time the fuse. For the most part the Confederate fuses were primitive in nature and unreliable as they were not properly standardized in production. Some shells burst when fired, some not at all. Sometimes the shell tumbled in flight which stopped the fuses from working. They were more effective fired from smoothbores than from rifles.

Grapeshot consisted of a canister with stacks of metal balls on stacked iron plates with a bolt down the middle to hold it together until fired. The effect is that of a giant shotgun firing a number of bullets at once. The 12-pounder Napoleon smoothbore grapeshot fired only nine large balls. As the war went on and the gun barrels became more reliable, artillerists switched to using canister instead.

Canister was akin to grapeshot but contained more balls in each shot. It consisted of a thin metal container containing layers of lead or iron balls packed in sawdust. On firing the container dissolved and the balls fanned out like a shotgun blast. It was useful only at ranges of less than 400 yards but was quite deadly. Each shot could kill dozens of enemy troops. Even more deadly was the use of double canister, when two containers were fired at one time. The canister round used by the 12-pounder Napoleon smoothbore cannon contained twenty-seven small metal balls in each container. When ammunition ran low that gunners jammed any scraps of metal they could find, such as nails, down a barrel after placing the powder and used it as a form of improvised canister.

*   *   *   *

A successful battery commander adequately provided all the equipment and nourishment for men and beasts to assure that his artillery was well supplied. He also needed to know the varieties of ammunition, effective ranges, and elevations for the guns, etc., in order to successfully employ his battery in the field. Furthermore, he needed to find the best location to position the battery. Ideally, each gun required a space of forty-seven yards from the mouth of the gun to the end of the ammunition caisson. Regulations also called for a space of fourteen yards between each gun. The ground could not be too wooded or obstructed by buildings or other objects such as hills, fences, etc. Nor could it be too soft given the weight of the guns, limbers, and caissons. It was no easy task.

The battery commander also needed to know when to use the variety of ammunition in his caissons. If he faced an infantry charge 650 to 1,400 yards away with a battery of 12-pounder smoothbore guns, such as the commonly used and versatile Napoleon, he would fire twenty rounds of spherical case or canister at fifty-three second intervals. As the infantry closed in between 350 and 650 yards and marched at the quick step he fired seven solid shot at twenty-nine second intervals. From 100 to 350 yards when the infantry was now double stepping he fired nine canister rounds at fifty-four second intervals. During the charge of the infantry in the last 100 yards he would fire two rounds of canister about forty seconds apart. Each battery needed to carry a variety of different rounds for use by each caliber of gun in the battery.

Needless to say, an artillery battery in an open field was rarely able to defend itself from an infantry assault. The unprotected gunners could be shot as they worked their pieces, and ultimately the guns could be over run and captured. In order to properly defend a position with artillery it must have adequate infantry support consisting of more than just a few men. The musketry of the infantry was needed to keep the enemy from easily overwhelming a battery in the field.

Even though Pendleton had not trained with field artillery in almost thirty years he quickly adapted and learned what was required to fight a modern war. Even when he ceded tactical command of the artillery to the Corps commanders in May 1863, Pendleton was still responsible for equipping and feeding all of the field artillery units. He was also able to keep his field artillery equipped and ready until the day Lee surrendered at Appomattox. In a time of shortages with want of food and fodder, this was an outstanding accomplishment.

7. "TO BE COMPELLED...TO MEET OUR FELLOW-MEN IN DEADLY SHOCK CANNOT BUT BE....PAINFUL TO A CHRISTIAN MIND."

[THE PENINSULAR CAMPAIGN, 1862]

O ALMIGHTY God, who art a strong tower of defence unto thy servants against the face of their enemies; We yield thee praise and thanksgiving for our deliverance from those great and apparent dangers wherewith we were compassed.

Episcopal Book of Common Prayer, 1789

During one of his visits to the army in the field near Manassas Pendleton heard the rumor that the Army planned to remain through the winter. When he returned to the field to resume command of the field artillery he found the Army settling in. As of October 19th he wrote that he had five artillery batteries in the Reserve Artillery Corps camped around his tent. All told, there were 600 men, 450 horses, and twenty-eight guns. During his absence the Provisional Army of Virginia was dissolved and merged into the Confederate States of America Army. With the change Pendleton remained a Colonel, but Sandie's commission with the Confederacy was late in coming. Pendleton intervened with the War Department to get Sandie commissioned. He also found multiple opportunities to preach to the men. He preferred using a large barn near Jackson's headquarters as the chapel as the weather worsened heading into winter.

He was invited to stay in the tent of "Stonewall" Jackson. They enjoyed each other's company sharing ideas on religion, tactics, and the war, probably in that order. Staying in the field as winter approached made Pendleton feel his age. He complained that "Camp-life, at all times a trial to one of my age and habits, is peculiarly so in weather like this, so damp and chilly," and "Camp-life is getting more trying as it becomes cold. These nights are very sharp in an open tent. The order now is to have a large fire before the tent and to leave the front open all night." The soldiers had it worse, many having only one blanket. Pendleton reported home that he slept well, had a good appetite, and was well. But by early November his health took a turn for the worse. Sandie wrote home that "Papa has jaundice very badly." Pendleton found that it was difficult to obtain the medicines he needed, and that what he had taken was ineffective. "I am as yellow as any white human being you ever saw." By November 16th he felt better and was able to ride around the camp for many hours.

In December Pendleton built a hut encampment for his reserve artillery a mile and a half from Jackson's headquarters. He hoped it would help as many soldiers were ill "from cold in various forms, fever, jaundice, pneumonia, etc." After occupation by an Army for several months the land around the camps was stripped. Fences, crops, livestock, and woods had been removed to feed the needs of the Army. In spite of this, Pendleton found a small wood in which he built his camp. Some of the trees were left standing on the weather side in the north to block the winds. Firewood was plentiful. He called it "quite a little city of cabins, with straight streets. The boys call it "New Centreville." Pendleton remained with Jackson while the camp was being built. Every morning he awoke at sunrise, ate breakfast when Jackson was ready, and then walked to his camp for the day unless he rode out inspecting breastworks and the terrain. After Jackson's departure on the ill-fated Romney campaign he moved into his own cabin. By January Pendleton erected a sixty foot by twenty five foot wooden chapel in which he held well attended regular services. Before it was completed he held services at the door of his cabin.

The New Year found Pendleton mired in paperwork. He was still trying to raise another Rockbridge Artillery battery in Lexington to form a Rockbridge Artillery Battalion but without much success. He also urged General Johnston to expel the writer "Bohemian" of the Richmond *Dispatch* from camp for "espionage and villainy." His articles included far too accurate details of the

Army's condition. "Bohemian" was *nom de plume* of the reputable Dr. William G. Shepperson, and Johnston quietly ignored Pendleton's request. In January Anzelotte arrived for a prolonged visit taking advantage of the winter lull in fighting. The couple stayed in a private home near Centreville. Anzelotte took charge of Pendleton's cabin, cleaning it out and putting in carpet for warmth and comfort. Meanwhile the nearby landscape was churned into mud by all the men and horses. The roads were impassable and it was difficult to feed and supply men and horses.

On March 26, 1862, Pendleton was promoted to the rank of Brigadier General of Artillery, the highest available rank in the Field Artillery branch. Pendleton heard it first from Longstreet. Sandie wrote his father that "no honor which has been conferred by the President has been better deserved or will be more prized..." Jackson's staff received news with "the liveliest satisfaction." Jackson passed along his "most cordial congratulations and love." Critics later maligned Pendleton for never being promoted to Major General but the fact remains that the Confederate Congress never created such a rank in the Field Artillery Corps, so no such promotion was possible. Congress also authorized sixteen batteries of six guns each, and eighty officers of artillery for ordnance duties, each army to have a Lieutenant Colonel of artillery responsible for ordnance, and each Corps to have one Major.

It was also about this time that he first heard the rumors being spread about his alleged cowardice at First Manassas. When Pendleton heard mutterings "that I had shrunk from my post and gone to the rear," he assiduously tracked them back to an artillery major, and then complained bitterly about the rumors in a long letter to Stonewall Jackson. Jackson replied that he spoke with Colonel Grigsby, one of the brigade's regimental commanders at the battle, and "He says he saw more of you during the battle and says you behaved bravely as an officer should and was impressed with your coolness and courage and speaks of your conduct in high terms and except when you went to rear to hitch your horse you were forward with your battery. Another artillery officer recalls you went forward with your battery in line of battle. Just before the pieces went to the rear you gave [instructions] respecting the firing." Pendleton, who was slightly wounded during the battle, was never able to shake off the rumor.

*   *   *   *

In addition to caring for the Army's field artillery Pendleton also needed to look after his family and their needs back in Lexington. For the most part Anzelotte handled many of the details of managing the household but there were still times when Pendleton became involved.

Since his departure in May Pendleton was pressed to find a teacher for his rectory attic school. In September 1861 he hired a P. Doddridge Thompson as the teacher. Thompson, however, refused to take on twelve students, and wanted the number of pupils reduced to no more than eight. He agreed to start on October 15th provided that he obtained his release from the army on health grounds. He also thought he might be delayed because he was teaching the regimental band.

During Jackson's Valley Campaign in the spring of 1862 Anzelotte asked Pendleton whether the family should stay in Lexington or flee. She did not want to give up her "sweet home" and prayed that Jackson would drive "the wretches back." Pendleton reassured her that Lexington would be the safest place to be. However, if she felt threatened she should keep her "attention alive for quick preparation and departure" for Lynchburg. Sandie also told her not to fret. When Jackson retreated up the valley Anzelotte prepared to leave but heavy rains raised the water levels in the James River bursting the walls of the James River Canal. Unable to take a boat she and daughter Susan P. Lee scurried about in the rain looking for any available wagon and found none. She abandoned her idea of flight and never sought to flee Lexington again.

In the midst of the Valley Campaign Jackson created a dispute when he ordered the arrest of General Robert Garnett for disobedience of orders. Garnett, horribly outnumbered, had withdrawn his men before they could be overwhelmed but Jackson did not care. Garnett's brother-in-law Colonel T. H. Williamson was a faculty member at VMI, a West Point classmate of Pendleton, and a member of Pendleton's congregation. The Williamsons asked why Garnett was arrested since he performed well in the battle. Anzelotte wrote home that she visited the Williamsons and found them despondent. They refused to allow Garnett to be made a scapegoat for Jackson's mistake in attacking a much larger force than expected and were convinced Jackson was insane.

117

In early June the "mad" General Jackson stopped at Brown's Gap in the Blue Ridge, close enough for Sandie to make a quick trip home. His mother took exception to the number, quality, and rough use of Sandie's horses, and complained to her husband about his spending habits. Pendleton replied that Sandie "was an extravagant dog about his horses. He must try to take better care of them."

By June 1862 the war consumed so much of Virginia's resources that hunger and deprivation loomed for portions of the civilian population. In Lexington Margaret Junkin Preston complained, "...Coffee is not to be bought. We have some on hand, and for eight months have drunk a poor mixture, half wheat, half coffee. Many persons have nothing but wheat and rye. ...For months we have had no service at night in any church in town owing to the scarcity of candles, or rather, to save lights and fuel." Coins became scarce following Say's Law of economics that cheap money pushes out valuable currency. The Bank of Rockbridge issued paper notes and warned users not to rely on notes from outside the County. This printing of money to meet needs exacerbated inflation, which sapped the income of everyone but particularly harmed the poor and elderly as it always does.

Conditions worsened in Lexington as the war dragged on. Refugees from northern Virginia consumed the shrinking available local resources. Residents survived on rye, sweet potatoes, corn, chestnuts, and coffee substitutes. City services failed. Roads, gutters, and sidewalks went without repair. Police and fire protection was inadequate. Smallpox and typhus struck the area, no doubt taking advantage of the weakened constitutions of the people. Inflation worsened. Firewood was $10 a cord at Jordan's Point on the river or $12 delivered in town. Wage earners were paid only $8 a day. Free blacks working in the niter mines were fed and paid 60 cents a day. Patrols of Home Guards maintained law and order to prevent the nighttime movements of slaves between plantations and town, which became fairly common during the war.

*   *   *   *

Winter still lingered when Pendleton received the order to abandon his little city in the woods and move south with Gustavus Smith's infantry division to Warrenton. The risk averse General Johnston, concerned that the defensive lines so laboriously built around Manassas would not repel the larger Federal Army, once again decided to retreat rather than face a larger force. He ordered

118

all food, baggage, and equipment, all collected through great hardship by the Confederacy, to be burned and the troops to fall back. Pendleton's Reserve Artillery departed on March 8th in severe late winter weather taking the turnpike towards Warrenton. Four days later they reached the outskirts of Culpepper. Each night on the march Pendleton made arrangements for foraging for food for the horses, posted guards, and made the men comfortable. Whenever he could Pendleton stayed out of the weather with a local rector for a good supper and a "most delightful bed," something which probably did not endear him to his men. Near Fauquier Warm Springs the column stopped at an old country bridge, which General Smith felt was not safe enough to cross. Pendleton examined it and disagreed and the column passed over it easily. On arrival at Louisa Courthouse they joined with Longstreet's division. At Orange Courthouse Pendleton's horse was stolen. Four men were later arrested using the horse as a pack animal to carry their possessions. In the meantime his staff made a gift to him of a new horse.

On April 11th Pendleton and his Reserve Artillery were ordered to Fredericksburg where the bulk of the Army was then gathering. He preached that morning to his own command and started out. The very next day he was ordered to return to Louisa Courthouse in the pouring cold and icy rain. On arrival he received orders to report to General Robert E. Lee, then Davis' military advisor, in Richmond. The trip took Pendleton near his family estate in Caroline County but he did not stop to visit. He arrived in the capital on April 14th and waited for orders. Two days later he and the Reserve Artillery were told to move down the Peninsula between the York and James River estuaries to Lebanon Mills, just southeast of Williamsburg.

The Federal Army of the Potomac under General McClellan moving swiftly landed at the tip of the Peninsula. From there McClellan could make a quick march of only eighty-one miles to undefended Richmond, but the overly cautious McClellan instead came to a halt. Johnston needed to move his Army to the Peninsula to defend Richmond, but the question was whether the Peninsula, a land of sunken dirt roads, woods, swamps, sand, and sluggish rivers, was suitable for large scale military operations. He sent Pendleton forward to Yorktown to report on the available terrain for defense. It did not take Pendleton long. After consulting with former Washington College professor, and Jackson in-law General Daniel

Harvey Hill, Pendleton concluded that the Lower Peninsula was not the place to fight a major battle. The area consisted of pine woods and dense undergrowth interlaced with marshes and occasional clearings. The soil was spongy, and became flooded after a heavy rain. Given the weight of the artillery and the heavy pine woods it was not a place where artillery could deploy. Rather, Pendleton recommended a retreat towards Richmond. Apart from the disadvantages of the terrain, the Federal Navy could easily sail up the York and James Rivers and bombard the Confederate defenses with their long range rifled naval guns. Using these waterways McClellan could easily land troops in the rear of the defending Confederate Army. Pendleton also recommended that Yorktown not be aggressively defended due to its exposure to heavy Federal artillery bombardment. On the positive side, Pendleton did feel that the terrain required the Federal artillery to limit itself to travel on the few well-constructed roads in the area which would prevent it from deploying, thereby depriving it of its normal advantage of greater and longer range firepower. On the whole, however, Pendleton feared that the Confederates would not be able to both defend Richmond and defeat McClellan on the Peninsula.

The defense of Yorktown was given to General John Bankhead Magruder, a childhood neighbor and West Point roommate of Pendleton. Magruder enjoyed theatricals and put on an impressive show of strength for McClellan to fret about despite the very low numbers of defenders in the town. McClellan, true to form, pulled up and slowly approached Yorktown opening siege lines and forts as though he were besieging a major fortress. The siege, which lasted a month, exhausted the vigilant defenders so Magruder asked Pendleton for help in replacing some of his artillerymen. He reported that some of his batteries needed to be relieved without delay due to physical exhaustion. Men from the Kentucky artillery "have slept on the platforms of their guns and been under fire without relief since the 4th of April continuously. They can keep no fires; many of them have chills and fevers; all of them should be put in the reserve for a short time." He asked that Pendleton swap them for his Reserve Artillery. Pendleton agreed and the Reserve Artillery began rotations into the front line. On April 16th McClellan launched an attack at Dam No. 1 on the Warwick River near Yorktown spawning a heavy exchange of artillery fire. During the battle Pendleton arrived and took command of the artillery as the Chief of Artillery for Johnston's Army. The Federals were readily repulsed.

When McClellan's lines were finished and his heavy artillery ready to fire, Magruder fired off a heavy artillery barrage and abandoned Yorktown, moving up the Peninsula towards Richmond. This charade bought the Confederacy precious time to gather forces. During the siege new artillery batteries arrived to assist in the defense of Richmond and were supplied by the new Confederate Ordnance Department.

The Reserve Artillery, the only field artillery still under Pendleton's direct tactical command and control, included ten batteries and Walton's battalion with fifty-six guns and 1,050 men. With Yorktown abandoned it needed to move down the primitive sandy roads towards Richmond from Lebanon Mills. The withdrawal of the artillery from the Lower Peninsula was rendered difficult by the constant rainfall which turned the roads into bottomless streams of mud. Without the assistance of the infantrymen on the road many of the guns would have been abandoned. By May 4, 1861, the Reserve Artillery had reached Hickory Neck Church in Toano. The next day they travelled only five miles to Barhamsville, and the day after made ten miles to New Kent Court House. There they stopped until the Army gathered. By May 9th the Army escaped what was called the "Peninsula Trap" by reaching the north bank of the Chickahominy River.

Pendleton advised Johnston in April that the defensive line needed to be on the north bank of the Chickahominy for the reasons discussed above. He felt it was the only proper position for a successful defense. He also advised Johnston not to waste too many field artillery batteries in the Peninsula because of its terrain and conditions. Instead, he recommended that Johnston use the artillery for redoubts and batteries in the Richmond defensive lines. Pendleton spent a great deal of time directing the construction of the lines at Richmond and positioning artillery there. The useless operations in the Lower Peninsula sapped the field artillery of equipment and horses. Even so, the terrain around the Chickahominy River was not much better. Given the swampy landscape and wide sluggish rivers the best use of artillery was to place it in earthworks dominating the river crossings and in support of the infantry. On May 30th Pendleton, anticipating Johnston's and Lee's later plans, wrote Johnston that:

I venture to offer a suggestion based upon some information respecting the Chickahominy River. It is said to rise immediately after a rain like this, and to continue in flood some twenty-four hours. Would not this seem a providence to place all the Yankee force this side that stream, almost certainly in your power? Might not an active, sudden, and adequate movement of troops to-night and at dawn in the morning so overwhelm the divisions confronting Gen. Hill as to crush and capture them with next to certainty? I submit it with great deference. Your judgment will, I know, determine sagaciously on the subject.

That same day General D. H. Hill reported that a Federal Army corps had crossed the river and was exposed. Johnston called his officers together that night and announced that he would attack the next day. For the first time in the war Joseph E. Johnston was going on the offensive, a rarity indeed for him. The attack, however, was a disaster. One division wandered off into the swamps, another took the wrong road and never reached its assigned position for the assault. Most of the fighting was by D. H. Hill with little to no support. Johnston, riding forward at the end of the day was struck by a bullet and a shell fragment. His wounds were serious enough to remove him from command. Pendleton and the Reserve Artillery waited in the rear for orders that never came. Here, for the first time, we see a flaw in Pendleton's military performance that would repeat itself. He lacked initiative; he disliked taking affirmative moves on his own without orders. He should have ascertained whether an additional battery here or there would have assisted the infantry attacks. Instead he complained that the mucky terrain made deployment difficult and that the Federal railroad artillery guns could fire too far. While Johnston may have tolerated such inactive behavior the new commander would not.

President Jefferson Davis arrived at the battlefield late in the day with his military advisor Robert E. Lee. When Johnston was wounded Davis turned to the next in command, Gustavus W. Smith, and asked about his plans. Smith had none and was flustered by the news he was now in charge. That night when riding back to

Richmond Davis informed Lee that he was now the commander of what became the Army of Northern Virginia.

　　　　*　　　　　*　　　　　*　　　　　*

After assuming command on June 2nd General R. E. Lee asked Pendleton to continue to act as Chief of Artillery, and he ordered Pendleton to bring the performance of the field artillery up to maximum efficiency. Lee did not seek to enlarge the field artillery but to re-organize it and improve the performance of each of the batteries. Pendleton was impressed with Lee as commander. They knew each other from West Point, but by 1862 that was well in the past. They also shared a common background as scions of the Tidewater gentry. Pendleton pleased with the assignment wrote that, "I liked very much his tone and bearing in the conference I had with him the evening before last….His head seems clear & his heart strong." Pendleton was also well aware of the burden Lee carried. Lee had to shield Richmond while at the same time trying to defeat McClellan. Richmond was like a millstone around his neck. "Few men ever borne a greater weight than that which now rests upon his shoulders."

The first thing Pendleton did was to augment his staff to ten officers, the number used by a brigade commander. It would not grow again for some time. He selected chiefs to oversee the functions of quartermaster (food, forage, and supplies), ordnance (guns and shells), medical care, inspector general (ensures compliance with Army regulations and law), adjutant general (paperwork), aide-de-camp (personal aide), and two others. The number of staff officers was required to keep all of the field artillery organized, reinforced, fed, and supplied. He made his nephew Captain Dudley Pendleton the Assistant Adjutant General. This raised the hackles of Anzelotte who complained that Pendleton should have promoted Sandie to Captain and given that position. Pendleton curtly replied that "It would not do to take him away from General Jackson." Soon after, Sandie was promoted to Captain by Jackson, although one of Jackson's regimental commanders felt that Sandie had earned an even higher rank.

Lee was not alone in thinking the artillery required re-organization. E. P. Alexander felt the same way. Batteries were assigned to each brigade and subject to the whims of the brigade commander. Too few batteries were placed in reserve. This scattering of artillery's firepower made the massing of guns impossible and the artillery tended to lose any real impact on the battlefield. Pendleton realized that the function of Reserve Artillery was not having a mass of guns waiting for action in the rear of an army. Rather, it meant having masses of artillery readily available for immediate use under the direction of the field commanders who knew the field of battle and could place the artillery where it would have the greatest possible impact.

As early as June 5th Pendleton began re-organizing the Army's field artillery command structure. Pendleton told Lee that the artillery required "more system." He was perplexed at the "the want of efficiency" shown by some of the batteries. He was also stymied in trying to procure accurate information regarding the status of the batteries and men. "Nothing is more certain than that I ought to have at all times and be ready to spread distribution and capacity for diffused or concentrated action." In the effort to place the artillery on a more effective footing, Pendleton attached one battalion to each of the two Army Corps, with an additional reserve battalion for each of these corps and a general reserve for the entire army. However, at the time the Army was not organized into Corps, something which would occur later. Through until the end of the Peninsular Campaign Lee would directly command the divisions.

Pendleton began his report to Lee by stating that "The artillery of the army is necessarily so extensively diffused that it becomes essential for its due efficiency there should be in its administration rigid system. Therefore, a Chief of Artillery should be assigned to the division level with his own reserve artillery battalion, and the batteries at the brigade level would report to the division chief as well as to the brigade commander." Pendleton proposed that at the Corps level there should be a Corps Chief of Artillery with his own reserve artillery battalion. Meanwhile, Pendleton, as the Army Chief of Artillery kept his "general charge of that branch of service and special direction of the general reserve. He will, under instructions from the commanding general, see that the batteries are kept in as efficient condition as practicable, and so distributed as to promise the best results. To this end, he will require from the several chiefs of artillery weekly returns exhibiting the condition of each battery, and where it is serving. He will, also, make to the commanding general a tri-monthly report of his entire charge." The gist of the change was that the artillery, apart from the Reserve Artillery, would be tactically commanded at the division and Corps level, and not the brigade level. Pendleton kept a general responsibility for maintaining all of the units but specifically kept tactical control only of the artillery reserve. A weekly return from all of the field artillery was to be sent to Pendleton, who in turn, reported directly to Lee. It was a revolutionary change, one later adopted by the Union armies and European armies.

Pendleton presented his plan for re-organization to Lee on June 22nd. Lee promptly approved it but the change took some time to implement. In the interim some of the artillery battalions had to be pried from the command of brigade or division commanders, such as Longstreet (still just a division commander) who wished to maintain sole control of the guns. Pendleton gathered batteries into battalions and over time assigned them to the division or Corps levels, and in some instances dissolved inefficient batteries and combined their best men into veteran units. In turn, Pendleton preferred to give each battalion commander or chief of artillery a great deal of latitude in the management of their batteries.

The new organization could not be implemented before the Seven Days battles began and was not formalized for months. For the campaign there was just the divisional artillery and Pendleton's Reserve. Longstreet commanded four divisions, Magruder was in charge of three divisions, and A. P. Hill, D. H. Hill, Holmes, Whiting, and Huger each had their own divisions. Stuart commanded the cavalry. Pendleton's artillery reserve consisted of four battalions of several batteries each, including the best rifled guns.

The Army also needed to resolve what to do with the large and inefficient heavy artillery batteries in the Richmond defenses. Pendleton and two other senior artillery officers were appointed to a board of inquiry to investigate "the efficiency of the unattached heavy artillery companies in the works around Richmond and the competency and qualifications of the officers…" The board was to ascertain which batteries and officers to keep and which to either disband or merge into light field artillery batteries.

*   *   *   *

The armies spent most of June sitting along the Chickahominy River eying each other nervously. Lee used the time to plan his next move. Jeb Stuart's cavalry rode around the Union Army in order to discover the extent of the Federal Army's positions. Meanwhile, Pendleton settled into a routine. On Sundays he held separate services with each of the units under his command. He greatly enjoyed preaching, noting that "Soldiers come to hear me much more freely than they seem to do the chaplains." Most of the week, he wrote Anzelotte, he rose near sunrise, meditated and prayed silently, dressed, straightened out his tent, read the Bible, and ate breakfast. Once his office paperwork was dispensed with, Pendleton spent each day in the saddle reconnoitering artillery positions, positioning field artillery, arming the Richmond lines, and conferring with his officers. He inspected the batteries, breaking up some which were inefficient and reducing officers to the private ranks. After dinner, he reviewed all the new paperwork, and then retired for the night. He moved his camp depending on where he was needed most. He was very pleased with his work and staff, "I have a nice military family, - not small." The whole ambiance was one of safety and calm, although he complained of the high price of food. Still, the Army remained well fed and the people in Richmond felt perfectly safe, despite McClellan being so close to the city that his men heard the church bells ringing.

Both Lee and McClellan refined their plans for an offensive and each was ready to attack towards the end of June. Lee's plan was audacious. He would bring Jackson's victorious Army of the Valley secretly to the Peninsula from the Shenandoah Valley and place it on McClellan's extreme right flank where two of the Federal corps were isolated from the rest of the Army by the wide, sluggish, and swampy Chickahominy River. Lee would swing to his left and smash into the isolated portion of the Federal Army destroying it in detail before McClellan could react.

Lee's orders to Pendleton for the campaign provided the Reserve Artillery with a limited defensive role, but an expanded personal role for Pendleton. He was to employ the Reserve Artillery as a reserve defense should McClellan strike out for Richmond. There it would deal with any emergency that might arise, man the defensive lines along the Chickahominy, and if ordered to do so, attack north of the river as occasion might require. In addition, Pendleton was also to supervise the artillery being used in support of the offensive on the left flank, which required some initiative on his part. A later order sent on the 21st stated that Lee expected Pendleton to have all his "reserve artillery parked on the different fronts, where it can be conveniently and rapidly brought into action when necessary. He will rely greatly upon the good use of artillery to hold the enemy in check should he advance against our weakened lines, and he *requests that you will give your constant and unremitting attention to this matter,*" [emphasis added] thereby emphasizing the limited and defensive role assigned. This defensive posture reflected more Davis' fears than Lee's. Lee was convinced McClellan was too cautious to launch a major attack while his flank was being battered. For a man of limited self-initiative on the battlefield the orders expected too much.

Pendleton spent the days before the attack consulting with the various commanders about their artillery needs and re-distributing resources. None of it became any easier when President Davis arrived on June 28th to help command the Army and observe the action. Davis added to Pendleton's concerns by choosing stay with Pendleton in his tent.

McClellan suspected that Lee was up to something and on June 25th launched a reconnaissance in force westward down the Williamsburg Road towards Richmond. The attack also sought to occupy a village named Old Tavern where McClellan planned to position his long range siege artillery for firing on the capital. The advance led to a clash at Oak Grove but by the end of the day the lines remained essentially in the same position.

The next day Lee's plan called for Jackson to start the battle on the far left of the Confederate line. Once he heard Jackson's gunfire A.P. Hill was to attack through Mechanicsville and on to Beaver Dam Creek. D. H. Hill and Longstreet were to provide support in their rear while Magruder and Huger held the lines on the right. Unfortunately for the Confederacy, Jackson experienced some kind of emotional and/or physical breakdown after weeks of hard campaigning in the Valley. By midafternoon Jackson still had not attacked so A. P. Hill launched his attack on his own initiative. The Federals of General Fitz-John Porter's Corps withdrew from the pressure of the assault and concentrated at Beaver Dam Creek where 14,000 entrenched Federal soldiers and thirty-two guns repulsed repeated attacks with heavy casualties. Jackson finally arrived but had his men camp for the night. Even that was too close for Porter. He withdrew another five miles that night. McClellan, acting defensively as Lee expected, focused on changing his supply line to run from the James River and not the York River on his threatened right rear, rather an adopting an offensive posture.

Pendleton spent the day on the right flank as that was where he expected McClellan to launch a reactive offensive against the weakened Confederate line. The attack never came. McClellan's innate paranoia led him to believe that Lee had 200,000 men in his army far outnumbering him, and that the Union Army needed to stay on the defensive. The newly organized Reserve Artillery battalions did not participate, and the desired experiment in concentrated masses of artillery fire was not conducted. Even though Napoleon used this concept for his many victorious campaigns it was a new concept in America for the tactical use of field artillery. With their inexperience both the artillery officers and the division commanders lacked the training to employ this new tactic.

On June 27th Porter continued his fighting withdrawal to safety on the south bank of the Chickahominy. McClellan ordered Porter to hold Gaines Mills to provide time for the Army to switch its base of supply. Lee attacked Porter with six divisions but was held up by Federal defenses at Boatswain's Swamp. Once again Jackson appeared too late to assist turning Porter's flank, and once again the Confederates sustained heavy casualties in trying to force the Union line back without help from Jackson. By 4:00 a.m. the next morning the entire Federal Army was safe on the south side of the Chickahominy and Lee's greatest opportunity to destroy the Army of the Potomac was lost. However, McClellan was badly frightened and broke off any effort to besiege Richmond. Instead, he started to concentrate his entire army at a defensive base on the James River at Harrison Landing.

Pendleton once again remained on the quiet battlefront on the right flank. Through a break in the woods he observed Federal troops in force east of Powhite near Gaines Mill, and reported it to Lee. He also was able to belatedly assist Magruder by advancing his long range guns towards the front. As Magruder's aide reported, "Great execution could have been done yesterday evening if pieces had been stationed there."

While McClellan now planned a defensive line based on the James River and Malvern Hill Lee still planned the campaign as though McClellan would fall back to the east to protect his base on the York River. It was not until the 28th that Lee firmly understood what McClellan was doing.

Most of June 28ᵗʰ was quiet but for some attacks on Garnett's & Golding's Farm by Magruder and Toombs on the right flank. Lee was now convinced he had McClellan on the run and ordered a pursuit. Once again Pendleton did little. He ordered Master's battery of long range rifled guns up to Garnett's Farm in support but it did not fire. Pendleton also coordinated with Magruder to set up heavy artillery to engage in counter battery fire against the entrenched Federal artillery. However, Magruder had no assigned engineering officer to handle the construction of the required works and Lee's engineers vetoed the proposal and removed all the tools needed for the job. Magruder asked Pendleton to see if Lee or Davis would send him an engineer officer with tools and he would see the job done. Lee did not reconsider his decision but ordered Pendleton to visit Magruder that night to urge the utmost vigilance in the outposts. Pendleton was also occupied as a messenger and guide for President Davis. As a result, Pendleton remained well removed from the battlefield on horseback with Davis. All he could later say was "The battle spectacle which I witnessed several miles on our left, across the river, was awfully impressive as well as greatly exciting."

On Sunday, June 29, McClellan's army remained centered on Savage's Station on the Richmond and York River Railroad where it crossed the White Oak Swamp. McClellan was not present on the field having withdrawn to Malvern Hill without leaving any clear directions for his field commanders. Lee was now committed to what he believed was an open pursuit of a fleeing enemy, a mistake that would cost him dearly at Malvern Hill. He told Jackson to link with Magruder on the south side of the Chickahominy and to launch a strong attack on the "fleeing" Federal army. Once again Jackson was late and Magruder attacked a force twice his size without assistance. After a fierce battle the positions remained unchanged.

Pendleton spent a portion of the day on horseback with Lee and Davis. When the Nelson Reserve Artillery battalion engaged in a hot counter battery fight Pendleton watched the combat under fire. Later in the day he came down with dysentery and fever. That evening he reported to Anzelotte, "You need not be uneasy about me. I am lying on a lounge under a shady tree in the yard of my headquarters…I feel better already, and hope a day's rest, a blue pill, etc., may make me quite well again tomorrow." We do not know what "blue pill, etc." he took. In all probability given the medicine of the time it included mercury and a purgative which made him even sicker, depriving him of energy for the next few days.

Finally, on June 30th the Reserve Artillery fully engaged the enemy. Lee ordered an assault on the rear of the Federal Army now bottlenecked between White Oak Swamp and Glendale. Jackson was to press the rear guard at White Oak swamp while the bulk of the army launched a smashing attack on the traffic bound Federals near Glendale. On the right Holmes was to take Malvern Hill. Once again the Confederate staff-work was shoddy, resulting in no coordination between the different parts of the army. Huger spent the day clearing tree blocked roads. Magruder marched in circles. Jackson remained north of the Chickahominy and made only feeble efforts to attack. Both Holmes and Magruder were repulsed at Malvern Hill, primarily because of the massed Federal artillery there supported by naval gunboat fire from the nearby James River. It should have been a lesson learned but Lee ignored the next day.

Only Longstreet and A.P. Hill attacked as ordered, and in doing so they initiated a heavy exchange of indirect artillery fire along the front. When shells landed among Davis, Lee, Longstreet, and their staffs, Longstreet tried to silence the enemy with counter battery fire. Given the longer range of most of the Federal guns the effort failed and an infantry charge was required to chase the enemy guns away. By 8:00 p.m. that night Longstreet's entire command was committed to the battle.

While the Reserve Artillery participated in the battle it had little impact on the outcome. Part of the Reserve Artillery was ordered forward but was told not to engage in the fighting. Other batteries could not see the enemy artillery. Instead, the gunners were told to fire toward the sounds of the enemy guns. Little damage came of it. While Longstreet finally made good use of the artillery it was a wasted effort. E. P. Alexander wrote fifty years later that, "The cannonade, which was kept up during all the rest of the day, was not only a delusion, but useless burning both of daylight and ammunition, for it was all random fire. The Federal and Confederate artillery could not see each other at all." As for the still recovering Pendleton, he spent the day adjusting the positions of the artillery and making sure that the three largest batteries would be ready for the next day.

*   *   *   *

130

The battle at Malvern Hill on July 1st was a preview of Lee's thinking a year later at Gettysburg on July 3, 1863. Lee believed the Federal Army was in disarray and could easily be pushed. He was still in a pursuit frame of mind notwithstanding the reality that the Federal Army was well positioned for the defense. Malvern Hill was a battle the Confederacy could not win regardless of what happened. But the enemy was there and Lee was going to strike them.

Malvern Hill lies eighteen miles southeast of Richmond on the James River. A geologic anomaly in an otherwise flat and swampy terrain, it stands 130 feet high and runs a mile and half long. From the summit there is a commanding view of the surrounding countryside. Days before, when McClellan shifted his base to the James River, he also strengthened the defenses at Malvern Hill. By July 1st its crown was lined with over fifty field artillery pieces lined up hub to hub with clear fields of fire supported by heavy guns to the rear and on the nearby warships on the James River. Asking the troops to take the hill was asking the impossible. Still, as a result of the defeat which followed there was a great deal of blame spread about within the Confederate command.

Lee, with Longstreet's assistance, planned the assault to develop like a Napoleonic battle map. The plan was to create grand batteries of artillery consisting of the artillery commanded by Magruder and Jackson on both flanks. Their fire was to break down the Federal lines to be followed by charging columns of infantry all moving in unison. The commencement of the infantry assault depended on the successful outcome of a massive artillery duel. Once the Federal guns were driven from the summit the assault could begin. Nothing of the sort even came close to happening. Once again, extremely poor staff-work on orders and planning by Lee's and Longstreet's staffs led to confusion among the commanders. No one thought to send orders to Pendleton, and so far as we know none were ever drafted. Lee would have abandoned the attack if he had realized that the assault could not have succeeded.

However, Lee thought he knew the area well from his childhood and failed to conduct a reconnaissance of the ground over which his assault would pass. His memory failed him. As he later noted, the area was covered by dense thickets of scrub pine trees and extremely mushy ground which would not bear the weight of the guns. It was impractical to bring up a sufficient amount of artillery to overcome the extraordinary artillery positions of the Federal Army. When D. H. Hill saw the Federal defenses he told Longstreet that any attack was useless, but was overruled. It did not help that all of Hill's artillery was sent to the rear to replenish their exhausted ammunition.

Pioneers were sent to open a road to the left flank to move the artillery forward but no one told Pendleton. As a result the only artillery deployed was the artillery under the command and control of the individual division commanders. Many of those guns were low on ammunition after a week of fighting but no effort was made to obtain additional ammunition from the rear, and Pendleton failed to inquire as to their status. During the morning of the 1st of July the Army slowly moved into position one division at a time. As each division deployed in the woods its divisional artillery was placed in a position to bombard the Federal line. Because of the thickness of the woods only half of the divisional artillery actually reached its assigned positions. The divisions acted independently of each other and at different times so that each divisional artillery battery deployed in a piecemeal fashion over time. As each battery appeared the entire Federal line of artillery directed all of its fire on it. While the Federal line was never seriously damaged the Confederate batteries were destroyed or crippled one by one. Some of the Confederate artillery officers requested replacements from the Reserve but no help came, and no requests for help were delivered to Pendleton. By 3:00 p.m. all the Confederate guns were silenced or withdrawn from the front line.

As mentioned, the infantry assault was to occur when the artillery succeeded in driving the Federal Army back or severely damaging it. Lee's first reaction was to call off the attack but then was persuaded that by shifting the attack slightly to the left the attack might succeed. D. H. Hill pushed his entire division forward on the left but was quickly beaten back. When Lee realized the effort was a failure he called off the attack, and so informed Longstreet, who was in nominal command of the assault. Apparently Longstreet failed to pass along the order and some of the divisional commanders charged on their own initiative, again in a piecemeal fashion. The resulting slaughter, as with Pickett a year later, was useless and accomplished nothing.

The night before the battle the still ailing Pendleton spent the evening chatting with President Davis and Generals Longstreet and Stuart about the campaign. There was no discussion of what role Pendleton would have in the morning. When dawn broke, Pendleton started looking for General Lee to get orders for the day but he never found him. There is no indication as to how hard he tried one way or the other except for his claim that he spent hours in the search. Certainly all of the twisting narrow dirt paths through the scrub pine forests and swamps made the task difficult. When he could not find Lee Pendleton started searching for some means to place his Reserve Artillery closer to the front line so as to be of some service. He spent time "examining positions near the two armies toward ascertaining what could be best done with a large artillery force, and especially whether any position could be reached whence our large guns could be used to good purpose. These endeavors had, of course, to be made again and again under the enemy's shells, yet no site was found from which the large guns could play upon the enemy without endangering our own troops, and no occasion was presented for bringing up the reserve artillery."

Pendleton moved his guns forward as far as feasible. One battery commander complained that while his command of seven guns was placed near the front line it never had the chance to participate. When he searched for an access for his guns through the swamp and woods he found that the weight of the guns made it impossible to move closer to the front line. Instead, Pendleton decided to "remain nearby … and await events and orders in readiness for whatever service might be called for…." While waiting he encountered Jefferson Davis, and they spent the afternoon together. Had anyone seriously looked for Pendleton or any of the Reserve Artillery they would not have been hard to find. They waited along nearly all of the roads just to the rear of the Army.

For the entire Peninsular Campaign the Reserve Artillery lost eight killed and thirty men wounded. The next day Major Cole, Lee's Inspector of Transportation, found Pendleton and told him that there had been a heavy loss in artillery horses in Magruder's division. Lee ordered additional horses up but Cole felt that given the condition of the Army it would be better to send up artillery batteries from the Reserve to replace the shattered batteries. "If I send a lot of unbroken horses over the crowded roads to hunt a division in our army at present, it will be nine to one if they reach their destination in two days." That same day McClellan retreated to Harrison Landing under the protection of the Navy and its big guns.

Pendleton wrote to Sandie, "The fighting was terrific – the most awful artillery fire I ever imagined-, and our men suffered terribly, rather more than the enemy, but we compelled them to fall back..." To his wife he wrote, "Owing to the movements of the enemy and the nature of the ground, no large artillery force could be placed by us anywhere. We had a vast deal that could not be used at all."

Lee admitted in his battle report some months later that the Federals occupied a "high range, extending obliquely across the road, in front of Malvern Hill. On this position of great natural strength he had concentrated his powerful artillery, supported by masses of infantry, partially protected by earthworks.... Immediately in his front the ground was open, varying in width from a quarter to half a mile, and, sloping gradually from the crest, was completely swept by the fire of his infantry and artillery. To reach this open ground our troops had to advance through a broken and thickly-wooded country, traversed nearly throughout its whole extent by a swamp passable at but few places and difficult at those. The whole was within range of the batteries on the heights and the gunboats in the river, under whose incessant fire our movements had to be executed....The obstacles presented by the woods and the swamps made it impracticable to bring up a sufficient amount of artillery to oppose successfully the extraordinary force of that arm employed by the enemy, while the field itself afforded us few positions favorable for its use and none for its proper concentration." Hindsight is a wonderful thing, but Lee tragically failed to understand the nature of the battlefield before launching such a hopeless and uncoordinated attack.

Once again, the Confederate field artillery was burdened by poor planning, poor control at the division level, poor understanding of the role of the Reserve Artillery, poor ammunition, and smaller guns with smaller ranges. Given that the entire plan relied on a heavy concentration of artillery it is odd that no staff officer or commander bothered to seek assistance from the nearby Pendleton. His five battalions of seventeen batteries literally clogged the few roads leading to the rear of the army while he was near the President. Pendleton concluded later that the divisional artillery organization also broke down since "not one-half of the division batteries were brought into action either Monday or Tuesday...." As he wrote then:

Too little was thrown into action at once [and]…too much was left in the rear unused…We needed more guns taking part, alike for our own protection and for crippling the enemy. With a powerful array opposed to his own, we divide his attention, shake his nerves, make him shoot at random, and more readily drive him from the field worsted and alarmed. A main cause of this error in the present case was no doubt a peculiar intricacy in the country, from the prevalence of woods and swamps. We could form little idea of positions, and were very generally ignorant of those chosen by the enemy and of the best modes of approaching them ; nor were good maps readily accessible by which in some measure to supply this deficiency; hence a considerable degree of perplexity, which nothing but careful reconnaissance, by skillful officers, experienced in such service, could have obviated, but being obviated, attack had been more cooperative, concentrated and effectual, the enemy's condition more crippled, and our success more triumphant, with less mourning in the land.

Could Pendleton have done more? Many of the officers involved blamed Pendleton for not bringing up his guns when needed, for not creating grand batteries, and for staying in the rear where no one could find him. Much of the criticism lacks any basis in fact. No one gave Pendleton orders for the day or told him he needed to assist with the grand batteries on the flanks. It appears that no message seeking relief was sent to him by the divisional commanders or by Longstreet, the officer in charge of the attack with whom Pendleton spent the previous evening. As for being lost, President Davis found Pendleton. His reserve guns were just to the rear of the front lines.

Even if Pendleton had assisted with the grand batteries or replaced batteries destroyed by enemy fire, would it have made a difference? The terrain rendered any effort to bring up guns to the front line nearly impossible. Only half of the divisional batteries were able to push their way through the thick woods before they were forced back or destroyed. Even if all the grand plans came true, would the Confederate artillery have been able to outshoot fifty superior Federal field artillery pieces backed by large caliber naval guns and heavy artillery? In all likelihood they would not. But the illusion that the battle might have been gloriously successful haunted Lee and the Army of Northern Virginia until the disaster of Pickett's Charge.

The one thing Pendleton might have done in the absence of orders was to contact the divisional commanders through his staff to see what help he could offer. He was still recovering from the gastrointestinal purge pill he took on the 29th and that may have limited his efforts. As it was he went as far forward as he dared given the condition of the newly hewn roads and the need for the Army to keep the roads to the rear open. Maybe he could have pushed his guns further forward without knowing why or where they should go. It would not have made any difference in the outcome.

Pendleton did not earn any accolades for the campaign, nor did he receive any serious criticism until years later. Lee, who followed Winfield Scott's practice of delegating the resolution of problems to subordinate officers, did not criticize Pendleton. In his report he mentioned at length the difficulties with the terrain hindering the deployment of artillery, inexperience, and disorganization, "The artillery failed to perform the rôle of that arm by reason of inexperience on the part of divisional leaders, the impetuosity of their attacks, defective organization, the topographical features of the terrain, and comparatively inferior material and for want of concert among the attacking columns their assaults were too weak to break the Federal line, and after struggling gallantly, sustaining and inflicting great loss, they were compelled successively to retire." Lee also named Pendleton as one of many for attending "unceasingly to their several departments." President Davis spoke well of Pendleton's performance, saying he was the "happy combination of a Christian soldier and patriot. He energetically strove to bring his long range guns and reserve artillery to into a position where they might be useful but the above referenced [terrain] difficulties made it impossible." Some of the younger officers felt that Pendleton lost a grand opportunity but their insight was not the best. E. P. Alexander, a senior artillery officer, waited fifty years to criticize Pendleton, when at the time he was in a position to help by sending to Pendleton for reinforcements and failed to do so.

Pendleton also displayed an inappropriate sense of self-importance. He firmly believed that no general in the army worked harder than he did in the campaign and that he had "done the utmost in my power." It is difficult to understand how Pendleton could have reached such a conclusion. The infantry generals launching assault after assault, day after day, were far busier. Certainly such an attitude could not have been well received by the officer corps of the Army.

Despite what really happened many in the ranks and the officer corps began to question Pendleton's value to the army. Many had no training or experience in artillery, nor were they aware of his many responsibilities. All they saw was an old general with a large staff who tended to be near the rear of the army in any battle. They were unaware of the failure of Lee's staff to properly issue orders and coordinate troop movements. Nor were many of these same men happy with his part time volunteer work as a chaplain. For the rest of the war the complaints followed Pendleton and grew in their scorn. One soldier from Georgia wrote, "Gen. Pendleton displayed an utter want of confidence & fearlessness…it was an absolute disgrace to the army…. [Pendleton] succumbed like a whipped puppy."

       *   *   *   *

The following day Lee ordered Pendleton to take all of the artillery not required by the divisions towards Richmond and examine and re-distribute all of the artillery guns and equipment taken from the Union Army. On the 3rd Pendleton was kicked in the leg by an artillery mule. The vicious kick struck so hard it seriously injured him and by one report broke a bone. In apparent ignorance of his Chief of Artillery's debilitating injury Lee wrote an acerbic note to E. P. Alexander when he could not find Pendleton two days later:

> General Lee directs me to say that General Pendleton is absent, and he [does] not know who is in charge of the Reserve Artillery; he therefore desires that you will go at once and ascertain the condition of the Reserve Artillery, and have it all put

in condition to move to Malvern Hill early to-morrow morning.

The artillery will be held in readiness to move; everything ready for active service, but you will not move the artillery without further orders from these headquarters. You will also see that your ordnance train is ready to move at the same time, if necessary. If the artillery is ordered down the general desires that you go with it.

It was not the last time Lee would go over Pendleton's head to give commands directly to his subordinates but this was the only occasion when it occurred because Pendleton's injury left the Reserve Artillery without a commander.

While recovering from his leg injury Pendleton re-equipped and re-organized the Army's entire artillery corps. Some batteries were shifted to new commands. The far superior captured Federal guns replaced many of the obsolete 6-pounders still in use in the Army of Northern Virginia. Inefficient batteries were broken up and the men, recruits, and returning soldiers were sent to batteries short of men. Pendleton was also told by Lee to make sure the field artillery stopped causing damage to the local farm crops.

Anzelotte arrived to help nurse the injured and still ailing Pendleton. She stayed with an aunt of one of the staff officers in Richmond where she was visited by Stonewall Jackson and Sandie. She also spent two days with Pendleton at his headquarters two miles out of town and shared with her husband the fear that Sandie was losing his religious faith to a boisterous camp life. Sandie was admonished by his mother to abandon the vices of card playing and liquor, "There is no security if you ever relax and think you may do so just a little. It can never be necessary for you to drink one drop of spirits, and it can not be for you to play cards." Pendleton merely suggested that Sandie, "watch and pray. If you do not make opportunity for prayer regularly you will spiritually die. Let nothing prevent this. My sure way of getting a certain time for prayer is to compel myself to awake early, and then employ the first waking hours in steady reflection and prayer. I find, too, that by dwelling on the several petitions of the Lord's Prayer until each word impresses on the mind its full force and stirs up feeling, I get more of the spirit of prayer than I have been able to secure in any other way. Be industrious here, and you will find spiritual health and strength."

Lee spent July repairing his battered Army. Completing the plan offered by Pendleton before the campaign on the Peninsula, Lee created two Army Corps under Longstreet and Jackson, thereby creating the Corps Artillery Reserves as well. The drawback remained that the roles and duties of the various Corps and divisional chiefs of artillery remained vague and ill-defined. Colonel Stapleton Crutchfield commanded the Second Corps Artillery under Jackson while Colonel E. P. Alexander took actual charge of Longstreet's First Corps artillery. Lee also rid the Army of commanders he found wanting, including Generals Magruder and Huger. He kept Pendleton.

       *   *   *   *

McClellan was ordered to move his Army back to Washington but was slow to respond. He gathered his Army around Harrison landing and Westover on the north bank of the James River but did not bother to occupy the southern bank of the river as his naval gunboats commanded the shoreline. Seeing this Lee ordered General D. H. Hill to strengthen the James River south bank defenses and strike at the enemy. Lee hoped to disrupt McClellan's lines of communication and supply, to otherwise compel him to abandon the Peninsula, or at the least, to freeze him in position so he could not assist General Pope. Since McClellan's naval strength gave him the power to cross the river anywhere at any time Lee's expectations to establish a permanent position on the south bank were unrealistic.

Lee told Hill to find points along the river opposite from Westover from which the Federal transport ships could be bombarded. On the 28th Hill personally reconnoitered the river and selected Coggins' Point and Maycock's from which to launch the attack. Pendleton was to cross the James with five of his Reserve batteries and some of his larger guns; the two 32-pounders, the long 32-pounder (Long Tom), and the 18-pounder, all carried on heavy and slow moving siege carriages. Lee's orders were specific. Hill was placed in overall command with Pendleton in command of all of the artillery. After making a personal reconnaissance Pendleton was to place the guns in the dark and as quietly as possible to ensure surprise. When the shooting began it was to be maintained until such time as the return fire became too dangerous. "Not more than one caisson will move with each battery, and those will be divested of two ammunition-chests which will be put where they can be easily replaced on the carriages….All noise, all fires, and approach during the day when a soldier can be seen by the enemy is forbidden, the whole being a secret expedition." Lee even told Hill to lie to the newspaper reporters as to where he was going to maintain the secrecy.

Pendleton reached Petersburg the night of July 29th where he met D. H. Hill's two infantry brigades and assorted field artillery batteries. Two of Pendleton's large rifled guns were transported there by rail. On the 30th Hill and Pendleton scouted out positions along the riverbank and were joined by General Samuel French's brigade of infantry at Perkinson's Mill. At this point Hill delegated command of the expedition to French. This was news to French, so once again Pendleton and French reconnoitered the south shore of the river until nine o'clock in the evening. Standing on the river bank Pendleton looked out across 1,000 yards of water to the other side and saw a lot of targets of opportunity; writing that, "the enemy's shipping lay crowded before us." But he also found that the "tour proved laborious and perplexing" and that the terrain approaching the south bank was "difficult of access and a night approach required great care." On their way back they encountered the head of the artillery column two miles south of the river. The column was halted for the night as it was too late to deploy the guns in their various positions for a night attack. Instead, the remainder of the night was spent in moving troops and guns into the shelter of the woods near the river to prevent them being seen by the Federal reconnaissance balloons the next day. The movement was delayed by the dark and rain, but locals finally helped guide the batteries into position. Some batteries were sent to Hood's Point or Claremont instead of Coggin's Point. By dawn everyone was in position.

Coggins Point is a peninsula sticking out into the James River which sweeps around it. The river at this point is narrowed down to only 1,000 yards bringing the opposite shore well into artillery range. Directly opposite was the Federal army's base camp at Harrison Landing. The shipping, feeding and supplying the enemy, stretched for two miles downriver. The 31st was spent in absolute quiet lest the Federals discover the attack force. The artillery officers placed firing stakes and calculated ranges to assist them in firing at night. Since the ground was swampy in some areas only forty-three of the more than seventy guns available were placed. Most of the ones left in the rear were lighter artillery pieces of dubious value at such a long range. Being a peninsula jutting into the river also meant that the federal warships could bombard the Confederate positions from three sides, and perhaps cut off their line of retreat.

After dusk the awaiting Confederates could see thousands of lights over the water illuminating the ships and tents that were to be the targets of the attack. At half past midnight all forty-three guns opened fire. General French heard "the screams, scenes of wild confusion must have followed, as sailors rushed on the decks of their vessels and soldiers flied from their tents in midnight darkness amid bursting shells falling fast around them." The Federal warships quickly returned fire followed a quarter of an hour later by Federal land batteries on the opposite bank. Pendleton wrote, "I never witnessed anything more terribly grand than that cannonade in the pitch dark." Most of the enemy shells passed well over the Confederate positions. One Confederate gun exploded after being hit, killing one, wounding two, and killing some horses. Another rolled over in the road injuring a few more.

Because of the rain soaked roads the reserve ammunition caissons had been left two miles to the rear. After fifteen to twenty minutes the guns ran out of shells and the firing by Pendleton's batteries slowly died down. The guns were withdrawn under fire but with the protection of the dark and a heavy rain. The dark also hid any evidence of the damage wrought on the Federal camp. After reaching camp the guns, caissons, and wagons were taken back to Petersburg. No guns were lost. On the Federal side there was a great deal of confusion but the losses were minimal, up to fifty men injured or killed, some horses killed, and some minor damage to the shipping.

Pendleton assuaged his Christian guilt arising from the "sneak" attack:

> To be compelled, resisting outrage, to meet our fellow-men in deadly shock cannot but be, under any circumstances, painful to a Christian mind. Especially is the trial grievous when we must be slain by or slay those who so lately were our countrymen, but who, having trampled upon our rights, now seek

to desolate our homes, appropriate our soil, kill off our young men, degrade our women, and subdue us into abject submission to their will, because we claim, under our own Government, exemption from their insults and their control. And still more distressing to find requisite toward contributing to avert the ruin threatened by malignant millions thus to send the sleeping, however unprepared, to their great account. But painful as it is, just as to snatch life from an assassin whose arm is uplifted against our best beloved, most sacred is the duty. As such was this attack made, the issue being committed to unerring wisdom. Such considerations imparted a mournful solemnity to the scene, share so many sudden flashes through thick and multiplied reverberations startling profound stillness constituted elements of grandeur rarely combined.

General French immediately telegraphed headquarters that "We attacked the shipping and camps of the enemy at Shirley last night at 1 a. m. with about forty guns very successfully. It was a complete surprise." Lee was less sanguine, noting, "This does not satisfy the object I had in view." Nevertheless, McClellan evacuated Westover and fortified Harrison's Landing. Two days after the attack he crossed the James and seized control of Coggins Point to protect his shipping. When he learned of the Federal occupation of Coggins Point Lee ordered D. H. Hill to keep an eye open for further troop movements to the south bank. Under the circumstances Lee allowed Hill to keep Pendleton on the south side of the river.

Soon after word of a stranded Federal gunboat reached Lee and he asked Pendleton to see if it could be destroyed before high tide lifted it off the sand bar. Pendleton replied that by the time he heard about it "Either all has been done against her that can be or she is off by the high tide and the aid of the other boats." Since the note was not an order Pendleton felt he could exercise his discretion to not act. Otherwise he feared exhausting a battery and its horses to no purpose. Lee followed up with another request. This time Pendleton responded at length. He advised Lee that senior artillery officers examined the ground and found that "there is not the remotest rational prospect of damaging the grounded gunboat without the probable destruction of every gun with me and horses that we get into position for the purpose." The approach to their positions by any artillery would be exposed to a "triple fire, direct and cross" from any number of enemy warships in the area. Pendleton concluded, "seeing the gunboat is comparatively worthless, and our guns, horses, and men are so valuable to run so great a risk of losing these is not warranted by the remote possibility of destroying" the gunboat. Nothing more was done, and by the end of August McClellan's army was gone.

When Robert E. Lee took a dislike to someone he usually never changed his mind. After the conclusion of operations in the Peninsula, and on the James River, Lee concluded that D. H. Hill was deficient in his performance as a commander. Despite being one of the Army's best combat officers Lee felt Hill lacked administrative ability, and was embarrassed and reluctant to act. On August 7th despite Pendleton's explanation Lee criticized Hill for failure to report on the condition and status of his cavalry primarily because the Federal gunboat escaped destruction. This showed a pettiness on Lee's part that ultimately deprived him of the services of one of the finest officers in his command.

*   *   *   *

Until his final evacuation Lee feared that McClellan might push towards the Confederate capital now that Jackson was pursuing John Pope's Army of Virginia in the northern area of the state. On the 10th Pendleton himself was ordered to return to Richmond the next day, but not before Pendleton managed to embarrass himself before the local citizenry before his departure.

Captain Lane of the Irvine Battery from Georgia was stationed a short distance outside of Petersburg near a farm owned by the Falconer family. One day he asked the farmer to provide him with two quarts of milk. The next morning he picked up the milk which he then took back to his camp. Three men of the mess drank the milk which they also shared with two of the black men of another mess as their entire breakfast. All five became violently ill and died later in the day. The treating doctor thought they had been poisoned by the milk. Pendleton arrested the farmer, his family, and his slaves and sent them under guard to Petersburg on the charge of selling poisoned milk. The magistrates trying the case reviewed all of the available facts but found no evidence that the farmer, or his slaves, poisoned the milk. All were acquitted.

Boteler's Ford 1862

8. "NOW CAME MY GREAT RESPONSIBILITY"

[THE MARYLAND CAMPAIGN, 1862]

When thou goest out to battle against thine enemies, and seest horses, and chariots, and a people more than thou, be not afraid of them: for the Lord thy God is with thee, which brought thee up out of the land of Egypt.

Deuteronomy 20:1, King James Version

After the Peninsular Campaign ended Sandie Pendleton came down with headaches, insomnia, and loss of appetite. Jackson's medical officer Hunter McGuire ordered him to go home to Lexington for rest on the 15th. There he was diagnosed with fever and exhaustion. By the 20th he was on the mend although feeling "still poorly." His pulse remained low but his appetite and sleep improved. He spent two days recuperating at Warm Springs where he was given two teaspoons of whiskey four times a day along with hydrangea, quinine, tea, buttermilk and a cup of chlorates. This was topped off with a dose of mercury. After three weeks his "Chickahominy fever" abated and he was cleared to return to duty on September 9, 1862. Assisting in his recovery was the news that his fiancée, a girl in Winchester, had broken off their engagement. Instead of being despondent Sandie was buoyed by the news. He realized for weeks he did not care for the girl any longer but felt it dishonorable to call off the wedding. In all probability, the girl sensed his loss of interest.

That same month the Grace Episcopal Church vestry asked for Pendleton's resignation. The congregation had swollen with a large number of Episcopalian refugees from northern Virginia and a full time priest was needed to meet their needs. The vestry hired the Reverend George Norton, a refugee priest from an Alexandria parish, for the duration of the war. Pendleton tendered his resignation just before the year's end.

*   *   *   *

General Pendleton's dysentery, jaundice, and fever lingered. Despite his illness he continued to report for duty. In the aftermath of the Peninsular Campaign Pendleton improved the Reserve Artillery still under his command. By August 1862 the Reserve had 100 guns in twenty-six batteries with most of the batteries well horsed. Among the guns were some of the finest pieces captured from McClellan's army, and a small number of Hotchkiss, Whitworth, Armstrong, and Blakely guns purchased abroad by foreign agents for the Confederate Bureau of Ordnance. Altogether, Pendleton directly commanded 3,000 men.

Lee had an ability to anticipate the moves the Federal generals would make. Realizing that McClellan was now largely toothless on the Peninsula, he turned his attention to the growing threat posed by the new Federal Army of Virginia under General John Pope. Pope was moving down the Orange and Alexandria Railroad towards Culpepper and Gordonsville, threatening to cut Lee off from his supplies in the Valley. In July 1862 Lee sent Jackson's Corps to central Virginia to confront the combative Pope. With McClellan still on the Peninsula Lee left the Reserve Artillery under Pendleton in the Richmond area attached to McLaw's division protecting the city. However, to strengthen the forces facing Pope Lee asked Pendleton to reinforce Jackson with several batteries from the Reserve Artillery. It was the first time Lee reduced the number of guns available to Pendleton in the Reserve in the campaign, but by no means would it be the last.

On the 15th Pendleton was preparing more batteries to reinforce Jackson when he was summoned to the Spotswood Hotel to meet Major General Gustavus Smith. Smith ordered him to move what portion of the Reserve Artillery was not needed at Petersburg towards Gordonville to join up with Lee's army. Pendleton did not move very far north of Richmond when on the 19th Pendleton's column reached Hanover Junction. There he was ordered by Lee to quickly advance with an infantry brigade and the artillery under his command to defend the North Anna River crossings from a rumored Federal advance south from Fredericksburg. On arrival at the river ford the next day Pendleton found nothing out of the ordinary.

Meanwhile Pope advanced to the Rapidan River crossings in the Piedmont region of Virginia on August 8th. Jackson, moving north from Gordonsville towards Culpepper in the midst of a severe heat wave attacked the Federals at Cedar Mountain on the 9th. Pope withdrew towards Culpepper and Jackson pulled back to Gordonsville. At this point Jackson decided to outflank Pope. With Lee's arrival at Gordonsville Jackson took his Corps over the Blue Ridge and into the Shenandoah Valley. Then shielded by the Blue Ridge, Jackson tuned north past Pope's right flank. Pope mistakenly thought Jackson was retreating. Jeb Stuart, embarrassed from being surprised by Federal cavalry on the Rapidan, struck Pope's lines of communication by seizing Manassas Junction and burning the supply depot there on the 22nd. Jackson also appeared in Pope's rear and attacked Bristoe Station on the 26th. Pope, now realizing his mistake, turned his army north in a desperate bid to destroy Jackson before he could escape. In doing so he lost track of what Lee was doing with the rest of his Army.

On August 24th, Lee advised Davis that Pope's army of 43,000 men was superior in artillery and the Federals planned to hold Lee in place until Pope was reinforced with 66,000 more troops from McClellan and Burnside. Lee also raised concerns that his Army was not being properly fed and asked the incompetent Commissary-General Northrop to forward more cattle. Otherwise the men were consuming gods and crops in an area previously undisturbed by war. Finally, Lee asked that the divisions of McLaws, D. H. Hill, and other available troops, including "Pendleton's usual battalions" be sent to him.

On Sunday, August 24th Pendleton preached at the Trinity Episcopalian Church and visited his aunt on her plantation at "Oakland." When Pendleton returned to camp he was accosted by D. H. Hill begged him to go to Richmond and ask President Davis to intervene and issue orders for Hill to advance to join Lee. Davis was less certain of McClellan's intentions than Lee and wanted to protect the capital. Pendleton took the train south arriving in Richmond by evening. He ate dinner and breakfast with Davis and the Secretary of War. After a conference consuming the morning of the 25th, Davis finally relented and agreed to send the troops on to Lee. Davis also asked Pendleton to submit "occasional confidential memoranda" on conditions in the Army without Lee's knowledge.

Pendleton returned north on a crowded train and stopped for the night in Bumpas Station near Beaverdam, Virginia between Hanover Junction and Gordonsville. While he was traveling the Reserve Artillery moved towards Lee on its own. By the 27th Pendleton and his artillery reached Louisa Courthouse. President Davis advised Lee on the 28th that the reinforcements he requested had already been sent forward and should have reached Lee. He also noted that, "General Pendleton left here fully possessed of my views and charged to communicate them to you." Unfortunately we have no idea what ideas Pendleton was to convey.

Meanwhile, Lee was on the move following Jackson around Pope's Army. Pope did not need to search far to find Jackson. Jackson's II Corps sat astride Pope's line of retreat as he withdrew towards Centreville and Fairfax County. On the 28th Jackson struck Pope at Groveton. On the 30th Lee pushed through Thoroughfare Gap and advanced undiscovered on Pope's left flank while Jackson beat back multiple assaults by the Federal Army at the Battle of Second Manassas. On the 31st Longstreet launched an attack on Pope's left flank. Thanks to Pendleton's new organization the Corps and divisional commanders made effective use of their field artillery for the first time. Totally surprised, the Union Army broke and fled back inside the fortifications of Washington, D.C. Half a century later E. P. Alexander cattily complained that if the Reserve Artillery had been present the results of the battle would have been better. Perhaps he forgot the Reserve Artillery had been ordered to linger around Richmond by Lee and President Davis.

At Davis' request Pendleton rode hard from Louisa Courthouse towards the battlefield at Manassas. He arrived just in time to watch the last two hours of the battle. Far behind him the Reserve Artillery rumbled forward at twenty miles a day. On arrival Pendleton was totally exhausted by his illness and effort. After Pendleton gave Lee the messages from President Davis, Lee took one look at Pendleton and urged him "in the kindest manner to find some comfortable place, rest and get well." Pendleton went to the Foote Plantation, recently plundered by the Federal Army, two miles north of Haymarket to rest. He wrote home that he suffered from a "crisis of diarrhea of some two weeks duration," undergoing blistering on his abdomen for treatment. He felt he could "with an easy mind rest and recruit" until the artillery arrived. Until then, "I am as comfortable as I could be anywhere in the world away from home." The Reserve Artillery, whittled down to fifty-eight guns and 1,000 men, arrived two days later.

About this time Pendleton jotted down his reflections on the war and his service to the Church in a letter to his daughter Susan P. Lee:

> When I contemplate my own part in the struggle here my feelings are solemn, yet trustful and hopeful. He who notes the fall of every sparrow holds in His hands my life on the battlefield as everywhere else. And I desire, harder though it then be, to realize this when the shells crash and the bullets whiz within a hair's-breadth as when all is quiet and peace around me. It is a strange position for a servant of the Prince of Peace and a minister of the Gospel of Peace. But as I do not delight in war, and would not hurt the hair of the head of any human being save under conviction of public duty; as by prayer, pleadings, and expostulation I have earnestly tried for peace, so I trust the blessing of the peace-maker will not be denied me, though as a soldier of the Cross I follow the example of old Abraham in endeavoring to defend my kindred against cruel outrage.

> He knows how truly I mourn over the wrongs which have compelled the best people of the South to resolve on resistance unto death, and how painful to me the alternative of seeing all that I most value on earth desolated, or of taking myself an humble part in the endeavor, at whatever cost, to resist oppression. He sees that I desire in all sincerity to be a faithful soldier of the Cross, while trying also to be a useful soldier of a much-wronged country. And He graciously accepts, I trust, my unworthy services, whatever error, whatever sin be chargeable against

me in this as in other portions of my life. The blood of Christ cleanseth from all sin.

On September 3rd, the still ailing Pendleton felt strong enough to re-join his command at Sudley Springs. In hindsight he should have gone home to recuperate. The upcoming campaign proved too difficult for an ailing fifty-four year old man. From Sudley Springs Pendleton and his artillery marched at the rear of the Army to a camp at Leesburg near White's Ferry across the Potomac River. There, Lee issued orders applicable to all of the Army's artillery. Extra or weakened horses were to be left behind, gunners were prohibited from riding the caissons in order to save the horses' strength, and the batteries were re-organized by Pendleton to render them more efficient. Despite his ongoing illness Pendleton reviewed his batteries and sifted out the inefficient units while strengthening the efficient ones in preparation for crossing into Maryland. Anticipating the future needs of his artillery corps he ordered Major Richardson to take some batteries, the weaker horses, and the damaged equipment to Winchester. There he was to establish a depot for the artillery where horses could recuperate and equipment repaired. The remaining artillery battalions of Lieutenant-Colonel Cutts and Major Nelson were prepared for the campaign.

The recent campaign left much of the artillery disorganized and under equipped. Pendleton concluded that some of the small and inefficient batteries used up too many horses. Some batteries' wagon trains arrived at the river crossings days ahead of their cannon. Pendleton's re-organization angered many of the affected officers. Fights broke out between the officers over the rights of way, and Pendleton intervened to stop the arguments. Pendleton asked one battery to send eleven horses to aid Jackson, who was already across the Potomac. The battery commander was already under arrest for another infraction and his acting commanding officer objected to the order, violently stalking the room and slamming doors. The next day Pendleton followed up his command with the delivery of written orders. The commanding officers refused to obey. Pendleton rode out to the battery and handed the commander his written order in front of the entire battery. Both the arrested commander and his acting commanding officer refused to obey. Pendleton arrested them and sent them under guard to his camp. He then asked for another officer but none came forward.

The senior non-commissioned officers also refused to step up. Pendleton ordered a roll call of the battery but was told there was no roll of the men. He then ordered the battery to fall into line but the men complained they were too ill to do so. Having expected such a reaction Pendleton brought his surgeon with him and the physician examined the men. The doctor found only four who were ill. The men starting yelling at Pendleton, complaining they had not been paid in months. He listened to their complaints but did not believe them.

Pendleton inspected the battery's camp and found the horses in a wretched condition. Only a few could be used for active campaigning. Pendleton ordered them to be taken to General Jackson and a few of the men in the battery volunteered to take them. He announced he would split up the rest of the men and assign them to various batteries throughout the army. Their Corps commander A. P. Hill intervened and asked Pendleton to keep the battery together. Pendleton agreed provided the arrested officers apologized after which he would release them. Instead, the officers wrote a justification for their actions which Pendleton deemed unsatisfactory. The battery, along with seventeen others, was disbanded. The officers later admitted they meant Pendleton no disrespect but that "disobedience was a necessity." Still unsatisfied Pendleton forwarded them to the Army command for court-martial. Any further records of the affair were lost and the outcome unknown.

*   *   *   *

On the 6th Pendleton wrote Lee that he was still ailing but was taking good care of himself. The blistering he underwent left his side sore and made riding uncomfortable. On the 7th he led his reduced command across the Potomac at White's Ford and moved on towards Frederick alongside Longstreet's I Corps artillery battalions. Pendleton did not break the march until they arrived at Frederick, reaching his old hometown on the 8th. There he reported to Lee and visited old friends in the community where he was received with "great kindness," and found food in abundance. He was not happy to find that his old congregation was poor and suffering, and had been unable after several years to find a replacement for Pendleton as their priest.

His command continued to be whittled down. Cutts' battalion of artillery had been temporarily assigned to D. H. Hill, who was guarding the approaches to Frederick from Washington. On arrival in Frederick Pendleton attempted to re-establish control of the battalion but Hill objected. An appeal to Lee proved useless. Lee wanted the guns where they were to guard the roads to Washington.

On the 9th the infamous Special Orders No. 191 were sent to Jackson, McLaws, Walker, Stuart, D. H. Hill, and Pendleton. The orders split Lee's army into five parts, each with their own mission to accomplish. Two copies were sent by accident to Hill, one from headquarters, the other from Jackson, his Corps commander. The latter was not found. Nor can it be confirmed that Pendleton, McLaws, or Stuart received their copies. At any rate, one copy was dropped in an orchard just outside town and was found by Union troops a day or so later. McClellan, with full knowledge of Lee's plans, began to move more aggressively than usual, but not fast enough to destroy the divided Confederate Army in detail as he hoped.

On the 10th, Pendleton's remaining command, consisting of the battalions of Colonel J. T. Brown, Major William Nelson, and of Colonel S. D. Lee, marched with the Army toward Hagerstown. From camp outside town he wrote home that he felt much better, "not quite sound and strong yet, but improving every day." The chowhound Pendleton was pleased there was no problem finding places to eat with "wholesome food," and found that sleeping in a tent suited him well. On the 13th he sent a "confidential memorandum" to President Davis reporting that Lee was "bold, prompt, energetic, sagacious," that the Army showed a high morale and food was ample. One concern Pendleton raised was his worry that the Army would linger in the Hagerstown area for too long.

On Sunday morning, the 14th, Pendleton was ordered by Lee to return to Boonsboro at the western base of South Mountain. Federal troops were advancing suddenly and unexpectedly to the eastern base of South Mountain and attacking D. H. Hill's lone division holding the passes over the mountain. A Federal breakthrough would isolate the various parts of the Army of Northern Virginia. Lee directed Pendleton to erect a defensive position on the heights of Beaver Creek. By nightfall Pendleton placed several batteries there. At midnight Lee summoned him again and ordered that Colonel S. D. Lee's Reserve Artillery battalion take the road towards Keedysville to join Longstreet's

Corps, and that that Pendleton, with the much reduced remainder of his command take the shortest route to Williamsport. There he was to cross the Potomac and establish defensive positions on the southern bank at Williamsport and Shepherdstown. With the Army of the Potomac closing in on the isolated portions of his command Lee's invasion of Maryland was quickly coming to an end. He needed to be sure his Army could re-cross the river in safety. Pendleton's command was sent for the job since Lee had all the artillery he thought he needed and because a force was needed to guard the fords on his line of retreat.

The remainder of Pendleton's Reserve Artillery departed in the middle of the night. By sunrise the head of the column approached an intersection of the Hagerstown, Sharpsburg, Boonsboro, and Williamsport roads just eight miles north of Sharpsburg, and there "received reliable intelligence of a large cavalry force of the enemy not far ahead of us. I immediately posted guns to the front and on the flank." He rounded up the thousands of stragglers tramping in the trail of Lee's fast moving columns for defense and sent out scouts. He sent to General Toombs in nearby Sharpsburg asking for additional infantry support. The scouts returned and reported that the road was clear for the next two miles. Under the circumstances, and without awaiting the infantry from Toombs, Pendleton advanced cautiously along the road. In addition to his own command he also provided protection for the Army's large ordnance wagon train under the command of Colonel E. P. Alexander moving along the same road. It turned out that the Federal cavalry consisted of Gregg's brigade of three regiments escaped from Jackson's seizure of Harpers Ferry. It passed through the same intersection going north just an hour before Pendleton arrived.

Pendleton and his command crossed the river at Williamsport on the 16th. Pendleton ordered Brown to keep his artillery battalion at Williamsport while he took the only remaining battalion under Nelson to Shepherdstown where they arrived by ten o'clock in the morning.

*   *   *   *

At the northern end of the Shenandoah Valley the Potomac River flows between rolling hills on both sides of the stream. In a few areas the rock ledges surviving the river's flow created fords for crossing the river from one side or the other. The ease of passage depended solely on the amount of water in the river. If it rained upstream in the mountains the Potomac would be high and the fords hidden beneath deeper waters. In mid-September 1862 the rains miles away swelled the river sufficiently so that the fords near Shepherdstown were deep and rocky. One Confederate recalled that the fords were slippery and full of deep crevices posing a danger to men and horses.

British colonists arrived in the area in the early 1730's. In 1734 settler Thomas Shepherd laid out a town on the southern bank of the Potomac for which he obtained a charter in 1762. He named it Mecklenburg but the locals changed it to Shepherdstown. Over time the town grew prosperous. A stream flowing constantly and reliably through the town made it ideal for mills of all sorts. Nearby the clay was perfect for the manufacture of bricks, and the river, and later the canal, enabled transport of anything made in town to the markets on the seaboard. A bridge was built at Shepherdstown on stone piers for crossing the river but below the bridge about a mile downstream lay Blackford's or Boteler's Ford. Other fords could be found both upstream and downstream, but at Boteler's Ford there was a road from the Virginia side to the crossing which was too narrow for a wagon and horse to use side by side.

Along the northern bank ran the Chesapeake & Ohio Canal carrying goods and passengers from the upper Potomac to the Chesapeake Bay. The canal was constructed in 1838, and a lock for the canal was built in Shepherdstown to enable the passage of the boats. The war had not ignored Shepherdstown. By 1862 the bridge over the Potomac was burned and the Canal's walls were pierced and its waters emptied. All that was left along the bank was a trench several feet deep which could provide protection to infantry assaulting the southern bank.

On the northern Maryland bank of the Potomac the hills gently reached down towards the river bank, but on the Virginia side the hills rose steeply from the river creating a series of heights overlooking the river and the fords. Confederate artillery officer Colonel E. P. Alexander felt the terrain favored guns placed on the Maryland side of the river as the rolling hills permitted easy placement and a commanding field of fire. On the other hand, the Virginia side, while higher, was steep and difficult to access for artillery, as Pendleton was to discover.

As soon as Pendleton and his remaining artillery battalion arrived in Shepherdstown on the morning of the 16th he began to construct defenses and place his guns. Even before the battle at Sharpsburg, Lee planned for a rapid evacuation from Maryland. In spite of the fact that Lee's avenue of escape to Williamsport upriver was blocked by Hooker's Corps of the Army of the Potomac, he opted to leave Brown's Reserve Artillery battalion in place there and focus his avenue of retreat on Boteler's Ford and Shepherdstown. Lee hoped to use the fords at Williamsport to re-cross back into Maryland and continue to carry the war northwards. That morning orders from Lee were delivered instructing Pendleton to construct a wide bridge across the canal, fill in the canal with dirt enough to create a roadway, or knock down the sides of the canal enough so that wagons could easily cross. An engineering officer was sent with the orders to help build the bridge. Pendleton also worked to widen the narrow road leading down to the ford from the heights on the Virginia side. The work on the bridge and the roads detained the Army's food and supply wagon trains going north to re-supply Lee before the battle on the 17th. The work kept Pendleton awake and busy through the night.

Colonel Alexander, acting as Chief of Ordnance, continued down to Harpers Ferry on the 16th to take control of the seventy-three artillery pieces captured by Jackson from the Union garrison along with a large supply of ammunition unsuited to the smaller Confederate field pieces. That day and the next Lee asked Pendleton and Alexander to forward as much of the heavy rifled long range guns as possible to the battlefield at Sharpsburg.

On the morning of September 17th the sounds of battle could be heard over four miles away in Sharpsburg. During the day A. P. Hill's division passed over the ford headed north to rescue Lee's collapsing lines. Lee sent Pendleton an urgent request; "If you have fifteen or twenty guns, suitable for our purpose, which you can spare, the general desires you to send them, with a sufficiency of ammunition. You must not take them from the fords if essential to their safety. Send up the stragglers. Take any cavalry about there and send up at the point of the sword. We want ammunition, guns, and provisions." Another request arrived in the afternoon asking for any long range guns which could be spared. Pendleton had no infantry or cavalry to employ but sent the guns requested.

Colonel Thompson Brown reported to Pendleton from Williamsport on the 17th that on arrival there he found only thirty cavalrymen and 800 infantry, although only half that number could be relied upon to fight. Jeb Stuart told Brown there was no enemy between Williamsport and Shepherdstown but Brown found a small column of Federal troops and wagons on the Maryland side and asked for permission to attack if he could use the infantry. Pendleton was probably too busy to reply. He later wrote that, "By night and day much labor was needed on the road, the passage of troops had to be facilitated and important dispatches forwarded in different directions, all rendered the more essential toward General Jackson hastening to Sharpsburg after capturing Harpers Ferry." The work continued all day long.

General Daniel Harvey Hill criticized Lee's use of field artillery during the battle at Sharpsburg. The smaller Confederate guns simply could not compete with "the superior weight, caliber, range, and number" of artillery pieces of the Federal army. Instead of using the Confederate cannons for counter battery fire they should have been spared for use against masses of infantry. Instead, Hill complained, "our guns were made to reply to the Yankee guns, and were smashed up or withdrawn before they could be effectually turned against massive columns of attack." Of course, this was not the fault of Pendleton as he was four miles away preparing the fords at Shepherdstown for the escape of the Army of Northern Virginia from Maryland. Rather, the Corps Chiefs of Artillery were in command of the field artillery on the battlefield.

As the sun began to dip toward the horizon on the 17th Pendleton established his headquarters high easily accessible from all points on a bluff in the middle of his lines. The location commanded a view of the area. That evening Pendleton had only forty-four guns left in his Reserve Artillery. He found places in the bluffs overlooking the river for only thirty-three of them; the rest had to be kept in reserve behind the lines. The guns consisted of eight Parrott rifled guns; a long-range Whitworth rifled cannon, several short-range howitzers, and a dozen obsolete 6-pounder smoothbores. All in all, very little with which to battle any superior Federal artillery force should the crossings come under attack. Fifteen guns were placed below the ford, and eighteen guns above the ford. The obsolete small smoothbore guns were put in the center closer to the river while the longer range rifled guns were placed on the flanks. Each gun had a clear field of fire at the roads and hills opposite them.

Despite still recovering from his dysentery Pendleton worked this second night through as well. Rumors spread through the night that Lee was defeated and retreating to the fords. Another rumor was that Longstreet had won the battle and defeated McClellan. The sounds of the battle were clearly heard. By late afternoon wounded soldiers appeared in the town seeking help. All night they were treated by exhausted surgeons working by candlelight in makeshift hospitals, each hour bringing more and more wounded. When the sun rose on the 19th the town was teeming with 5,000 to 8,000 wounded Confederate soldiers. Every house, building, factory, and church filled with the wounded and dying soldiers.

Federal troops were reported to be at Shepherd's Ford some four miles upstream from Pendleton. He arranged for some infantry and cavalry to round up stragglers and organize them as a force to attack the enemy. Along with them he sent Ancell's Battery from his artillery. He also worked at improving the roadway across the canal, the river, and up through the heights on the Virginia side. He worked so hard he could "scarcely steal a nap."

In the midst of all this activity, Pendleton had to deal with a Yankee spy. Captain William Palmer of the Pennsylvania cavalry volunteered to cross the Potomac in disguise to discover Lee's plans for the future, especially if he planned to re-cross the river and re-invade Maryland. Palmer and another spy crossed the river and found their way to the home of a sympathetic Union miller in Shepherdstown. While Palmer's cohort escaped the Confederate pickets and made his way back into Maryland, Palmer lingered at the miller's house and changed into civilian disguise. On the night of the 18th the house was surrounded by Confederate soldiers and Palmer was captured. He was interviewed by Pendleton. Palmer felt his answers clever enough to fool Pendleton, but he was wrong. Pendleton concluded that Palmer was a spy and ordered him confined. He was shipped to Richmond for trial along with a long, and probably verbose, report from Pendleton. On his arrival in Richmond the jailor felt Pendleton's report too long to read, and just filed it. With the guards ignorant that he was considered a spy, Palmer was tossed in with other routine prisoners of war. He was able to escape later on and resumed his duties as a cavalry officer.

*   *   *   *

All day on the 18th Lee's army faced the far larger Federal Army across Antietam Creek. If McClellan had been more courageous he could easily have crushed Lee's Army that day and brought the war to a faster finish. But he hesitated, and Lee sensed that he would. For Lee, it was a day to consider the next step. First, Lee had to evacuate the wagons and the wounded, and then the army, to the safety of Virginia. From there he could plan his next campaign. In the late afternoon thunderstorms swept off the mountains and through the valley turning the roads to mud. The rain turned into a steady drizzle towards evening, and fell all night long. In the dark and drizzly night Lee quietly withdrew his troops from Sharpsburg and turned south towards Boteler's Ford. Orders were sent to Pendleton to halt all northbound traffic and keep it in Virginia. The Maryland campaign was coming to an end.

Campfires were left burning to fool the Federal pickets. The wagon trains so laboriously hauled to Sharpsburg the day or two before were now the first to depart. Longstreet's Corps followed at 9:00 p.m., and then Jackson's Corps. A. P. Hill provided the rearguard. Last of all to leave was Fitzhugh Lee's cavalry division. The orders were to go to Martinsburg, Virginia, and then to double back to Williamsport on the Potomac. There was not enough time to evacuate all of the wagons and some were left behind. Even so the narrow roads and lanes choked with wagons, horses, and men stumbling south in the damp and dark.

As the Army reached the Potomac River they were met by a wondrous sight. Torches and bonfires were lit to show the way through the trees and down onto the river. Amidst the cool mists rising from the river sat cavalrymen on horseback with torches in hand to guide them. The wagons and men first crossed the canal over a makeshift bridge, and then slid down the steep bank to the river. The riverbed was rocky and strewn with boulders. The river was 200 yards wide at this point and the men had to use their feet to find the narrow rock ledge of the ford while walking waist deep in cold water. Looking up they could see the guns and men of the batteries placed to defend the fords. Once across, they climbed up another steep bank and followed the narrow farm lane winding up through the bluffs overlooking the river.

The hero of the hour was the II Corps Quartermaster Major John Harman, who exhausted his colorful vocabulary encouraging

158

the men, horses, and wagons cross the river. Pendleton was busy, too, now for the third night in a row. He "had to work like a beaver, as did all my officers and men, promoting the safe passage of the army, with its immense trains of artillery and wagons, hence no rest that night." Officers and men in his batteries were employed that night "removing obstructions, preventing collisions, having lights at hand as needed, and promoting the orderly movement of vehicles on the several routes." Nevertheless, several wagons fell into the canal and a gun slipped in the mud over into a ravine on the Virginia side.

Once the wagons crossed the more disciplined and maneuverable infantry came next. Longstreet crossed first and set up a defensive line behind the bluffs as the remainder of the army crossed over. As each unit reached the heights behind the bluffs they were stopped and re-organized by their NCO's and officers. The men were exhausted after actively campaigning since mid-July and fighting in several battles. Some observers felt the army was demoralized and exhausted. Many of the units, having worn themselves out crossing the river dawdled on the rolling hills south of the river to rest and recuperate until morning.

Longstreet's Corps crossed the river starting at 2:00 a.m. By 8:00 a.m. the ford was clear of wagons and the rearguard under A. P. Hill began to cross. At dawn the rising sun found Robert E. Lee sitting astride his horse in mid-river watching the last of his men reach safety in Virginia. As the last brigade crossed a band struck up the old song "Carry me back to Old Virginny." On their way across the tail end of the army stopped to rescue wounded men stuck helplessly in a broken wagon in mid-stream. Lee was assured by General John G. Walker, the division commander, that all that was left in Maryland was one artillery battery and the severely wounded. Lee sighed out, "Thank God."

As relieved as Lee must have been he was still looking ahead to re-crossing the river soon. He sent Stuart and his cavalry to Williamsport to ensure passage across the Potomac and a report to President Davis that he intended to continue the campaign. After all, Lee was confident that McClellan was too slow and too defensively minded to pursue the scattered and battered men of the Army of Northern Virginia. In all probability, McClellan would send out some cavalry to be sure Lee did actually cross the river, so the defenses at the ford need not be overwhelming, just enough to stop a cavalry brigade or two.

Artillery in the field requires a force of infantry to support and defend the gunners while they work. Lee knew this, and assigned Pendleton the Armistead and Lawton infantry brigades to assist him. Pendleton had never commanded infantry before. He had no training or experience in combined arms warfare. Lee knew this, but accepted the risk that the Federals would not aggressively seize the river crossing and attack his weary and scattered troops. Pendleton could not have known at the time just how small the brigades assigned to the defense were after the Maryland Campaign. Told he had two infantry brigades he must have assumed he had over 3,000 men at his disposal. When the new brigade commanders reported to Pendleton neither mentioned how few men they had under their command. And Pendleton never bothered to ask.

Brigadier General Armistead was assigned to Provost Marshal duty during the campaign along with the bulk of his brigade. It was their duty to try to control the straggling that sucked such strength out of the Army during the campaign. Instead, what was left of the brigade was under the command of Colonel John Lamar Hodges, an inexperienced officer. Lee should have been aware of this. On paper Armistead commanded 3,000 men when the campaign began. The brigade sat out the Battle of Second Manassas and while it fought at Antietam its losses were minimal. The brigade suffered only thirty-six casualties. Yet somehow, more than 2,500 of the men carried on paper were not present at Shepherdstown. They may have been on Provost Marshal duty, or they may have joined the thousands of stragglers and deserters trailing in the Army's wake. All we know for sure is that by the 19th no more than 300 or 350 were present for duty.

It was even worse with Lawton's Brigade. Lawton had assumed division command when Ewell was wounded at Second Manassas and at Antietam the brigade was commanded by Colonel James Hodges, yet another inexperienced infantry officer. The brigade carried 1,213 men into the Cornfield at Antietam where half of them were killed or wounded. What was left of the brigade was seriously demoralized and no longer willing to stand and fight against serious opposition. On its way south in the drizzly night even more straggled off or deserted. When it reported for duty on the 19th it too had no more than 300 to 350 men. Altogether,

Pendleton had a battered group of 600 to 650 men under inexperienced officers with which to defend the ford and provide infantry support for the thirty-three mostly obsolete cannons remaining in the Reserve Artillery.

As Pendleton later wrote to Anzelotte, "now came my great responsibility." Lee fully understood the risk he took in leaving a skeletal force under an inexperienced combat general to hold the fords. Lee's intent was to give Pendleton discretion to withdraw if pressured and allow a cavalry screen, with a few batteries, to fight a delaying action. In written orders left for Pendleton on the 19th Lee's aide-de-camp wrote:

> The Commanding General says that if the enemy is in force in your front you must retire tonight. If not in force, being merely an artillery force, withdraw the infantry forces, directing them to rejoin their respective divisions on the march tomorrow, a few guns, and a small cavalry force being sufficient to guard the fords.

Pendleton understood that "I received instructions to hold the position all that day and the night succeeding, unless the pressure should become too great, in which event I was, at my discretion, to withdraw after dark, it being most unlikely that a discreet commander would then risk the destruction of his entire army by getting it across in the night, and being assailed when in disorder next morning, with such a river behind him. Should I find it best at nightfall to withdraw, I was to follow the track of our army." Both Lee and Pendleton expected that the Federal Army would not aggressively follow Lee across the river, nor did they expect the Federal commander to risk a night time assault. Pendleton's mission was to stop the Federal troops from crossing behind Lee on the 19th.

The rain stopped late at night on the 18th and the morning of the 19th dawned clear, bright, but damp. In the saddle by sunrise, Pendleton carefully reviewed the placement of his batteries and felt they were where they would do the most good. As batteries crossed the Potomac on the night of the 18th Pendleton stopped some of them and placed them in positions to cover the opposite bank. Maurin's Battery with three rifled pieces was placed about 250 yards from the river on the right; and Maddox's Battery with just one

161

piece remaining on the left. Upstream Pendleton placed Milledge's Battery with four rifles and a howitzer, and Chapman's Battery with one rifle and one Napoleon. Overlooking the ford he put Johnson's Battery with two obsolete 6-pounders and two short range howitzers. Covering the road up from the river was Kirkpatrick's Battery with two 6-pounders and two 12-pounder howitzers. Alongside was Huckstep's Battery of four 6-pounder guns. To his left Braxton's Battery, and then Hardaway's contingent of the Washington Artillery with a 12-pounder Whitworth and two 10-pounder Parrotts. Two other batteries from the Washington Artillery were posted on the edge of a ravine coming up from the river. Pendleton had forty-four guns deployed, most too small in caliber to be effective against the Federal artillery.

Some of the infantry was placed to cover the ford from concealed positions, and to act as sharpshooters. The brigade commanders were told by Pendleton to keep the force at the ford as strong as possible. The remainder was placed in reserve behind some hills for protection until needed, probably no more than 400 men. The sharpshooters were ordered to fire at the enemy only in reply to shooting from the opposite bank, and to repel any efforts by the Federals to cross the river. Pendleton similarly told the field artillery to conserve their ammunition and to fire only when fired upon. When everything was ready Pendleton found "a point central, moderately protected by conformation of ground, at the same time commanding the general view and accessible from every direction, with a little exposure of messengers as any one place in such a scene could be. And here, except when some personal inspection or order had to be given requiring temporary absence, I remained for best service throughout the day." Pendleton remained on horseback through the day. Two of his staff officers acted as couriers and carried messages to his subordinates on the battlefield.

* * * *

When McClellan awoke on the 19th to find that Lee fled in the night he ordered Federal cavalry to pursue Lee towards Virginia. On route to Boteler's Ford Union General Alfred Pleasonton captured Confederate stragglers and one abandoned cannon. By 9:00 a.m. Pleasonton's cavalry appeared on the hills opposite Pendleton just as his final defensive arrangements were made. Pleasonton halted at the Douglas house on a high hill about a mile upstream from the ford to scout the Confederate position. When the

Confederate batteries opened on the advancing Union skirmishers the Federal horse artillery of eighteen guns unleashed a barrage across the river, with most of the shells landing in the hills behind Pendleton's lines. For the Confederates lingering behind once they crossed the river, including Alexander, his ordnance wagon train and the last of the rearguard from Longstreet's Corps, this was a rude awakening. They suddenly found motivation to quickly move further south. Even as the Federals set up their horse artillery batteries to fire, the lost Confederate artillery battery suddenly appeared and clattered its way across the ford. Pendleton halted the battery and put it into the line.

The Federal artillery, consisting of 12-pounder smoothbore Napoleons, was "planted on more commanding heights on the other side," a number of powerful batteries compared to which "ours were but pop-guns." They battered the Confederate positions. Even though the gunnery fire was well downstream the town of Shepherdstown panicked. Some shells landed in the town. Escaping the battle civilians and military wagons jammed the roads heading south. Under cover of the "furious cannonade" Federal sharpshooters filed into the trench offered by the empty canal and picked off the exposed Confederate gunners in the open forward batteries. The battery commanders asked for more infantry support to suppress the Union riflemen. Pendleton sent 200 men from his infantry reserve, which unknown to him severely depleted it. The Federal barrage lasted through the morning.

Federal cavalry approached another ford about two miles below Boteler's Ford and started to shell the small Confederate cavalry force there under Colonel Munford. Pendleton quickly dispatched 200 more infantry to oppose their crossing. That morning Stuart arrived at Pendleton's headquarters. The Reserve Artillery battalion at Williamsport withdrew without orders, leaving the ford there in Union hands. Jeb Stuart, looking for a place to re-cross the river, wanted to drive the enemy away from Williamsport. Pendleton lent him one of his batteries and by noon Stuart was successful in re-taking the fords.

Pleasonton was ordered by the cautious McClellan not to cross the Potomac "unless you see a splendid opportunity to inflict great damage upon the enemy without loss to yourself." After exchanging artillery and smalls arms fire with the southern bank Pleasonton concluded that the Virginia side, defended only by a small infantry force, fifteen light rifle guns, and nineteen obsolete smooth-bore guns, was too strong for his cavalry division to attempt a crossing. This was the scenario Lee expected, a less than aggressive follow up by Union cavalry making sure Lee was gone. The force he left behind was adequate enough to keep the enemy cavalry on the northern bank. However, Lee's expectations were shattered when the V Corps of the Army of the Potomac under Major General Fitz John Porter arrived on the Maryland side of the river about noon.

Porter was an experienced and competent West Point officer. Having seen action in the Mexican War and serving in the 1857 Mormon War, he had considerable experience at battlefield command. He also was thoroughly trained in the use of field artillery. It was Porter's V Corps that fought off the constant and heavy assaults of Lee's Army in the Peninsular Campaign giving McClellan ample time to shift his base and save his army. The V Corps was kept out of the battle at Sharpsburg by McClellan for use as a final reserve should the Army of the Potomac be routed. It was fresh and fit for battle. Porter was a favorite of McClellan's, something which hurt him after McClellan was removed from command. Unfortunately for the Union this was to be his final battle. Radical Republicans convinced that Porter abandoned Pope at Second Manassas, court martialed him and dismissed him from the service. E. P. Alexander wrote that Confederates who knew Porter respected him greatly and considered his dismissal "one of the best fruits of their victory."

McClellan sent Porter's V Corps towards the Potomac with orders not to cross the river without further orders. If he found the enemy Porter was to damage them as much as possible with artillery and small arms fire. Another Army Corps was sent to Williamsport with the same orders. The V Corps, which was at full strength, had 12,750 men with added elements of the Pennsylvania Reserves and two new regiments. Porter's total force of 16,780 men and seventy superior cannons dwarfed Pendleton's little army.

      *   *   *   *

As the sun reached its zenith in the sky Porter deployed his seventy field artillery guns on the Maryland hills overlooking the river and commenced to smother the inferior Confederate batteries with shells. The firing was fast and furious. Confederate gunners fled their batteries and hid behind any cover they could find. Maurin's Battery sent their three small 6-pounders to the rear as they were ineffective against the Federal artillery. The battery's 3-inch rifle lacked long range fuses and could not be used. The battery was left with just two 10-pounder Parrott rifles to return fire. The battery also lost twenty horses and a caisson. The other Confederate batteries were similarly affected. While the Confederate cannon fire withered it did not stop. Some of the Confederate counter battery fire succeeded in causing minimal damage to the Union guns. The fury of the cannonade died down, and through the afternoon the two sides traded a desultory but constant exchange of cannon fire.

The commander of the 38th Virginia reported to Pendleton that the Confederate artillery fire in front of him at Boteler's Ford, all smoothbores, had stopped shooting, and that twenty Federal guns were still shooting at his men. He also informed Pendleton that the only forces present to stop the Federals troops from crossing the ford were his sharpshooters. Pendleton issued orders for 200 men from his reserves to reinforce the ford. After another request from the right for reinforcements he ordered an additional 100 to 200 men to help. In all probability the reserve left was too small to comply. By now his reserve force was totally depleted and he did not know it. By sending reinforcements to his flanks Pendleton had only 300 men left to protect Boteler's Ford. Some of the isolated Confederate batteries left their guns in the open and sought shelter. The guns still shooting ran low on ammunition. Some of the battery commanders asked permission to withdraw for lack of ammunition. Pendleton told them to remain a bit longer. Pendleton was reluctant to retreat in the open daylight for fear of encouraging a Federal assault across the Potomac. Dusk was approaching and Pendleton planned to pull out after dark and allow the cavalry and a small artillery force to delay the Federal forces if they crossed the river, just as Lee planned.

Still ignorant of the exhaustion of his reserves, Pendleton planned his evening withdrawal from the river. Any battery concealed from view could pull out immediately. The balance needed to remain in place for the moment. Once it got dark the batteries would pull out of their advanced positions and head down the road. Colonel Munford promised to arrive with his small cavalry unit and Chew's Battery at sunset when he would assume control of the delaying actions while the artillery and infantry moved south down the roads. When the batteries withdrew the cavalry would cover their rear on their march south deeper into Virginia. In this fashion Pendleton would have successfully completed his mission of resisting the Federals through the daylight. No thought was given as to what the Federals might do after sunset. As historian Douglas Southall Freeman later noted, "This plan, I judged ...under the circumstances, the best on the whole to adopt" given the discretion given to Pendleton. Nothing justified the sacrifice required to try to stop any crossing by a strong Federal force.

By now the sun was within an hour of setting, a time which Pendleton referred to later as a "critical and anxious hour." Maurin's Battery withdrew before dusk. The infantry at the ford ran out of ammunition and the officers asked for permission to retire. With both his artillery and infantry running out of ammunition and unable to defend the ford from the overwhelming firepower of the Federal troops, and no longer having any reserve force to plug any gap in his lines, Pendleton took a huge risk by waiting for complete dark to retire. Troop movements over unknown terrain in the dark are very difficult and time consuming. It is easy for confusion and panic to strike any force which is retiring under fire and lost in the night. It is even worse if while retiring the enemy launches an assault.

Across the river Porter observed that the Confederate fire had appreciably slackened and that abandoned guns could be seen on the heights above the river. Orders or not, Porter decided it was the perfect opportunity to storm the ford and seize the heights on the Virginia side of the river. As the sun began to set the 4th Michigan advanced and filed into the canal. Fifty men of the 118th Pennsylvania, the Corn Exchange Regiment, joined them. Colonel Hodges spotted them and reported to Pendleton that the enemy had moved downstream and thrown out skirmishers in his front. Men from the 1st U.S. Sharpshooters under Captain John B. Isler were to spearhead the attack, followed by the 4th Michigan.

As Pendleton recalled, "I was not aware of infantry weakness for the ford itself. This was, however, as the evening progressed, made to me only too certain. The enemy's fire, which had for a season relaxed, became fiercer than before, and so directed as to rake most of the hollows, as well as the hills, we occupied. At the same time their infantry at the canal breastwork was much increased, and the crack of their sharpshooters became a continuous roll of musketry." He later called the lack of adequate infantry support to be "a woeful condition of affairs." Pendleton's artillery had just begun to pull back in the deepening dusk while some of the batteries continued to fire to provide cover for the retirement.

At 5:30 p.m. Porter launched his assault. The sharpshooters crossed first under the supporting fire of the 4th Michigan. Once the sharpshooters were across the 4th Michigan followed. Some of the Michiganders became lost in the river and ended up soaking wet with useless ammunition. Only four Union soldiers were lost in the crossing. When the Federals reached the southern bank they charged.

The Confederate soldiers at the ford, without ammunition, under inexperienced leadership, and already seriously demoralized, ran for their lives. Pendleton's first inkling that anything was wrong was when "men rushed rapidly by the point I occupied. Arresting them, I learned that they were of the sharpshooters who held guard at the ford; that their body had all given way, and that some of the enemy were already on our side of the river. Worn as were these men, their state of disorder, akin to panic, was not, justly, to be met with harshness." Pendleton tried to steady the men and use them as a rear guard but they kept running. Without a reserve he had no means to stop the Union assault through the middle of his line. At the time all but two of his staff was absent. He sent one of the aides toward the ford to ascertain the actual conditions while he sent the other "to secure the orderly retirement of the last batteries and of everything attached to my own headquarters."

One exhausted soldier, whose 6-pounder battery had already pulled back from enemy fire, was sleeping when the assault began. He awoke to find the hills on the Maryland side "ablaze with the fire of heavy guns." Some of the enemy shellfire had found their targets and made it "most uncomfortable" for him to remain any longer. Worse still he could see what appeared to be "a 'million' Yankee infantrymen were massing to cross the river" He and his comrades became "mixed in helter skelter race for the road-" crowded with "men, guns, horses, limber chests without the guns, caissons, officers on horseback and on foot, all in a confused mass and all making the best possible time to….the rear of General Lee's army." Milledge's and Johnson's Batteries each lost a 12-pounder howitzer and Huskstep's Battery lost one of the old 6-pounder smoothbores in the rush to get away.

Pendleton feared that the Union cavalry would sweep through at any moment and capture him. "The arrival of our own cavalry being now unlikely, I had to determine, at once, what duty required of myself." If the Federal troops stopped and advanced no further than Pendleton figured that he had already given orders to his artillery that should allow them time to escape. If the enemy aggressively pursued the artillery then there was nothing he could do. Instead of staying and sending a staff officer for help from the infantry divisions that crossed the night before, Pendleton decided to ride for help by himself.

*   *   *   *

Pendleton's mental and physical fatigue caught up with him. His failure to discover how small his infantry support was left him with no reserve force to push forward to defend the artillery batteries and fleeing infantry from pursuit. And then he fled the battlefield all alone on the pretext of seeking help. Even after he started his flight he had the opportunity to rejoin his command and send messengers but failed to do so. Perhaps his lingering illness and three nights with no or little sleep explain his mental confusion and mistakes. But he was not alone in being exhausted and worn out. The same was true for most of the officer corps. Perhaps his advanced age for a field officer rendered Pendleton more vulnerable to such mental fatigue. A lot of the criticism of his conduct that day is pointed at his command mistakes, but had he not fled the battlefield these criticisms may have been more muted. His flight appeared to justify every criticism of him to date.

Pendleton "proceeded to a point in the road probably not then reached by any party of the enemy, on foot and leading my horse, and accompanied by my adjutant and ordnance sergeant, who had rejoined me, along a path still thundered over by the enemy's shells and crossing the road inland from the river." He later claimed that "[t]hose shells were obviously indicative of no intended advance of any considerable body of the enemy; firing on their own troops thus would scarcely be risked," but that did not stop his flight. On the road Pendleton found "the rear of our artillery column properly moving. Mounting here, I rode with the column and employed the two young officers in moving our hospital camp and enforcing order along the entire column." He told the officers to keep the column moving and to bring the hospital as well. Pendleton concluded that the column would find its way south on its own, and if not, then it would be captured along with the rest of Nelson's Reserve Artillery battalion. Then he took off south.

As Pendleton rode south his Reserve Artillery under the command of Major Nelson re-organized and dragged their guns and wagons out of danger. Maurin's Battery found that the only road south was swept by enemy fire, so they headed across the fields without maps or a guide. One of the Parrott rifles had to be abandoned when the horses pulling it gave out. The gun was spiked and left for the enemy. At some point the remainder of Lawton's brigade pulled together and fired long enough to give the artillery time to escape. In the end Pendleton lost only four guns, five killed, nine wounded, and ten captured. Twenty-six horses were lost. The Union forces which crossed the river took their time scaling the bluffs giving the Confederates ample time to hitch up and escape. The Federals found some of the more forward guns left on the field. By 10:30 p.m. all of the Federal troops were recalled to the Maryland side of the river in compliance with McClellan's orders that morning. They brought back some Richmond newspaper reporters left behind in the flight of the Confederate forces. The Union lost five killed and fifteen wounded. Still, the ford was in Union hands, a ready access point to launch an offensive at Lee's scattered and exhausted army.

Pendleton continued down the dark country lanes on his own. Someone told him that Anderson's division was nearby so Pendleton diverted from the road to find it. About two miles from the river he found Brigadier General Roger Pryor, then temporarily in command of the division, resting in his tent. Pryor had been one of the rabid newspapermen calling for secession before the war and lacked any military training or experience. Pendleton reported what happened and asked Pryor to give him enough men to repel the Federal cavalry he still imagined were in pursuit and to recover his guns. With his division battered in the recent battle Pryor was reticent about trying to mount a counter-attack in the dark. Pryor told Pendleton that the situation was too serious for him to make a decision, and suggested that Pendleton find Major General John Bell Hood and seek his assistance. Pryor's response is baffling. Had Pendleton's fears of a Federal cavalry pursuit been true the first unit they would strike would have been Pryor's.

Still riding in the night Pendleton returned to the road south to find Hood, Longstreet, or someone with authority to react. He found Hood's staff but was told the general could not be disturbed as he was unwell. Once more, Pendleton struck out in the dark on unmapped lanes. He found regiments and brigades scattered and lost. The entire Army was in disarray. Pendleton now felt it was his duty to find General Lee. Having passed through Longstreet's I Corps he travelled on towards Jackson's II Corps. Around midnight he arrived at the headquarters of his old friend Major General D. H. Hill. Pendleton told Hill what happened, including that he lost thirty guns, and asked after General Lee. Hill advised him that Lee was not very far away, although Hill later claimed he believed that Lee was so exhausted he could not summon his powers of decision. Hill had been asking for orders from Lee through the night and was finally told to just follow the division in front of him down the road.

Finally, after an odyssey of seven hours Pendleton rode into Lee's headquarters where he found Lee sound asleep. Lee awoke to find Pendleton leaning over him. Pendleton appeared to be shaken and bewildered, which is not surprising considering this was his fourth night of sleeplessness and illness. Pendleton told Lee that the Federal Army brought up heavy guns and forced their way across the river. All of the Reserve Artillery guns at the ford were lost. Lee sat up, "All?" he asked. Pendleton sheepishly replied, "Yes, General, I fear all." Lee was disturbed, but also exhausted. He told Pendleton to get some sleep, and to do no more until morning when "measures would be taken."

The record of that night is confusing. D. H. Hill's biographer Hal Bridges dedicated an entire chapter to the episode and concluded that of all the reports given that of Pendleton's was the most accurate. Some reports, but not Pendleton's, state that Pendleton arrived at Jackson's headquarters nearby either before or after his visit to Lee, and made a similar report. D.H. Hill wrote that he alerted Jackson to the news. The versions having Pendleton speak with Jackson comment that Jackson was angry, and questioned Pendleton about the size of the enemy force which crossed. Pendleton was uncertain but offered he did not think it sizable.

In any event, after reporting to Lee, his mind unburdened and his body exhausted, Pendleton found a bed of straw under the open skies, lay down, pulled over his overcoat, and went soundly to sleep. He was comforted by the fact that by holding out until dusk he had fulfilled his mission. One of Lee's staff officers was outraged. Pendleton's report "lifted me off my blanket, and I moved right away, fearful I might betray my feelings."

Jackson was also thoroughly disgusted by the news. His widow later said it was one of the worst moments for him in military service. He awakened the staff and began to issue orders. Dawn of the 20th came cool and cloudy. By 6:30 a.m. the divisions of Jackson's Corps began to march back towards the river to "punish the enemy," as Jubal Early put it. Early and D. H. Hill became lost. Boteler's Ford had many names, and the name Boteler was unknown to them. Pendleton awoke early and rather than locate his Artillery Reserve and order it to assist in the battle he became just an observer by accompanying Hill. However, A. P. Hill, with Pendleton in tow, headed straight towards the ford with Jackson well in front scouting out the enemy.

*   *   *   *

Back on the Potomac River crossing Porter woke his troops early. The 4th Michigan, 62nd Pennsylvania, and elements of the 5th U.S. Artillery crossed the river and returned with four captured cannons and a battle flag left behind the night before in the dark and confusion. No one was pursuing Pendleton. Meanwhile the rest of the men cooked breakfast and formed up to cross the river. The 118th Pennsylvania, 2nd Maine, 18th and 22nd Massachusetts, 1st Michigan, 13th and 25th New York, and some Massachusetts sharpshooters under the command of Colonel James Barnes, a West Point classmate of Robert E. Lee, prepared to cross the river.

When George McClellan heard of the battle at Shepherdstown he sensed an opportunity too good to miss. He sent a message to Porter the night of the 19th that "General Pleasonton has been directed to have his cavalry and artillery at the river by daylight, and has been informed that you intend to cross at that time, and would co-operate with him." McClellan also sent an order to Pleasonton to conduct a reconnaissance in force. He was to "push your command forward after the enemy as rapidly as possible, using your artillery upon them whenever an opportunity presents, doing them all the damage in your power without incurring too much risk to your command. If great results can be obtained do not spare your men or horses." Even though the idea was aggressive for McClellan it amounted to no more than the harassment of a defeated foe.

The order to Pleasonton also ignored reality. Pleasonton was within a mile of McClellan's tent, not at the river. That morning Pleasonton also awoke early and fired off a reply message to

McClellan complaining that Porter sent him back to Sharpsburg without food or forage, and that his men had now gone without food for two full days. He would leave the camp soon with an advance force while the rest of his cavalry followed (presumably after breakfast for man and beast). He told McClellan he hoped Porter would not interfere with his operations again. Porter's plan to allow the cavalry to cross in pursuit followed by two brigades of infantry support fell apart. McClellan revised his initial order allowing only half of Pleasonton's division to return to the river. McClellan then wrote Porter that, "The reason why no cavalry reported to you this morning is that they were ordered by you back to their camps…it is presumed [they] must have reported to you before this time."

Long before he received this message Porter ordered some of his Corps across the Potomac to scout for the Confederate Army after the expected early arrival of the cavalry. At 7:00 a.m. Union Brigadier General Sykes, commanding a regular infantry division, decided the cavalry was not coming. He sent his 3,000 men across the Potomac without cavalry support. The men playfully splashed water and laughed as they crossed, re-formed on the Virginia bank and marched south. Barnes' brigade now headed for the ford. The troops took off their shoes and socks, rolled up their pant legs, and waded into the water. Others splashed, paddled, or fell into deeper water. While crossing they passed a small group of cavalry headed north. This cavalry arrived just after Sykes crossed and since no cavalry pursuit was in the offing, turned around and headed back to their camps in Maryland. Sykes' regulars moved carefully about one and half miles down the road into Virginia when they blundered into a Confederate skirmish line, something the cavalry would have discovered. The regulars quickly deployed across the road and formed a line of battle.

Stonewall Jackson had not rested overnight. He and his staff stayed in their saddles organizing a counter-attack by his Corps. When Lee awoke he looked for Jackson but was told Jackson was already on his way to Boteler's Ford to drive the enemy back across the Potomac. Lee sat down and wrote a report to President Davis about the loss of the forty-four guns of the Artillery Reserve while Jackson rode ahead to reconnoiter the battlefield personally. By the time A. P. Hill's division came up Jackson's plan was complete. Hill's vanguard reached the area of the ford by 8:15 a.m. Pender's brigade took the left of the line, Gregg's the center, and Thomas' brigade took on the right. An hour later Hill's battle line was in position and prepared to attack. Jackson's counter attack could be heard at Lee's headquarters about the same time Jackson's message arrived, "with the blessings of God they will soon be driven back."

Sykes sent a skirmish line forward to discover the nature of the Confederate threat. He quickly ascertained that a large Confederate force was forming to drive him back into the river in a repeat of the Ball's Bluff disaster a year before. He ordered a slow retreat in battle order back towards the ford. As he withdrew Sykes came upon Barnes' brigade coming up the bluff from the riverbank. He ordered Barnes to form a defensive line on the bluffs facing south to provide cover for the retreating regulars.

Hill launched his assault at 9:15 a.m. He drove the Federals back towards the river but took tremendous casualties from the Federal artillery firing across the river from the northern side. The artillery fire was so furious that Hill lost well over 200 men in fifteen minutes. Pender wrote his wife that it "...the most terrible artillery fire I ever saw troops exposed to. They continued to shell us all day. It was as hot a place as I wish to get in. It is considered even by Jackson as the most brilliant thing of the war." Pendleton recalled, "The furious fire of the enemy from beyond the Potomac, though necessarily harmful at first, proved far less damaging than it must otherwise have been, because such direction had to be given their pieces as to spare their own troops receiving the charge." Translating the "Pendletonese," the Federal artillery let up their shelling lest they kill their own troops. Hill's divisional artillery was insufficient to counter their fire and Nelson had moved the Reserve Artillery too far south down the road to be of any assistance. Just behind Hill, Jubal Early's division began to deploy.

The Confederate attack reached the Union lines just as the Federals received reinforcements from Colonel G. K. Warren's Pennsylvania brigade. Warren stood on the left of the line, Lovell's brigade of Sykes' division in the center on the road, and Barnes' brigade on the right. As the Federals were pressed back towards the Potomac Union stragglers ran and hid along the bluffs only to be hit by their own artillery. Federal shell fuses were too short, and the shells exploded too soon. Porter crossed the river to see the situation and immediately ordered a retreat back across the ford. For some reason the order to withdraw was ignored by the regimental commander of the 118th Pennsylvania. He wanted the orders coming through official chain of command and Colonel Barnes had already left the field.

This totally green one month old regiment had never been under fire before. Even worse, apparently due to the negligence of their officers, they discovered for the first time in the middle of the battle that half their muskets did not work. Men fled and scrambled down the bluffs towards the river. Many fell to their deaths, while many others were shot by the Confederates while re-crossing the river. Of the 767 men in the regiment who reported that morning only 468 returned unscathed. The Confederates continued shooting at the retreating Union soldiers as they splashed back to the northern bank. Four Federal cannons could not be brought down the bluffs so they were spiked and rolled over the edge of the heights. Finally the intense fire of the Federal guns on the northern bank forced the Confederates to pull back and seek shelter. It was, as Jackson reported, "inflicting upon him a very severe punishment for his rashness in undertaking to pursue us and making him pay very dearly for the guns he had taken."

The battle lasted three to four hours ending by 2:30 p.m., although heavy picket firing lasted the day. Of the approximately 9,000 men involved on both sides the Federals later claimed only 367 killed or wounded although their casualties were much higher. The Confederates lost forty-one killed, 162 wounded and four missing, a total of 310. All but four guns lost by Pendleton were recovered. The 21st was spent rendering aid to the wounded still alive on the battlefield and burying the dead. Many of the Confederate dead were buried in Shepherdstown's Elmwood Cemetery.

Around noon Pendleton finally found his "missing" artillery column four miles south of Shepherdstown on the road towards Winchester. Pendleton's reaction displayed unlikeable characteristics of arrogance and bombast. He noted that because Major Nelson followed his orders on the 19th that the artillery was safe, "With others, similarly instructed by myself, he had been diligently engaged the previous evening in causing batteries to be withdrawn in order, as directed, and the anticipated caution of the enemy had allowed them all to get back with no further damage than the leaving of one guns apiece by each of four batteries…" Later that day he received orders to move further south, and the battalion marched through the night until they arrived near Opequon. By the 22nd he was stationed at Darkesville distributing the cannon captured by Jackson at Harpers Ferry and still recovering from his ailments.

*　　　　　*　　　　　*　　　　　*

The entire episode finally persuaded Lee that he had pushed his army beyond endurance. It was disorganized, demoralized, scattered, and short of ammunition, forage, and food. The Army needed time to allow stragglers to rejoin their units and to count the losses. Lee decided he would not re-cross the Potomac to force another battle. The end of the Maryland campaign also convinced McClellan not to pursue Lee across the river for fear of losing a battle. This failure on McClellan's part to pursue Lee was the final straw persuading Lincoln that McClellan needed to be removed from command.

At first Pendleton did not realize that his behavior placed him in a precarious position within the Army. He wrote home two days later that despite some personal embarrassment, "While I regret the loss and the occasion for Yankee glorification, I am so conscious of having done well my duty, and so thankful to God for ordering so remarkable a preservation, that any temporary cloud over myself I am more than willing to compound." From Pendleton's perspective, that with "the men at his disposal" he had accomplished "a great deal" by keeping "the powerful army of the enemy at bay for ten hours despite a tremendous ordeal." As he explained to Anzelotte "No blame that I ever heard of is attached to me by any body. On the contrary, it is felt, I think, that with the means at my disposal, a great deal was accomplished." He could not have been more wrong.

General Lee sensed at once that his Chief of Artillery had to explain his conduct. He told Pendleton, while giving him other orders, to quickly file a report giving Pendleton's version of events "as well for my own sake, as for his satisfaction and the truth of history." A few weeks after the battle Pendleton was more contrite asking Anzelotte and his family to "join me in special prayer for divine guidance—as to what God would have me do. May not my mission as a soldier have been fulfilled in two campaigns? May it not be my sacred duty...to resume exclusively the sword of the Spirit?"

Any sense of contriteness expressed in Pendleton's letters home was not to be found in his official reports. Instead, he noted that "that so much was done with such partial loss." He commended his officers, especially Major Nelson, the officer actually responsible for commanding the withdrawal after Pendleton fled, for "cool courage and persistent vigor throughout the day, and in the trying hour at its close, deserve especial mention. His services were of great value." He also commended the two infantry commanders, "credit is justly due for the persevering determination with which they bore during all the day a fire, doubly galling, of case shot from the enemy's cannon and of musketry from the vastly outnumbering infantry force sheltered by the canal bank across the river. Not until overwork did the handful of our sharpshooters at all give way, and that would probably have been prevented could a double number, partly sheltered by trees, & etc., have allowed relief in action." He then concluded with a series of excuses, outlining all his other duties commanding the artillery of the Army which kept him constantly busy all that day.

Lee's first report to President Davis included the hasty report that the guns of the Artillery Reserve were probably lost to enemy cavalry. After Jackson drove the Union Army back across the Potomac Lee sent another report. In it Lee inexplicably protected Pendleton by sending reports that simply ignored what had happened. His short report on the 20th satisfied Pendleton's desire to avoid criticism. Lee only reported that:

> After the army had safely reached the Virginia shore with such of the wounded as could be removed and all its trains, General Porter's corps, with a number of batteries and some cavalry, appeared on the opposite side. General Pendleton was left to guard the ford with the reserve artillery and about 600 infantry. That night the enemy crossed the river above General Pendleton's position, and his infantry support giving way, four of his guns were taken. A considerable force took position on the right bank, under cover of their artillery on the commanding hills on the opposite side. The next morning General A. P. Hill was ordered to return with his division and dislodge them.

The next day Lee reiterated this reporting that, "Only one or two brigades of the enemy's infantry with cavalry had crossed the river, none of whom had entered Shepherdstown. They displayed a large force of artillery on the opposite bank. ...Only four pieces of artillery fell into the hands of the enemy, which they had carried across the river before they were attacked by A. P. Hill." Lee added that the primary reason there was so little infantry to assist Pendleton in the battle was because of the horrible problem of straggling. The infantry had been moving and fighting for two months and were exhausted and demoralized.

However, General Lee had not forgotten what had happened. His disappointment in Pendleton appears two weeks later in a letter to him that "you will still be accessible to the points I have named, and perfectly safe by exercising care and attention." Looking to Pendleton's continual health problems, Lee suggestively offered to Pendleton that "relaxation might benefit you," and perhaps Pendleton should take a furlough home for his recovery. Nevertheless, Lee kept Pendleton throughout the war. Perhaps Lee wished to take advantage of Pendleton's tremendous skill at organization and supply while assigning the more fatiguing and combat related tasks to younger subordinates. Shepherdstown was to be the last time Pendleton commanded troops in combat until the final weeks of the war.

Pendleton's old friend Stonewall Jackson was especially displeased. His open anger and irritation towards Pendleton was omitted from the official reports, but his widow later wrote that the news "of this appalling disaster caused Jackson more anxiety than he had ever shown during the war." In his report Jackson only noted that "In the evening the Federals commenced crossing under the protection of their guns, driving off Lawton's brigade and General Pendleton's artillery."

Not surprisingly, the officer corps of the Army of Northern Virginia held a generally negative view of Pendleton after the battle. Even before Shepherdstown Pendleton's reputation was shaky. Other Confederate officers scorned Pendleton. A Jackson staff officer reported that "Pendleton was dreadfully stampeded and almost in tears." A Virginia cavalry colonel, who was nowhere near the battlefield, described Pendleton as "all day" being "in the rear in a well sheltered place, and entirely out of danger." A Virginia artillery captain wrote tartly that his chief had "managed...to lose four pieces." An officer in Longstreet's Corps called Pendleton "a stupid old useless fool." One battery commander said that,

"Pendleton is an absurd humbug; a fool and a coward. Well known to be so among those who see and know."

Pendleton's biggest public relations problem arose because the officers and soldiers of the Army had little to no idea of his constant attention to providing the equipment, food, forage, and ammunition for his large command. Most soldiers pay no attention to such things provided they are well cared for. Instead, they look for dash and glory in battle, something Pendleton lacked. As one historian noted, "The faithful performance of the drudgery of the service adds little to the lustre of a military name."

Despite the accusations of cowardice levelled against Pendleton, his subordinates for the most part defended him. One historian inquired of the junior artillery officers if they thought Pendleton was a coward and found that they all agreed that "no evidence of the truth of the scandalous charges has been found." Fellow Lexingtonian Captain William T. Poague of the Rockbridge Artillery noted that having witnessed Pendleton under fire on numerous occasions that Pendleton "remained as calm, self-possessed, and apparently as courageous, as any man could well be."

The disrespectful attitude towards Pendleton drifted well down into the ranks. There were many reports that while the troops would cheer other general officers as they rode by, they would not cheer Pendleton, even when prompted. Later in the war Lee rode by a column of infantry, and the troops cheered him as loudly as they could. Then Pendleton and his staff rode by. A "lone soldier yelled 'three cheers for General Pendleton'—to which not a soul responded. The embarrassed trooper "then very faintly cried Oh! whereupon the whole column broke out in a laugh."

As Max Sorrel, Longstreet's aide-de-camp, noted, Pendleton's part time job preaching made him appear ludicrous to many; "I am not so averse to hearing the General as others but am always sorry to see him officiate, because I know how the soldiers will talk about him." Pendleton's overall reputation affected the Army's response to his preaching. But there were exceptions. Some troops even at the end of the war were impressed by his "noble" and "dignified" appearance. Another soldier attending services felt that Pendleton was "large and tall...with rough, shaggy iron gray beard, dark complexion, rich, full, sonorous voice, fertile imagination, rapid utterance, easy flow of language...fine effect."

In early October 1862 a Court of Inquiry convened to analyze the hasty flight of Lawton's brigade from the fords at Shepherdstown. It may have been requested by one of the infantry officers in Lawton's brigade. After fully investigating the incident the Court did not assign blame to any of the artillery officers, a sign that the high command did not blame Pendleton for the disaster. Still, it did not resurrect his military reputation.

One junior artillery officer, probably Lieutenant John Hampden Chamberlayne, wrote a complaint about Pendleton's conduct at the battle to the Richmond Whig newspaper on October 13, 1862. Chamberlayne was not present during Pendleton's defense of the ford or the retreat. However, as he was seconded at the time as an aide to A. P. Hill, he was present during the counter-attack the next morning. Chamberlayne was also a good friend of artillery Captain Greenlee Davidson of Lexington, who was not an admirer of Pendleton. Entitled, "The Affair at Shepherdstown," Chamberlayne wrote, "By the way Pendleton is Lee's weakness. Pendleton is like the elephant, we have him & we don't know what on earth to do with him, and it costs a devil of a sight to feed him." He went on to say that the Army ridiculed Pendleton and referred to him as "Old Mother Pendleton." He further wrote that at Shepherdstown Pendleton "withdrew in confusion, losing four guns. Gen. Pendleton thought he had lost almost all his guns, but such was not the case….General Pendleton, it seems, retreated without sufficient cause." In another letter Chamberlayne referred to Pendleton as "an absurd humbug, a fool, and a coward."

A few weeks later a rejoinder was published in the same paper under the pen name "Justice," probably written by Pendleton himself given the verbiage and pomposity of its phrasing. It offered a lengthy bloviated defense of Pendleton, citing "ten hours" of "stern endurance, without food, water or respite." The outcome of the battle was the best which could be expected given "so small a force and so little loss." Instead of a retreat without cause, the "[t]he withdrawal of the guns at nightfall was not an unadvised retreat but an arranged removal, according to instructions received from the Commanding General [Pendleton]." Furthermore, in a complete misstatement of facts, "Justice" wrote that "General Pendleton did not think he had lost nearly all his guns, but knew that the extended column, which, on personally reaching the road he met and accompanied, was safe." Chamberlayne heard of the response but may not have seen the article. In any event, he made no further comments.

The initial newspaper reports the next day merely reported that the "Troops having crossed the river safely the enemy soon appeared on the thither bank and commenced heavy cannonading." It was answered by "our own batteries" placed by Pendleton. The artillery duel went on all day without any attempts of the Federal army to try to cross the river. Subsequently "one or two brigades crossed…..Our loss was small and of enemy great." More recent historians feel differently.

*   *   *   *

The dean of any study of the Army of Northern Virginia was Douglas Southall Freeman. In his books on Lee Freeman is slightly critical of Pendleton stating that circumstances and a certain aptitude for administration made him the Chief of Artillery. Yet, younger men wondered if he had the basic qualities needed by a commander. He also noted that Pendleton suffered from "cacoethes scribendi," Latin for diarrhea of the pen. Freeman's private views were a bit more jaundiced. In 1939 he wrote in his private diary that he "[w]orked on that pompously-pathetic old fraud, Pendleton" that day. Unfortunately, this harsh opinion of Pendleton echoes on in newer histories, despite the actual facts. It amuses any historian to excoriate Pendleton because of his religious views and pomposity, regardless of the truth. By the time Freeman wrote *Lee's Lieutenants* in the early 1940's his views were somewhat more ameliorated.

Other historians have been more forgiving. Some feel that Pendleton, who lacked any combat experience with a command over the size of a small battery, and without any experience in infantry or combined arms tactics, just panicked. Because of his position on the battlefield he did not see his batteries withdrawing under fire, and in the dark, did not know that enemy infantry (not cavalry) had crossed in force. Rather than ascertain what happened, Pendleton fled for help, something he should have sent an aide to do. Commanding generals should never be the first man to arrive reporting a disaster to the troops under his command.

The fault initially lies with Lee for his mistaken assumption that no one in the Union Army would aggressively pursue him. Lee, who prided himself on knowing his enemy, concluded that McClellan would not aggressively pursue him across the river. He was right; McClellan ordered his corps commanders and cavalry not to cross the Potomac. In this vein Lee chose Pendleton and his Reserve Artillery to protect the retreat simply because Lee did not expect anything to happen beyond the arrival of a Federal cavalry reconnaissance. Given this line of thinking Pendleton's artillery was the best unit left as it had not been in battle and had not used its available ammunition. Lee did not know that he trusted his rear guard to obsolete artillery guns and a handful of exhausted, demoralized, and poorly led infantry.

Despite McClellan, the war was turning out some fine Union officers, including Pleasanton and Porter. Furthermore, Lee had whittled away at the Reserve Artillery during the campaign, and most of what remained was the old and obsolete 6-pounder smoothbore guns. Lee knew they could not compete one to one with Federal field artillery. Lee and Longstreet are also responsible for detailing too few infantry to support Pendleton. This was caused by the harshness of the campaign lasting two months during which the Army engaged in three major battles. Lee's Army was literally scattered. After the hard campaign many of these units were commanded by less experienced junior officers, which is what happened at Shepherdstown.

Despite the harsh criticism of many of his contemporary fellow officers and historians, in all probability no officer in the Army of Northern Virginia would have been able to stop Porter from crossing the river with the same force given Pendleton. After all, in addition to more than seventy pieces of modern artillery, Porter had the entire V Army Corps of more than 16,000 men up against Pendleton's 650 infantry and some old cannons.

That said, Pendleton's behavior in the withdrawal was a breach of his military duty and a potential court-martial offense. As a commander he should have remained to make sure that his commands were obeyed and the guns withdrawn to safety. He should have sent a staff officer to seek help, and have done so hours before the crossing by the Federal troops. His personal flight continued even after he reached his own retreating column, and after he located Pryor, Hood's staff, and D. H. Hill. He then gave a false and frightened news report to his commander that contradicted what he had just told D. H. Hill. He told Hill he lost thirty guns, but by the time he reached Lee it was all forty guns. Pendleton had no clue as to what had actually occurred to the troops under his command and instead spilled out his greatest fears.

Still, Pendleton inadvertently accomplished his mission. After he fled the field the Union troops withdrew back across the river and Lee's Army escaped. Students of the war readily overlook Jackson's complete failure in the Seven Days, Stuart's failure at Gettysburg, Lee's failure in West Virginia or at Gettysburg. Pendleton's failure was not forgotten because of his reputation as a pompous and ineffective leader and because of his precipitous flight that night.

Lee expected his officers to show discretion in following orders. While Pendleton clung to his orders not to withdraw until dark he allowed his defenses to collapse and his guns to become endangered. Pendleton, albeit weak, ill, and fatigued for lack of sleep, made three mistakes. First, he failed to count his infantry, as Freeman noted. Had he known their weakness he should have immediately asked for more. Second, he knew, or should have known, that he had insufficient artillery ammunition to engage in a day long artillery duel with a far better supplied enemy. While Pendleton ordered the shells to be used sparingly it was not enough. By the time of the withdrawal many of the guns lacked ammunition with which to fight. Third, he should have withdrawn sooner, probably by mid-afternoon. Then he could have used some of the infantry and batteries as a rearguard while he slowly pulled back. Pendleton's reliance on cavalry was unfortunate. Despite Munford's promise his cavalry never arrived to provide cover for the withdrawal. Instead, Pendleton clung to the literal content of his orders and began to withdraw at dusk, just as the Federal attack began. His withdrawal could not have come at a worse time.

For a few weeks after Shepherdstown Pendleton considered resignation. He knew he was too old and sick to be an active combat officer, but he also believed that his services were needed if the Confederacy was to survive. On October 2nd he was still feeling sick and thought about taking Lee's offer to go home for a month to recover. A few days later he changed his mind, writing that "there is a good deal to do in my department which no one else can do as well…." He felt well enough to stay and embarked on yet another series of recommendations for the improvement of Lee's field artillery.

For the remainder of the war, and for a long time after, the ghost of Shepherdstown haunted Pendleton and his military reputation. Pendleton never complained about the way he was treated by many of the soldiers and officers in the Army. He was buoyed not only by his religious faith but in the knowledge of having the respect of Robert E. Lee as an officer, organizer, supplier, and as a clergyman. He was sure of himself and of fulfilling his duties. While his enemies complained about him, Pendleton, ever the Christian Virginia gentleman and officer, always treated them with respect, and he urged recognition of valiant service and promotion for some of his critics because he knew it was the right thing to do.

General W. N. Pendleton

9. "ON ALL THE BATTLEFIELDS I HAVE SEEN NOTHING LIKE IT"

[FREDERICKSBURG, 1862]

ALMIGHTY God, the supreme Governor of all things, whose power no creature is able to resist, to whom it belongeth justly to punish sinners, and to be merciful to those who truly repent; Save and deliver us, we humbly beseech thee, from the hands of our enemies; that we, being armed with thy defence, may be preserved evermore from all perils, to glorify thee, who art the only giver of all victory; through the merits of thy Son, Jesus Christ our Lord. Amen.

1789 Episcopal Book of Common Prayer

The debacle at Shepherdstown and the Army of Northern Virginia's dulled reaction to it, apart from Jackson's rapid counterattack, highlighted for Lee that his Army was exhausted, hungry, scattered, disorganized, and demoralized. He would not be able to re-invade Maryland and attack McClellan as he hoped. He put away his dream of carrying the war to the North for another time.

Lee admitted to President Davis that straggling was a serious problem in the Army, and was a big reason for Pendleton's lack of strength at Shepherdstown. As soon as the shooting stopped at Boteler's Ford, Lee asked for a roll call of those present for duty in the Army. He must have been shocked when only 37,000 men reported as present. The remainder was wounded, lost, or milling about the lower Shenandoah Valley wreaking havoc on the farms, abusing the farmers, and stealing their food. From the lower Shenandoah Valley Lee advised Davis that the Army's:

> ...present efficiency is greatly paralyzed by the loss to its ranks of the numerous stragglers. I have taken every means in my power from the beginning to correct this evil, which has increased instead of diminished. A great many men belonging to the army never entered Maryland at all; many returned after getting there, while others who crossed the river kept aloof. The stream has not lessened since crossing the Potomac, though the cavalry has been constantly employed in endeavoring to arrest it.

Lee sent troops to round up the stragglers as far south as Winchester. Pendleton joined in the effort even before the battle at Shepherdstown by instructing officers to put the stragglers under the control of some cavalry and an infantry battalion to march them towards the battlefield. When some of the straggling officers refused to comply they were arrested. On the 23rd Lee urged that Pendleton employ even harsher measures:

> As to the stragglers, you cannot do better than to carry out your proposition, sending out armed detachments to rid the country of this annoyance of stragglers, using the most stringent measures, punishing them as severely as you choose, handing them over to your men, to do your pleasure on them.

As the Army slowly gathered, rested, and replenished, Pendleton was also asked by Lee to find a source of winter clothing for the Army. Pendleton contacted the woolen manufacturers in the area to make the necessary arrangements. Otherwise, Pendleton settled back into camp life at Darkesville. Most of his letters home at this time were gossipy. In October Pendleton complained again of feeling poorly, this time with a bronchial complaint. He wrote Anzelotte that a "small army" of enslaved blacks was "happy" living the camp life as there was less work to do than on a plantation.

However, one enslaved black named George from his Aunt's plantation at "Oakland" complained that he was broken down and could not stand being in a "wide ocean."

Yet Pendleton focused most of his time in the autumn of 1862 on his beloved artillery corps. He distributed the cannons captured at Harpers Ferry and re-organized the Army's field artillery once again. The matter of the fair distribution of the seventy-three captured guns was a sensitive one. Everyone wanted some, and demands and suggestions came from all of the officers from Lee on down to the individual battery commanders. One wrote that there were "guns going in every direction and fear I won't get any...." One of the captured guns belonged to VMI and had been taken by the Federals early in the war. VMI wanted it back. In December Lee sent a note to Jackson that his Corps seemed to have more than its fair share of the captured guns. Jackson sharply replied that since his "Army of the Valley" had captured all of the guns it was entitled to keep as much as needed.

On top of it all, due to the confusion of the campaign, all the batteries, guns, soldiers, and battalions were mixed up, and they had to be sorted out as well. The Maryland Campaign left the Army's field artillery in a chaotic condition. Guns and men lost in battle needed to be replenished. Poorly performing batteries were broken up and their men and equipment distributed to other batteries. No sooner had Pendleton settled in with his Reserve Artillery after Shepherdstown than he fired off requests for reports on the condition of the artillery from the two Corps Chiefs of Artillery. Once more, all of the officers, especially from the division level up, made demands to save or break up various batteries. Colonel Crutchfield of the II Corps reported that in D. H. Hill's division all of the artillery was unfit for duty. Early's divisional artillery officers had helped themselves to the captured guns and stores at Harpers Ferry and were fine. Jackson's division needed hundreds of horses and new forges for their batteries. As for the Corps Reserve Artillery, Crutchfield was not able to report its condition until he consulted with Jackson. In the I Corps the McLaws division batteries needed newer cannons. On the whole, Longstreet's Corps had 117 guns, of which fifty-nine were modern, compared to Jackson's 127, of which seventy were modern cannons. Pendleton supplemented the supply of captured guns with two 20-pounder Parrott rifled cannon from Richmond and two rifled Whitworths capable of firing up to five miles. Pendleton felt that finally the Confederate artillery might match the long reach of the firepower of the Federal artillery.

Through the end of September and into October Pendleton worked hard to re-organize the field artillery at Lee's request. The proposal further strengthened Corps artillery allowing more concentrations of firepower by creating sixteen-gun four battery artillery battalions at the Corps and divisional levels. Pendleton presented the proposal to Lee on October 2nd. After a thorough inspection of the artillery Pendleton concluded:

> It is clear that our service is now encumbered by too many artillery companies, of which some have never been strong enough, some are commanded by inadequate officers, and some, though well officered and entitled to honor for excellent service, are so reduced in men and horses as scarcely to leave room for a hope of their restoration to efficiency....
>
> I have sought with great care the actual merit and condition of the several batteries connected with this army; and though it were vainly presumptuous to suppose that I had escaped error, I feel assured there is as little mistake at the complexity of the case and the limited time for investigation fairly admit.

Pendleton applied a standard of his own creation to the process. In looking at a depleted battery Pendleton first considered "laudable service" unless it was rendered impracticable by other criteria. The next criterion was "thoroughly efficient" officers after excellent service through "the season." Third, if these criteria were not met, these batteries would be merged with another exemplary battery. Another factor Pendleton was required to consider was "the rule of proportion for State quotas, the proper preference of State troops, and the legal provision which prohibits the mingling of citizens of different States in the same military organization," one of the government imposed requirements so that Virginians did not appear to be running everything. This was a difficult requirement to meet. Most of the better field artillery officers were VMI graduates, and no other state had anything comparable to VMI. He also considered the number and availability of horses to pull the guns and wagons. Some batteries could not be returned to efficiency simply because of the expense of re-fitting an enormous number of horses.

Pendleton also made recommendations for the promotion or demotion of officers. The surviving officers were to "select for the portions retained the best horses and equipments of those distributed, and to turn over the surplus of ordnance to the ordnance department, and of horses to the quartermaster's department." The changes reduced the Field Artillery Corps by nineteen batteries, leaving the Army with fifty-one batteries for service. Pendleton's Reserve Artillery was reduced to twelve batteries of three battalions consisting of sixteen rifled guns, twenty smoothbore guns, and 900 men.

Lee approved the proposals on October 4, 1862 and issued an order stating that "The necessity of the service requires an immediate reorganization of the artillery of this army." Many of the batteries were to be disbanded despite their gallantry and efficiency in battle simply because "their enfeebled condition is attributable to the dangers and hardships they have encountered. Whenever circumstances will permit, the batteries will again be restored….." He also sent a copy of the paperwork to the Secretary of War George Randolph. Lee described the action as "imperatively necessary" and asked for authorization if it was required. On October 8th Randolph responded. While the Secretary agreed with Lee's actions he concluded they were illegal. Instead of authorizing the orders he asked President Davis to initiate legislation approving of the changes.

The War Department advised Lee on October 25th that it required Lee and Pendleton to name officers fit for promotion. However, the Secretary warned, "You are allowed a brigadier-general for every eighty guns; a colonel for every forty; a lieutenant-colonel for every twenty-four, and a major for every sixteen…." Pendleton supplied a list of Captains for promotion in order of ability on November 1st, including Captain William T. Poague of the Rockbridge Battery. In so doing he wanted it understood that the rankings were "only approximating justice." He was open to new information. His recommendations provided for three brigadier-generals, seven colonels, eleven lieutenant-colonels, and eighteen majors, more than the numbers allowed. Poague did not receive a promotion and blamed his old college roommate Sandie Pendleton for undercutting him although there is no evidence of this. In all likelihood, the War Department was reluctant to promote any more Virginians for political reasons. While Longstreet was happy with the changes, Jackson was not. He resented any interference within his Corps regarding command assignments and promotions.

It was not just the men who were exhausted by the campaign. The horses necessary to move all of the guns and wagons of the Army were broken down and exhausted as well. Just as a modern army requires oil and gas to move, the Civil War armies required horsepower. Pendleton was not able to provide to the Army field artillery all of the horses it needed. Some horses were re-shod and allowed to recuperate for a week to ten days. Others were replaced with horses from the disbanded batteries and the worn out horses and older replaced guns sent to Staunton. More than most officers in the Army, Pendleton understood the fragile nature of the horses and the need to lessen their loads and provide them rest.

Lee also took steps to remedy the problems created by having too few quality horses. Even though there were a large number of horses in the South, the Army was only able to procure inferior animals described as "almost without exception worthless." Another problem was procuring forage for the horses to eat. The quartermasters tended to send the forage to the existing camps, so that if there was a troop movement the animals arrived at their new camps without any food. Given the destruction of agriculture by the war throughout Virginia more often than not on arrival at a new camp there was no local forage to allow for the quartermaster's mistakes. As the winter of 1862-1863 progressed there was less and less forage available and the horses began to starve. Pendleton scrambled to find enough horses just to move the artillery.

To try to prevent these problems Lee issued an order on October 1, 1862 regarding the maintenance and care of the horses. He urged those caring for the animals to provide "energetic and unwearied care of their animals, and of preventing their neglect and abuse." Teams were not to be overdriven, misused, or neglected." He placed the burden of the care for the artillery horses on Pendleton requiring that the "Artillery horses especially must be kept in good condition." Pendleton was to correct every instance of neglect and punish offenders when necessary. He was also to ensure that the horses were adequately fed "with sufficient and suitable

190

food, sparing no effort or reasonable expense." Horses attached to the batteries were not to be ridden except by NCO's in the commission of their duties. Pendleton was authorized to arrest any offenders. The broken down horses were turned into the chief quartermaster who sent them to "good pasturage" where they would be cared for by responsible government agents, or disposed of otherwise.

*   *   *   *

By late October all of Pendleton's labors in re-organization were completed. It was just in time. Finally, after much urging from Lincoln, McClellan began to move the enormous Army of the Potomac across the Potomac River and into Virginia on the eastern side of the Blue Ridge. As usual, McClellan moved very slowly taking eleven days to go from Sharpsburg, Maryland to Warrenton, Virginia, a distance of sixty-six miles.   McClellan's goal was Culpeper. The sloth like movement gave Lee ample time to contemplate his next move.

Aware that the forage available in the lower Shenandoah Valley was exhausted, Lee sent Pendleton to scout routes through the Blue Ridge and to find available pasturage in the rolling hills of the Piedmont. When Pendleton reported back to Lee the Army started eastwards. On November 1st Pendleton and his Reserve Artillery marched alongside Lee and Longstreet's I Corps through Front Royal, Chester Gap, through Sperryville, and on to Culpeper on the eastern side of the Blue Ridge arriving on November 4th. Pendleton ordered his men to not overburden the horses during the march and to help with the wheels of the guns, caissons, and wagons over difficult stretches of the path. Straggling was forbidden. During the march Pendleton was forced to find food and forage wherever he camped as the quartermasters failed to provide any. The camp chosen by Pendleton at Culpeper was a mile from town and offered fresh meadows and running streams. The woods nearby were used to shelter the animals from the cold north winds.

McClellan's slow movements, his perpetual complaining, and his misplaced paranoia about a superior Confederate force finally exhausted Lincoln's patience. On November 7th Major-General Ambrose Burnside replaced McClellan in command of the Army of the Potomac. Burnside then did something that only few ever did; he slipped around Lee's right flank and moved quickly down to the town of Fredericksburg on the Rappahannock River. Having beaten

Lee to the river Burnside had the advantage and could cut Lee off from Richmond and his supply lines. But then Burnside dithered for weeks waiting for his pontoon trains to arrive to cross the river in style. He could have moved a slight distance westward and crossed the fords, or go a bit east and allow the Navy to ferry him over. Instead, Burnside foolishly surrendered all of his advantage and was faced across a wide river with an entrenched and strong foe. In the meanwhile Lee gathered his scattered divisions and moved them towards Fredericksburg as fast as possible.

On November 18th Pendleton received orders to move in the rear of Longstreet's column towards Fredericksburg. Quartermasters were tasked with preceding the column to arrange for food and forage. Pendleton ordered that each battalion's wagon train keep in the rear of the battalion and not fall behind. He was especially concerned about the horses, "There must be no going ahead nor falling behind, and no straggling; at all hard pulls the horses must be aided by judicious lifting at the wheels, & etc. As we are about to march through muddy roads, special care will be needed in grooming the horses."

The weather was brutal, rainy, and cold. Some of the men went barefoot and without winter clothing, but morale nevertheless remained high. After a five day grueling march over the sticky clayish dirt roads of Virginia the command finally reached Fredericksburg on November 23, 1862. On his arrival at Fredericksburg Pendleton ordered Moore's battalion to continue moving south to the North Anna River. There Moore was to construct a defensive position in the event the Army needed to retreat. Jackson's II Corps was still in the Valley and Lee faced a horde of Federal troops with just Stuart's cavalry, Longstreet's I Corps, and Pendleton's Reserve Artillery to oppose any crossing.

Fredericksburg was an old colonial town founded at the fall line of the Rappahannock, where the tidal current met the fast flowing streams pouring down out of the mountains and rolling hills of the Piedmont. Ocean going vessels could go no further up the river, making the site an ideal port. The town sat on the river's edge in a wide valley with slopes running up to the heights above the river on both sides. It was best known as the childhood home of George Washington across the river in Stafford County. In 1860 the town had a population of 5,000 and bridges across the river. By December

1862 the bridges were gone, and most of the people were leaving town as fast as they could.

The day after his arrival Lee ordered Pendleton and Alexander, now Chief of Artillery for the I Corps, to scout the positions of Burnside's Army of 121,000 men across the Rappahannock in Stafford County. The Federal Army was there in large numbers, with batteries deployed and in the process of constructing fieldworks. In fact, Pendleton reported that the enemy was better dug in than the far outnumbered Confederates. He placed a number of batteries to cover Lee's position but additional help was needed to finish the defense works. He placed other batteries downstream to repel any Union gunboats trying to come up the river. As usual, Pendleton complained about how much work he put in having ridden over thirty miles in two days

The early cold spell continued as the winter weather turned more bitter and cold than normal in early December. Food was scarce, at times there just enough for only one meal a day. The only tents available were used by the headquarters so the men slept in the open without shelter. Pendleton wrote home asking that blankets, curtains, carpets, anything that could be used to provide warmth for the soldiers be collected and hurried to Fredericksburg. Collection points were placed throughout Lexington and Rockbridge County. In a short time blankets and other coverings, pairs of socks, shoes, with leather for more, and $750 in cash was raised and sent to the Army.

In the mornings Pendleton awoke to find his tent cold and sheeted in ice. He ate breakfasts of fried middling, a coarse wheat and flour mix, cornbread, and bacon. Once in a while there was coffee. He was a bit tired of beef, on which the Army so heavily relied since it was easy to herd cattle with an Army, "A great thing for the eatables of an army to transport themselves," mused Pendleton. He grew out his beard, probably to avoid cold water shaving, and took on a resemblance to General Lee for whom he was often later mistaken.

Lee accompanied Pendleton and Alexander on a tour of the defensive lines on December 1st. When Lee criticized some of the artillery positions as being too far back from the front Alexander showed Lee how the positioning preserved these batteries from Federal artillery but allowed them to rake the field over which the Federal infantry would pass. Lee was so impressed he afterwards often asked Alexander, rather than Pendleton, to place some of the artillery.

Soon afterwards, Alexander, as Chief of Artillery for Longstreet, was ordered to replace Pendleton's artillery in the redoubts with his I Corps Artillery Reserve instead. If he needed more guns he had to look to the I Corps brigade artillery batteries for assistance. As a consequence it was Alexander and his artillery that provided the support mowing down the Federal lines as they approached Marye's Heights. At the time of the battle Pendleton had twelve batteries in three battalions with thirty-six guns and 752 men under his direct command. Many were placed in various locations about the field to provide long range artillery fire support. About twenty guns and Pendleton were placed behind Longstreet's lines behind Marye's Heights to provide support if needed. The artillery fields of fire were carefully marked with the maximum fields of fire set out by the engineering officers. The gunners and slave gangs were used as labor to dig the dirt fieldworks protecting the guns. The lack of tools and the frozen soil made the effort difficult. By the time the battle began there were forty entrenchments for the guns but no shelters yet for the ammunition or infantry support.

*   *   *   *

On December 11th Pendleton was wakened by the booms of signal guns announcing a Federal crossing of the Rappahannock. The Federals crossed on pontoons built while under fire and in a dense fog. They occupied Fredericksburg while covered by their long range artillery on Stafford Heights. Lee asked Pendleton to bring forwards some of his bigger guns and fire disrupting shells over the Federal advance. Smoke and fog made it difficult to find targets, and there was only an occasional response from Lee's artillery. Pendleton spent the day checking all his batteries to be sure everything was ready for a heavy infantry assault. On the right flank near Deep Run the Federal artillery found the range of some of the Confederate batteries which were forced to pull back. Near town Pendleton sent his Whitworth long range rifled guns to replace some shorter range guns Alexander was using.

Burnside's Army took two full days to cross the river and assemble on the southern bank. On the morning of the 13th Burnside launched nearly suicidal frontal assaults up the slope from the river towards Marye's Heights and Lee's well entrenched left flank. But Burnside also thrusted from the river into the woods and ravines near Deep Run penetrating Jackson's line. Pendleton and his staff rode beneath the shellfire from the Federal batteries to the central command post near Lee. There he sat most of the day, occasionally directing fire and moving batteries at Lee's request, but otherwise just observing. During the firing one of the two 30-pounder Parrott rifles near the gaggle of commanders exploded after its thirty-ninth discharge not more than ten or twenty feet from Lee, Longstreet, and Pendleton. Fortunately, no one was hurt.

On the right flank Meade's V Corps drove into Jackson's line at Deep Run. Meade advanced to within 800 yards of the Confederate batteries and Major Pelham's small horse artillery battery. The Confederate artillery opened up against Meade's attack with its forty-seven guns and with eight additional guns sent by Pendleton from his Artillery Reserve as reinforcement. Portions of Meade's line pulled back, and an artillery duel commenced that lasted over an hour until the Federals withdrew and the Confederate batteries ran out of ammunition. On another occasion Colonel Alexander needed to ride beneath the Confederate gunfire on the left flank and ordered the shelling stopped lest he be killed by a Confederate fuse misfiring early, which was a constant concern. Late in the afternoon Pendleton sent up batteries from his Reserve to relieve some batteries which had exhausted their ammunition and suffered severe losses. During the lulls in the assaults the ammunition caissons were replenished from the Reserves.

Later Pendleton recalled that the Federals were driven back so easily that it seemed to be more of a skirmish than a real battle. After Burnside sought a truce to attend to the wounded, Pendleton "rode over the field, and the sight of his dead and dying, in such amazing numbers, was absolutely sickening." From Lee's command post they could see the entire field. When one assault was driven back Lee merely looked on and solemnly said, "It is well war is so terrible or we should get too fond of it." Most of the West Point trained generals had no idea that the warfare of the past was obsolete, and failed to grasp the futility of massed infantry assaults on an entrenched enemy. The firepower of rifled muskets, minie balls, and cannon swept the battlefield clear of such attacks. Such erroneous tactics were repeated time and again through the end of the First World War.

Pendleton remained with Lee through the day and into the darkening night. Lee expected Burnside to renew the assaults in the morning. If Burnside had his way he would have attacked again but his senior officers convinced him of the futility of further assaults on the heights. Pendleton worked into the frozen night below the shining aurora borealis re-distributing artillery to where it was most needed. He moved every gun he could spare to covered positions to fire directly on the avenues of approach. Long lines of reserve caissons were positioned just behind the ridge to ease the re-supplying of ammunition. The only batteries left in reserve were those which were so depleted or exhausted by the day's battle that they were temporarily unfit for further service. Pendleton also had incendiary shells sent to some batteries in the event of a night attack so as to reveal Federal movements, but nothing happened. For once the Army and Pendleton used a reserve artillery force as intended.

All the next day the two sides faced each other and fired occasionally, but little happened. Pendleton sent even more artillery to the right flank after a potential threat appeared there but nothing came of it. The same pattern repeated on December 15th. Pendleton spent the day consulting with the general officers and re-arranging artillery positions on the right flank. Once more there was merely desultory firing. The only excitement occurred when the second 30-pounder Parrot rifled cannon exploded after its fifty-fourth discharge. By early the next morning, the 16th, the Confederate scouts reported that Burnside was retreating to the north side of the river. For all intents and purposes the battle was over. Pendleton ordered the long range Whitworth to fire at the retreating Federals. The Federal artillery returned fire using their huge 30-pound shells. Pendleton was amused when each time one of these large shells exploded all the Confederate generals would squat and hide.

Pendleton later reported that, "all the batteries of the general reserve, as well as those of the two army corps, were posted on the lines, and, though not called by the enemy's mode of attack to bear the brunt of close and concentrated action, they were all, more or less, and some quite severely, under fire." Nevertheless, casualties were small. Pendleton concluded with, "an expression of gratitude for the Divine guidance and guardianship under which these duties were discharged, and especially that so much was achieved by the army and its leaders with so little to regret, and a loss of valuable life so much less than usual to lament." His letters home were graphic. After writing, Well, the Yankees are gone!" he described the terrific destruction and "terrible loss of life….On all the battlefields I have seen nothing like it." The ground was "wet with blood."

The Federal commanders were well aware of the role the Confederate artillery played in their defeat. The official reports from Generals Burnside, his Corps and division commanders down to the officers commanding brigades and regiments, and especially the field artillery officers, commented that it was "murderous, deadly, terrific, destructive, continuous, severe, galling, vigorous, furious, heavy, enfilading, cross, and concentrated." The Confederates had so much time to prepare their fields of fire for their artillery that it covered every square yard of the battlefield from many different angles. As Colonel Alexander told Longstreet, "General, we cover that ground now so well that we will comb it as with a fine-tooth comb. A chicken could not live on that field when we open on it." There could be no better proof of the power of artillery when massed and given adequate time to prepare a defense.

*   *   *   *

After the battle Jackson re-located his headquarters to the manor of Moss Neck, about twelve miles east of Fredericksburg and two miles south of the Rappahannock. The large country manor was the home to the Richard Corbin Family, which was still in residence. Jackson opted to use a smaller outbuilding for his headquarters so that the family would not be disturbed. The news that the famous "Stonewall" Jackson was present brought locals to visit, many of whom made gifts of food to Jackson and his staff. Jackson chose to use some of this bounty to entertain some of the senior Army officers on Christmas Day. The Corbins happily allowed the dinner to be enjoyed within the manor house, and the entire family joined in. Jackson's personal slave Jim Lewis and another enslaved black wore white aprons and served turkeys, oysters, ham, fresh biscuits, vegetables, pickles, and a large bottle of wine for the twelve guests. Lee, Jeb Stuart, Pendleton, and their staffs were invited. Lee and Stuart teased Jackson about the opulence of his surroundings and Pendleton offered grace. The meal was a great success.

The guests left by afternoon leaving Jackson and his staff, including Sandie Pendleton, as the family's guests for supper. Sandie enjoyed his evening with young Catherine "Kate" Corbin, and by February 1863 they were in love. The story is not so happy for the rest of the Corbin family. Just before the Battle of Chancellorsville three of the small children, including a little girl Jackson doted on, had died from scarlet fever.

Pendleton continued to be harangued by commanders unhappy with their share of the Army's artillery. D. H. Hill asked for more Napoleon 12-pounders. Longstreet thought Jackson should surrender some of his guns. Lee finally resolved the dilemma by ordering guns up from Richmond. Elisha Paxton, a lawyer from Lexington, was made Brigadier-General and given command of the Stonewall Brigade. Pendleton thought it, "a blunder. Paxton is a fearless man but very obstinate and impracticable. Sure to be disliked & so far not to be fully efficient. It is in such matters that Jackson makes mistakes. His prejudices and partialities mislead him as to the merits or demerits of individuals." Sandie Pendleton resented that he had not been promoted Major despite his service record and responsibilities in logistics as an assistant adjutant general. Pendleton's son-in-law Ned Lee was still unhealthy but wished to contribute to the fight. He finally found a quiet billet in Richmond and later in the Valley.

Before the end of December Lee scattered the artillery in order to find sufficient forage for the horses through the winter. Pendleton's headquarters moved southwards towards the northern bank of the North Anna River near his childhood home. Pendleton was instructed to ensure that all of the artillery's horses received proper care so that no batteries would need to be disbanded in the spring for lack of horsepower. The Army Reserve Artillery under Pendleton's direct command now consisted of five batteries, thirty guns, 437 horses, and 778 men. The winter was cold and wet, and the country lanes around the camp became impassable for the artillery. Pendleton ordered that new bridges and roads be built in the area enabling the artillery to move if necessary. Pendleton also arranged lodging for his wife and daughter at a minister's home near the camp. One day out riding his horse refused to cross an icy stream. Pendleton dismounted, crossed the stream, and called on the horse to come to him, but instead the horse turned around and returned to his dry, warm stable.

Prices were rising as Confederate finances collapsed and its currency lost value. Inflation drove the price of food and clothing, if it was available at all, sky high. The Pendletons had to make do. Late that month Major Page of Pendleton's staff found the General working away with a needle and thread. "What are you doing,

General?" Page asked. "Mending my trousers," Pendleton replied. "The only thing I could find for a patch was this old piece of collar." "Well," replied Page, "it's a great waste of time, for nobody will ever be able to tell one end of your shirt from the other."

*   *   *   *

Early in January Pendleton finally decided to delegate some of his duties to younger officers. He appointed junior officers as Inspectors General to each Corps and the Reserve, and tasked them with checking the condition of horses, guns, harness, ammunition, and wagons; the strength of each battery; the supply of forage, its source, and prospects in future; whether the camps were located in healthy spots; protecting the local citizens; and reporting all absences without leave. They were also to inspect field hospitals and arrange for the disposition of the condemned horses.

Pendleton also continued his ongoing project of improving the field artillery organization. Working with the Corps Chiefs of Artillery Colonels Crutchfield and Alexander, he prepared yet another comprehensive reorganization. The three senior artillery officers concluded that batteries should no longer be assigned to the brigade level. Such assignments burdened the brigade commanders and limited the usefulness of the individual batteries. The scattering of batteries required for brigade level units also overburdened the supply officers trying to keep the units fully supplied with the necessary artillery rounds. "[M]ost injuriously of all, this system hinders unity and concentration in battle." There could be no massive artillery firepower directed at a single key point.

Going forward the artillery was to be arranged in battalions of four batteries each. The battalions could "ordinarily to attend to a certain division, and to report to, and receive orders from, its commander, though liable to be divided, detached, etc., as to the commanding general or corps commanders may seem best." The plan was to arm each battalion with good rifled cannons and Napoleon 12-pounders in equal numbers. The reserve batteries were to keep the largest guns. The Army Reserve Artillery was to consist of two battalions, of three batteries each, with a total of thirty-six guns. Some of the remaining obsolete 6-pounder smoothbores were sent to Tredegar Ironworks to be re-cast as 12-pounder Napoleons. The new arrangement would leave the handling of artillery tactics in the hands of trained artillery officers and not at the whim of untrained infantry commanders. Once accomplished, the plan left the Army with fourteen artillery battalions, and a total of 264 guns excluding Stuart's horse artillery. Pendleton forwarded the plan to Lee on February 11th.

Lee approved the plan and issued the required orders. He reported to President Davis that despite Richmond's misgivings, every battalion required two field officers (Majors and up) so that one could reconnoiter an appropriate position to place the guns while the other brought them up. The same was true of batteries, so there had to be two company grade officers (Lieutenants and Captains) for each. Pendleton never asked for a promotion, and never received one since the law permitted no rank for Major General of Artillery. Nor did Pendleton ever express any disappointment in not receiving a promotion. He got what he wanted when Lee authorized him a staff and wagon train equivalent to that of a Major General.

The trio of senior artillery officers also made recommendations for promotions. In making these recommendations Pendleton was sure to add, "The proportion between the number of field officers of artillery thus proposed belonging to Virginia and those from other States is very nearly coincident with that between the number of batteries from Virginia and those from other States." Once again he recommended William Poague of Lexington for promotion. Pendleton wrote Poague, "is a superior officer, whose services have been scarcely surpassed. He has been recommended for promotion, and should justly receive it." This time Poague received his well merited promotion. Another Lexingtonian was excluded from the list. Captain Greenlee Davidson bitterly complained to Governor Letcher of Virginia of his lack of promotion, and complained that "Old Granny" and the "Reverend General" Pendleton ignored his rightful claims. Jackson typically objected to the list of recommended promotions stating it contained too many incompetent officers whom he would not tolerate. He insisted that all of the promotions within his Corps be awarded to officers in his Corps and not to outsiders. Lee refused, saying, "I regret I do not concur altogether with the principle there laid down regulating claims to promotion. I think the interest of the service, as well as justice to individuals, re-quires the selection of the best men to fill vacant positions." In the end, though, Jackson got his way.

*   *   *   *

The effort to collect new horses continued but was hampered by the lack of food. The War Department halted a shipment of 400 horses for the Army at the border of North Carolina in order to be sure to find forage for them. Other droves were collected but forage for them was not available. Pendleton ordered agents into the counties along the Virginia Central Railroad, and the James River Canal to collect grain and use the available transportation to bring it to the Army as quickly as possible. This shortage of horses and forage was a major problem, and one that may have prevented Lee from assuming the offensive in February 1863. The horses and mules of the Army were scattered too widely to gather together quickly for a movement, and not strong enough because of hunger to pull the Army's guns and wagons.

Pendleton felt that there were three causes of the deficiency in horses. First, there was a loss of horses in battle and arduous campaigns. Second, many horses sickened and died from hauling forage while underfed, cold, and sick. Third, the adoption by the Army of larger and more modern guns required more horses to pull them. Instead of a four-horse team per gun and limber, there would have to be a six-horse team.

In February 1863 the II Corps complained that its horses had to carry forage from as far away as sixty miles over wretched back country roads. Lee was not pleased, and sent what was, for him, a rebuke to Jackson. Lee learned that "one-half of the hay brought by the General Railroad from Augusta and Albemarle, the only places from which it can be obtained. The Army was promised 90,000 pounds per day by railroad but never received more than 30,000 per day and that irregularly, which was only sufficient to feed half of the animals. Lee concluded that the horses, "if nothing better can be done, turned out during the day, that they may browse on the stubble, twigs, & etc. Life at least can be preserved with other forage that can be procured."

By the end of March the need for new horses grew acute as the weather warmed for campaigning. Pendleton needed 1,200 horses with which to fully equip all of the Army's artillery. In the Army Reserve Artillery alone he needed another 170 horses. Lee tried to calm Pendleton, telling him "Do not, however, distress your horses." It was better to leave the horses in the rear areas and send for them when the weather and road conditions allowed. Lee cautioned Pendleton not to bring up more horses than he could feed. In the meantime "every exertion will be made to bring up full supplies of corn and hay." Fortunately, spring arrived in early April, and many of the horses could be turned out to pasture to feed.

Pendleton arranged for the corn brought by rail to be delivered to the artillery camps. He also lightened the burden and need for horses by asking the entire artillery corps to reduce the number of wagons used in the Army. Pendleton noted that "General Jackson takes no trunk himself and allows none in his corps." The clerks in Lee's headquarters did not have horses, and "for all his voluminous papers & all the accommodations of his staff only three or four wagons are employed."

Nevertheless, the equine problem persisted. Pendleton ordered that transportation in each battalion the staff be reduced to one four horse wagon for mess outfit, desks, papers, and tents and one two horse wagon for the medical team. This time he met with resistance from his Corps Chiefs of Artillery. Crutchfield in particular objected strenuously, pointing out that by eliminating too many wagons the efficiency of the artillery corps would be hurt. The limits made it impossible for batteries to carry forage or forges, carry sufficient supplies for the medical corps, or what could be used as kitchens. For Crutchfield the better solution meant finding more forage. Lee joined in the discussion, noting that his orders regarding reducing the load for horses did not apply to the supply wagon trains. Still, the lack of horses remained. Lee wrote that "The difficulty of procuring horses renders it necessary to reduce the transportation as low as possible…. The destruction of horses in the army is so great that I fear it will be impossible to supply our wants. There are not enough in the country."

*   *   *   *

The winter chill exacerbated Pendleton's rheumatism. Being so close to his old home, Pendleton enjoyed the time he spent with family, and as one officer noted, "no one enjoyed the dinner and the ladies… more than the old General did." He was happy to baptize E. P. Alexander's new baby when his family visited. And Sandie finally received his deserved promotion to Major. Pendleton also spent a lot of his time leading the religious revival which swept the Army with the active encouragement of Lee and Jackson. Lee was fully persuaded that his Army needed all the help God could provide. Pendleton was convinced that Lee "is deeply concerned for the spiritual welfare of the soldiers." Many soldiers heard Pendleton preach during this revival and most credited him with instilling faith in them. One gunner recollected "the men were sitting on their guns and listening very attentively to the words of God uttered by General Pendleton." One Lieutenant believed that Pendleton's sermons were "searching, eloquent, and just." As spring approached Pendleton sent Anzelotte home to Lexington and pondered the future. He believed somewhat pessimistically that the war would last another four years. Hearing this prediction one soldier acerbically noted, "My only consolation is that I believe him to 'be neither a prophet nor the son of one.'"

In mid-March Federal cavalry probed the outer Confederate defenses, testing for weakness, and to discover the strength behind the Confederate defenses. Pendleton placed his guns so they could command any approach to the area where Lee's Army was camping. He also sped the completion of the artillery's re-organization although many of the promotions had yet to be approved in Richmond. On March 21st, Lee asked that as much artillery as possible re-join the Army. The bulk of the I Corps under Longstreet was on campaign in Suffolk, Virginia, as well as collecting food and forage, so the Army was shorthanded. At first, Pendleton brought up too many horses causing Lee to caution him that "we shall be injured instead of being benefited by the fresh horses." Finally, Lee moved the artillery corps to three miles west of Guiney's Station where it would be centrally located to meet any threat by the Union Army.

On April 15th Jeb Stuart reported a large movement of Federal cavalry at Kelly's Ford across the Rappahannock twenty-five miles upriver from Fredericksburg. Then, on April 29th reports came in that the Federal Army was crossing the Rappahannock at Fredericksburg. Pendleton ordered the Reserve Artillery to move as quickly as possible to Fredericksburg while preserving the strength of the available horses as much as possible. The Confederacy's most famous victory and its most lamented loss were about to occur.

10. "OUR WEAKENED LINE
MET THEM WITH SPIRIT"

[CHANCELLORSVILLE, 1863]

*MERCIFUL God and heavenly Father, ….look with pity, we beseech thee,
upon the sorrows of thy servant for whom our prayers are desired. In thy wisdom
thou hast seen fit to visit him with trouble, and to bring distress upon him.
Remember him O Lord in mercy; sanctify thy fatherly correction to him; endue
his soul with patience under his affliction, and with resignation to thy blessed
will; comfort him with a sense of thy goodness; lift up thy countenance upon him,
and give him peace….*

1789 Episcopal Book of Common Prayer

In January 1863 Burnside attempted a rapid flanking movement around Lee's left flank. He started his troops up the Rappahannock River in a driving storm resulting in the infamous Mud March. After the Army bogged down and any hope of surprise banished Burnside abandoned the effort. Some of his unhappy senior generals approached Lincoln and asked for a new commander. Lincoln obliged them by appointing Major General Joseph Hooker as the commander of the Army of the Potomac, a man well known for braggadocio and hard fighting. While Hooker was an excellent corps commander the command of the entire army seemed to upset his sense of self-confidence. Nevertheless, with a far better system of collecting intelligence than that employed by McClellan or Burnside, Hooker came up with a brilliant campaign strategy. His only problem, in the long run, was whether he would have the moral courage to execute it successfully.

Hooker's first move sent General Stoneman and 10,000 cavalry well around Lee's left flank to raid Lee's line of supply back to Richmond in an effort to compel Lee to withdraw to protect his lines of communication. The movement began on April 13, 1863 but quickly came to a halt when rains swelled the rivers too high for the horses to cross the fords. Hooker altered the plan and on April 27th launched Stoneman's cavalry on a raid once more, but this time sent three Army Corps of 42,000 men in their wake across the Rappahannock and the Rapidan Rivers and into the area known locally as the Wilderness. Hooker left three Army Corps at Falmouth under General John Sedgwick across the Rappahannock from Fredericksburg as a diversion to pin Lee down there and to guard his lines of communications and supply back to Washington. When half of the Army successfully crossed into the Wilderness Hooker ordered one of these three Corps march to join him, leaving only General Sedgwick with his VI Corps and Reynolds' I Corps, a total of 40,000 men in front of Fredericksburg. While the Federal Army passed through the Wilderness to cut Lee off from Richmond, Sedgwick was to launch diversionary feints at Fredericksburg.

Once again a Federal commander had the jump on Lee, and once again he surrendered whatever advantage he held. Lee's Army was scattered and the bulk of one of his two Army Corps (Longstreet's) was over a hundred miles away. Now he had large enemy forces on both of his flanks threatening to cut him off from Richmond or make him fall back in panic. Perhaps that was Hooker's wish, as once he entered the Wilderness Hooker's courage abandoned him. As soon as the two opposing armies came into contact in the Wilderness on May 1, 1863, Hooker stopped his advance near the crossroads at Chancellorsville and began to dig defensive entrenchments. In stopping Hooker ceded his military advantage and passed the initiative to Lee. Lee did not hesitate to make the most of this opportunity. Rather than retreat he launched one of the boldest flank attacks in American military history.

This area of Virginia was once covered by a dense broadleaf tree forest. Colonial settlers removed the forest for fuel to operate their small iron furnaces. When the wood was exhausted the iron furnaces closed, and the once lush forest grew back with a secondary forest of densely packed vegetation and pine trees, brambles, thickets, and vines. The only easy passage through the Wilderness was on one of the few narrow country lanes, or one of the broader roads; the Orange Plank Road, Orange Turnpike, or River Road. The density of the foliage made it nearly impossible to deploy field artillery and prevented the Union Army from readily deploying its superior artillery arm. For the most part, any battle within the Wilderness would be an infantry battle.

The situation on the Fredericksburg front was entirely different. Once again, the Federal troops would have to cross the river and storm the heights to push the Confederate forces back towards Richmond and envelop the rear of Lee's Army, which was now turned to face Hooker in the Wilderness. It was on this front that Pendleton's Reserve Artillery and Major General Jubal Early's infantry division were deployed behind the entrenchments atop Marye's Heights. And once more Pendleton's conduct in the battle became enmeshed in controversy.

On the morning of the 29th Lee learned that Hooker had turned his left flank and threatened his lines of communication and supply. The correct military solution was to attack the isolated Union wing at Fredericksburg as it was the closest. But both Lee and Jackson felt that it would be impossible to cross the river and drive Sedgwick back, primarily due to the dual hurdles presented by the river and the well-entrenched and superior Federal artillery batteries. Instead of retreating, Lee split his army in two although he was already outnumbered by two to one. He left Barksdale's brigade of McLaw's division and Jubal Early's division under Early's command in Fredericksburg, and ordered Pendleton to come up from Guiney's Station and provide artillery support. The force defending the town would number only 10,000 men while faced across the river by three Federal Army Corps. As E. P. Alexander later wrote of the defending Confederates that, "this force averaged about one man to each yard, and nine guns to each mile." The remainder of the Army moved west towards Hooker and Chancellorsville.

That morning Federal troops crossed the Rappahannock downstream from Fredericksburg at Deep Run, just as they had in December. General Early moved his division to his right flank to block any further movement from the river crossing. Pendleton was at Chesterfield Station that day when he received word that his artillery was needed at Fredericksburg. By afternoon most of the

206

Reserve Artillery was on the roads leading to the Rappahannock. That night a heavy rain pelted the men and turned the dirt roads into mush making the movement difficult at best. Pendleton travelled with the rear guard of the Reserve to Massaponax Church, nine miles south of Fredericksburg, arriving there by noon the next day. Walton's field artillery battalion, having made a late start to garner enough horses to pull the guns, lost their way and were somewhere in the darkness and storm.

Pendleton arrived in Fredericksburg on the 30th, and reported to General Early. Together they made a brief reconnaissance of their lines. Both felt that the lines were weak; using 10,000 men to defend a line six miles wide would be difficult. Pendleton turned over the command of the artillery on the right flank by Deep Run to the artillery battalion commander from II Corps present, and turned his focus on the left flank defended by Barksdale lone infantry brigade at Marye's Heights. Barksdale's defensive line spanned three miles. By mid-morning Pendleton placed his guns with Nelson's battalion in the gap north of Deep Run, and Cabell's and Cutts' battalions on Marye's Heights where they could place crossfire onto the slope approaching the heights. When Walton and the Washington Artillery arrived on the afternoon of the 1st they were placed on Marye's Heights with some of its batteries sent to replace those at Port Royal. With many of his batteries previously deployed to reinforce the main Army, Pendleton committed his entire reserve to the front line in order to comply army artillery reserve as all of the guns were committed.

The next morning, Friday the 1st, Pendleton joined Early at his command post. General Early ordered Pendleton to send no more batteries to the main Army. He also turned over the command of all of the artillery, about fifty-six guns, at Fredericksburg to Pendleton. Together they confirmed the number of guns protecting the right flank was sufficient. Pendleton and Early then rode to Lee Hill to chat with Barksdale on the left flank. While there they were joined by Lee. Lee told Pendleton to send some batteries to Port Royal where it was rumored two Federal gunboats were shelling the port. At this time Walton had not yet arrived, and Pendleton had to pull some of Cutts' batteries out of the line and send them. Lee approved the disposition of the troops, and advised the officers to be prepared to meet any attacks with "the utmost energy and determination." If Sedgwick left Falmouth and moved west up the north bank towards Hooker then Early was to join Lee. Lee followed this command with additional orders. If Early was forced back he was to retire down the road towards Richmond and set up a defense at Guiney's Station, about ten miles south, where the Army had its main supply base.

That evening General Sickles' Federal III Corps departed from Falmouth to join Hooker's force upstream. Meanwhile, Sedgwick's two Corps began to move about their camps. Pendleton decided that since the wagon trains remained in place the movement was a mere feint. Jubal Early remained distinctly uncomfortable with the force at his disposal. Outnumbered four to one across a front several miles long there were left large gaps guarded only by a thin picket line. That same evening, Lee and Jackson met at a crossroads campfire to decide their next move. Jackson proposed a daring run around Hooker's right flank in the Wilderness with his entire Corps. He would strike Hooker from his right rear and drive him back into the Rapidan River. Lee agreed, and now split his vastly outnumbered Army into three isolated pieces.

*   *   *   *

Saturday, May 2nd, dawned quietly at Fredericksburg apart from some desultory exchanges of artillery firing on the right flank by Deep Run. Pendleton met Early at a heavy battery position where they discussed Lee's most recent order to open on the Federal troops with the long range artillery to see their reaction. Early asked Pendleton to fire the long range Parrott rifled cannons on the left flank. If the Union Army failed to do anything aggressive, then Early was to send Lee half of his already small force. By the time Pendleton reached the guns on the left, Early had already commenced a desultory exchange of firing on the right flank. Pendleton found on his arrival that there were no decent targets within range and decided not to waste the ammunition. Even so, he could see the Federal troops massing on the opposite bank near the river crossings from Falmouth into Fredericksburg.

Pendleton rode to Marye's Hill to further confer with Jubal Early. He hoped to move some guns to the far left flank and fire on the Federal columns massing near Falmouth as he and Early thought the Federals were moving upstream to assist Hooker. On his arrival at Marye's Heights he found Lee's Chief of Staff Colonel Robert Chilton talking with General Early. Chilton repeated his comments to Pendleton as well. Chilton ordered them that "all of the artillery, except some eight or ten pieces, and especially the heaviest guns, should be sent down the Telegraph road toward Chesterfield, and most of the infantry force withdrawn and moved up to the commanding general; that the small force left should keep up a demonstration as well as it could, to detain the enemy and check his advance, and when it could do this no longer should retire...." The only units to be left behind were a brigade of infantry and a part of the Reserve Artillery to be selected by General Pendleton. If the enemy advanced with force this rearguard was to retreat southwest towards Spotsylvania Court-House. In the meantime Pendleton was "required to send the greater part of his Reserve Artillery to the rear at once." During the conversation they could hear the sound of heavy artillery firing off to the west.

Neither Pendleton nor Early could believe what they were hearing. This would leave a tiny skeleton force defending the rear against Sedgwick's two Federal Army Corps. Any withdrawal would be clearly observed by the Federals on the ground and in their observation balloons. Both generals protested the command but Chilton was adamant. Lee had considered all of their objections, Chilton responded. Lee needed infantry for the battle in the Wilderness, and since artillery could not be usefully employed there, it was to retire towards Richmond. Pendleton reiterated his objection, "I reminded General Chilton that the force left could really make no fight on such a line and against such odds, and that all we could do would be to make a show of fighting as long as possible, and then get away as sagaciously as we might. I also asked him how long he expected us to hold the ground if the enemy pressed with all his force." Chilton remained adamant. The defenses need hold only long enough for the "artillery and trains sent to the rear get beyond danger." And orders were orders.

It was not quite noon. Orders were sent to Nelson's battalion and the three 20-pounder Parrots to pull back as soon as possible towards Richmond. The batteries would be temporarily replaced by smaller guns. Other batteries were to follow behind Nelson in order. Six guns of the Washington Artillery were left with Barksdale's brigade, and nine others, including two Parrotts, were left in the defenses while twenty-two guns moved south on the Telegraph Road. Pendleton tried to mask the movements by having some batteries moving back and forth as though advancing to the lines of defense. At the same time Early's division and Barksdale's brigade began to file past and head west towards Salem Church. Left behind in command of the infantry was General Hays with his Louisiana brigade of Early's division, and one regiment of Barksdale's Mississippi brigade. By two o'clock, Early was gone, leaving a very nervous Pendleton and Hays confronting tens of thousands of Federal troops.

It was then that the Federals crossed the Rappahannock in division strength and pressed forward a strong line of skirmishers. Pendleton later wrote "Our weakened line met them with spirit, but could not long maintain the unequal contest. It therefore fell back." Another debacle like Shepherdstown loomed. Once again Pendleton's guns were inadequately protected by an insufficient number of infantry against a much larger enemy force. More Federal troops began to deploy on the southern bank of the river while even more massed at the bridgeheads on the northern side. Pendleton estimated that between 15,000 and 20,000 men were moving to the attack. He ordered any of the batteries still in the area to return to their positions. Yet, in spite of everything the Union Army halted.

At the outset of the campaign Sedgwick was ordered to engage in a diversion but to not seriously attack the Confederate lines at Fredericksburg. That changed on May 1st when late in the afternoon he was told by Hooker to attack if Sedgwick thought it would be successful. The next day Hooker changed his mind. He wanted the I Corps in Chancellorsville while the VI Corps remained in Falmouth on the north bank of the Rappahannock. Sedgwick replied that he had divisions across the river already and if they withdrew the Confederates would realize there was no real threat. And then Hooker changed his mind yet again. On the afternoon of the 2nd he again ordered Sedgwick to attack if in his discretion he would succeed. Sedgwick, like Pendleton, did not like discretionary orders. So he did nothing, just when the Confederate troops began to depart Fredericksburg, and even after reports of the Confederate withdrawal reached him.

Pendleton and Hays were at the Marye House making arrangements to complete the withdrawal of the forces remaining when Barksdale returned. He heard about the Federal threat and thought that everyone needed to return to Fredericksburg. He issued an order to his brigade, already on the road west, to reverse course, and then sent a messenger to Early explaining what had happened. Word reached Early when he and his division was a mile down the

Plank Road. Early also ordered his men to turn around and return to Fredericksburg. Pendleton sent orders to the scattered batteries to return, but was only able to reach Walker, Cabell, and Fraser. Nelson's battalion and another battery were too far down the Telegraph Road on their way towards Richmond to return in time. By dark most of the other batteries were back where they began the day, and Walker's battalion was parked just behind the lines on the Telegraph Road.

Pendleton and Hays anxiously awaited Early's return. There had been no confirmed reports that he was returning and so they decided to abandon the position if Early had not arrived by 11:00 p.m. When Early returned that night the Federals on the south bank had not moved any further south and were still north of the Richmond Stage Road and Marye's Heights. Generals Hays and Pendleton found Jubal Early about 11:00 p.m. along the railroad line just south of the town. General Early commented that he had returned because Barksdale reported a threat. Early then took them to his tent and showed them a letter from Lee that Early received just as it was getting dark. Lee had not intended Early to abandon his position but left it to his discretion whether or not the threat from Sedgwick was real. Pendleton expressed regret that so many guns had been sent away and were now beyond recall, leaving their defensive line weaker than before with just fifteen guns.

Out in the Wilderness Jackson's flank attack was a success. His men drove the Federal Army back onto the Chancellorsville clearing but had failed to defeat it. Jackson was still separated from Lee by the Federal III Corps. The 70,000 men of the Army of the Potomac also still held their entrenchments. While scouting out another attack Jackson was returning through the lines in the evening gloom when he was shot by some anxious North Carolinians. When A. P. Hill was also wounded Jeb Stuart took command of the II Corps. Lee spent the night organizing an assault with the 43,000 men he commanded on two wings against the Union lines. He hoped to drive them back into the river and re-unite the separated wings of the main army. Meanwhile, Hooker, having heard the reports of Early's withdrawal now believed that Lee was in full retreat. He directly ordered Sedgwick to assault the Confederate lines at Fredericksburg the next morning and then march west to join him near Chancellorsville. The idea of assaulting the heights was daunting for the Federal officers. One wrote that the Confederate position was "protected by strong works and supported by well served artillery."

*   *   *   *

In Fredericksburg the night passed fairly quietly except for the occasional picket firing at something moving in the dark. Barksdale placed the 1,500 men of his brigade in a tiered defensive position on the left flank. There were enough men for one man to cover five yards of defensive line. There were no defending troops on the far left of the Plank Road running along the crest of the heights and overlooking the fields and canal below. Pendleton placed some of his guns in entrenchments on Marye's Hill, and the rest on Lee's Hill at the military crest. Additional guns to the right covered the gaps between Barksdale and Early's positions on the right.

Jubal Early was shaken awake by an excited Barksdale at 2:00 a.m. Barksdale reported that bridges had been thrown across the river at Fredericksburg and the enemy were coming across in strong numbers. Early was confronted with four Union divisions arrayed in line on the south bank from one end of the Confederate defensive line to the other. Most of the Confederate strength was on the right flank at Deep Run where Jackson had been driven back by Meade in December.

By then Pendleton had been on the move for twenty hours "nearly without food" and was exhausted. He lay down for nap in one of the houses behind the lines. Ninety minutes later he was up again and headed for Lee's Hill attending to his flock of batteries. He placed Walton in command of the guns posted on Marye's Heights and Cabell in command of the guns on Howison's and Lee's Hills. Below he could see the Federal VI Corps, some 20,000 strong, massed south of the river between Deep Run and into the town. Large Federal batteries were already deployed on the south bank and on the fields below the heights. At sunrise he re-positioned batteries on Marye's Heights and in front of the graveyard to the right of Marye's house. A section of Parrotts were positioned in the works on the extreme right of Marye's Heights. At 8:00 a.m. when the Federals began to demonstrate near the town, Pendleton placed two 12-pounder howitzers in two small and incomplete works on the brow of the hill in front of the main line of redoubts and to the left of the plank road. At Barksdale's request Pendleton sent two more guns to the advanced works on the left. Critically, Barksdale also

212

moved a battery out of the works commanding the Plank Road without telling Pendleton. Pendleton assumed throughout the battle that the battery was still there to block any attacks on that flank. Barksdale also moved some of Walton's guns to Marye's Heights in the middle of the night to cover a different part of the Plank Road and the causeway. Walton objected that there was insufficient infantry to protect the guns from assault but was ordered to comply.

The first major assault occurred on Early's right flank along Deep Run. Federal infantry managed to move into the ravines where they were protected from Confederate artillery fire from their left or right. From across the Rappahannock enemy guns began to play on the Confederate batteries and a brisk duel ensued. After a while one of Early's infantry brigades dislodged the Union infantry and drove it back. The Confederate artillery shelled the withdrawing Federal troops. The Union effort now shifted upstream towards Barksdale's flank and Marye's Heights.

At 8:00 a.m. Sedgwick's attack began against Marye's Heights with a heavy artillery fire on the Confederate positions while his troops gathered for an assault. When the Federal light artillery deployed in advance of its infantry Pendleton sent additional guns to the most advanced works on the left. Concerned with what he saw Pendleton advised Early that the main Federal effort would be made on the left flank. General Early ordered Hays' brigade moved from the right flank to reinforce Barksdale on the left.

The Union lines advanced up the Marye's Heights towards the stone wall at the crest, just as they had in December. As they moved forward Federal skirmishers pushed the Confederate skirmish line back up slope to their defensive lines. Pendleton ordered the rifled artillery to shell the enemy at a distance causing the Federal lines to advance with great caution. Another Federal column moved upriver towards Taylor Hill to outflank the Confederates on their left, and Hays' brigade was sent to stop them. The Union assault came in three columns of 20,000 men. Pendleton's artillery opened on them "with fine effect, and soon caused them to disperse and lie concealed." Federal artillery fire began to concentrate on Marye's Heights, confirming in Pendleton's mind that it was the focus of further attacks. He asked Hays to send any troops he could spare to reinforce the line behind the stone wall.

Sedgwick launched two large scale attacks directly uphill against the sunken road and its stone wall atop Marye's Heights, but both times they were blunted by rifle fire and because "Pendleton's batteries poured shell and canister into their ranks with dreadful effect...." An attempt to turn the right of the Confederate lines by moving up the Hazel Run ravine was stymied by Pendleton's artillery. The repulse of each attack gave both Pendleton and Barksdale confidence that their line could hold, and they so advised Early. At the same time news arrived that Lee had been successful in defeating Hooker off to the west in the Wilderness. Quiet descended on the battlefield. By this time Federal losses before Marye's Heights were estimated to be between 1,000 and 2,000 killed and wounded.

However, it was now to be the kindness of Colonel Thomas Griffin, commander of the 18th Mississippi in the forward trenches, which cost the Confederates dear. When the local Federal commanders requested a truce to aid their wounded, Griffin readily agreed without referring the request up his chain of command. Union soldiers and officers used the opportunity to come up to the Confederate defenses, and they easily observed just how few men were behind the stone wall. When the truce ended the Confederates on the right flank noticed masses of Federal troops moving to their left towards Marye's Heights to reinforce yet another assault on the stone wall. Early sent a warning to Barksdale and Pendleton, and not hearing any response, sent a staff officer to investigate the conditions on the left flank.

General Sedgwick now knew that the Union masses could overwhelm the feeble Confederate resistance. All of the Confederate mistakes were coming home to roost; Chilton's erroneous order to withdraw, Barksdale's removal of batteries from the Plank Road, and Griffin's approval of the truce combined to grant the Federal Army the easy opportunity to win the day. Sedgwick arranged for a massive assault in which his men outnumbered the defenders by twenty to one. As Pendleton later observed, had the guns sent to the rear by Chilton's error been in position the Federals would probably have been repulsed. Instead, the Confederate lines "were, however, at the critical point too weak in guns as in infantry." At 11:00 a.m. Pendleton observed a sudden combined assault from "along the streets, and by a line of battle toward the stone fence, and also another toward Howison's house. The gun to play upon one of the streets had been removed, the remainder, supporting the small force of infantry, could not repel the attack at all points....."

The Federal infantry pushed through the feeble resistance of the Mississippians at the stone wall, capturing many of them. Barksdale noted afterwards "many of this noble little band resisted to the death with clubbed guns even after his vast hordes had swept over and around the walls." Barksdale pulled back the rest of his brigade to save as many as possible and set up a new defensive line further back. Confederate batteries defending the position were also overwhelmed, and seven guns were taken. Chaos and confusion reigned in the collapsing Confederate lines.

Pendleton saw the success of the Federal assault with "mortification." He directed that the guns on Lee's Hill fire on the Union troops swarming around Marye's Heights. He then went back to untether his horse from a ravine behind the hill, and returned to Lee's Hill. As new batteries arrived he gave them targets on Marye's Heights. The Confederate batteries along the line turned their guns on the Union infantry and fired quickly and effectively at the enemy on Marye's Heights. Their fire slowed the Federal advance and gave the Confederates a chance to pull back and re-form a mile or two behind their original lines.

Hearing nothing from the staff officer sent earlier, Jubal Early rode towards his left flank to discover its condition for himself. On the way he encountered a messenger from Pendleton reporting that the lines were holding, but just then his staff officer returned with the report that enemy troops were atop Marye's Heights. He ordered reinforcements from his right flank to attack the victorious Federals on his left. Meanwhile, the Federal infantry on Marye's Heights turned to their left and advanced towards Lee's Hill, driving back the Confederate infantry protecting the batteries there. When General Early arrived at Lee's Hill he met Barksdale rallying his men.

Pendleton rode all around the battlefield rallying his men and preserving his artillery. At some point he rode to Signal Hill to observe the battlefield. He remained for some time on or near Lee's Hill slowly withdrawing the guns when they exhausted their ammunition. One battery, Fraser's, stayed on Lee's Hill until the bitter end. Having exhausted all his available canister shells the Fraser resorted to solid shot. Another battery barely escaped capture, leaving one gun behind as it lacked the horses to pull it. Just as some of his guns were pulling out of their positions on Lee's Hill Pendleton encountered General Early. The commanding general concluded that Pendleton was moving rapidly to the rear with his artillery, making it appear that Pendleton was pulling out too soon. It was the accepted practice at the time for an artillery officer to save as many guns as possible, and also to pull back out of harm's way any battery which had no more ammunition in their limbers and caissons. Early ordered one battery to stop and deploy, which it did. But it did not fire. When Early asked the battery commander why he did not shoot at the enemy he was told the ammunition was exhausted from shelling the Federal infantry. It had not helped that only one in fifteen Confederate shells actually exploded over their targets.

The artillery leaving Lee's Hill, the remainder of Barksdale's brigade, and one regiment from Hays' Brigade now joined the defensive stand along Telegraph Road about two miles behind Lee's Hill. Pendleton rode along the new defensive line on Telegraph Road re-positioning the artillery. Pendleton was not told that more reinforcements were on their way, and fearful of being flanked by enemy advances up the ravines on both flanks of the position at Telegraph Road moved his guns further south down Telegraph Road. The new Confederate line along Telegraph Road did not stand for long. As Pendleton feared, Union troops, using the shelter provided by the local ravines on both sides of the line, quickly outflanked the position. The remaining men and guns were withdrawn further down Telegraph Road.

As the Confederate batteries withdrew Pendleton ordered Colonel Walton to find "the first proper and commanding position," and to stay there. Colonel Walton selected the intersection of Military and Telegraph Roads, and it was near there that Early set up his new defensive line. However, Jubal Early countermanded Pendleton's orders placing some of the artillery to the new line selected by Walton. Pendleton remained at the new line commanding the guns while under fire from Federal batteries. When Confederate shelling broke up the enemy formations it led to a prolonged artillery duel.

Meanwhile, the Union infantry stopped to eat lunch. When done they re-grouped and moved west down Plank Road towards Chancellorsville and not south down Telegraph Road towards Richmond. Sedgwick was strictly complying with his orders to cross the river and advance on Chancellorsville. He had no further interest in Early's lines and ignored them while he moved his Corps to the west. Later that night when some of the Union artillery wagons and forges at the rear of the Federal column came too near the Confederate lines Colonel Walton shelled them until they fled in the dark.

Early later reported his losses that day as, "Ten guns were lost in all, including those taken at Marye's Hill, but two were subsequently recovered, making our final loss in that respect eight pieces." The Reserve Artillery also lost seventy men killed, wounded, or missing, along with the eight guns and limbers, four caissons, and sixty-four horses.

*   *   *   *

After re-grouping following the victorious assault of Marye's Heights, the Federal VI Corps moved west down the Plank Road seeking a merger with Hooker's forces at Chancellorsville. Sedgwick's orders had not changed; he was to pursue the now retreating Confederates towards Chancellorsville, except the Confederate Army was not retreating as expected. General Lafayette McLaws halted his division at Salem Church on the Plank Road and turned to face the Union advance. Sedgwick attacked the position at 3:25 p.m. but after a couple of hours the Union Army was repulsed. Nevertheless, Sedgwick successfully pushed Wilcox's brigade off of Taylor's Hill, a commanding point controlling access to the river fords and Sedgwick's line of supply and retreat. Sedgwick was now alone on the southern bank of the Rappahannock between two enemy forces of unknown size; Early to the south and Lee to the west. Hooker, still confused from his wounds, was unable to tell Sedgwick what to do. Another Union general suggested Sedgwick safeguard his line of retreat over the river and head towards the fords upriver from Fredericksburg guarded by Taylor's Hill.

Reports came in late to Early and Pendleton on the 3rd that Sedgwick was moving up the Plank Road towards Chancellorsville to attack Lee in the rear, and the reports were soon confirmed by a personal reconnaissance conducted by Early and Pendleton. General Early also received news that McLaws and his division were approaching Fredericksburg from the Wilderness along the Plank Road. Together, they were to push Sedgwick back across the river.

When dawn broke on May 4th Early launched his division at Sedgwick's rear guard defending the approaches to Fredericksburg. Pendleton rode along to provide any assistance from the artillery which Early required. Pendleton observed that the Union troops abandoned the line at Telegraph Road but remained in some force on Plank Road and on Marye's Heights. He ordered that long range artillery fire shell the Union position driving the bulk of the enemy off of the ridge. By 7:00 a.m. General Gordon's Brigade seized Lee's Hill and cut Sedgwick off from Fredericksburg. As the federals withdrew Barksdale's Brigade and some of Pendleton's artillery re-occupied the same trenches where they started the day before. The Federals were pushed back to the bank of the Rappahannock and to the safety from attack provided by the Federal artillery on Stafford Heights north of the river,

However, the fighting on May 4th was far from over. General Early charged the hills immediately to the west of the Telegraph Road. The attack was nearly successful but was stymied by a threat from the right flank. Pendleton felt that Early's division, consisting of 8,400 men by this point, was in a dangerous position given the massing of Federal troops on both sides of the river. He sent an aide to McLaws requesting assistance. But the remainder of the offensive languished. Upriver, Sedgwick pulled back towards the river in a horseshoe shaped line protecting his escape across the Rappahannock over some fords. McLaws failed to attack. He believed that General Anderson's division was to join him, and he waited in vain for its arrival before attacking. He did not even bother to advise Early of the change of his plans, nor did he scout out the location of Sedgwick's lines. When Lee arrived on the scene at mid-day his anger at the lack of initiative by McLaws was evident. Lee visited his generals and organized an assault on Sedgwick's forces for late that afternoon.

Pendleton now worked to cooperate in the plan to launch McLaws and Early at Sedgwick's horseshoe defense line to prevent him from re-crossing the river in safety. He placed some batteries "as far forward as practicable, between the Telegraph Road and Guest's house, and sought, but could not find a fit position for the Whitworth." The Confederate attack began in the gathering gloom of late afternoon. Pendleton felt that the batteries "rendered some service in annoying the enemy while Hoke's brigade made its brilliant charge," but the Confederates were repulsed. So far as Pendleton was concerned, "Nothing further was left to the artillery on this line." Sedgwick pulled out of his defenses overnight and successfully re-crossed the Rappahannock to safety. On the night of the 4th the Federal troops re-crossed the Rappahannock at Fredericksburg and on May 5th, Fredericksburg was re-occupied by Barksdale. The Chancellorsville campaign reached its anti-climactic conclusion.

*   *   *   *

When it was over Pendleton was exhausted. During the battle he managed to find one to two hours in which to sleep each night and had hardly anything to eat, a situation that he admitted was "too common in the army to be thought of." His artillery, Barksdale, and Early were tasked the next day to keep watch over the crossings from Bank's Ford to below Fredericksburg while the Lee's Army slowly gathered itself. In his report General Lee commented that the artillery on his left flank was skillfully and efficiently managed despite the unfavorable ground (The Wilderness). He also wrote that "The batteries under General Pendleton also acted with great gallantry." Even with this somewhat favorable comment Pendleton's critics attacked him anyway. He was criticized for withdrawing his guns too early, and attacked for leaving them in the battle too long. For the embattled Pendleton it must have been frustrating, he was damned if he did, and damned if he didn't.

It did not help that by comparison E. Porter Alexander conducted himself brilliantly. Utilizing Pendleton's scheme of concentrated Corps artillery firepower, Alexander took advantage of the open area at Hazel Grove in the Wilderness to collect his guns and shell the apex of the Federal defenses until it broke. On the last day, Lee relied on Alexander to similarly concentrate his guns on Sedgwick's forces, and Alexander even used indirect fire to harass the enemy while they moved to safety north of the river. Pendleton received no credit for this use of his idea and his re-organization.

Despite his commendation of Pendleton it appears that Lee was actually displeased with Pendleton's conduct. In September 1863 Pendleton heard rumors that Lee felt Pendleton had withdrawn his guns too quickly from Marye's Heights on May 2nd after Chilton's erroneous order, and that Lee showed his dissatisfaction by turning his back on Pendleton's staff officer. Pendleton asked in writing for an explanation. Lee's reply was an understatement of support:

I think the report of my dissatisfaction at your conduct is given upon small grounds, the statement apparently of your courier, upon whom I turned my back. I must acknowledge I have no recollection of the circumstances, or of anything upon which it could have been based. The guns were withdrawn from the heights of Fredericksburg under general instructions given by me. *It is difficult now to say, with the after knowledge of events, whether these instructions could, at the time, have been better executed, or whether if all the guns had remained in position, as you state there was not enough infantry supports for those retained, more might not have been captured.*
[Italics added.]

In re-occupying Marye's Heights late on May 2nd Pendleton had not sought to have the heavier guns under Nelson returned from their withdrawal towards Richmond as ordered by Chilton. Pendleton felt they had gone too far to return in time to be of assistance, and General Early apparently concurred, saying they would not be needed. It is difficult now to say, but in all probability both generals were correct in their assessment.

Once again the dean of the history of the Army of Northern Virginia, Douglas Southall Freeman, posited that Pendleton fell short in his duties. Freeman saw Lee's commendation as meant for the battery commanders and not for Pendleton personally. He also noted that Jubal Early's commendation of Pendleton was similarly casual. There were unofficial criticisms that on the 3rd Pendleton made faulty dispositions in the defense of Salem Church but the records show he was not on the battlefield but with Early south on Telegraph Road at the time. Others criticized him for obeying Lee's order as conveyed by Chilton. The truth is that Early and Pendleton objected vigorously to the order but both generals were told to follow the order by Lee's representative. The general feeling against Pendleton was that while not disgracing himself he did not shine either, hardly a fair test.

Freeman also wrote that Lee sought to replace Pendleton after the battle with Major General Arnold Elzey. Pendleton would have been sent down to the II Corps to command the Corps Reserve Artillery after Crutchfield was severely wounded at

220

Chancellorsville. It would not have been legal to do so. The highest field artillery rank remained Brigadier General throughout the war, so Elzcy would have had to accept a demotion. If true, the logic behind the request is lost in the mists of time. According to Freeman, President Davis rejected the request out of hand.

These criticisms of Pendleton at Chancellorsville are without any merit. It was Pendleton's misfortune to be present when the artillery was withdrawn before Sedgwick's attack. As one historian noted, "Not only was he absolutely free of blame on this occasion, but as has been shown and testified to by Gen. Early, who was with him, the guns were removed over the protest of the Chief of Artillery. The withdrawal on this occasion was the result of a serious mistake on the part of one of Gen. Lee's own staff officers." The critics ignored the fact that Early, who was in fact the commanding general at Fredericksburg, also pulled out his troops at the same time. The criticism was simply the manifestation of an overall dissatisfaction with the older, pedantic, and generally absent artillery general. Freeman concluded that all of Lee's misgivings about Pendleton from the Peninsular Campaign and Shepherdstown deepened but did not yet provide a positive reason to warrant Pendleton's removal.

Pendleton was aware of the attacks. His staff officers were constantly circulating through the Army on behalf of the administration of the Field Artillery Corps, and they were fully aware of the attacks on their commander. They told him what they heard and insisted he bring it to Lee's attention to defend himself from such "gross injustices." When Pendleton wrote to Lee in October 1863 he received the reply noted above, hardly a staunch defense of his artillery chief. This left Pendleton unhappy and discouraged. He wrote Anzelotte, "Few men have worked these two years as I have! And yet poor the reward if the applause of men were my motive!"

*   *   *   *

Thomas J. Jackson, the immortal "Stonewall", came down with pneumonia while recovering from severe wounds and died at Guiney's Station on May 10, 1863. The day before Pendleton rode out to Moss Neck with Sandie for a visit, but on that mournful Sunday Sandie was with his dying General. Jackson awoke briefly and greeted the grieving young man with "unfailing courtesy." Jackson asked who was preaching that morning and Sandie replied that it was Mr. Lacy as previously ordered. Sandie added, "The

221

whole army is praying for you, General." "Thank God. They are very kind," Jackson replied. "It is the Lord's Day. My wish is fulfilled. I have always desired to die on a Sunday." When Sandie walked out of the house his body was racked with sobbing. In Jackson's last feverish moments his sub conscience returned to Sandie, "Hasten the columns! Pendleton, you take charge of that! Where's Pendleton? Tell him to push up the column!" He finished with the famous, "Let us cross over the river and rest under the shade of the trees."

Lee sent Sandie Pendleton to Richmond to accompany Jackson on his final journey. There Jackson lay in state in the Capitol. Sandie accompanied the casket to Lexington using the James River Canal, arriving on the 14th. The next day the VMI Corps of Cadets placed Jackson's casket to lie in state in his old classroom protected by an Honor Guard. The following day the Cadets bore Jackson's remains to the Presbyterian Church where he had worshipped and afterwards on to the Lexington town cemetery to lie in rest with his first wife. The funeral procession was accompanied by local politicians, educators, clergymen, members of the Rockbridge Battery, the Bible Society of Rockbridge, and the Franklin Society. The Jackson family traveled by carriage but Sandie walked alongside the casket. After it was over Sandie stayed in town with his family for a few more days.

After Jackson died Pendleton met with the Army's chaplains and addressed them on Jackson's death and the Reverend Lacy described Jackson's last hours. Jackson's death shattered Lee. Lee turned to his old friend and clergyman General Pendleton for comfort, speaking to each other of their religious faith. Lee wept for many days afterwards whenever he spoke of Jackson to Pendleton.

*　　　　*　　　　*　　　　*

As happened after each great Confederate victory it was up to Pendleton to divide the spoils of war. In doing so he reviewed the needs of each battery and the type of guns captured. Furthermore, new Napoleons cast in Richmond were delivered to the Army and needed to be distributed where needed. This time the squeaky wheel was Jeb Stuart. His Horse Artillery had captured guns and wished to keep them. Lee intervened to allow Stuart two of the three rifled guns captured. The other went to Pendleton for distribution. After the distribution was completed the Army of Northern Virginia had 105 rifled guns, 99 Napoleons, 30 howitzers, and 2 "independent" guns, a total of 236 canons of all types outside of the Horse Artillery. Gone were the obsolete small 6-pounders with which the Army began the war. Of this amount the Army Reserve Artillery had sixteen rifled guns, eleven Napoleons, and nine howitzers, a total of only thirty-six guns. Stuart's Horse Artillery had thirty-five guns.

Pendleton found it difficult to achieve exact equity between the Corps artillery battalions. He wrote Lee that, "Some have rifles in excess, others Napoleons. This difficulty dates back to irregular appropriations of captured guns last summer and fall. It has been deemed a less evil to let it remain than to create other difficulties by enforcing an equalization."

Once the Army settled down after the Battle of Chancellorsville, Pendleton embarked on yet another re-organization of the Army's Artillery Corps, one which would have a profound impact on him. The impetus for the changes came from the death of Jackson. His old II Corps was just too large for any other commander, and Lee split it into two Corps. Now the I Corps would be led by Longstreet, the II Corps by Lieutenant General Richard Ewell, and the III Corps by Lieutenant General Ambrose P. Hill. Each Corps was to consist of three infantry divisions and was assigned five battalions of field artillery, with three used at the division level and two kept in reserve.

The I Corps Chief of Artillery was Colonel James B. Walton, although in reality it was his assistant Colonel E. Porter Alexander. With Crutchfield's injury Colonel J. Thompson Brown was appointed the II Corps Chief of Artillery, and the III Corps Chief of Artillery was Colonel R. Lindsay Walker. In making these recommendations Pendleton also noted that promotions in the Field Artillery branch had not kept pace with what the law allowed, "From which it appears that while we have two majors more, we have two brigadier-generals less, five lieutenant-colonels and one colonel less than the law allows; that is, 6 general and field officers less than allowed."

The need to create another Corps Artillery Reserve meant the dissolution of Pendleton's Army Reserve Artillery. As Alexander later noted, "although our reserve under Pendleton had never found the opportunity to render much service, its being discontinued was due to our poverty of guns, not to dissatisfaction with the system." Unsaid was the fact that rarely had the Reserve Artillery ever been given adequate infantry support with which to accomplish its mission, or that many of the field artillery officers preferred to keep Pendleton away from the battlefield. The change also meant that no longer would there be battalions of field artillery waiting in the rear and rarely ever usefully employed. Additionally, no longer would batteries be assigned to a division but to each of the Corps Chiefs of Artillery.

This created a system of three army corps fulfilling the Emperor Napoleon's intentions in organizing his armies. Each Corps was a separate little army taking with it the means and men to supply every need an army might have. It is critical for any historian to fully understand the meaning of this change. There were now three Corps Chiefs of Artillery, each fully responsible to their Corps commander for the tactical command and control of their artillery. They each had no responsibility for the other Corps artillery, and none of them had a superior in the field artillery branch to provide command and control. Their orders came from their Corps commanders.

From this point on Pendleton had no means to influence or command the tactical decisions of the individual Corps artillery chiefs. However, as he noted, he would still be able to influence tactics in individual and independent circumstances where appropriate. We will see in the next campaign instances where Pendleton moved a piece here or there or made suggestions, but we will also see how Lee's orders for artillery actions descended from Lee to the individual Corps commanders, and only then to the individual Corps Chiefs of Artillery. Far too many historians have missed this key point and made it a launching pad for unfair and inaccurate criticism of Pendleton. Lee approved the changes in an order dated June 2, 1863.

No longer would Pendleton have tactical command over artillery units in battle. He, like many others of Lee's staff officers, was now just merely an administrator for the Artillery Corps. For a moment Pendleton was considered as a replacement for Elisha Paxton, the commander of the Stonewall Brigade killed at Chancellorsville. Pendleton shied away from the assignment. He preferred administering the over 4,400 men, 234 guns, and hundreds of horses, wagons, forges, etc., than to keep up with an infantry brigade in the field. He preferred to have no special charge, and be allowed to superintend the artillery and only direct it in battle "such portions as may most need my personal attention." He concluded,

"This is a better arrangement, I think. My work will be much as it has been, but freer, as none of the petty details of one or two battalions will require my care."

Of course, the administrative needs of the artillery were always among Pendleton's biggest concerns. Immediately after the conclusion of the Chancellorsville campaign he ordered that all of the battery commanders report on their status, and to otherwise re-fit and prepare for the next campaign. One of the big problems, not surprisingly, was a shortage of horses, especially with the universal use of larger field guns. He made a tremendous effort to maintain the batteries at a serviceable strength, in guns, men, and horses. Many of the Corps Artillery Chiefs reported that if they had more horses they could add more guns to their organization. The II Corps Chief Colonel Brown reported he sent out "two men from each battalion to buy horses, amply supplied with money, with directions also to offer as inducement the sale of condemned horses in any neighborhood where horses can be bought." Pendleton also chided battalion commanders who failed to separate themselves from their previously assigned divisions to find new camps with better forage. Guns without adequate horses were to remain at the front since they could not be moved easily. By the end of the month no more than an additional 400 horses were incorporated into the artillery.

Pendleton chastised Alexander about his management of horses, writing "Horses are our great difficulty. You know this so well that suggestion as to the best care of yours must be almost superfluous..... You were mistaken in supposing I would favor another company at the expense of one of yours." Pendleton and Lee also criticized Alexander for moving too far south to find grazing, a criticism Lee would later recall to Alexander's cost. However, given the expense in horseflesh to move closer to the Army, and finding sufficient forage where he was located, Pendleton told Alexander he was better off staying there. Pendleton also mentioned that the distance between Alexander and the Army would hamper Alexander's participation in a Board of Officers considering the Army's artillery ammunition supply.

The ammunition used by the field artillery also remained a problem. Fuses did not always work well, and exploded at times a second later, having already passed over their target. The fuses were handmade and there was no uniformity in production. For example, shells for the Parrots were miscast so they exploded closer to the muzzle of the gun and not above the enemy. Other shells passed over the enemy and exploded over the enemy's rear area. On June 8th Lee and Pendleton created a special Board of Officers to investigate the situation to be headed by the experienced Alexander. The Board was to report each month on the "material, ammunition, and any other matters concerning the Artillery, and to make recommendations for its improvement." It was also "compile range tables for the various types of guns in use."

          *   *   *   *

Through May 1863 Sandie continued to grieve the loss of Jackson. He questioned whether it would be better to be assigned to a line unit. Pendleton told him that he had better "do his duty in the post assigned by Providence." The Pendletons continued to worry about Sandie's faith, "we are in danger of worldly elation for Sandie, and my prayer to God is not to expose him to vanity, ambition, pride, or worldliness in any form, but to give him an humble, godly, faithful heart."

On June 1st Sandie fell seriously ill with dysentery. Pendleton visited him often, finding him in a camp tent since no houses could be found to lodge him. Pendleton moved Sandie to his own tent and continued to search for a homeowner unfearful of catching the disease and sympathetic enough to allow him to heal. One woman Pendleton asked was "a selfish, hard hearted creature....a seventy-six year old, vulgar & worthless as humanity can well be without degrading vice." Ultimately, Sandie was allowed to recover in the same room where his hero General Jackson died. By the time the Army began to move again he was able to ride in an ambulance or occasionally ride on horseback.

By June Lee's Army was recuperated, re-equipped, and re-organized. He had 80,000 well equipped, well officered, and highly motivated men at his command. By June 5th Lee's new invasion of the North was already underway. Pendleton began that day visiting Ewell's headquarters with Bishop John of Virginia. In the midst of a service he was summoned to deal with a new threat. Hooker threw a pontoon bridge across the Rappahannock under the cover of a heavy artillery barrage. Pendleton spent that evening and into the following morning working with the new III Corps Chief of Artillery in adjusting the positioning of the guns. By mid-day it was apparent that the Federal move was a feint and not the start of a new attack. Lee's staff, including the now troop-less Pendleton, decamped and headed north, arriving in Culpeper early on Sunday morning, June 7th. Pendleton was off on a campaign for which, even though he had no command or control, he is still criticized today for the misuse of Lee's field artillery.

DRAGGING ARTILLERY THROUGH THE MUD.—[Sketched by A. R. Waud.]

11. "SO MIGHTY AN ARTILLERY CONTEST HAS PERHAPS NEVER BEEN WAGED."

[GETTYSBURG, 1863]

The fear of the Lord is the instruction of wisdom; and before honor is humility.

Proverbs 15:33, King James Version

I will say unto God my rock, Why hast thou forgotten me? Why go I mourning because of the oppression of the enemy?

Psalms 42:9, King James Version

Lee's new invasion of the northern states began with an ill omen. The hubris of the Army of Northern Virginia combined with a hard lesson in the vast improvement of their enemy's ability to wage war bode ill for the future of the Confederacy.

Jeb Stuart was very proud of his cavalry. For the first two years of the war it rode rings around the Federal cavalry and created a record of glorious adventures and victories. Stuart, a dandy all dressed up in finery and plumes, also loved to entertain the ladies and impress the gentlemen. When Stuart's Cavalry Corps arrived at Brandy Station near Culpeper Stuart decided to display his men and horses in lavish style. He invited all the important people in Virginia to come to Brandy Station on June 5th on the Orange & Alexandria

Railroad to watch a grand review of his cavalry. The day concluded with a fine dinner and a lavish dance. Every officer sported a new uniform, and the horses were brushed to perfection. Men and women from all over Virginia arrived by rail and watched the horses and men ride by in review, and then gallop. Some of the cavalry put on charges with blank artillery shells fired overhead creating an atmosphere of actual battle. The crowd was thrilled. That evening the dinner and dance were the most brilliant of the season.

Robert E. Lee was invited to the festivities but could not come as his military duties required attention. However, on the 7th it was announced he would arrive the next day for a proper military review. Lee and his staff, including Pendleton, arrived on horseback to review the entire cavalry corps waiting for him in formation. Lee set a lively pace for the group, but it was unpleasant for Pendleton and some of the others not used to hard riding. Pendleton complained that they "had to sit on our horses in the dust half a day…." Lee enjoyed himself immensely. When the Corps rode by Lee in review the commanding general made certain that there was no galloping, yelling, or shooting as before. He wanted it all saved for the campaign.

The next morning Stuart was packing up camp for the start of the campaign when he received news that Federal cavalry was approaching from Beverly Ford. At first he did not treat the report with any alarm as he was convinced it could not be a major attack. He was shocked into reality when more news arrived that masses of Federal cavalry were also off his right flank and already in possession of Brandy Station. The vaunted Jeb Stuart and his renowned cavalry were caught napping. Cavalry charge after cavalry charge swept over the hills and plains around Brandy Station and at the end of the day Stuart finally beat off the attack. Even so, it was embarrassing for Stuart to be caught by surprise, and it was concerning that the Federal cavalry fought so hard and rode so well. One could say the enemy cavalry, the laughingstock since the war began, was now as good as Stuart's cavalry. The Richmond papers lambasted Stuart for chasing the girls when he should have been on guard. The sensitive Stuart took it very personally, and his compulsion to show off some glorious adventure in the new campaign severely hampered Lee's campaign.

After two years of war the wheel was turning. The Army of Northern Virginia was no longer invincible and superior. Lee's constant preference to launch infantry assaults bled the ranks from Corporal up to Lieutenant General. Too many quality high ranking officers had been lost, and their replacements were but pale imitations. For example, Jackson was replaced by the uncertain Richard Ewell and the chronically ailing A. P. Hill. Furthermore, the North's vast superiority in manpower and industrial strength was asserting itself. The Army of the Potomac shed its reputation as toy soldiers, a parade army, led by incompetent and political generals. Men like Meade, Hancock, Buford, and Reynolds were taking charge of experienced veteran units while commanders like Howard, Slocum, or Sickles lost influence. The next major battle on Northern soil would see a vastly improved Army of the Potomac vying against a weakened but still arrogant Army of Northern Virginia.

         *   *   *   *

Ewell's II Corps led the way down the Shenandoah Valley, pushing the Federals back in battles at Winchester and Berryville. Jenkins' cavalry crossed the Potomac on the 15th with infantry following the next day. The II Corps moved quickly on the western side of the Blue Ridge, and unlike the year before, there was hardly any straggling. Ewell focused on capturing Harrisburg, and he greatly enjoyed his independent command. Longstreet's I Corps followed behind Ewell, but with a course to the east of the Blue Ridge. The two Corps crossed the Potomac on the 25th at Williamsport and Shepherdstown. Hill's III Corps finally pulled out of the trenches at Fredericksburg on the 15th and headed north.

After a week administering the artillery's logistics Pendleton left Culpeper on the 16th with Lee and headed for Berryville just inside the lower Shenandoah Valley. While there Pendleton preached at a service attended by Lee and Longstreet, and gave a parishioner $100 Confederate to buy dry goods for his wife once the Army reached Maryland. He also gathered cherries and delivered them to Lee and his staff. From Berryville Pendleton travelled to Darkesville and Martinsburg, and crossed the river at Williamsport on the 24th. He camped a half mile north of the fords in Maryland. The next day Lee and his staff, with Pendleton in tow, reached Hagerstown, where one soldier found "the men sullen and the women obsequious." Lee needed a guide and some maps, and Pendleton was able to find an old parishioner to assist. On the 26th they rode in a heavy rain into Pennsylvania and camped two miles north of the Mason-Dixon Line. Pendleton proudly observed that the Confederate soldiers behaved well, "Our men are entirely forbearing. No private property taken by violence, no quiet person molested. A great exhibition of forbearance after all the outrage perpetuated by the Yankees on our soil and our friends." The men were "ragged, shoeless, filthy" but "well armed" and "under perfect discipline"

His parishioner returned the $100 as all the shops in Maryland were closed and shuttered. When he could buy anything he was forced to buy at U. S. currency prices with devalued Confederate money. Sandie Pendleton had greater success. Women's shoes seized from a U.S. Army sutler in Winchester were sent to his mother and sisters back in Lexington. When he reached Chambersburg, Sandie paid $75.00 for additional women's apparel for his sisters, mother, and his fiancée Kate.

Meanwhile, so far as the Confederacy was concerned, Jeb Stuart and his cavalry disappeared from the face of the earth. After effectively guarding Lee's movements out of Virginia, Lee gave Stuart discretionary authority to "pass around their army without hindrance…." However, "after crossing the river, you must move on and feel the right of Ewell's Corps." Stuart used this discretion with license to try to reclaim his former glory. Instead of adhering to Ewell after crossing the Potomac, he went hundreds of miles out of the way, feeling towards Washington, and passing through York to finally reach Carlisle on July 1st, where Ewell had been a couple of days earlier. By then the battle at Gettysburg was already underway. He did not return to the Army until late on July 2, 1863. During this entire time Lee had no idea what was happening to his east, the location of the Union Army, or its movements. Lee's last news was that the enemy was still somewhere south of the Potomac.

So it must have been a shock on June 28th when Longstreet's "spy" Harrison appeared in camp announcing that the Federals were not only north of the Potomac, they were not very far away. In addition, Harrison reported that they had a new commander, Major General George Meade, the V Corps commander and like Lee, a veteran West Point Army engineer. Galvanized, Lee issued rapid orders for his Army to concentrate in the area of Chambersburg and Cashtown, a little more than eight miles from Gettsyburg. Two days later Pettigrew's Brigade of Heth's Division, of Hill's III Corps, encountered a Federal cavalry screen while on its way to Gettysburg to collect shoes rumored to be there. Uncertain what to do,

Pettigrew returned to camp. The next day Heth started out with his whole division to gather up the badly needed shoes.

*   *   *   *

At the crack of dawn on July 1st, Heth was on the road to Gettysburg with Archer's Brigade in the van. The day turned out to be warm and little water was found on the route, but otherwise the march was pleasant. Just before reaching Gettysburg they encountered some Federal cavalry videttes, which soon disappeared down the road towards the town. As Heth approached Willoughby Run he shook out two infantry brigades into a battle line, one on each side of the road, and then slowly advanced towards Gettysburg. They were greeted by the rapid fire of the repeating Spencer rifles of Buford's Cavalry Brigade and the infantry rifled muskets of the Iron Brigade of the I Corps spread out along Seminary Ridge. The Confederate brigades were badly mauled and pulled back. Heth decided to wait for assistance before launching a full assault. Pender's Division of Hill's III Corps came up and also went into a battle line preparing to charge. Meanwhile more and more Federal troops from I and XI Corps arrived on the field until they appeared to outnumber the two Confederate divisions. Suddenly, at mid-day, the Federals turned their right flank ninety degrees to face Ewell's II Corps arriving at the battlefield from the north. After Rodes' and Early's divisions of II Corps were fully engaged with the re-adjusted Union line the two divisions from the III Corps on the west attacked.

Pendleton rode with Lee and his staff towards the battlefield. As soon as they passed through the hills west of Gettysburg they could hear the distant sounds of artillery fire:

> Its significance, however, was not then fully understood. It might be only a passing skirmish; it might be more serious. After a brief pause near Cashtown, to see how it would prove, the commanding general, finding the cannonade to continue and increase, moved rapidly forward. I did the same, and, at his request, rode near him for instructions. Arriving near the crest of an eminence more than a mile west of the town, dismounting and leaving horses under cover, on foot we took position

232

overlooking the field. It was, perhaps, 2 o'clock, and the battle was raging with considerable violence.

After watching the battle for a while Lee asked if Pendleton could place batteries so that they could enfilade the Federal lines. Pendleton immediately placed a cordon of guns running from Fairfield Road to Rock Creek. The battery to the furthest right was placed without infantry support and came under fire immediately. There was some delay as infantry was placed protecting the exposed battery. Pendleton's placement was nearly complete when the Confederates launched their assault. The Union lines folded and the enemy fled back through the town onto some hills on the other side. Cemetery Hill, just southeast out of town, was at the end of a long ridge reaching back south to two larger hills, Big Round Top and Little Round Top. Just east of Cemetery Hill was the even higher Culp's Hill. Major General Otis Howard nominally commanded the routed Federals on the hills but made no definitive move to fortify the positions. His panicked troops would not tolerate another Confederate onslaught. During the rout of the Federal troops Pendleton assisted in placing artillery batteries for the most effective shelling of the frightened men.

Pendleton sent some of his staff officers to scout a road heading south into some woods on the Confederate right. Based on their report Pendleton moved batteries to a position on Seminary Ridge, a long ridge running from the west of town towards the south paralleling Cemetery Ridge. From these positions the guns could shell the routed Federals as they milled about on Cemetery Hill and Ridge where the Federal artillery was already setting up. However, Confederate Major General Ramseur asked them not to fire as it would bring Federal artillery counter-battery fire down on his men waiting in the nearby woods. Afterwards Pendleton and his staff scouted Seminary Ridge as far south as the Emmitsburg Pike through the Peach Orchard and Devil's Den. On his return Pendleton chatted with Colonel Walker, the III Corps Chief of Artillery, about what he had seen and done. He suggested Walker bring his guns forward. Then Pendleton rode back to Lee's headquarters to present a fully detailed oral report to Lee on what he had seen. He emphasized to Lee that the road going south could be used to flank the Federal left as it then existed.

When he concluded his report Pendleton rode around to Ewell's II Corps on the left flank of the Army facing Culp's Hill and Cemetery Hill. During his visit the II Corps Chief of Artillery Colonel Brown was absent searching for a means to place guns on a "wooded height commanding the enemy's right." Pendleton inspected the ground in front of Ewell's troops and found it much less "difficult" at the southern end of Cemetery Hill than that faced on the right by Hills' Corps. He later reported this as well to Lee. According to Alexander, "Gen. Pendleton declared that Lee told him when he reported the result of his second reconnaissance that he had already ordered Longstreet to attack by way of the Peach Orchard at sunrise the next morning, and requested him to re-examine the ground in that direction at dawn."

Alexander wrote this commentary after the controversy created by Jubal Early and Pendleton following Lee's death during which this order to attack at dawn was first mentioned. Longstreet and most officers from Lee's staff then living denied it. We will delve into this controversy in its proper time, but will note here Douglas S. Freeman's conclusion that the only scenario that does not run counter to any of the evidence is that Longstreet had already left the headquarters for the night when Lee voiced his opinion to Pendleton.

Lee's style of command was to give his Corps commanders goals and allow them to create the means to achieve them. When the Federals were routed through town Lee sent a message to Ewell to pursue and capture Culp's Hill and Cemetery Hill "if he thought it possible." Either Ewell was unaware of Lee's style, or he was afraid to make a mistake, but the attack was never made. Ewell's staff officers and division commanders were appalled. Assistant Chief of Staff Captain Sandie Pendleton burst out with, "Oh, for the presence and inspiration of Old Jack for just one hour." Ewell was concerned that Rodes' division had been shattered in the fighting that day and Johnson's was not yet on the field. Nor had the Corps Chief of Artillery located any satisfactory positions for his guns. When Lee arrived later that night Ewell told him he could not attack as the enemy had dug in, but that if Hill attacked on the right in the morning he would support him.

Had Ewell attacked the hills early in the evening of the 1st before the Union defenses were set he should have been able to sweep the Union Army all the way down Cemetery Ridge. His delay meant that the Confederates could no longer easily seize possession of the high terrain on the Union right. While Ewell dithered Federal Major General Winfield S. Hancock arrived on the battlefield and took charge of the Union lines. He ordered the troops to dig in and sent reinforcements for the defenses up on Culp's Hill. From this point on, despite some close calls on the 2nd, any hope of a Confederate victory at Gettysburg slipped away.

Lee turned his focus to his right flank. He expected Longstreet's I Corps to arrive early in the morning since they were encamped a few miles away. But there was no way they could be in position for a dawn attack. Moving troops along unknown roads and woods in the dark and then deploying them for an assault is a nearly impossible task. Longstreet urged Lee to slip around the Federal left and build a defensive line for Meade to attack. While tempting Lee had other concerns; his supply line ran stretched back to Virginia; his cavalry was absent and he really had no idea what was around the Federal left; he could not remain on the defensive in a foreign land; and he could not place his Army where it could be cut off from Virginia. Lee did not explain any of this to Longstreet, he probably felt it obvious to a Lieutenant General, and just refused his request.

Armistead Long of Lee's staff rode the evening of the 1st to the right flank of the Confederate Army and reached the same conclusion as Pendleton, that the way was open that night to out-flank Meade on his left. Lee knew he had to attack somewhere as he told Major General Hood, "The enemy is here, and if we do not whip him, he will whip us." After visiting Ewell, Lee returned to his headquarters and announced to Longstreet and Hill that they would attack as early in the morning as possible, but did not say where. He advised both Hill and Longstreet to "make the necessary preparations and be ready for prompt action" the next day. When Longstreet left very late that night no decision had yet been made as to where the attack would be focused.

Lee held the outside line of a long curve, his Army was outnumbered eight to five in men, the Federals had fifteen men per yard over their shorter three mile long line while Lee's outer lines ran for five miles. In artillery Meade had 354 guns to Lee's 272 guns, 118 guns per mile for the Federals and only 54 per mile for Lee. If Lee pulled divisions out of the line anywhere on the exterior curve to create a mass of infantry to use in an assault it would dangerously thin his line. Yet, Lee definitely decided to attack as early as possible in the morning. For Lee and his staff, including Pendleton, the night's rest was very short indeed.

*   *   *   *

After marching all day to reach Gettysburg McLaws' and Hood's divisions of Longstreet's I Corps, and its field artillery, camped about four miles west of town. Lee's expectations of an early morning attack assumed they would move forward in the darkness through unknown terrain to find their jump off positions in the dark or early dawn, which was unrealistic. Still, they could be placed for an attack by no later than mid-morning. At 1:00 a.m. word reached the camp they were expected to advance in the morning. After breakfast and coffee the troops moved forward and halted about 9:00 a.m. still a mile short of Seminary Ridge to await orders from Longstreet.

Lee was up before dawn still undecided about his plans for the day. He sent two staff officers, one of them Captain S. R. Johnston, to the right on a reconnaissance mission. Longstreet was up by 3:00 a.m. He met Lee early on Seminary Ridge for the first time that morning and once again objected to any attack. He again urged a move to the right to flank Meade's left. Once more Lee turned him down. Lee, with a growing concern about the strength of the Union position on Cemetery Ridge, wanted to attack and rout the Federal Army before it grew any stronger.

When Pendleton awoke "at the first blush of dawn" on the 2nd he noticed that the Federal troops had strongly entrenched Cemetery and Culp's Hills overnight. In his report two months later Pendleton said that he rode out on an inspection of the lines with Colonel Armistead Long, a veteran artillery officer, and Captain R. S. Johnston, an engineer, both of Lee's staff. As with nearly everything involving Gettysburg and Pendleton there is some controversy about this claim. Pendleton wrote close to the time of the events concerned. Most of those who later commented on it waited until many years later to do so. Pendleton was a truthful man, although as Douglas S. Freeman pointed out he "never minimized his exploits." In all probability, Pendleton rode with Johnston part of the way since Johnston scouted all the way to Little Round Top without finding any enemies, and returned by 7:00 a.m. Long did not mention a companion on his inspection ride, but it is likely that the two set off from Lee's headquarters together as they were on the same mission to inspect the Army's artillery positions. Along the way Pendleton made minor adjustments to some of the battery's locations.

Pendleton went to "the farthest occupied point on the right and front," which would have been an artillery position in Wilcox's Brigade of Anderson's Division of Hill's III Corps. In other words, he probably did not venture any further south than the area of Spangler's Woods, a point a half mile north of north of where the Seminary Ridge crosses the Emmitsburg Pike. He then "surveyed the enemy's position toward some estimate of the ground and the best mode of attack. So far as judgment could be formed from such a view, assault on the enemy's left by our extreme right might succeed, should the mountain there offer no insuperable obstacle. To attack on that side, if practicable, I understood to be the purpose of the commanding general." On his way back to headquarters he passed along the road through a ravine behind Seminary Ridge he noticed the night before. He and his staff came across "two armed dismounted cavalrymen," probably from Buford's cavalry brigade operating that morning near the Round Tops. The cavalrymen were surprised and immediately surrendered to Pendleton's staff and sent to the rear as prisoners. Nearly thirty years later Johnston recalled capturing four Federal troopers on his way back, so perhaps it was this last leg of the ride during which Pendleton and Johnston rode together.

Riding back near Lee's headquarters on Seminary Ridge Pendleton crossed the Fairfield Road and looked back towards the enemy lines. From this vantage point he could see that "Between this point and the Emmitsburg road, the enemy's cavalry were seen in considerable force, and, moving up along that road toward the enemy's main position, bodies of infantry and artillery, accompanied by their trains." He sent messages to Lee reporting that he found no "insuperable" difficulties in attacking on the right but that he saw "large masses of the enemy's infantry in the rear of the hostile line." Pendleton urged both Longstreet and Lee that prompt action should be taken to make an assault on the Federal left. Colonel Long's report agreed with Pendleton's assessment. However, Captain Johnston, who claimed to have ridden all the way to the Round Tops, reported no large enemy forces in the area.

After his discussion with Longstreet Lee left headquarters around 9:00 a.m. to visit his left flank and confer with General Ewell. He conferred once more with Ewell and Early about attacking the hills on the Union right flank. They discouraged Lee and urged that Longstreet attack on the right. Lee rode back to his camp where he received the reports from Long and Pendleton about the conditions on his right flank. Lee wondered why there had been no assault yet on his right flank, and decided to seek Longstreet out for an explanation. Lee finally caught up with Longstreet around 11:00 a.m. and expressed disappointment that Longstreet had not yet attacked. Having lost his patience Lee deviated from his normal practice and explicitly ordered that the attack take place on the right and in a certain manner, a rolling oblique attack in echelon all across the front.

Longstreet asked Pendleton to show his Corps Chief of Artillery Colonel Alexander "the best view he then could of the front." Pendleton volunteered to personally escort Alexander and took him to "the advanced point of observation previously visited," presumably the furthest right artillery battery. Its approach was now "more hazardous from the fire of the enemy's sharpshooters so that special caution was necessary in making the desired observation." They arrived just as portions of Hill's III Corps pushed the Federal scouting parties and skirmishers out of some woods behind them and to their right. "These woods having been thus cleared of the enemy, some view of the ground beyond them, and much farther to the right than had yet been examined, seemed practicable. I therefore rode in that direction, and, when about to enter the woods, met the commanding general, en route himself for a survey of the ground." By now Pendleton and his companions were riding beyond the protection of Wilcox's Brigade, the unit furthest to the right in the Army at that moment. With the constant and nearby firing by Federal sharpshooters they proceeded with caution. With Wilcox riding "shotgun" Pendleton rode to "the farm-house at the summit, where the cross-road from Fairfield, &c., emerges."

Longstreet had only two divisions near the battlefield on the 2nd, those of Hood and McLaws. Pickett's division was still coming up. Since the I Corps officers and staff were still unfamiliar with the area they required guides to take them to their positions. Captain S. R. Johnston, Lee's staff officer, led them to a point in the road where the column was visible to the enemy. The entire column of two divisions reversed course and returned towards the Army's center. When the column reversed track to return to the right flank Pendleton volunteered his staff as guides. They took the ravine road scouted by Pendleton that morning as it was out of the view of the Federal Army. "Members of my staff were also dispatched to remedy, as far as practicable, the delay." Pendleton also assisted Alexander in placing the artillery. As the artillery deployed it was targeted by Federal guns. Pendleton scouted out spots where the artillery might be better protected but ultimately it was Alexander, as I Corps Chief of Artillery, who made the placements. In assisting Alexander Pendleton saw the Union Army waiting 500 yards away for an attack.

Lee's plan was to place the I Corps in a position to attack obliquely across and down the Emmitsburg Pike towards the center of the Federal line on Cemetery Ridge. Each brigade and each division would attack by echelon, which meant that Hood on the far right would attack first with his furthest right brigade, followed slightly to the left by his second brigade, and so forth. Once Hood committed then the next division would similarly attack. This attack was to include all of the I Corps on the field (Hood and McLaws) and portions of Hill's III Corps including the divisions of Anderson and Pender. On the left Ewell was to attack with Early's and Rodes's divisions.

Douglas S. Freeman questioned why the Confederate III Corps artillery did not participate with Alexander in finding a single point on Cemetery Ridge to target with the guns. The reason is not the lack of coordination suggested by Freeman but the nature of Lee's plan of attack. There was no *point d' appui* to target, rather there was a wide scale frontal assault planned. The attack was to start on the far right and move slowly, brigade by brigade, to the left. If this was an error the fault lies with Lee.

But Lee's plan was already obsolete. Federal troops had occupied Little Round Top shortly after S. R. Johnston's scouting trip in the early morning hours. Of greater immediate importance, McLaws' line of advance had been occupied by Union General Sickles' III Corps.

Union Major General Daniel Sickles was a dandy, ladies' man, patent lawyer, and politician all rolled up into one. Flamboyant and controversial after his acquittal for shooting his wife's lover, he had no military training but finagled a high ranking commission from the Lincoln government all the same as a prominent pro-war Democrat and recruiter. When he arrived on the battlefield late on July 1st he was ordered by Hancock to defend the southern slope of

Cemetery Ridge where it almost levels out before reaching the Round Tops. On the morning of the 2nd he looked out across the fields and thought that he was not in the right spot. If you go to Gettysburg and stand where he stood it is easy to understand why he felt the need to advance into the Peach Orchard. From that low point on Cemetery Ridge one has every sense that the Peach Orchard is a higher and more commanding ground. So, at about 2:00 p.m. that afternoon, Sickles moved his entire Corps, with bands playing, drums rolling, and flags flying up to the Peach Orchard and the Emmitsburg Pike. Some of the experienced Union officers recognized Sickles' error right away. Sickles had extended the Federal line out at an angle and left an exposed salient. Hancock told an aide, "Wait a moment you'll see them tumbling back."

Now Sickles sat astride McLaws' line of attack towards the Cemetery Ridge. McLaws asked to cancel or to re-direct the assault. On the far right of the line Hood had similar doubts. His line of advance would run right in front of and nearly parallel to the Federal troops on Little Round Top. His men would be attacked on their right flank during the whole charge. Hood asked for permission to charge to the right around Little Round Top where no Federals had been seen. But Longstreet was pouting and uncooperative. He disagreed with Lee's order to attack and because of Lee's explicit order felt that he had no choice in the matter. As he told Hood, "We must obey the orders of General Lee." However, every American Army officer is taught, including in the mid-19th Century, that when the military situation changes and the original order is no longer applicable the officer must use his discretion to alter, cancel or seek clarification of the order with an explanation. Longstreet did none of these things. Despite the proximity of Lee, Longstreet ordered an attack now designed to fail. Furthermore, contrary to Lee's expectation, Longstreet did not provide any guidance to his commanders as to how to launch their attacks. Consequently, the attack tended to go more directly against the Federal lines than the oblique assault intended by Lee. Hood angled some of his men to his right to guard from a flank attack. This is the group that attacked the 20th Maine on Little Round Top. The rest charged the main enemy lines.

The assault commenced about 4:00 p.m. Hood's attack quickly bogged down into confusion, exacerbated when Hood was grievously wounded. McLaws swept Sickles out of the Peach

Orchard and sent his III Corps "tumbling back." Anderson's division of Hill's Corps was able to actually reach Cemetery Ridge, but once there realized it was receiving no help and were under heavy by Federal troops. The brigades under General Posey and General Mahone flinched and failed to advance. Anderson was soon driven off the ridge and the attack failed. The entire effort was uncoordinated and spastic without any effort by Longstreet to control events. As Douglas S. Freeman noted, the chaos resembled the confusion caused by the inexperienced officer and staff corps during the Peninsular Campaign. Pendleton watched the attack from the area of the III Corps, occasionally venturing forward to observe the impact of the artillery fire.

On the left Ewell similarly launched an uncoordinated assault. His guns opened up at 4:00 p.m. and an assault was made by only half of Early's division against Culp's Hill. Rodes' attack on Cemetery Hill really never commenced. One of Early's brigades was able to cling to a position atop Culp's Hill, and was still there when nightfall ended the battle. From his vantage point in the center Pendleton could see that the Federal artillery was massed on Cemetery Hill. "Thus," Pendleton wrote in his report, "stood affairs at nightfall, the 2d: On the left and in the center, nothing gained; on the right, batteries and lines well advanced, the enemy meanwhile strengthening himself in a position naturally formidable and everywhere difficult of approach."

*   *   *   *

After two days of ferocious battle both armies paused to recuperate. For the field artillery this meant watering and feeding men and horses, and re-loading the gun limbers and caissons with new ammunition from the ordnance trains. Each type of gun required a unique set of ammunition. Each Corps' artillery was supplied with ammunition from that Corps' individual ordnance train. When the Corps ordnance train ran low on ammunition, it could replenish its supply of ammunition from the Army ordnance wagons. The Corps ordnance trains and the Army ordnance wagons were under the command of an Ordnance Corps officer, not a Field Artillery Corps officer. All along the Confederate lines the individual batteries re-positioned, re-organized, and sent off for new supplies of ammunition. When the ammunition arrived at each battery the shells, fuses, and primers had to be unboxed and sorted for each gun, limber, and caisson. Once this was accomplished the men could try to sleep.

Each artillery piece carried with it in its caissons and limbers into Pennsylvania a supply of 130 to 150 rounds of shells, including a number of canister rounds used for targeting enemies charging the guns. Each Corps ordnance train carried another 100 shells per gun. Each gun could fire between 30 and 100 shells per hour. The Army's ordnance wagon train carried additional rounds. The supply line ran all the way back to Staunton, Virginia, 181 miles away. Following two days of fierce combat, and given the very long and exposed supply line unprotected by Stuart's cavalry, the ammunition for the artillery was quickly running out. The Corps ordnance trains had mostly canister shells left to use against infantry and needed to replenish their stock from the Army wagon trains.

Lee decided on the night of the 2nd that he would attack Meade in his defensive positions again the next day, and so advised A. P. Hill and Ewell, but not Longstreet. He wished to launch a two prong offensive on his two flanks by Ewell and Longstreet, with Hill left in support. Separately, he told Pendleton to make sure "the artillery along our entire line was to be prepared for opening, as early as possible on the morning of the 3d, a concentrated and destructive fire, consequent upon which a general advance was to be made. The right, especially, was, if practicable, to sweep the enemy from his stronghold on that flank." However, Pendleton was never tasked with arranging the artillery and its targeting for the assault. That would be the task of each Corps Chief of Artillery.

The sun rose over the battlefield on the July 3rd promising another warm, muggy summer day. The dead men and horses, others wounded, lay bloating and strewn about the landscape. The Confederates sensed that the day could decide the outcome of their invasion of the North, and perhaps the war. When Lee met Longstreet early that morning Longstreet continued his opposition to any form of attack, and suggested once more they move around Meade's left flank. Longstreet sent scouts out to his right flank to explore the opportunities that might be there and instructed his staff to write orders for such a move. Lee rejected the idea and asked Longstreet to make the attack with his entire Corps now that Pickett's small division of 4,800 troops had arrived. Longstreet demurred. The divisions used the day before were torn to shreds and one of its commanders severely wounded. If they were

242

withdrawn it would open Lee's right to a flank attack. Lee gave Longstreet command of two of Hill's divisions instead; Pender's, with a temporary commander after Pender was wounded the day before, and Heth's, which had been torn up in the battle on the first day. On paper the charge would include 15,000 men, in reality it was more like 12,000. Longstreet protested that no 15,000 men alive could succeed in charging an entrenched enemy for 1,400 yards over open fields. Lee overruled him. With the change in the composition of those involved in making the charge, Lee agreed to move the point of attack from the right flank to the center of the enemy line along Cemetery Ridge where a clump of trees could be seen on the horizon.

Lee wanted as much of the Army's artillery as possible to make a prolonged bombardment before the charge with the intent of driving the Federals either off the ridge or causing chaos and dis-organization among them. Of course, the howitzers were useless for this purpose as they only fired indirectly at closer targets. Lee hoped to have about 143 guns from I and III Corps artillery firing at the clump of trees. Only some of the artillery officers involved then realized that at no time during the war had Confederate artillery driven Federal artillery off the field.

After receiving orders for the attack from Lee, Longstreet appointed Colonel Alexander, his Corps Chief of Artillery, as the "director of artillery" for the upcoming assault. Longstreet also instructed him to coordinate the bombardment with the adjacent III Corps Chief of Artillery but there is no indication Alexander did so. He had enough on his plate. Alexander was up by 3:00 a.m. positioning the batteries in the dark, unable to be sure exactly where the enemy lines lay.

Pendleton was up early as well, and in the company of Colonel Long rode the entire length of the lines inspecting the artillery preparations. He found that Alexander needed little encouragement or advice, although he did suggest re-positioning some of the batteries, later noting "there appeared little room for improvement, so judiciously had they been adjusted." Pendleton reminded each of the battery and battalion commanders that ammunition was low and that as little as possible should be wasted. It was probably at this time he also passed along the location of the Corps and Army ordnance wagons for re-supply. Alexander noted that he received "quite specific" orders from both Longstreet and

Pendleton, which were "carried out to the letter." They were identical with the usual practice; cripple the enemy as much as possible with an effective cannonade and advance the artillery to provide support to the infantry once the attack succeeded.

Pendleton and Long also visited the II and III Corps artillery positions in the center and left and provided similar warnings and suggestions. Pendleton noted that "each group having specific instructions from its chief" there was little for him to do. Pendleton also made sure each Corps ordnance trains were positioned in the best possible location. During his visit to the III Corps Pendleton was told that it had Richardson's battery of nine 12-pounder howitzers which could not be used and offered it to Pendleton. Pendleton, in turn, offered it to Alexander, who placed it in a hollow behind the lines so as to advance and support the infantry after the charge. When Pendleton completed his mission the positions of the artillery in the II and III Corps were essentially unchanged from the day before. The exception was the massing of the batteries of the I Corps along the ridge at the Peach Orchard. Alexander placed eighty-three of Longstreet's guns, eight covering the right flank, and the remaining seventy-five guns were placed in a 1,300 yard staggered line running from the Peach Orchard to the northeast corner of Spangler's Woods. Alexander spread the batteries out so they were not clumped together providing the Federal artillery with targets. Oddly, the Federal guns were mostly silent while the Confederates deployed their batteries. Other than an occasional shot, to which the Confederates did not respond, the lines were quiet. Afterwards Alexander wondered if the enemy remained silent to encourage the Confederates to attack.

There was no coordination between the various Corps Chiefs of Artillery. Each pursued their own idea as to the best use of their guns. This was not Pendleton's fault. Both he and the individual Corps commanders passed along Lee's instructions. As Douglas S. Freeman pointed out, following the recent changes in the command structure Pendleton had no legal command authority to order compliance other than his lowly rank as a one star general, and he lacked the prestige in the Army to make the officers want to otherwise obey him. In any event, before the bombardment Lee and Longstreet also rode along the lines to make sure the guns were properly positioned and changed nothing.

Pickett's men woke up at dawn and by 9:00 a.m. filed into their positions behind Seminary Ridge. While Longstreet slowly assembled his men for the charge Lee's plans once again began to go awry. On the far left Early's lone brigade atop Culp's Hill came under intense artillery and infantry fire. Despite support from Johnson's Division, the Confederates were slowly driven off the hill. During the fight the II Corps artillery provided support, expending a great deal of ammunition. The Federal batteries forced some of the Confederate batteries to abandon their positions or be destroyed. Now on the defensive Ewell could no longer participate in the planned attack on both flanks. In front of the III Corps a group of Federal sharpshooters attacked a farmhouse occupied by Confederates. This small firefight launched a furious artillery exchange, wasting even more of the precious ammunition.

Only three of the ten brigades in the charge were to be from Longstreet's Corps, the rest coming from Hill's Corps. Longstreet's detached and fatalistic attitude affected the manner in which the attack was prepared. For the most part the division commanders were left on their own in forming their men for the attack, and in the end the attack formation was skewed and flawed with a second line ill positioned to provide adequate support to the front line. While Pickett was totally sanguine about his anticipated successful assault, his brigade commanders were pessimistic, calling it a "cul-de-sac of death," or "a desperate thing to attempt." One noted he had reached Cemetery Ridge the day before. The problem was not in getting there, the problem was staying there. Another felt after watching the Battle of Solferino in Italy in 1859 that the minie ball and rifled cannon made infantry charges obsolete.

Lee's plan called for the artillery to quickly follow the infantry so it could set up as soon as possible on Cemetery Ridge to protect the conquered ridgeline. Since the howitzers were useless for the bombardment, Alexander placed them under close cover at the rear of the assault formations with orders to stay until sent to follow the column as it advanced. One of the batteries selected for this task was the Richardson battery offered by Pendleton from the III Corps. The artillery was not to fire over the heads of the charging infantry since the shells were extremely unreliable and could kill more friends than foe.

Alexander found a spot where he watched the bombardment's impact on the Federal lines. He expected that the cannonading should last less than twenty minutes in order to save ammunition. Alexander would signal the bombardment with two shots from a battery of Whitworth rifled guns.

*   *   *   *

At 1:07 p.m. the Whitworths fired, followed by salvo after salvo of cannonading from between 150 and 163 guns. Pendleton wrote that the "salvos by battery being much practiced, as directed, to secure greater deliberation and power." All of the seventy-five guns of the I Corps were joined by sixty-three guns from the III Corps artillery and perhaps twenty-five guns in the II Corps, although they were mostly reduced to using solid shot and firing indirectly as they could not see their target on the other side of Culp's Hill. Some fifty-six guns remained silent, although there is no evidence suggesting their participation would have changed the outcome. Federal artillery all along the line responded. The level of noise was terrific. Pendleton wrote:

> So mighty an artillery contest has perhaps never been waged, estimating together the number and character of guns and the duration of the conflict. The average distance between contestants was about 1,400 yards, and the effect was necessarily serious on both sides. With the enemy, there was advantage of elevation and protection from earthworks; but his fire was unavoidably more or less divergent, while ours was convergent. His troops were massed, ours diffused. We, therefore, suffered apparently much less. Great commotion was produced in his ranks, and his batteries were to such extent driven off or silenced as to have insured his defeat but for the extraordinary strength of his position.

Both sides fired over the heads of their primary targets. For the Confederates the inaccurate shooting was caused by varying fuses, unreliable shells, as well as the tail of the guns digging into the ground with each shot. Smoke from the guns and shells on both sides obscured the targets and made it impossible to ascertain what effect the bombardment was having. Most of the Confederate shelling wreaked havoc on the men in the Union rear lines, killing horses and men of the reserve artillery, support wagons, and troops, and passing through Meade's headquarters; what a contemporary soldier would call the "rear echelon pukes." Meade's efficient Chief of Artillery Henry Hunt noted that "Most of the enemy's projectiles passed overhead, the effect being to sweep all the open ground in our rear, which was of little benefit to the Confederates,—a mere waste of ammunition, for everything there could seek shelter...."

The Federal shells fell on the Confederate rear hitting the ordnance trains and the howitzers left in the rear to follow up the charge. Shells also exploded over Pickett and his waiting columns. Pendleton moved part of Richardson's battery to safety, while Richardson withdrew the rest on his own initiative. Meanwhile, someone else, not Pendleton as some have charged, probably an ordnance officer, pulled the ordnance trains further away from the front lines. They were now too far away to re-supply the artillery. When limbers and wagons went to fetch more shells at the points designated by Pendleton they found nothing.

The firing went on and on.....twenty minutes.....thirty minutes....Alexander began to worry about his ammunition supply. Pendleton observed that the bombardment was starting to have an impact on the Federal line, "Great commotion was produced in his ranks, and his batteries were to such extent driven off or silenced as to have insured his defeat but for the extraordinary strength of his position." Alexander thought that while the Federal guns were not withdrawn, they simply stopped shooting back in order to save ammunition. The bombardment went on.

Pendleton rode out to see why the howitzers and other batteries ordered to follow the charge had not deployed behind the infantry. He discovered that many of the batteries in the bombardment were either out of or getting low on shells. When the ordnance train pulled back it lengthened the time required for each battery to re-fill its caissons. "What was worse, the train itself was very limited, so that its stock was soon exhausted, rendering requisite demand upon the reserve train, farther off. The whole amount was thus being rapidly reduced. With our means, to keep up supply at the rate required for such a conflict proved practically impossible. There had to be, therefore, some relaxation of the protracted fire, and some lack of support for the deferred and attempted advance."

Longstreet assigned to Alexander the authority to decide when the assault should begin. The devolution of Corps level command on a Colonel had an effect on Alexander. He began to doubt the very nature of the assault, and doubted it would succeed. He did not believe the Federals were weakened by the barrage but on the other hand he knew the attack should be made before the ammunition was exhausted. Before the shooting started, Longstreet wrote Alexander that "if the artillery fire does not have the effect to drive off or greatly demoralize [the enemy] so as to make our efforts pretty certain, I would prefer that you should not advise General Pickett to make the charge." After nearly an hour of cannonading Alexander failed to see the Federals either driven off or demoralized, and wrote to Pickett to come immediately as he could not continue to provide artillery support. Pickett went to Longstreet and obtained his nod to approve the assault. Longstreet then rode to where Alexander was observing the impact of his artillery barrage. Alexander repeated that he had insufficient rounds to continue firing and that Pickett had to attack now. Longstreet peremptorily ordered Alexander to stop Pickett and replenish his ammunition supply. Alexander replied, "We can't do that, sir. The train has but little. It would take an hour to distribute it, and meanwhile the enemy would improve all the time." Exasperated Longstreet blurted out, "I don't want to make this charge; I don't believe it can succeed. I would stop Pickett now, but that General Lee has ordered it and expects it." After nearly two hours of firing the guns fell momentarily silent. The die was cast.

Just as Longstreet finished his outburst men in long lines bearing Confederate battle flags emerged from the woods, seven men to a yard on a mile long front. Awaiting them some 1,400 yards away, were six Union infantry brigades, while additional enfilading fire would hit them from left and right as they progressed towards the clump of trees. The advancing columns passed by the exhausted field artillery batteries deployed in their front. As they passed Alexander went from gun to gun to find out how many rounds each gun had remaining. If they had more than fifteen long range shells remaining they were told to limber up and prepare to follow Pickett as support once the infantry held the crest. About one gun in four qualified. The field artillery needed to be careful in going forward too soon. If just one horse in a team is killed, the entire team and gun come to a halt, and this wide open battlefield offered a clear shot at everything on it. Every battery going forward would attract fire from the enemy lines. The rest of the guns were to resume firing well over the heads of the advancing columns until they exhausted their ammunition.

The columns moved forward under fierce firing from the Federal lines, advancing about 100 yards a minute for twenty minutes. As they neared the Emmitsburg Road they stopped to dress their lines while under heavy fire. The formations began to fall apart as they crossed the road. Some of the regiments, struck hard in the flank, ran as fast as they could for the safety of the woods they just departed. But a mass of men charged ahead. Pickett sent back word he would reach the crest and needed reinforcements. When the message reached Longstreet he only advanced Wilcox's Brigade in support. Pickett needed another division at least. His men broke through the Union lines but were too few to beat off the repeated attacks from Federal units rushing to the scene. The Confederates wavered, and then retreated. Seeing the repulse Alexander ceased all firing.

Everyone in the Confederate lines expected Meade to launch a devastating counter attack. As the men streamed past one of the batteries, Pickett stopped to tell the battery commander to save his guns. After the men had stumbled past the artillery Alexander resumed firing once more to forestall any attack. Occasionally, they fired canister when pushy Federal skirmishers drew too near. Some of the batteries that left the field when the charge started now returned with full caissons of ammunition. Others were forced to pull back as their ammunition was exhausted. The guns remained in their advanced deployment until late in the day. What Pendleton later called "the most tremendous artillery conflict ever known thus far on earth" was over. As one Virginia veteran of the charge observed, "we gained nothing but glory and lost our bravest men."

       *   *   *   *

Gettysburg and Pickett's Charge resulted in many criticisms of Lee, Longstreet, Ewell, and Hill, as well as of Pendleton. To keep this chapter on point and short we will address those against Pendleton only.

Most of the time we read that Pendleton as Chief of Artillery should have commanded all the artillery to do something, whether to all fire at a single point, or all fire in unison. Let us quickly dispense with these…. Pendleton was not in charge of the tactical use, command, and control of any of the artillery employed at

Gettysburg. Thus, he could not have pleased those critics come hell or high water.

One criticism is that his reconnaissance on the 1st and/or 2nd day did not go as far as he reported. Actually, he was very accurate in describing what he did. He went as far to the right as the Confederate lines then existed. From there he had a clear view of the terrain between himself and the Round Tops. Another criticism is that he failed to advise Lee that enemy troops were present in this terrain in strength, but he did, and warned Lee that time was running short to take advantage of the weakness of the Federal left. Lee ignored this advice from both Pendleton and Armistead Long, preferring to rely on Captain Johnston's rather improbable report that he rode to the Round Tops and saw no enemy force.

Pendleton is criticized for the use of the artillery on the third day. Yet, Lee placed Longstreet and Alexander in charge of the attack on the right. His plan to attack on the left was abandoned when Ewell's positions were heavily attacked that morning. Pendleton had no authority to coordinate the three Corps Chiefs of Artillery other than as a direct order from Lee or based on a moral leadership Pendleton did not have. It should also be noted that Colonel Armistead Long was Lee's senior staff artillery officer, and the Corps Chiefs of Artillery ignored him as well. Nor should it be forgotten that on July 3, 1863 no one complained that too few guns were employed, and given their inaccuracy, more guns would have made no difference. As for positioning the guns on the second or third day, Long and Pendleton, both senior artillery officers, examined their placement and approved of it. On the third day Longstreet and Lee also examined the placement of the batteries and approved.

It was not Pendleton's position to command where the attack should be made. That was entirely up to the commanding general. So, he could not have moved the focus of the attack on either the second or third day as some suggest. Nor was he responsible for the movements of the Corps ordnance trains with the shells to re-supply the guns firing in the front line. When the Federal counter-battery fire shells rained down behind Seminary Ridge landing amongst these wagons full of explosives, someone had the good sense to move them. No one knows who ordered them moved, not even Pendleton, but they were probably moved by the ordnance officers in charge. However, the ordnance officers should have advised the Corps Chiefs of Artillery of their actions and failed to do so.

Pendleton is faulted for moving five of Richardson's nine guns out of harm's way as well. It was the right thing to do, although one critic says he should have notified Alexander. However, Alexander found out somehow, and it may have been from Pendleton. Richardson took it upon himself to remove the rest to safety. Pendleton is also faulted for not advancing guns in support of the infantry charge. This criticism arises from a failure to understand the tactics involved. The artillery could not move and shoot while following the infantry charge, it took too much time to deploy and re-limber. The idea was that once the infantry charge succeeded the guns would arrive on Cemetery Ridge to help repulse any counter-attacks. As one battery commander observed, by the time he was finally limbered up to go forward the charge had been repulsed and the men were streaming back to Seminary Ridge.

Pendleton is criticized for not having the II Corps artillery co-ordinate in the bombardment and attack. Ewell made the decision to leave fifty-six of his guns idle and there was nothing Pendleton could have done. The premature firing that morning by Ewell and Hill's artillery were also out of his control. Alexander felt fifty years later that Pendleton should have spent the day with the II Corps but there is nothing suggesting that he could have changed Ewell's mindset. It should be noted that Alexander never sought any help from Pendleton, or advised him of any developments during the day.

Nor could Pendleton have provided more ammunition. What ammunition the Army possessed at the start of the battle was what it had to plan to use. In the mid-19th Century three day long battles were unusual, and Lee did not anticipate exhausting his supply when he invaded the North. By the end of the third day the supply was so low that not even the Army wagon trains had enough to provide for every battery. Most of what was left was canister intended for use against an infantry charge.

Finally, there is Lee's implied criticism in the report on the battle he turned into the War Department in January 1864. In regards to the third day Lee commented on the artillery that, "Our own, having nearly exhausted their ammunition in the protracted cannonade that preceded the advance of the infantry, were unable to reply or render the necessary support to the attacking party. Owing to this fact, which was unknown to me when the assault took place, the enemy was enabled to throw a strong force of infantry against our left, already wavering under a concentrated fire of arty from the ridge in front and from Cemetery Hill on the left." This is unfair. First, as a commander of an army in battle for three days it must have occurred to Lee that his supply of ammunition so far from his base of supply must be limited. Additionally, both Colonel Armistead Long, a senior field artillery officer on Lee's staff, and Pendleton knew that the amount of available ammunition was low, so it is hard to believe that neither mentioned this to Lee.

*   *   *   *

When the firing died down after the failure of the charge Pendleton shifted his focus to preparing a defensive posture should Meade attack. The officers in both armies had been taught that after an enemy assault was repulsed it was the best time to make a counter-attack, and the Confederates expected the Union Army to seek to destroy them so far from home. Lee called upon everyone for a supreme effort in preparing a defense, and Pendleton and his staff whole heartedly joined in. With Lee's authority Pendleton spent the day making preparations for such an attack. The batteries on the right and left flanks were pulled back and kept as an emergency reserve. Others were directed to accompany the long wagon train back to the Potomac fords at Williamsport. The rest remained in their positions.

Visiting British Colonel Arthur Fremantle had a long visit with Pendleton that evening. Pendleton told him the exact number of guns in action on the 3rd, and expressed the universal opinion that the 12-pounder Napoleon was the "best and simplest sort of ordnance for field purposes." Fremantle learned that nearly all of the artillery in Lee's Army had "either been captured from the enemy or cast from old 6-pounders taken at the early part of the war." In the battle Lee's field artillery lost 608 men and five guns. Seven enemy guns were captured. Sandie Pendleton did some visiting of his own that night. He carried the report for the day from II Corps to Lee's headquarters and handed them to Lee directly. Emboldened, Sandie remarked, "I hope, General, that the other two Corps are in as good a condition for work as ours is this morning." Lee stared at Sandie and icily replied, "What reason have you, young man, to suppose they are not?" Sandie wrote later that he had never felt so small.

The Army of Northern Virginia was low on food and ammunition. Retreat was the only option. A steady rain began in the afternoon of the 4th. That night Lee began the slow trek back to Virginia with an Army described by Sandie as "in fine spirits though dirty, ragged, barefooted, and furious at the thought of being whipped." The first to leave were the wagons filled with the wounded, then Longstreet's Corps, followed by A. P. Hill and then Ewell. Lee issued orders that "The artillery of each corps will move under the charge of their respective chiefs of artillery, the whole under the general superintendence of the commander of the artillery of the army." There had been a tremendous loss of horses in the field artillery during the battle, but the limbers and caissons were mostly empty and easier to pull, so the large but inefficient Pennsylvania farm horses were impressed into Confederate service. The wagons reached the Potomac on July 6th where the cavalry held off a spirited Federal attack. That same day the bulk of the Army reached Hagerstown, and the next day reached the Potomac after what Pendleton described as a "most laborious and fatiguing night and day."

Rains swelled the Potomac making passage impossible. The Army turned around and waited for Meade to attack. Pendleton wrote, "Accordingly, for three days, during which the enemy was waited for, my best energies were given, with those of others, to the work of arrangement and preparation. The enemy, however, prudently forbore, and, it being undesirable to await him longer, our army was, on the night of the 13th, withdrawn to the south bank of the Potomac." Ewell's Corps passed over the fords at Williamsport while the rest of the Army crossed at Falling Waters. Major Harman laid a pontoon bridge was laid across the Potomac with Heth's Division guarding the crossing. Alexander later recalled:

> The night movement on the part of the Confederates entailed the utmost hardship upon the Army, especially upon the Artillery. A heavy rainstorm had set in before dusk, and continued almost until morning. The routes to the crossings generally lay over narrow farm roads, rough and hilly, which were soon churned into all but impassable mires by the leading artillery carriages. No moon lit the way and the night was unusually dark, but large bonfires along

253

the shore illuminated the crossings. From sunset to sunrise the artillery battalions, in spite of the most tremendous exertions on the part of the men, were able to cover but three or four miles, and many horses perished from exhaustion.

After crossing some of the guns and infantry were detailed to guard the south bank of the Potomac. While Heth was in overall command, Pendleton personally conducted the use of the artillery in defense of the crossing as he had at Shepherdstown the year before. In the hardest rain he posted batteries in their positions on the southern bank. After losing two howitzers stuck in the mud the last Confederates crossed over into Virginia by that afternoon. During this time Pendleton remained on duty unaided by a single member of his staff. They were without horses or broken down by their exertions of the past two weeks. For twenty-eight hours Pendleton was in the saddle and without food and rest for forty hours. Soon after the guns were placed into position on the Virginia Pendleton fired them at enemy skirmishers halting their movement to seize the pontoon bridge over the river. These guns kept up an irregular fire until evening when it was clear that the Federals had no intention to cross the river, and "their formations not being sufficiently large to warrant the further expenditure of ammunition...."

Pendleton remained vigilant as the river started to fall making a Federal attack across the river more likely. George Armstrong Custer's cavalry found a way across the river but Heth stopped him before he got far and drove him back to Maryland. Fortunately, for the most part the Federals were just happy to see the Confederates back across the river. While at the riverbank Pendleton found time to send an aide off with the packages he bought for Anzelotte while in the North, sending with it a letter describing his "labors of all in responsible positions were great. Mine were herculean." Feeling down Pendleton told his wife, "Our cause is, undoubtedly, at serious disadvantage just now." His letter home was welcome. The newspapers in Lexington reported him among the killed at Gettysburg causing Anzelotte to be prostrated by shock for several days.

The Army of Northern Virginia's sense of invincibility in the campaign led Lee to attempt attacks unlikely to succeed. Furthermore, the failure in leadership by the Corps commanders left

Lee with an uncoordinated and flawed command structure incapable of the brilliance and aggressive nature of Jackson. The "what ifs" have accumulated in the more than a century and a half since the battle, but the bottom line is that the Army of Northern Virginia was no longer the efficient fighting machine it once was and the Army of the Potomac had evolved into a well officered and well-oiled machine. The tide of war had turned against the Confederacy.

12. "IT IS UNDOUBTEDLY A TIME TO TRY OUR FAITH AND FORTITUDE"

[NORTHERN VIRGINIA AND GEORGIA, 1863-1864]

What doth it profit, my brethren, though a man says he hath faith, and have not works? Can faith save him?

James 2:14, King James Version

Once across the Potomac and safe on Virginia soil the Army of Northern Virginia counted its losses and re-built its strength. The Army lost over 28,000 men killed, wounded, or missing in the campaign. The losses in the officer corps over the prior twelve months were horrendous. Only five of the thirty-eight brigade commanders were still leading their brigades, and only three of the nine division commanders were still present for duty. This was a loss which over time slowly ate away at the fiber of the Army, weakening it and rendering it less efficient.

While some of the wounded returned to their ranks in short order it did not stop the decline in the number of men present for duty. Once again straggling led to desertion, sometimes quite serious. Whole sections of regiments or brigades disappeared into the night. By the end of July the Army's strength excluding the cavalry was down to 53,286 men. At first Lee urged clemency. He asked President Davis to issue an amnesty for anyone returning to duty. It did not help, and the desertions increased. Finally, Lee had to deal harshly with desertion, executing those who deserved it. The more severe treatment stopped the drain, at least for the present.

For some, the need to return to service was dire. One former artillery officer begged Pendleton to find a post for him to ease the hunger his family faced, "Aunt Judy is nearly eaten out of house & home. She is killing her sheep, calves & has no bacon & cannot buy for less than 2 1/2 $ per pound. She has to buy Flour at 4 – $ per bbl & has made little or no wheat & will not make corn – enough to last 6 mos. the next year. So you see she cannot afford to keep me & my family, unless I can get something to do."

When the Army returned to Southern soil it initially camped in the area around Bunker Hill in the lower Shenandoah Valley. From there Pendleton wrote home about the conditions for the Army. It rained much of the time, leaving the roads all mud and the men miserable and damp. Food was hard to find, and provisions were irregular at best. His enslaved black servant baked two fresh loaves of bread which were delicious with tea. For the most part they ate dry bread, a little "poor meat," little salt, and no vegetables. He also apologized for the packet of Northern goods sent home at the end of the Pennsylvania campaign. He agreed it included shoes of the wrong size and odd patterns, but urged they be traded for something better. He regretted that "with so much blood and death to bestow much effort on earthly things" he was not able to spend a lot of time deciding what to buy.

Lee knew he could not linger in the lower Shenandoah Valley. His men were hungry and barefoot and the area was completely devastated and unable to feed an Army. That left Lee reliant on the criminally negligent handling of commissary stores by Lucius Northrop in Richmond. In order to take care of his Army Lee needed to draw closer to Richmond. All of this frustrated the combative nature of Robert E. Lee. He wanted to resume the offensive but knew his Army was too weak to do so, in fact, he realized it might never again have the strength to take the battle to the enemy.

*   *   *   *

The horses suffered just as much as the men. Promises were made by Richmond that they would provide the Army with 3,000 bushels of feed a day for the horses, but that number was never met. By November the supply dropped off drastically to 1,000 bushels a day. Horses resorted to eating anything at hand; tree bark, paper, and camp debris; and they died from fever or hunger. Even worse, Lee calculated he needed another 10,000 horses for the Army, and very few were now available east of the Union dominated Mississippi River.

General Pendleton worked strenuously to improve the condition of the Army's horses. He arranged for infirmaries to care for the sick horses, and conducted a thorough investigation of the problems faced by the Army. He concluded that the Army's Quartermaster General was not doing enough to care for the horses through neglect. The horses lacked salt and proper care, and were not being supplied with the food, water, and other things needed. He was also concerned that diseased horses were permitted freely to circulate among a large herd "with the certainty of spreading contagion, suffering, and loss."

He recommended to Lee on August 13th that horses unfit for active field service be turned over to individual farmers for light work. In this manner any contagion would no longer be spread by herding them all together. The farmer would also work harder to feed and nurture the horses. In turn, healthy horses could be collected from the farms. Pendleton recommended that artillery officers be responsible for obtaining the horses, and not the Quartermaster General office which had less interest in the abilities of the horse. In this way Pendleton felt that good horses could be purchased for $600 Confederate dollars each, or by trade for the ailing horses. Ultimately, it might be necessary to resort to impressing healthy horses into active duty. It appears that his recommendations were not acted upon.

On September 3, 1863, Pendleton issued a new set of recommendations and submitted them to Lee and the Superintendent of Transportation in Richmond. He noted that:

> The preservation of our horses, after all we can do in battling against the intrinsic difficulties of our situation and the common negligence of officers and men, leaves many things yet to be desired. Multitudes of those left too long in the field because of inadequate provisions for relieving them, and too far gone for restoration before they are relieved, are, when relieved, committed to unskilled or unfaithful agents, and either perish on the way to the point where they are to be permanently provided for, or

die after reaching those points through lack of the care, food, &c., essential for their resuscitation.

In order to address these needs horse districts would be established throughout Virginia under the care of a responsible agent, complete with depots and stables for the horses. Second, the agent in each district would acquire new horses and keep them at the depots along with the renovated veteran horses ready to return to the field. These horses would be subject to call up when needed. Third, the agent would create suitable places of accommodations for the horses sent to the district for renewal, and to provide for their care while in transit. The depots were to be established in areas unspoiled by the war and teeming with adequate forage. Pendleton felt that there existed "a supply of serviceable horses now, much exhaustion has been experienced, I am aware, but careful inquiry satisfies me that there are still horses enough for the army and for agriculture, & etc."

These recommendations were adopted and an officer appointed to organize the remount service out of Lynchburg. Even though one fifth of the horses still died the arrangement was a vast improvement on the prior system. At the same time, Pendleton, mindful of the need to move the Army's wagons, sent his agents to the Cotton South to acquire mules.

Pendleton also took direct action within the Army. Once winter quarters were established at Louisa Court House he sent several officers from his staff to examine the available forage between the railroad and the James River in the Piedmont. They were to report by December 10th on the available supply of corn, oats, hay, straw, and fodder, and the capabilities of the area's grist mills for the production of food. In issuing orders for the field artillery units Pendleton included instructions to march in reasonable stages to preserve the horses, forage their horses, and if required, buy corn feed for them.

In mid-February 1864 Pendleton reported on the results of the program. He found that disease still persisted among the horses between Lynchburg and North Carolina, and he urged steps be taken to control and limit the spread of any disease. Given the spread of disease, he recommended that new horses not be delivered from the depot to the Army until needed for the next campaign. However, he felt that the system "in parceling, protecting foraging,

259

and improving" worked well. Additionally, the effort to find and acquire new healthy horses looked promising. Pendleton had high hopes for finding the 1,000 horses he needed for the artillery come spring, but was less sanguine about finding horses for transportation. Once more, he urged using mules as an acceptable replacement. Lee agreed.

*   *   *   *

On July 21st the Army moved southeast through Front Royal and the Blue Ridge into Culpeper once more. The march took four days and at times there was no food for dinner or supper, and there was little rest. Pendleton believed the Army would remain there for a while. He was pessimistic and depressed about the future after the losses at Gettysburg and Vicksburg but wrote home that they should find comfort in God notwithstanding "the unfavorable turn in our national affairs….It is undoubtedly a time to try our faith and fortitude."

By August the Army settled around Orange Court House south of the winding Rapidan River. Mrs. Pendleton and a daughter were able to visit Pendleton staying for a couple of weeks with a cousin. Ned Lee was able to bring them hard to find goods from his family home in Shepherdstown on the Potomac; adamantine candles, coal oil, tea, sugar, coffee, shoes, dress, winter dress and sewing materials. Sandie was nearby as well. He finally received promotion to Chief of Staff of the II Corps and Lieutenant Colonel. Sandie felt it was as far as he would rise in the war. On September 1st a gala picnic was held at Montpelier, the home of the late President James Madison. Pendleton's wife and daughter attended but he was too busy to go. It was spoiled when a downpour struck just as the guests sat down to eat. They told him of the damage to the ladies' silk and the lawns. Everyone scrambled for cover in any available wagon. Meanwhile, Pendleton spent one evening reading an entire novel entitled *Aurora Floyd*, a sensational romantic novel about the moral derangement of contemporary society.

Sandie Pendleton also caught up on his letters home. He wrote that he enjoyed the convenience of a proper fireplace on the cold nights, and that he was beginning to really enjoy his military trade. It provided him with excitement during battles and campaigns, and he enjoyed the authority of his position as a staff officer; which he found gratifying to his ambition. Sandie also wrote his sister Susan and her husband Ned Lee that there were vacancies in the II Corps judicial panels and that Ned needed to go to Richmond and apply for a position. Ned eventually obtained a quiet position in 1864 as a camp commander for newly drafted soldiers.

Army camp life proceeded apace. Pendleton preached often and usually to large congregations seated on rough seats in the woods in the dark, the only light coming from a few candlesticks. On one occasion, he rode back to camp alone through the dark woods. Given the large number of civilian refugees in the area Pendleton also ministered to them with baptisms, communions, and funerals.

Occasionally the war intruded. On the 14th he rode to a forward artillery post on the Rapidan as a Federal attack seemed imminent. He stayed all day but "From what I saw I do not judge a fight so near." There were the occasional disciplinary matters to handle. On the 23rd a Lieutenant Haskell and a Sergeant galloped into Pendleton's camp after a drinking bout. This incurred Pendleton's "displeasure," and the men were referred to their commander for discipline. Haskell offered the weak excuses that he neither knew he was not supposed to gallop through camp or that his companion was drunk. The outcome of their punishment is not known. And there were the administrative and logistical matters to handle. By the end of September the Army had 267 guns and 4,929 men to work them, the size of an Army division.

In early September most of Longstreet's I Corps was detached from the Army of Northern Virginia and sent to Georgia to reinforce Braxton Bragg's Army of Tennessee. Soon after arriving Longstreet and the Army of Tennessee defeated and routed Rosecrans' Federal Army at Chickamauga and drove it back into Chattanooga. The victory was hailed throughout the South. The Pendletons, father and son, greeted it with the hope that Bragg would follow the victory up and destroy the Union Army of the Tennessee. They were to be disappointed. The failure to pursue Rosecrans after the victory angered Bragg's generals, and any sense of unity in the Army's command was lost. Daniel Harvey Hill was removed as a Corps commander while Longstreet took his I Corps on an expedition to re-capture Knoxville at the very time Grant was reinforcing Chattanooga. By the end of November Longstreet was repulsed at Knoxville and Bragg was driven by Grant and Thomas back into Georgia where he finally and belatedly resigned his command.

261

Left without Longstreet's Corps Lee had few options but to watch Meade and wait. In late September Lee discovered that two of the Federal Army Corps opposing him had been sent away from his front and decided that the imbalance in strength was not too much to risk an offensive. On October 8th Lee sent out a warning order for the Army to prepare to move from their camps. Pendleton wrote home to his daughter Nan that his correspondence might be irregular, He added, "You I have not seen for more than two years. My head is now never touched by a razor, so that you would hardly know me if I were unexpectedly to stand before you. This full gray beard adds considerably to the venerableness of my appearance making me look somewhat of a patriarch." Pendleton reported being "healthy, active, & cheerful."

Armistead Long, Pendleton's partner at Gettysburg, was promoted to Brigadier General of artillery and made the Chief of Artillery for the II Corps. Pendleton assisted him in filling out his staff. He also issued orders for the new campaign for the artillery batteries left behind in Virginia by Longstreet, telling Cabell to move his battalion of artillery to Gordonsville to protect the Army's flank, and Haskell's battalion to move to Liberty Mills. Lee started his offensive with his two remaining Corps by sending them north of the Orange & Alexandria Railroad, approximately where U.S. Route 29 now runs, with Ewell to the north and Hill to the south.

Pendleton left camp on the 9th and spent a long day riding towards Gordonsville until well after dark. On arriving he posted the artillery in a defensive position. While on the road a farm family mistook him for Robert E. Lee and invited him in for dinner. As the offensive began Lee, Pendleton, and their staffs rode with Ewell and his II Corps. As they approached Federal positions on the 11th Lee ordered Pendleton to ride ahead and position the artillery for an attack. On the 12th they found some Federal troops and artillery dug in at Warrenton Springs on the Rappahannock River. Pendleton carefully deployed sixteen guns along the south bank unseen by the enemy. When all sixteen guns opened up on the Federals across the river they scurried off. Outflanked, Meade quickly pulled back, but the Federals left a trap waiting for Hill at Bristoe Station.

When the Union Army withdrew northeast contact was lost. On the 14th Hill thought he saw an opportunity to crush isolated units of the Federal III Corps on the south side of the Broad Run near Manassas. Without making any reconnaissance, he launched two divisions at the milling Union troops, failing to notice the Federal II Corps waiting behind the embankment of the railroad on their right flank. Two of his brigades were chewed up, and he was fortunate to escape further damage. The Federals withdrew further northeast towards the protective cordon of fortifications around Washington, D.C.

On October 18th Pendleton boarded a train in Manassas and headed back towards Rappahannock Station. The brief offensive was over. Through a heavy rain he looked through the windows at the desolation left behind in northern Virginia after three years of brutal warfare. The entire route, he wrote, was one of "unbroken devastation." The day before he had arrived in Manassas and found it totally destroyed but for one dilapidated shanty occupied by a poor Irishwoman. From the train he saw that "The whole way from Manassas to this point is one unbroken scene of desolation. Not a house left standing! Not a living thing save a few partridges and other small birds! No horse or cow, no hog or sheep, no dog or cat, - of course, no man or woman, or child!....not a soul remained." Even the churches were defaced and desecrated. Any kind of farm equipment had been piled up and burned by the Federals. They even torched the shanties in which the enslaved blacks were living.

After the Army settled down again, Pendleton had a "strange call of duty." He was approached by a "good looking Negro" who was held as a slave by the Army's Chief Quartermaster. He asked if Pendleton would marry him that evening at 9:00 p.m. some four miles away. Pendleton and an aide rode out to the wedding in a heavy rain and found a large party of blacks gathered for the ceremony and feast. Pendleton officiated, "The groom said "I will" and the bride stayed silent." He and his aide joined the celebration feast at which they were served ham, turkey, fowl, bread, butter, cake, and rye coffee in abundance. The groom offered to pay Pendleton for his services, but Pendleton refused, telling him that the only compensation he desired was for the couple to fulfill their wedding vows and live happily ever after. The next day he preached in a church attended by Lee and President Davis.

Pendleton ended the month of October resolving some contretemps with Armistead Long, hunting down the returns for the artillery to give to Lee's staff, and writing home. Pendleton was homesick, and he wrote Anzelotte that he could only hope when the Army entered winter quarters that he could ask for a furlough back to Lexington. Yet, he could report that "My living is right hard yet am in good health and as cheerful for a man of my years."

The month of November opened with a debacle for the Army of Northern Virginia. General Early, temporarily in command of the II Corps, left two brigades in fortifications on the north bank of the Rappahannock near Kelly's Ford. The forts were connected to the south bank and the remainder of the Army by one pontoon bridge. On the 7th the Federals launched a well-planned night attack that killed, wounded, or captured most of the 2,000 men in the fortifications. It turned out that neither Lee nor Jubal Early ever expected the Army of the Potomac to make a well-coordinated night assault. Sandie Pendleton was appalled, "it is absolutely sickening and I feel personally disgraced by the issue of the late campaign, as does everyone in the command. Oh how every day is proving the value of General Jackson to us." Once again the Federals proved their experience and skill in warfare to the cost of the Confederates. General Pendleton felt that "there seems much suffering in store for us. The difficulty of feeding our animals where we have to meet the enemy is almost insuperable, and with difficulty others increase as feeding our men, whose food horses must draw and using our cannon, which must by horses be moved from place to place."

Meanwhile Sandie's future seemed clouded as well. His Corps commander General Ewell finally married his sweetheart Mrs. Brown and brought her and her two adult children to headquarters where the blushing groom introduced her to all as "this is my wife, Mrs. Brown." The new Mrs. Ewell hoped that when the Congress passed a new law allowing Ewell to appoint a Colonel as a staff officer that the appointment would go to her son, who had little military experience. If so this would block any hopes Sandie had of further promotion. Nor did it help when Ewell coddled his step-son and refused to put him in harm's way. To make matters worse, Mrs. Ewell's daughter became engaged to another of the staff officers. There was no doubt as to who controlled the headquarters, and it wasn't the General.

Even worse, Lee cancelled all leaves on November 10th preventing Sandie from appearing for his wedding to Kate Corbin on November 25th as planned at Moss Neck near Fredericksburg. The wedding had been postponed twice already for military exigencies, and Sandie's request for leave was declined again although preparations for the wedding were already underway.

General Pendleton felt that it was best if the family waited to before gathering at Moss Neck, telling his daughter Rose that "If we whip the Yankees, as we take for granted, & no harm comes to me or Sandie, as we hope" then there would be no problems. But if Lee lost or one of the Pendleton men was hurt, it was best if Rose waited at home. Pendleton felt that Sandie would need to "content himself for a month or so, as the season of active operations may be expected to last so long." Despite Pendleton's misgivings about an upcoming major battle Rose Pendleton left Lexington on the James River canal boat for Richmond and train connections up to Fredericksburg. On arrival she reported that Kate was "not pretty" but sweet. News of the postponement left a gloom at Moss Neck and left Rose stranded there. Nor had the news reached everyone since guests for the wedding began to arrive for the wedding.

Meade took the offensive before winter set in. News of his advance arrived on the 26th during a spell so cold that icicles formed on the beards of the men. The Federal Army crossed the Rappahannock and Rapidan Rivers and quickly found Lee's Army near the Wilderness area where the Battle of Chancellorsville was fought that spring. In terrain similar to the Wilderness the left of the Confederate Army contacted the Union troops near Payne's Farm. After a severe repulse the Federal Army pulled back and the two armies faced each other across Mine Run. Portions of the southern bank had a slight command of the northern, and so Lee had entrenchments dug for defense. Pendleton worked incessantly situating the artillery for the upcoming battle, although he had some time for a brief visit with Sandie. After his work was done he felt that the Confederates were in a good defensive position and that everything was ready for a Union attack. At some places the lines were just a quarter mile apart. Lee planned to assault the Union right and turn it. Meade had a similar plan but having closely examined Lee's works opted to avoid any slaughter. When Lee awoke on the morning of December 2nd the Union Army was gone, looting and burning as it went. Any food found was seized from the local families and their furniture and clothing shredded and broken up. The devastated families faced a bleak winter of starvation and lack of warm shelters.

Sandie applied for leave on December 14th to marry on the 16th but was denied. Jubal Early was taking some troops into the Shenandoah Valley in response to a Federal cavalry raid towards

Salem. Since Sandie knew the area he was ordered to go as well. Bereft of any hope that Sandie would be allowed to have leave General Pendleton finally took his long awaited leave and made his first visit to his home in Lexington since August 1861, well over two years earlier. Before leaving he made arrangements for the artillery sending it further south for adequate forage for the horses. The Chief Quartermaster for the artillery was designated to "supervise the operations of his department with the artillery in winter quarters, so as to have irregularities corrected and all requisite supplies appropriately furnished." The Chief Commissary was similarly given responsibilities in his department.

Pendleton must have conveyed his concerns about Sandie to Lee. On December 18th Lee's aide wrote a letter to General Ewell that Pendleton had asked about whether "his son will be able to return in time to go on leave next Monday." It must have worked. Pendleton attended Grace Episcopal in Lexington on Christmas Day. When he arrived home after the service he found a telegram advising him that Sandie obtained his leave and hoped to marry at Moss Neck on the 28th. Pendleton ate Christmas dinner with his family at home and then boarded a stage in a driving snowstorm for Staunton and the railroad to Richmond. He arrived the next morning. Sandie arrived unannounced in Moss Neck on the 27[th.] He went to Richmond to meet his father to escort him to Moss Neck after a delay in the rail traffic. There, the wedding was finally held on December 29, 1863. Rose was the only other Pendleton present.

The bridal party and General Pendleton departed Moss Neck and arrived back in Lexington on January 1, 1864. They celebrated with a Christmas pudding made of dried cherries and sorghum molasses. The entire Pendleton family, other than Ned Lee, enjoyed almost two weeks together. Friends in town dropped by to visit and monopolized their time. Pendleton was able to preach in Grace Church with the permission of Rector Norton. His robes were missing from the vestry forcing him to dress in uniform for the service, causing some titters in the congregation. Susan Lee left on January 12th to join Ned in Richmond, Sandie and Kate departed on the 19th.

The rapid depreciation of Confederate currency caused hardships for everyone. Pendleton made arrangements for food and fuel to carry the family through the winter, including the sale of his theodolite and compass to the Navy to pay for food. Pendleton remained at home until the end of January, reporting back to duty on February 3, 1864. There he found the Army had only 206 serviceable guns and only 3,842 artillerymen.

Ensconced in his tent Pendleton spent a comfortable winter. He continued to preach whenever an opportunity presented itself, and attended services of other Protestant faiths when able to do so. He spent some time seeking a job for his daughter Mary to increase the income for the family but failed to find anything. Jobs were reserved for the war refugees who were now homeless. This was, thought Pendleton "right and proper," and that "God's blessings will suffice." Anzelotte visited for two weeks lodging a mile and a half from the Pendleton's headquarters.

There were occasional skirmishes with Federal cavalry probing the lines, and in late February there was the controversial Dahlgren raid on Richmond. Meade sent cavalry around Lee's flank to capture Richmond and the chief officers of the Confederate government. It failed miserably. Pendleton acted directly in seeking reinforcements, in particular infantry, to support the II Corps artillery at Frederick Hall when enemy cavalry approached at the start of the raid. Pendleton made sure that accurate information on the raid was sent immediately to Richmond. He also continued to keep tabs on the well-being of his horses and men, checking for good shelter, adequate food, and a healthy environment for all. Even so, he received reports from battalion officers that their horses were sick and dying, and that new horses were required. He also sought to increase the number of guns in the Army until the full quota was met.

        *   *   *   *

Pendleton also spent the winter months seeking promotions for the officers of the Field Artillery Corps. It was a constant struggle since promotions in the branch were naturally slower than for the infantry or cavalry. There were fewer officers and the highest ranks were granted to only a few men. Consequently, many able officers left the artillery for the infantry seeking faster promotion.

First, however, he sought to procure a promotion for himself. The highest grade allowed by law in the artillery was Brigadier-General, a rank Pendleton held since August 1861. After more than two years of active service he felt he deserved more. On October 3rd he wrote to the Adjutant General of the Army in Richmond stating that "I ought not to be silent on subject of own situation." He touted his services and noted his current responsibilities as head of a very large artillery department which was the equivalent of handling an infantry division. In this he was not wrong. He was administratively responsible for a force as large as a division along with all the horses and equipment an infantry division did not have. Pendleton finished by asking to be granted the same grade as a division commander, that of Major General. Lee never recommended Pendleton for a promotion. In consolation Lee granted Pendleton the right to carry a staff the size of a divisional staff so as to accomplish his job. Pendleton appeared pleased with this compromise, and ignored the catcalls of those ignorant few who criticized him for having such a large staff.

One historian speculated that in the winter of 1863-1864 Lee still entertained the idea of replacing Pendleton with Colonel Thomas Carter, one of the battalion commanders, skipping over both Armistead Long and E. P. Alexander. The evidence for this is a letter from Carter to his wife "It would be an advantage to the Artillery of this Army should he do so." In all likelihood this would never have happened. Lee seemed satisfied to keep Pendleton as he was limited to the administrative role in which he excelled. Nor would Lee have jumped over two very brilliant and experienced artillery officers by promoting a mere battalion commander. In all probability Carter's letter referred to Pendleton's recommendation that he be made the Chief of Artillery for the Army of Tennessee, as will be discussed later.

On November 20, 1863 Pendleton provided Lee with his list of recommendations for promotion. There were quite a few names on the list headed by E. P. Alexander, who was to be made a Brigadier General. He prepared the list in consultation with General Armistead Long of the II Corps, Colonel Walker of the III Corps, and Jeb Stuart for the batteries serving with the cavalry. Each recommendation was made carefully as it was certain to offend any officer passed over. In this regard Pendleton and Lee both made every effort to avoid offending anyone, but at times the needs of the service and fairness required that one be selected and another left behind.

He began with a review of the status of the artillery. There were 244 guns available on a table of organization and equipment calling for 276. The primary reason for the shortage was that the number of Napoleon 12-pounder smoothbore guns turned out at

Tredegar was insufficient to replace the obsolete 6-pounders turned in for re-casting. Additional losses came through arduous service and combat. Nevertheless, Pendleton's scheme for promotion assumed that the table of organization and equipment would be fully supplied.

Two of the Corps Chiefs of Artillery required replacement. Colonel Crutchfield of the II Corps had served honorably and well but his severe wound at Chancellorsville limited him to a less arduous service. Alexander had been the acting Chief of Artillery for the I Corps for some time. His superior Colonel Walton asked to be re-assigned to a position near Mobile for health reasons. Colonel Walker, the III Corps Chief of Artillery, would not be promoted to General as no more promotions would be allowed. Other senior officers would be re-assigned for failure to perform at a level required and expected in the service either for reasons of health or incompetence. Pendleton nominated dozens of officers for promotion to fill in the ranks, all in line with the wishes of the new Corps Chiefs of Artillery. Even with the recommended promotions "the number of artillery field officers will be only about three-fourths of those belonging to three brigades of cavalry, or infantry having anything like the number of men, companies, & etc., constituting the artillery."

The Congress sat on the nominations of the senior officers for some time, frustrating Lee by the delays. He wrote Longstreet in East Tennessee on January 17, 1864 of his inability to push the promotions through, "This I could not accomplish at the time, nor have I been able to do so since. Not wishing the officers in the other corps to be promoted without advancing those in yours, so that their relative rank might be preserved, I have refrained from sending in the recommendations, but the season of active operations is approaching, and I wish the organization perfected."

When the promotions were not quickly made Pendleton followed up his recommendations on February 22, 1864 with a plaintive missive to Lee. He reminded Lee that the artillery service was losing quality officers to the line because they were not receiving deserved promotions:

> Men the most devoted must be expected to value
> rank alike, as an evidence that their services are
> appreciated, and as an important condition toward

269

more extended service. No man of merit ever disregards the question of promotion, and much as officers may be willing to sacrifice at times like these, they cannot ignore so universal and powerful a sentiment as that associated with martial honor.... Even those officers who have no idea of seeking other service, and whose simple sense of duty will keep them steadfast until the end, in spite of disproportionate reward, are compelled to consider themselves and their commands regarded with less than justice, and after all that can be allowed for high principle, we must conclude that it is not in human nature not to be more or less disturbed by such a reflection, nor can such disturbance be without its injurious effects upon the public service.

Pendleton added that some of the artillery battalions suffered so much loss through attrition or service that there was only one field officer in the entire battalion. Such a situation could not be allowed when the next campaign began in the spring. The promotions finally were approved by Congress before March 1864.

*   *   *   *

The vestry of Grace Episcopal Church in Lexington asked that the Pendletons vacate the Rectory for the new rector Reverend Norton, but allowed the family to keep their church pew at Anzelotte's request. In late September 1863 Pendleton rented a home from Mrs. Withrow in town for the family. The Reverend Norton came to the family's rescue and asked Pendleton if he wished to rent the Rectory from the Church for $600 paid quarterly in advance. The next morning while Pendleton sat at the breakfast table Reverend Norton arrived in an agitated manner and asked if the Pendletons would agree to rent the Rectory for the amount quoted. He responded in the affirmative, and the move to the Withrow house was cancelled. Instead, Pendleton sub-leased the Withrow house. He also promised that he would make the Rectory comfortable for Anzelotte by "knocking a hole in the wall in old dining room" and installing a steam pipe. Meanwhile the food supplies in Lexington dwindled. The family lived on what daughter Susan P. Lee called an "improper and insufficient diet.... Have had plenty but could not enjoy eating vegetables and fruit. Of course like other people we have to do without sugar."

Pendleton's son-in-law's mother remained behind in Shepherdstown after the Confederate departure in the summer of 1863. Federal troops moved into the area. In mid-October she wrote her son and daughter-in-law of an encounter with roaming Union soldiers. She was awakened "at midnight and heard efforts to get into parlor window and tramping of many feet upon the pavement. I asked who was there and a man with an Irish accent answered, "Open the door, we have business in this house." Mrs. Lee asked again who was there and was told if she did not open the door it would be broken down. She replied she needed time to dress and was given permission. She returned to her room to put on clothing and slipped two revolvers into her pockets. She lit a candle and shaking badly and "white as death" she opened the door. Some Irish men entered. "Riley, again?" she asked. He denied it but she knew he was lying. "Riley" said, "Take me to the room where the two rebels are sleeping." She replied there were none in the house and that all good Confederate soldiers were at their posts of duty. He repeated the demand, to which she offered to show him where her "two little Confederate soldiers" were sleeping. They went upstairs and she opened the door to the room where two little boys slept. "Riley" said, "Ah, the little fellows! Don't disturb them." Instead they searched the cellar and finding no one, cursed the information given them that there were Confederates in the house, and left.

The lack of food at home in Lexington concerned Pendleton. He felt that an insufficient diet and lack of rest adversely affected Anzelotte's health. His concern mounted when she wrote to him of the theft of seven joints of bacon from the family smokehouse. Nevertheless, he reassured her that the theft meant little in loss of money and that she should be thankful it was no worse. He urged her to rest her strength and eat well, "cherish all the health, strength and flesh you can by diet....even though it cost more. What will property or anything else be to me if you languish or lose health from lack of adequate nourishment?" He suggested that she try to make up any deficiencies in tea, coffee, sugar, and desserts, for "...at our age nature needs some help."

*   *   *   *

When Braxton Bragg resigned his command of the Army of Tennessee his position was taken by the senior Corps commander

271

Lieutenant General William Hardee. Hardee worked diligently rebuilding the shattered Army, including improving and augmenting the artillery. When he was replaced by General Joseph E. Johnston he left behind a glowing report on the condition of the Army. After an initial inspection Johnston disagreed. The horses were in poor condition, there were few wagons to carry supplies, and he felt he could not take the offensive without being able to provide supplies for the Army on the march. He needed 600 horses to pull his artillery or he would have to leave 64 guns behind.

This exacerbated another ongoing problem. President Davis and Johnston did not like or respect each other. Davis appointed Johnston against his better judgment as there was no one else he deemed qualified. The two men immediately began a bitter dispute over the mission of the Army of Tennessee. Davis wanted it to go on the offensive, carrying the war north and liberating Tennessee and Kentucky. In the belief that the Federal armies were moving men to Virginia to confront Lee, he felt there was an opportunity to strike at a weakened foe. Davis assumed that if Johnston went around the right flank of Sherman and crossed into Tennessee that Sherman would be required to retreat. He promoted John Bell Hood to Corps commander and assigned him to the Army of Tennessee after whispering in his ear the advantages of such an offensive. Johnston pointed out that he could not take the offensive without reinforcements. Johnston felt that the Confederate government was blind to the ever increasing size of the enemy armies, including the 300,000 freed slaves who had enlisted. Unless he received help he would be forced to go on the defensive.

At the same time Johnston wanted a new Army Chief of Artillery, and he asked Richmond, in the person of Davis' military advisor Braxton Bragg, that General E. P. Alexander be appointed. In two separate letters dated March 4 and 7, 1864 Bragg advised Johnston why his request could not be met. And with this we step into yet another controversy regarding General Pendleton.

Bragg initially told Johnston that he was surprised by Johnston's report on the deficiency of his artillery after reading Hardee's glowing report, and "hopes are entertained there must be some error on your part. Prompt measures should be taken by you, however, to supply the real want, whatever it may be." The request for Alexander was denied by Lee as he was "deemed necessary by General Lee in his present position." Instead, "Brigadier General W.

N. Pendleton, an experienced officer of artillery, has been ordered to your headquarters to inspect that part of your command and report on its condition. Should his services be acceptable to you, I am authorized to say you can retain him." If not, then it was still possible to have Alexander re-assigned. Some historians read into this an effort by Lee to dump Pendleton and hold onto the highly qualified Alexander. Alexander certainly felt that way. In his memoirs he finds great comfort in the thought that Lee preferred him to Pendleton. But it just wasn't so, as Bragg clarified in his next letter.

On March 7th Bragg wrote Johnston again stating that if Pendleton was not satisfactory he was not sure who would be. Bragg reviewed some possibilities. It is here that Lee must have remembered Alexander's negligent care of his horses, for Bragg writes that another officer was "a good judge and fond of good horses, which is a qualification Alexander is especially deficient in." He concluded with the reminder that Johnston needed to bring up supplies for his Army and that the preferred role for the Army of Tennessee was to attack Sherman before he was ready to start his offensive towards Atlanta.

There is no clear reason for why Lee offered Pendleton. He knew that Pendleton could whip the Army's artillery into shape better and faster than any other officer. He also knew that Davis was urging that Lee go himself to Georgia, something Lee did everything he could to avoid. Perhaps since Pendleton's role was now merely administrative he might be easier to replace. Perhaps Lee knew Pendleton would refuse the assignment, or that Johnston would not want him. Was it for these reasons he was apparently willing to sacrifice Pendleton? We will never know. It was certainly not because he prized Alexander more.

Pendleton received orders on March 4, 1864 to inspect the artillery of the Army of Tennessee and report back on its conditions. It was a delicate mission which, as Douglas S. Freeman acknowledged, Pendleton handled very well. He telegraphed ahead to his daughter Susan Lee in Richmond that he and her mother would be coming to stay the night. He knew it would be difficult for her to procure adequate food to feed him. The normal diet in Richmond at this time was salt beef, fat middling, and beans. Turkeys sold for $50 Confederate each. Half the Lee's monthly pay went to renting just three rooms. Susan was able to scrounge up some turkey, bean soup, and coffee.

While he was being briefed in Richmond Pendleton was stopped on the street by a drunken Irishman. The drunk harangued and gesticulated violently towards Pendleton for some fancied grievance. The Pendleton women wanted to ignore the drunk but Pendleton stopped, listened, and replied, "My friend you are talking to the wrong person." The drunk responded "Why ain't you Mass' Bob?" Pendleton patiently told him "No, look and see if you don't know me." The drunk stared at him, slapped his leg, and said "I'll swear if it ain't old Artillery!" The man apologized and stumbled on. People at St. Paul's Church were similarly confused not having seen Pendleton since he grew his beard.

On the 11th he reached Atlanta by train with two of his staff officers and his enslaved personal servant. He telegraphed ahead to Dalton of his upcoming arrival. Yet, when he arrived at the station no one was there to greet him. He waited through the night under the depot roof and walked to Johnston's headquarters the next morning. There he was cordially greeted by Johnston, his old mentor from the Valley. He washed up and ate breakfast in the headquarters mess with real coffee, butter from Johnston's cow, toast, and cornbread. Then with a happier stomach he sat down to confer with Johnston. Afterwards he went straight to work.

That same day he inspected the three battalions of the Army Reserve Artillery, which constituted about one third of the guns in the Army. On one of Johnston's mounts he made a thorough inspection, including harness, field transportation, horses and stables. Surprisingly, and despite Johnston's report, he found the horses to be in fairly good condition, the guns and equipment in good order, and in every respect this reflected the diligent care and attention provided by the officers and men. Pendleton felt the problem lay with some of the senior officers. Pendleton recommended that Colonel Thomas Carter of the Army of Northern Virginia be appointed as Chief of Artillery, but was later disappointed to find another officer named for the post. He worked on paperwork for the inspection, including a series of questions for every battalion commander. They sought information on the officers and men, their combat experience, length of service, and whether they needed commendation or condemnation. He asked about the armaments, equipment and condition of each battery; diseases and

274

vermin among the horses; want of care and grooming for the horses; and what equipment, guns, men, and horses were needed by each battery.

It was bitterly cold the next morning. Pendleton watched as both Hardee's and Hood's Corps passed in review. In the days following he conducted an inspection of every battery in the Army. On Sunday the 15th he remained indoors and read parts of the Bible, Prayer Book, and Bradley's Sermons. By the 16th he was done with his initial inspection and paperwork. Hood put on a sham battle for Pendleton with an imposing drill of his Corps followed by combat exercises involving infantry, artillery, and cavalry using blank rounds. The sight of 15,000 to 20,000 men with artillery impressed him, a scene "wildly enlivened" when some horses bucked their riders and took off. Hardee later put on another show with his Corps, but it was less entertaining than Hood's. However, he was impressed that Hardee's new bride kept her saddle when all the guns went off.

While waiting for replies to his inquiries he visited with old friends and preached to the troops. On the 20th he preached to a large congregation on Jesus' agony in Garden of Gethsemane. The congregation remained attentive to the end. He wrote home that he hoped to leave by the 22nd, "The long jaunt in crowded cars day and night for nearly a week is anything but attractive in prospect, and will be worse in experience. Still, evils much greater can be endured."

On March 21, 1864 Pendleton submitted his report to General Johnston with the results in the form of comments, a tabular report, and a proposed order. Pendleton concluded that the horses pulling the artillery were in a "better than average condition; the wagons for the most part strong, and the animals quite serviceable." The horses, as to be expected at the end of winter, were thin but they have been in the main obviously well cared for, are in promisingly good health....." The anticipated arrival of new cannons would improve the armament and make it "quite efficient." He found the officers to be "earnest, capable, experienced, and generally efficient." Pendleton found the organization acceptable although he preferred the battalions to consist of four batteries and not the current three. He felt that proper promotions should be made as soon as practicable and named some deserving of such an accolade. In all, Pendleton found that the Army of Tennessee's artillery "well commanded will prove greatly efficient and powerfully contribute to the great victory…." Johnston was pleased with the report.

Pendleton left the next day. On his way home he inspected the harbor defenses at Charleston as requested by Richmond. By the 29th he was back in the capital. He submitted his review to Davis, Bragg, and the Secretary of War. He also provided a copy of the report for Lee. It differed in tone from the one given to Johnston. He told them that Johnston had only 111 guns of which only 69 were serviceable. The rest were obsolete or useless. Johnston and his commanders expressed concern over the condition of the artillery and wanted it ready for spring. They felt it had "defective armament, insufficient strength in animals, and want alike of adequate chiefs and of suitable organization." Pendleton found that the armament was "less strong than is desirable," the fifteen 6-pounders were obsolete and useless, the twenty-seven 12-pounder howitzers were not much better and he hoped that by April 10th these guns would be replaced with more modern weaponry as promised by the Ordnance Department. The horses were "certainly thin; some had died from hard usage and disease not uncommon in our artillery service, and others were worn down below the standard for use." He recognized that active campaigning and the winter take their toll on horses, and that they now needed plenty of adequate forage to fight off diseases. However, despite all this, it was not unusual a condition for an artillery corps in the Confederate service. He asked that 500 new horses be sent. Pendleton also noted that the current battalion organization needed revision to reflect more that of the Army of Northern Virginia, and that better senior officers needed to be supplied.

Davis found the report inconclusive. He also needed to impress upon Johnston the need for a spring offensive. So he sent Pendleton back to Georgia for further conferences. Before he left, Pendleton visited with his family and Robert E. Lee. He met his wife in Richmond and they travelled together to Gordonsville by train. He went on alone to Orange Court House to meet Sandie. Sandie left the station to find horses while Pendleton walked in the mud and rain to Lee's quarters. Pendleton spent over two hours discussing the situation with Lee. Lee questioned the reasons Johnston gave for not attacking, but admitted he was not in a position to pass judgment. After Pendleton departed Lee wrote optimistically to Davis that "As far as I can judge, the contemplated

276

expedition offers the fairest prospects of valuable results within the limits of the Confederacy, and its success would be attended with the greatest relief." When Pendleton got up to leave he was asked to remain the night, but Pendleton needed to return his borrowed horse and planned to stay with a cousin nearby. He got lost finding his way and was helped by a courier. Although he arrived late he was greeted with a hot meal of the "most beautiful bread" and two beef tongues. As for the region in which the Army was camped, he concluded that "The whole country is one vast bed of mud."

Davis urgently wanted Johnston to pressure the Federal forces in the West in order to relieve the pressure on Lee caused by the presence of Grant and his ever larger armies. Lee concurred, urging Pendleton to do his best to persuade Johnston to attack. In the meantime, both Johnston and Davis sent emissaries to each other. First, Davis and Bragg sent Colonel John B. Sale to Dalton, Georgia on March 12, 1864. Johnston told Sale that he needed Longstreet to join him with his Corps before he could launch an offensive severing the Union's line of communications between Knoxville and Chattanooga and thereby force Sherman in Chattanooga to attack Johnston in a solid defensive position. However, it would be best not to risk a defeat north of the Tennessee River, so the offensive should be made through northern Alabama instead. Johnston preferred to force Sherman to attack him and incur severe casualties to try to even the odds.

Davis next sent Lieutenant Colonel Arthur Cole, an Inspector General of field transport. His inspection disclosed startling deficiencies in fodder rations and supply wagons which hampered Johnston's ability to move. In return, when Pendleton was on his way again to Georgia Johnston sent Colonel Benjamin Ewell to answer questions raised by Davis. Johnston was prepared to take the offensive but not into East Tennessee. That direction was fraught with risk should the Army be defeated. Ewell tried to convince Davis that Johnston's transport was inadequate and that he needed more men as well. While Bragg was convinced the transport was deficient he disagreed about the manpower. Both he and Davis were focused on Virginia.

Pendleton departed Orange Court House on April 7th on the accommodation train for Richmond. The derailment of a freight train on the war worn tracks delayed his arrival in Richmond until late at night at his daughter's rented rooms. The next day he spent hours in conference with President Davis and General Bragg. His departure south was held up by botched paperwork, allowing him to linger in the capital for worship services on Sunday. He arrived in Georgia at midnight on the 14th. The next day he met with Johnston and his cavalry commander Joe Wheeler, an ally of President Davis. Pendleton passed along Davis' message. The enemy in East Tennessee was weakened by the movement of troops to Virginia, and an invasion of Tennessee could garner much needed supplies for the Confederacy. Pendleton added on his own that an inactive Army was simply a waste of assets.

Johnston bombarded Pendleton with evidence that his Army was ill prepared to do what Davis desired. Surprisingly, Wheeler supported Johnston for the most part. Sherman had 103,000 men around Chattanooga alone, while Johnston had but 77,000 infantry. Instead, Johnston offered his own plan. Pendleton sent a report to Bragg on the 16th conveying that Johnston "cordially approved of an aggressive movement" but not into East Tennessee on account of its "hazard of ruin." Johnston was unwilling to do as Davis wanted since "The enemy is, in fact, not weakened in Tennessee, but is, if anything, stronger than at Missionary Ridge." Johnston's Army was too small "to advance at once into Tennessee." Johnston's "immense trains essential for supporting the army through such a wilderness" would be exposed to constant attack. Nor would the transport be ready for at least a month. Even if Johnston reached Middle Tennessee he lacked the means to gather the supplies Davis hoped to find. Sherman's preparations were advancing and he would probably attack before Johnston could, and force him on the defensive. It would be "ruinous" should the Army be destroyed in a defeat north of the Tennessee River.

Instead Johnston intended to "stand on the defensive till strengthened; to watch, prepare, and then strike as soon as possible." In order to do this he needed reinforcements. Once reinforced, he would advance and attack Sherman and move north on the south bank of the Tennessee to Cleveland, cut the railroad and isolate East Tennessee. "This would probably force the enemy to a general battle this side of the Tennessee." At the same time the cavalry would cross into Middle Tennessee attacking Sherman's line of communications and hopefully force him to retreat north. Perhaps then Johnston could defeat Sherman and advance to the Ohio River.

After hearing this Pendleton "did not feel justified in pertinaciously advocating the particular movement into Tennessee, and could not but admit that the mode of attack preferred by General Johnston might, on the whole, prove most proper....Having accomplished all I could" Pendleton took a train back to Richmond. After a delay due to the poor condition of the tracks in Danville, Pendleton arrived in Richmond on April 20th, the same day Colonel Ewell last met with Davis before returning to Georgia. Ewell reminded Davis that Johnston could not move without adequate transport, and therefore needed another 1,000 wagons and horses to pull them. Furthermore, Johnston was in desperate need of reinforcements. Pendleton conferred with Davis and Bragg on April 21st. In the end Bragg first offered a division from General Leonidas Polk's independent Corps in Alabama, but eventually Polk's entire Corps united with the Army of Tennessee. The entire discussion was mooted when Sherman launched his offensive on May 4, 1864 with Johnston surrendering the military initiative and engaging in a fighting retreat towards Atlanta.

The experience gave Pendleton a new prestige. Both Davis and Johnston were impressed by his handling of the situation and the professionalism of his conduct. When Leonidas Polk, an Episcopalian clergyman like Pendleton, was killed in June 1864 at Kennesaw Mountain President Davis asked Lee if Pendleton should be promoted to Lieutenant General and sent to replace Polk as a corps commander. Lee's response was chilling:

> I am unable to recommend a successor. As much as I esteem and admire General Pendleton, I would not select him to command a corps in this army. I do not mean to say by that he is not competent, but from what I have seen of him, I do not know that he is. I can spare him, if in your good judgment, you decide he is the best available.....

Given his own self-assessment Pendleton would probably have agreed.

VMI After Hunter Raid 1864

13. "I HAVE NEVER BEEN MORE IN PRAYER THAN DURING THIS CAMPAIGN."

[THE OVERLAND CAMPAIGN AND HUNTER'S RAID, 1864]

From lightning and tempest; from plague, pestilence, and famine; from battle and murder, and from sudden death, Good Lord deliver us.

Episcopalian Book of Common Prayer, 1789

In the spring of 1864 the opposing armies in Virginia camped close to where they began the campaigns of 1862 and 1863. After three years of arduous fighting the surrounding landscape was desolate. The soldiers of both armies used all of the available wood for fires and shelter, and all of the local livestock for food. There were no growing crops, no animal stock, no people, and few buildings left standing. But this time there would be a difference in the outcome of the campaign. The Army of Northern Virginia was no longer the efficient machine Lee created in 1862. The quality of the officer corps was diminished; there were fewer men in the ranks, and less hopeful of winning the war. This time, too, Lee faced a larger enemy force commanded by a much improved officer corps, and controlled by an opponent who knew how to use his strength to his advantage and rarely made mistakes.

Upon Pendleton's return to Virginia he returned to the chronic fine tuning of his artillery corps. He visited the various Corps Chiefs of Artillery at their remote winter camps, often staying overnight in their tents. He wrote home that nothing was stirring on the front but that active campaigning was soon expected. Overall he reported that, "The enemy all quiet still on this line. All our officers and men are hopeful." On May 3rd the weather turned unusually cold with wind and rain. When he awoke the next morning he saw the Blue Ridge to the northwest covered with snow.

Business affairs in Lexington also demanded his attention. He asked Anzelotte to insist that the farmer renting one of their lots by the fairgrounds manure the soil properly for cultivation. With Pendleton absent from town other farmers had taken advantage of his absence and broken the gates of some of his acreage out of town to feed their cattle on his crop land. He wanted a warning sign posted and any cattle found on his lots shot. The family desperately needed the vegetables grown there for "abundant health." He also leased the Rectory for another year.

Pendleton fought off a proposal by the Chief Ordnance officer of the Confederacy, Josiah Gorgas. Gorgas had asked Braxton Bragg, the de facto national military chief by virtue of his role as advisor to President Davis, to make changes in the overall national artillery organizational structure. Primarily he sought equality in the number and type of artillery pieces throughout the Army by diminishing Lee's overall superiority in field artillery and adding them to the Army of Tennessee. Lee had more and better guns because his Army captured them in battle while the Army of Tennessee tended to lose them. Gorgas proposed that for every 1,000 men there be a battery of three guns, not to exceed five pieces per brigade. If adopted this would upset Pendleton's creation of massed artillery battalions in each Corps. Gorgas also intended to reduce the overall number of guns allowed since providing all the equipment and ammunition for the artillery was severely taxing the resources of the Ordnance Department. As a result, "the artillery of General Lee would be reduced to about 170, including Eshleman at Petersburg, instead of 213. Besides, an increase of thirty pieces has been asked and is preparing under the requisition of General Pendleton, approved by General Lee." For whatever reason, Gorgas' proposals were never adopted.

At some point Pendleton was offended by the reception he received at the Army's national headquarters in Richmond as not befitting his senior rank. In order to meet with the Army Adjutant General Samuel Cooper he had to pass through the "exclusive & extremely invidious obstruction placed at the door of your Department," forcing him to undergo "the indignity of seeking admittance through permission circuitously obtained." Cooper, holding the highest rank in the Confederate Army, refused to respond to the complaint, writing on Pendleton's letter that "I cannot permit myself to reply to so intemperate & insubordinate a letter as this."

Pendleton met with Lee to sort out issues pertaining to the Army's artillery organization. General Long, the II Corps Chief of Artillery, had asked that any connection between the individual artillery battalions and the infantry divisions be severed. Lee and Pendleton disagreed. Pendleton advised all the Corps Chiefs of Artillery of Lee's new requirements. Lee preferred to "not wholly to break off associations which have more or less obtained during the war between certain organizations of the infantry and artillery arms, because such associations are considered salutary. A wise regard to proprieties of intercourse between officers the general thinks may obviate all difficulties." Pendleton also asked them to turn over two or three batteries to serve with the cavalry, and to "equalize batteries and battalions as nearly as may be without needless disturbance." This could best be accomplished by limiting every battery to just four guns each. The surplus men could be armed with muskets and used as guards.

*   *   *   *

In early May the Army of the Potomac under General Ulysses S. Grant stirred. Confederate signal stations on the nearby hills spotted movement in the Federal camps both day and night towards the fords of the Rappahannock. On May 4th the Army of the Potomac crossed the Rapidan and entered the Wilderness area where the Battle of Chancellorsville was fought just one year before. Pendleton wrote home that day to announce that the Army was "moving to the great struggle…Our army is in good condition & it feels reasonably confident.….We go to the lines on Mine Run." The curtain was about to open on the Overland Campaign which ended with Lee pinned to the defenses of Richmond.

Grant planned to pass through the Wilderness as quickly as possible. Any battle in the impenetrable thickets there would prevent him from exploiting his superior numbers and artillery. Grant had 113,000 men at his disposal while Lee had only 64,000. Grant knew that victory would not come easily and fully understood that Lee would fight him as tenaciously as possible. He was also fully aware that Lee was far better than his Confederate opponents in the West. Grant fully expected Lee to attack him as soon as he crossed the Rapidan, and in this respect he was not disappointed. As Grant's Army entered the woods Lee moved up to strike Grant's right flank. By mid-morning on May 5th General Ewell found the Federal columns marching southeast on Brock Road. He sent his Chief of Staff Sandie Pendleton to Lee asking for permission to attack. Lee refused the request; more time was required to bring up the entire Confederate Army so that the attack was not made in a piecemeal fashion. Ewell deployed to the left and A. P. Hill to the right facing Brock Road, and waited for Longstreet's Corps to come up before attacking.

Grant had other ideas. He knew Lee was coming and expected a hard fight. As soon as Federal troops spotted the Confederate lines in the woods they were ordered to "pitch into a part of Lee's army, do so without giving time for dispositions." The battle reached Ewell first. Surprised by the vehemence of the Federal attack Ewell held on with desperate fighting. Then on the right flank the once again ailing Hill was attacked. For the individual soldier the fight narrowed down to just the few yards around him. Soldiers could not see targets as they were obscured by gun smoke and woods. Around them lay the skeletal remains of those unburied from the previous spring. Hill's lines began to buckle but he did not withdraw in the expectation that Longstreet would be up soon in support. He wasn't; Longstreet was once again plodding into battle.

The battle seesawed back and forth all day until darkness fell. The night was illuminated by the many fires sparked by the muskets firing in the dry thickets. The fires could not be contained and soon consumed those wounded unable to escape. Their screams mingled with the crackling of the flames and rattle of the musketry. Pendleton was frustrated as there were only a few clearings where artillery could be deployed. He placed the battalion of twelve guns commanded by fellow Lexingtonian William Poague on a rise behind Hill's front on the Widow Tapp's farm, the only open ground in sight on the Orange Plank Road. There his guns were "effectively used in the bloody repulse given by Heth and Wilcox to a very heavy assault of the enemy." Pendleton spent the night with Hill's Corps artillery, the men sleeping with their arms at their side.

The morning of the 6th found both armies still fighting in the Wilderness. It was purely an infantry battle. As early as 5:00 a.m. the Union center attacked and found a gap between Hill and Ewell. Hill's line folded on the Orange Plank Road and Longstreet was still not on the battlefield to assist. Lee and his staff stood alone with Poague's artillery battalion confronting the Union assault. Pendleton wrote after the battle that he went to the cannon on the far right of Poague's line just as the Confederate infantry broke and fled past them. Pendleton dismounted and spoke with Poague. He then walked along the line telling each gunner to load their cannons with canister for shooting at charging infantry. Poague, writing forty years after the war and twenty years after Pendleton's death, does not mention Pendleton. He recalled that he loaded the guns with short range shells and fired slowly and obliquely at the Federal charge. One observer reported that Poague's cannon worked with speed, the twelve pieces "blending their discharges in one continuous roar." The Federal charge ground to a halt. Nearby Lee sat astride his horse attentively watching.

Just then the head of Longstreet's column appeared down the Orange Plank Road. Longstreet issued orders for his Corps to deploy in line of battle to meet the Federal assault. Lee rode up to the nearest brigade, and asked "Who are you my boys?"

"Texas boys," came the reply. Lee stood up in his stirrups and, waved his hat, and shouted, "Hurrah for Texas, hurrah for Texas." As more men came up Lee placed himself on their left and ordered a charge. The Texans hesitated. They would not endanger their beloved commander. "General Lee to the rear," they shouted, but Lee stayed. "Charge, boys" he called out again. An older graying veteran came out of the mass of soldiers and grabbed Lee's reins. He spoke respectfully to Lee, "General Lee if you do not go back we will not go forward." Lee allowed himself to be pulled back out of danger, and the charge drove the Federals back. Lee rode over to where Pendleton stood and asked him to send two guns down the road with Longstreet. Pendleton selected two guns, and after they limbered up rode with them towards the front lines. After 200 yards they came across the gravely wounded Longstreet, shot by North

Carolinians a short distance from where Jackson had been shot the year before. Pendleton and others placed Longstreet into an ambulance and sent him to the rear. Pendleton feared that Longstreet was dying.

Longstreet's arrival stabilized the lines. Lee now worked on a plan to flank Grant and drive him back into the Rapidan as he had Hooker the year before. It was not to be. Grant extended his line and the attempt to flank him proved a failure. Pendleton jotted a note to Anzelotte, "we had hard fighting..... an important success. The Yankees have been seriously beaten" He could not have been more wrong. The next day was quiet as each army collected itself and their wounded.

On the morning of the 7th Lee called Pendleton to his headquarters and asked him to build a road through the Wilderness southeast towards Spotsylvania Court House. Lee sensed his opponent was not deterred by the battle and would continue to attack in that direction. He wanted an avenue permitting Confederate troops to arrive before Grant could reach the crossroads village. The road was to pass through the woods due south from the army's right flank on the Orange Plank Road down to Shady Grove Church on the Catharpin Furnace Road. It was a rush job through dense forest, but Pendleton got it done. The road ran about six miles. It was not a perfect job, the new I Corps commander, General Richard Anderson, found tree stumps above ground level and other trunks left lying in the passage, but it was usable.

Pendleton arrived at Anderson's headquarters about midnight on the 7th and gave specific instructions as to the location and direction of the road. One of Pendleton's staff officers remained behind as a guide. Anderson did not intend to leave for Spotsylvania until morning, but when he saw the condition of the road he changed his mind. "I found the woods in every direction on fire and burning furiously, and there was no suitable place to rest." The road was narrow and due to the tree stumps the passage would be slow. Anderson broke camp immediately. The I Corps marched all night in total darkness down the newly hewn and rough road. As they entered the open fields at the end of the road the I Corps stopped for breakfast. Off in the distance gunfire could be heard in the direction of Spotsylvania Court House. A courier arrived at a gallop and presented Anderson with an urgent plea for help from

Jeb Stuart. He and his cavalry were trying to keep the Federal infantry from taking Spotsylvania Court House cutting Lee off from the roads connecting him to Richmond. Anderson's men hurried towards the sound of battle and arrived just sixty yards ahead of the enemy. Pendleton's road and Anderson's decision to move earlier saved the day.

*   *   *   *

Anderson spent most of the 8th fending off Federal assaults in the muggy heat at Spotsylvania Court House. By late afternoon Ewell's Corps arrived in support. Grant, observing that Lee was fully entrenched in the Wilderness wanted to move around his flank to force him out into the open, but failed to do so. May 9th was relatively quiet although there was heavy skirmishing between the armies. Both sides extended their lines while Lee dug deep trenches for a defensive line. One observer concluded that in one day an army could build a solid line of rifle pits, in two days it would convert these into deep trenches with a proper parapet, and in three days it could add abatis in front and well entrenched artillery in the rear. Pendleton re-capped to Anzelotte that evening from the Orange Plank Road, "We have had hard fighting and an important success. But there is nothing yet really decisive. Important movements are on foot today...."

Late in the day of the 10th Grant attacked again, this time hitting Lee's left flank and center. The attempt to flank Lee on the left was stopped by two Confederate divisions. During this fighting Pendleton placed himself with Cabell's artillery battalion of the I Corps on high ground behind the lines. During the Confederate attack the Federal artillery focused on Early's division on the left flank of the Army placing it under heavy fire. Pendleton re-directed Cabell's fire to suppress the enemy's guns. The effect was instant and Early enabled to advance.

That night the Confederate pickets reported troops moving while cavalry scouts reported enemy movement to the rear. Lee erroneously concluded that Grant was retreating towards Fredericksburg, and he wanted the Army ready for pursuit. All the next day it rained, cold and dreary, on both armies. Lee ordered Pendleton to remove all of the guns from the front line to be ready to move quickly in pursuit of Grant. Lee even rode to Ewell's position in the Mule Shoe, a salient located at the center of the line, and suggested that due to the rain and mud it might be better to remove the guns to prepare them for pursuit before nightfall made the task harder. As a result the II Corps Chief of Artillery Armistead Long pulled his guns out of the Mule Shoe salient in the center of the Army's lines as did the III Corps artillery.

That night the Confederate pickets in the Mule Shoe heard the rumbling noise of an approaching mass of troops. They alerted Ewell, but the artillery chief Armistead Long did not get the message until 3:30 a.m. that morning, too late to return the guns to their positions. The dense fog lying on the meadows between the lines slowly started to lift, but the field of vision remained dim for the pickets. At 4:30 a.m. Federal General Hancock launched an assault at the Mule Shoe without any prior warning. His troops overwhelmed the infantry still in position, capturing 2,000 men of Johnson's division, including nearly all of the old Stonewall Brigade. The twenty guns withdrawn the day before returned just in time to be captured. General John B. Gordon rallied the II Corps in a counterattack driving the Federals back to the toe of the salient, known now as the Bloody Angle. The trench warfare there was fierce hand to hand combat. Soldiers pushed their muskets over the parapet and into another trench before pulling the trigger. Others were stabbed by bayonet thrusts through the chinks in the logs. The fighting went on all day and well into the night. It was a muddy, bloody mess. Afterwards one Union officer counted 150 bodies in a space no more than twelve feet by fifteen feet. As midnight neared the Confederates fell back to a new defensive trench dug at the base of the salient while the Federals remained clinging to the outer walls of the Mule Shoe. Pendleton later wrote, "Thus passed and closed this eventful day." Lee was disabused of the idea that Grant had given up. He may have sensed that he had lost the military initiative and was doomed to merely react to whatever Grant chose to do.

Sandie Pendleton was under fire the entire day and had two horses shot out from under him. General Pendleton wrote to his new daughter-in-law Kate that Sandie was mercifully spared in what was "almost a miracle," but was "worn out and sleepy." He appealed once more to God to remedy the situation. Kate, now pregnant, was staying in Richmond with Pendleton's daughter Susan Pendleton Lee. Federal cavalry again raided to the limits of the city, killing Jeb Stuart in the process. With the capital under attack Pendleton suggested perhaps they might be safer if they went home to Lexington. He reassured Kate about Sandie; "Kate, my darling …, I like him better for loving you." He wrote separately to Susan on the 13th, claiming that the Army had been quite successful against "General Ulysses," beating him continuously for the past ten days. He told her about the debacle at the Bloody Angle on the 12th, noting it a "mishap of consequence." Still, the Federal losses were immense and Lee's troops had suffered nothing in comparison to it.

The next two days it rained buckets of water forestalling any attempts by Grant to attack again. The rains made the Confederates miserable, as Pendleton described, "The most constant rains add much to our difficulties, exposing the men all the time to wet and mud, and rendering the roads almost impassable." He wrote home that "We have all been many times in the utmost danger of hot battles, yet almost as by miracle not one has therefore received a scratch….we have a good deal of real hardship, short rations, little sleep, constant labors and more or less all the time. Still the spirit of officers and men are wonderful." Pendleton was up all night the 15th "putting some guns into position to meet an attack reported as likely." However, Grant showed every sign of sidling off to the eastward again. On the 16th Lee sent Pendleton and other officers to the east, "exploring a new position to head Grant off if he moves that way." Along with the other officers, Pendleton "had a long ride last night through as bad roads as I ever travelled…I manage, however, to get along pretty well, and feel this morning quite fresh. Grant is in the mud too, and will find it next to impossible to move till we have some dry weather." As for the death of Jeb Stuart, he commented to Anzelotte that the news was "very sad."

*　　　　　*　　　　　*　　　　　*

On May 17th Pendleton sent his aide Lieutenant George Peterkin with a message to President Davis in Richmond. Given the recent Federal cavalry raids he did not trust the mail to reach the addressee in safety. We do not know what he reported, but we do know that Pendleton believed that Lee was not well. His lack of sleep affected his health through the Wilderness and Spotsylvania battles and weakened him. On the 18th Pendleton advised General Alexander at the I Corps that an attack was imminent near the Court House where the line was weakest. Even though all the other senior artillery officers had examined the defensives, he asked that Alexander do so also, and to bring some extra batteries with him. Indeed, Pendleton later reported that the shelling was "pretty lively all about the Court-House, and between there and the Frazier house."

Recalling the debacle on the third day at Gettysburg Pendleton took the time to count how many shells remained in the Army's supply trains after several days of combat. As of the 18th there were 7,466 left in all three Corps, no more than thirty-seven shells per gun. He also reported that there were only twenty-nine guns in defensive positions since the Army was prepared to move as quickly as possible once Grant's next move was made. The seventeen days of nearly constant battle wore both armies down. Along with crucial senior officers wounded and killed, Lee lost 16,000 men he would not be able to replace. He was heartened by the thought that Grant was even more damaged, but it did not matter. Grant's losses of 36,000 men would be quickly made up by new recruits, draftees, and reassigned units.

Pendleton noted that the Confederates expected a heavy attack soon. But it was Lee who made the next move. On the 19th Ewell struck around the Federal right in an endeavor to reach Grant's wagon trains. His attack was botched at the outset and failed miserably. Early in the evening of May 20th the Army of the Potomac gathered its equipment and trains and took the road to the southeast towards the North Anna River and the Confederate supply base at Hanover Junction. Lee expected the move. By 4:30 a.m. the next morning Ewell's II Corps left camp headed for the North Anna.

Lee reached the North Anna River first and entrenched in an inverted "V" on the south bank. Pendleton reached Hanover Junction just south of the North Anna after a hard march. Other than a break in the middle of the night the column moved south until it reached the Junction at 9:00 in the morning. Pendleton dined at the headquarters of General John C. Breckinridge and enjoyed the hospitality of a "superb lunch and delightful nap." He wrote Anzelotte a letter while leaning on a stump outside Sandie's tent, surrounded by the Army. The sun was hot but a pleasant breeze made the day tolerable. He had been asked to preach in the I Corps and was "very happy for the opportunity unless military duties interfered." Pendleton also commented on his faith in God. "During the beat of battle my mind has been so exercised, and it is wonderful what calm it impacts amid the storm. I cannot believe a holy God would sanction the enormous wickedness involved in the whole programme of our enemies. We certainly deserve his displeasure and are justly punished for our sins, yet the impiety, treachery, falsehood, impurity, covetousness" of the "shameless Yankees must ever be abominable in God's sight."

It was Lee's hope to re-gain the initiative and drive Grant back to Washington as he had so many others. But Lee was betrayed by his own body. On top of his history of heart ailments and exhaustion he was bedridden with a gastro-intestinal illness. The doddering Ewell, the ailing Hill, and the neophyte Anderson were incapable of leading the Army.

Lee hoped Grant would cross the river and attack one flank of the "V" or the other. This would enable Lee to use his shorter interior lines to mass troops for an attack driving that isolated wing of the Federal Army back into the river crushing it. Pendleton spent the night choosing a defensive line and adjusting some of the artillery positions. Occasionally a Federal picket would shoot in his direction. On May 23rd Grant took the bait and sent two Corps across the North Anna on the western side of the "V" where they were isolated and attacked Hill's Corps. Hill held them off but failed to launch the planned counter-assault. On the 25th Grant doubled down on his mistake by sending Hancock's Corps alone across the river on the east to face two Confederate Corps. Neither Anderson nor Ewell acted as Jackson, Lee, or Longstreet would have done, and the opportunity to defeat Grant in detail was lost.

That day Pendleton wrote home, this time he sat in a "humble building" near the railroad station during a lull in the fighting. Once again the Confederates had "headed off Grant" and there had been some "sharp skirmishing." However, the "strong fortification" prepared by the Confederates prevented any real assault. Pendleton believed that the "Federals have vastly less fight in them than at Wilderness." Pendleton reported that Lee was unwell but that a "little rest and good diet will see him restored….He is unceasing in his care and labors, and is animated by a most cheering Christian trust….He expresses full assurance that the Judge of all the earth will do right…." Pendleton was less sanguine about the runaway inflation depreciating Confederate currency. A recently received package consisting of a barrel of molasses, salt, sugar, ten pieces of cloth, along with shipping charges, cost him $1,400.

Grant reached a similar conclusion about his enemy. He reported to Washington that in his opinion "Lee's army is whipped." On May 27th Grant packed up again and moved southeast down the northern bank of the North Anna. A frustrated and still ailing Lee was concerned that Grant was edging ever closer to Richmond and told Jubal Early that "We must destroy this Army of Grant's before he gets to the James River. If he gets there it will become a siege, and then it will be a mere question of time."

  *   *   *   *

General Pendleton spent the 27th inspecting the horses of the horse artillery under Major General Fitzhugh Lee. His findings were gloomy, "Thirty horses are needed to put this battery in efficient condition. ….The horses reported are in such an exhausted condition that they are unfit for severe marching or rapid movement, but are still worked in harness. Under these circumstances, I have not directed them to be turned in. A few days of rest would make some of them efficient again. Others are totally unfit for service as horse artillery horses."

He also spent part of the day scouting down the North Anna River. What he found disturbed him. He reported to Lee's headquarters that "the whole body of the enemy that was visible on the opposite side of the river to our right of the railroad move off obliquely by their right flank toward the Telegraph road." He was "certain that they were moving in that direction to get on a road in the rear out of view, and follow the rest of the army to the Pamunkey." Pendleton ordered an artillery battery to fire at the Union line of march. Meanwhile, General Kershaw informed Pendleton that there was still a considerable force opposite his position…and across the river. No movement had been observed in this body at the time Pendleton departed for Lee's headquarters.

The two armies moved southeast towards Hanovertown on the Pamunkey River, just fifteen miles from Richmond. On the 28th Lee sent a cavalry force to conduct a reconnaissance in force to Hanovertown to see if Grant had crossed the river. They encountered Union cavalry and infantry at Haw's Shop south of the Pamunkey, confirming Lee's fears. That day Pendleton remained at the still ailing Lee's headquarters near Atlee Station. Pendleton was exhausted and sleepy having had no rest the night before. The Army had arrived at Atlee Station the night before chasing Grant as he "slipped off again." Pendleton noted that Grant was closing in on the same "track" McClellan took in 1862, and the Confederates had come "squarely upon his force today." The following day he and Lee moved to Totopotomy Creek amidst "such destruction as you never saw" left in the wake of the Federal Army.

Once there Pendleton continued his inspection of the horse artillery. He discovered that the horses in some batteries "are much worn down and many of them unfit for service," although now being adequately fed. The 100 new horses requested had not yet arrived. Pendleton also sent any broken or damaged equipment to nearby Richmond for repair. For some reason Pendleton asked Lee's staff for a reliable road map of the area and was told none could be found, but one had been sent for from Richmond. It was a Sunday, so Pendleton performed his devotions, rested, and refreshed. Lee was beginning to mend and rode about his Army in a carriage.

The armies maneuvered towards Cold Harbor in an excessively muggy heat. Lee determined to control the critical crossroads at Cold Harbor and sent his cavalry to hold it until the rest of the Army arrived. But Grant's infantry and cavalry drove them out. Lee saw an opportunity to launch a flank attack to roll up Grant's lines but the assault was badly managed by inexperienced brigade and division level officers without proper reconnaissance and failed miserably. Lee's Army could only dig in. The heat may have affected Pendleton as he felt unwell. He wrote home that Grant kept fortifying his positions and sliding to the left, and was getting close to the York River. The Confederate right now extended to Cold Harbor. Pendleton feared that Grant "may go on till he reaches James River below Chaffins Bluff and then for aught I know cross to the south side and we must still head him off." However, he opposed any attack on Grant before he did so. Pendleton reiterated his faith that Grant was destined to fail because of the wisdom, goodness, and power of God. The next day he wrote Anzelotte again, commenting that the war was replicating itself, placing Grant where McClellan had been in 1862.

On June 2nd Pendleton requested that batteries from the Richmond defenses on Drewry's Bluff be sent to Cold Harbor to augment Lee's artillery. It rained heavily that night. On the 3rd and 4th he made a thorough reconnaissance of the fords of the Chickahominy River beyond the right wing of the Confederate Army in the expectation that the two armies would soon move that direction. That afternoon Grant launched his suicidal assaults against

Lee's entrenched Army at Cold Harbor. Even Grant recognized afterwards that his losses were enormous and futile. It is a mark as to how deteriorated the Army of Northern Virginia had become that there was no thought given to making a counter-attack to rout the disorganized and demoralized Federals once their assaults failed. Then for the first time since Grant crossed the Rapidan the campaign came to a halt. During the lull Lee and Grant dithered over terms of a truce wounded men suffered and died in the hot sun between their lines.

While waiting for Grant's next move, Pendleton learned from his son in law that Virginia born General David Hunter's Federal army had reached Staunton, just forty miles north down the Shenandoah Valley from Lexington. He anxiously wrote his daughter Susan in Richmond from near Gaines Mills on the 7th that there was nothing to keep Hunter from heading further south. For now she and Kate were safer remaining in Richmond. He did not know "what outrages they may perpetuate there none can say." He relied on his faith that his family would be "sustained" and he "cannot suppose that even Yankee villainy will be allowed to indulge itself in …disgraces to my family. They may destroy property, and so inflict a good deal of suffering. But all that could be remedied." Pendleton just hoped that the treasonous and "despicable" Hunter would "be punished as he deserves…"

Two days later he addressed a letter to his wife in Lexington although he did not know if it would arrive given the Federal invasion. He told her to have faith, but cautioned her about the Federals, "Restrained as they are of no principle of right, the customs of civilized war, no limit can be expected to their outrages wherever they can make their way….the raiders may in the wantonness of their malice destroy my books and break up furniture…..and destroy all your present means of subsistence." Yet he believed that God would protect them.

Over the next few days Pendleton occupied his mind with administrative details. Beauregard's new artillery chief asked Pendleton for charts showing how he organized his artillery corps so he could follow the same pattern. Pendleton inspected more of the horse artillery, this time discovering that "the general condition of the batteries is very good." Lee's staff sent some instructions for the artillery, and he spent time trying to find some Napoleon 12-pounder guns for the Army. Pendleton also rode the front line and laid out the positions for the mortars. Mortars are short stubby bronze or iron tubes used to shoot a high arc into an enemy trench, a return to the 17th Century siege tactics and a precursor to trench warfare in the 20th Century. He asked Alexander and the Chief Ordnance officer about using "stink shells" with toxic or annoying gases in them and wondered if they could be inserted into the fuse for the shell. Pendleton wondered if the shell should combine a destructive explosion with suffocating gases or to avoid the explosion and just let the gases out. On the title page of a romantic and sensational novel "Eleanor's Victory" Pendleton wrote the answer, the shell should combine both. He also approved of the use of hand grenades provided the men were not afraid to use them, and thought it worth the experiment.

There was still no news from Lexington although Lee told him that conditions in the Shenandoah were improving. Pendleton preferred to believe that the Federals had not reached Lexington. On the 11th he and Sandie rode into Richmond to visit with Susan Lee and Kate Pendleton. Still, his anxieties consumed him. "I have never been more in prayer than during this campaign." It soothed him to "lay hold of unerring wisdom, infinite power, and unfailing goodness" of God and faith.

On June 13th Jubal Early, along with his Chief of Staff Lieutenant Colonel Sandie Pendleton, pulled the II Corps out of the lines and headed west to defend Lynchburg. That same day Confederate skirmishers slowly crept forward and were surprised to learn that Grant was gone. No one knew where. Having exhausted his Army in the Overland Campaign Grant determined on a siege of Richmond by crossing the James River and attacking Petersburg to cut off rail traffic from the south. On the 14th Grant rode down to the James and crossed the river on a 2,000 foot long pontoon bridge. The next day he attacked the woefully undermanned Petersburg defenses, which were saved only by the genius of Pierre Beauregard and the timidity of the Federal commanders on the ground. Parts of Lee's Army reached Petersburg the next day and prevented the loss of the city. Lee was now pinned down in trenches defending Richmond, Petersburg, and the railroad lifelines to the South. The war was entering its final stages.

    *   *   *   *

Grant's first attempt to occupy and destroy Lee's breadbasket in the Shenandoah Valley ended in disaster at New

Market when Franz Sigel's superior Federal force was defeated piecemeal by General Breckinridge with the heroic charge by the VMI Corps of Cadets. On May 21st the Virginia born abolitionist General David Hunter assumed command of the defeated Union force of 9,000 men. Five days later he started up the valley, burning farms and grain as he went. On June 5th he routed three raw brigades assembled by the Confederacy at Piedmont and the next day occupied the railhead of Staunton. He was joined by additional forces coming from the west on the 8th. With an army of 18,000 men and only a scattering of Confederates to oppose him he started to burn his way further south towards Lexington. As Susan Pendleton Lee wrote, "The progress of this army was marked by devastation and destruction." While it was impossible to burn all the crops in the field, the Federal troops burned all the mills and structures in their path.

The advance of a Union army towards Lexington threw the residents into a panic. Rumors flew, "people moving flour, goods, etc.; driving their cows; ladies flying about in a high state of excitement." Books were moved from VMI to Washington College. Arms, munitions, and supplies were put on canal boats and floated down to Lynchburg. Families hid their jewelry and silver. Livestock and enslaved blacks were sent to the mountains for safekeeping, while white men went to escape capture. The Pendletons stashed, with the aid of their enslaved black servants, two guns under the porch and one buried in the cellar. They had some trunks of other Confederate officers and cadets which they hid as well. They packed a box with valuable clothing and hid it in the tall grass in a corner of garden. However, it could be seen by passersby, and so they dug a hole and buried it.

Hunter's army approached on four parallel roads towards Lexington, sustaining his army with what it could seize from the residents rather than its own supply line. Consequently, the Federals were chronically short of food provisions and fresh horses, and simply lived off the land they passed through. The small Confederate army under General Imboden harassed the Federals but could no more than slow their advance up the Valley. There was hit and run fighting between the opposing forces from Brownsburg to Fairfield.

Late on June 10, 1864, the small Confederate army camped for the night across the river from Lexington, the campfires visible to the frightened townsfolk, while the Federals bivouacked at Hays Creek and Brownsburg. The Confederate commander warned VMI officials that he could not prevent the Union army from occupying Lexington, however, he intended to delay the Federal troops at the river for a few hours. The VMI Corps of Cadets were in Lynchburg when they heard of Hunter's advance towards Lexington. The cadets took the canal boats back to help defend the town where they spent the night under arms. Their howitzer was ordered to cover the bridge across the North (now Maury) River at Jordan's Point with an infantry company in close support. On the following morning, June 11, 1864, the Confederates slowly withdrew their pickets across the bridge and into town, placing them on the bluffs and in stores surrounding the bridge in support of the cadets. A Union attempt to cut the rear guard off from the bridge was foiled by the fire of the troops from the southern bank.

The Confederates burned the bridge and defended the crossing with artillery fire and sharpshooters. Union field batteries on the hills on the northern bank of river began shelling the defenses and the town. The fight was a "very noisy affair, but not dangerous." Federal cavalry scouted up and down the river for a crossing in order to flank the Confederate line. When the Federals destroyed the James River canal locks downstream the level of the river dropped, allowing for the Federal troops to easily ford the river. The shelling continued for what seemed hours, striking twenty houses. The Confederates withdrew south when the Federal infantry crossed the river at the town and cavalry approached from the west after fording the river upstream.

During the shelling the Lexingtonians huddled in their basements for protection. Luckily, no one in town was injured. One shell landed in the Rectory garden. As Anzelotte recalled "The wretches shelled the town for hours. Shells fell everywhere in town – in Colonel Williamson's yard, into Mr. John Campbell's house, into Miss Baxter's house. One struck Colonel Reid's front door and almost struck his daughter ...one fell in the garden here; one struck somewhere near us, as several small bullets were found in the upper porch here and at Captain Moore's." To the west the Federal cavalry crossed the river at Leyburn's Mill and came in by way of Mulberry Hill.

As the Federals entered what one described as a "beautiful town" singing "John Brown's Body," the curious villagers watched them through drawn blinds. Mrs. Pendleton and daughter Mary sat on their porch as the Federal cavalry came from behind their house and rode past into town. The invaders sacked and burned VMI while looting Washington College next door. Some of the cottages at VMI housing the families of Confederate officers and the home of Virginia Governor John Letcher were burned. Other Union soldiers went house to house looking for food, tearing up gardens for turnips and other vegetables. Hunter made the home of the VMI Commandant his headquarters, later saving it from destruction.

One Union officer noted his surprise that the whites felt that the enslaved blacks were loyal to them and would not leave them on any terms. Yet the blacks were "wild with joy…thronging our camps, giving information, proffering assistance….The Negroes take the first opportunity they find of running into our lines and giving information as to where their masters are hidden and conduct our foragers to their retreats. In this way our supply of cattle has been kept up. Negroes were continually running to us with information of all kinds and are the only persons upon whose correct truth we can rely." Many blacks escaped to the Union army as it paraded through town. Many others participated in the looting. All five houses on the street where the Pendletons lived were ransacked. At the Reids and Moores the soldiers seized 1500 pounds of bacon, five barrels of flour, preserves, buttermilk, and lard. They tore up clothing of the young boys and enslaved blacks. Every little particle of food was gone, except at the Pendleton house.

The Pendleton ladies' ordeal was just beginning. At home were Anzolette, and daughters Mary, Rose, Nancy and Hughella. Rose Pendleton wrote a week later they were over run by "thieving wretches." The women locked up the house except for the front door where two or three kept guard while Mrs. Pendleton was stationed at the back door into the kitchen. One trooper crawled over the fence from the Reid's yard with his pistol in hand. One of the Pendletons described him as "one of the most ruffianly I saw." He asked for milk and was given some buttermilk instead. He claimed he had orders to search the house but Mrs. Pendleton told him she would wait for officers before she allowed a search. The soldier left, but five more came up to the house demanding bread and meat, and were given a shoulder of bacon. One asked, "How do you feel about this war?" The response was a curt "I should think by this time you would know how every Dixie woman felt on that subject." Mrs. Pendleton went to Hunter's headquarters and asked for a guard for the house. When she returned she found a guard from the 20th Pennsylvania Cavalry mounted on his horse in the front yard.

They ate no supper. One Yankee opened the dining room window and broke into a flour barrel stored there. He was caught with his hands full of flour and meekly asked "May I have some?" One of the daughters replied "I can't prevent it since you've broken the barrel open, but who do you think wants to eat out of it after you have put your dirty hands in it." One of the guards told the man to put the flour back but he left with it anyway. Hundreds more came in the evening. At night all the women slept in the Pendleton's bedroom for safety.

On Sunday morning they fed the guard breakfast on the front porch and held their Sunday service, including reading the prayer for Jefferson Davis. The enslaved blacks stayed in the kitchen baking bread for the Union soldiers. Anzelotte remained on guard on the front porch. Some of the wandering soldiers threatened to burn the house down. The threat was taken seriously since the Pendletons could see the fires burning at VMI. Some officers came by and asked to buy strawberries but the Pendletons had none to sell. In the afternoon an officer and a squad came to search for munitions of war and provisions. Anzelotte told the officer that "one man ought to be enough to search the house." The officer left his armed men on the porch. Anzelotte escorted him to "every hole and corner," but nothing was found. On the whole the officer behaved respectfully, and refused to seize Pendleton's Confederate coat as he had been in the old pre-war Army. Their milk cows, which had been taken away, were returned.

The next day the soldiers returned to search as they learned of the guns hidden under porch and a cache of VMI uniforms hidden in the house, probably from one of the enslaved servants. The second search revealed more hidden items. They removed ten pounds of bacon, two bushels of meal, and salt. One daughter heard the slaves asking each other if they would leave with the Yankees. One said she would rather stay in the nice house and make the whites wait on her. A black man walked into the kitchen on Sunday morning and introduced himself as a "colored gentleman from headquarters." He was ordered out, and after about the third command that he could not stay, he went away, saying "Them's coming, and of my color too, that will go where they please."

On Sunday evening the guard asked what General Pendleton would have thought of a Yankee sitting on his porch. No one answered. The guards talked about Grant's losses in the Overland campaign. Anzelotte commented that "Grant lost those 70,000 men before he left the Wilderness, and I must say one thing, that though we are the most wonderful people on the earth, still how we with our five million can always lose two to one against you with your twenty millions, and still have plenty of men to oppose you is more than wonderful."

"Oh, the guard replied, "you get men from England."

"Pray" queried Rose, "at which of the blockaded ports do they come in?" The response, "They came before the war."

The guards said they would be gone by Monday but were still there in the morning insisting on getting the key to search the cellar. Rose asked if a non-commissioned officer authorized the search and was told, "Sis, We are the provost guard and have authority to look where ever we suspect." It was apparent one of the enslaved servants told them where to look. They went straight to the guns and the trunk of clothing. One of the guards insisted they had been informed that the Pendletons owned a beautiful silver mounted rifle to shoot at Federals. A neighbor insisted that since Pendleton was artillery he would have no use for one. The guard responded that Mrs. Pendleton was a liar and that he would not take her word under oath. Mary Pendleton told the guards they could not have the trunk of clothing without a written order from the Provost Marshal. She accompanied the guards back to the Provost Marshal. On the way Mary asked how they knew about the guns, and the guard said "we happened to fall upon the very person who knew all about it, a Negro." The Provost Marshal told Mary to raise her veil so he could see her face. He then refused to hear Mary's request, and rudely ordered the house searched again and the trunk seized.

This time the soldiers looked under the beds, and into the drawers, book cases, trunks, boxes, wardrobes, and bureaus. During the search the women had some of the cadet uniforms under their skirts with the rest tossed over the kitchen roof. During the search one man claimed Lee's men stole jewelry off the women in Pennsylvania. Rose shouted out, "I believe no such talk." He then turned to Anzelotte and said, "Lincoln put out his Proclamation to you to free your niggers and come back into the Union, and you wouldn't do it, and this serves you right." One man asked to exchange sugar for some bread, but Anzelotte proudly said, "We Dixie women do without sugar" He fired back, "and coffee too." She retorted with "yes, everything but independence and that we will have." Once the guards took the trunk they wanted to open it right away, probably to loot, but Mary insisted they return to the Provost Marshal with it first. On their way back to the Rectory the guard told Mary "You treat those niggers good, they is as free as you." Mary replied. "Do you suppose they have to wait for you to tell them that?"

Hunter spent an extra day in Lexington waiting not only for reinforcements but also for a 200 wagon train carrying much needed supplies. The delay was "enough to prove the salvation of Lynchburg." On the morning of Tuesday the 14th Hunter and his army left town. The Pendletons were still in bed when they heard the noises of their departure. Leaving with them were 300 to 500 newly freed blacks. For Mrs. Pendleton it was an "inexpressible relief." She later told her son-in-law that, "My horror of the American Yankees is great, but of the African Yankee! It is impossible to express it." She felt that Hunter's army was "wicked" and "wild beasts" stealing all the food they could. The enemy left behind piles of abandoned items stolen in the heat of the moment but now of no interest to the looters. The Union occupation caused damage of at least $3 million to the town.

Hunter arrived at Lynchburg just after Jubal Early and his II Corps. Hunter retreated towards the Ohio River. On its way down the Valley General Early's men camped on June 23rd at Buffalo Forge. Lieutenant Colonel Sandie Pendleton, now Early's chief of staff, was suffering from dysentery and rode ahead to his home in Lexington. A group of officers joined him the next morning for a breakfast of fresh raspberries, and for dinner they had cold ham, lettuce, and rice, an amazing menu given the pillaging a handful of days before. The next day when the Confederate Army reached the outskirts of Lexington, Jackson's old Corps marched past his grave with guns reversed and heads uncovered. Hunter's men had removed the head and footboards of the grave, but the silk flag, a gift from England, was preserved and flew above it. After passing the cemetery Early's army received an enthusiastic welcome as it marched down Main Street through town.

General Edwin Lee

Susan Pendleton Lee

Alexander 'Sandie' Pendleton

Kate Corbin Pendleton

Confederate lines at Petersburg

14. "NEVER WILL MY HEART CEASE TO FEEL THE SORROW"

[PETERSBURG, 1864-1865]

In the midst of life we are in death: of whom may we seek for succour, but of thee, O Lord, who for our sins art justly displeased?

1789 Episcopal Book of Common Prayer

Thus saith the Lord; A voice was heard in Ramah, lamentation, and bitter weeping; Rachel weeping for her children refused to be comforted for her children, because they were not.

Jeremiah 31:15, King James Version

For nearly a fortnight Pendleton was in a state of constant anxiety about the safety of his family and home in Lexington. Initially he drew comfort from the thought that God would protect his family. But as the days wore on his concern grew. He visited his brother Hugh Pendleton and cousin Robert Nelson, and rode into Richmond to visit daughter Susan, and to visit a barber. Even though the mails had not yet been re-established with the Valley, on the 12th he wrote home that he was still uncertain as to the fate of Lexington and was encouraged to believe that Hunter never reached the town. On the 18th Sandie sent his father a telegram announcing that Anzelotte and her daughters were well, but provided no details on how the invading Union soldiers treated them. Pendleton received the cable three days later. Susan wrote her father from Richmond that her husband General Ned Lee had visited in Lexington just before the occupation and reported that Mrs. Pendleton was "all wonderfully calm and unterrified."

Relieved, Pendleton pressed for more details. He asked if the enemy troops left any food for them to eat, since he found that he could not believe anything the Federal authorities reported to be accurate. This made it so "that it will be difficult to have the truth recorded in history, or to make mankind believe that a people calling itself Christian could perpetuate such enormities." He reported that when Federal troops arrived in Prince George's County, Virginia, that they "let loose their Negro soldiers to indulge at their pleasure their brutal passions, and the result beggars description..." He wondered if the people of Lexington suffered similarly.

A letter from Anzelotte finally reached Pendleton in late June. She described the actions of the Confederates and VMI Corps of Cadets, and then the occupation by Hunter's men. Pendleton referred to Hunter's actions as "Yankee insolence." On the other hand, he also was relieved, "I hardly dared you would come off so easily." For him it was proof that God answered prayers from the faithful. To make up for the food stores lost he believed that there would be enough bread until the next wheat harvest and they could also live off the vegetables grown in the garden and milk and butter from the cows. Pendleton arranged for 100 pounds of sugar, a half barrel of molasses and some cotton cloth be sent from Georgia to help his family. In early July the Tidewater turned excessively muggy and hot. Combined with an extreme drought the weather was unbearable. With the Federal armies encircling Richmond and the suffering from the heat, Pendleton sent his daughter Susan to Lexington's higher altitude and cooler weather for her own ease, comfort, and safety. She was joined there by Sandie's wife Kate, now expecting their first child.

    *   *   *   *

In the meantime Pendleton once again scouted the area east and southeast of Richmond in the hope of finding Grant's main Army. Initially, he thought he found Grant near Harrison's Landing on the north bank of the James, but by the 18th realized that Grant had moved his entire army to the southern bank around Petersburg where he was certain to "bring trouble." Pendleton was "off again.

Grant has taken all his army to the south side. We go to meet him as usual." On Sunday he preached to former Governor and now General Henry Wise. Wise thoroughly enjoyed the sermon, telling Pendleton that it was soothing. For his part Pendleton found Wise to be "a strange but interesting man."

With the merger of Beauregard's Army with Lee's at Petersburg his artillery corps came under Pendleton's management. On the 19th Pendleton inspected the lines around Petersburg with General Beauregard. For two days he adjusted the various artillery positions. On the north side of the Appomattox, the river flowing through Petersburg to the tidal waters of the Chesapeake, Pendleton arranged for rifled guns to enfilade the Federal lines. Other guns were placed on a commanding hill at the Archer house, while upriver more guns were placed. On the 20th these guns opened up on the Federal flank, causing it to fall back to a new position. The Federals later responded with an extensive shelling of these new positions from their newly sited batteries and gunboats.

For the next few days there was a "good deal" of artillery exchanges every day along with continuous infantry skirmishing between the lines. The Federals shelled the civilian areas of Petersburg, an "outrage" borne by the citizens with "great fortitude and dignity." With the competing armies locked into trench warfare Pendleton found little to do. The lines he rode along were generally fixed and no adjustments were needed. Pendleton wrote that the "Armies hurling defiance at each other day and night from their trenches," using missiles of all sorts. The heat remained "stifling" and the "very earth seems parched." Water became hard to find which was especially trying on the horses. The food was costly but "rough," with the rations available "not half enough." There was no coffee, and the troops lived on bread, bacon, and water.

By mid-July there were 6,472 men and officers in the artillery corps, 3,000 short of what the table of organization allowed. The battery by battery inspections were renewed by Pendleton with the assistance of his staff. An aide and later writer John Esten Cooke inspected the horse artillery and found that some of the horses were broken down by severe marching and badly galled on their back and shoulders. Most just required some rest and forage. Their equipment was worn out and ruinous to the horses, and Pendleton asked that it all be condemned. His initial request for ammunition for Coehorn trench mortars was answered by the military bureaucrats in

Richmond with a three page explanation as to why they could not be provided. Pendleton patiently replied that the ammunition be sent forward as soon as possible. By July 8th distribution of the rounds commenced. Pendleton also re-organized various batteries, placing them back in their proper Army Corps for supply and command, and eliminating unnecessary organizations. His task was further burdened when General E. P. Alexander was wounded on June 30th. Pendleton was so busy he forgot to wish Anzelotte a happy anniversary. He apologized to her by confessing that she was God's gift for "eternal good and earthly happiness."

Throughout June and July Grant kept up pressure on the Petersburg lines while reaching ever westwards towards the railroad lifelines to Richmond and Lee's Army. Sharp skirmishing lasted day and night along with desultory artillery exchanges. In the area of A. P. Hill's III corps sentries detected mining underneath by the Union Army, and began to countermine. On July 22nd the front was unusually quiet, and Confederate troops were shocked to see ladies in carriages riding behind the enemy lines. On the night of the 26th enemy forces were spotted moving north of the James River near Richmond. Over the next two days an enemy assault there succeeded in capturing guns from the Rockbridge Battery but was forced back. Two days later enemy forces gathered opposite the III Corps on the Petersburg lines.

As day dawned on the 30th a large mine was set off beneath a battery in Hill's Corps, blowing a gap 170 feet long and 70 feet wide in the Confederate line. The Federal assault at first occupied the gap but failed to exploit the breach. Cowardice, incompetence, and lack of command and control led to a Federal fiasco. By 10:00 a.m. the Confederates re-captured their lines after killing or wounding 3,500 Federal troops and capturing some 1,500. The killing was fueled by the presence of black troops amongst the assaulting units left stranded in the Crater. Lee's artillery contributed to the victory by guns pre-positioned to defend the area where the blast occurred. Pendleton appeared on the scene directing the artillery fire. In the midst of the battle he surrendered his horse so that a wounded officer could reach medical assistance. Large enemy shells exploded within yards, but Pendleton remained in the front lines to repel the second assault made by the Federal divisions. Many Federals were killed and the Confederates "chased them like sheep." As Pendleton later reported, "The enemy, unable either to advance or retreat, and by the co-operating fire of all our artillery on this front, crouching into the crater to escape this deadly fire, were literally crushed and torn asunder by mortar shells."

For the next week the Union Army strengthened their entrenchments in the summer heat and dust. Pendleton spent mornings on paperwork and the afternoons inspecting the lines at Lee's request. He urgently pressed Lee's staff to promote J. H. Chamberlayne, his harsh critic from Shepherdstown, to command a battery at a critical point in the lines. In his recommendation he referred to Chamberlayne's "extraordinary gallantry & skill." In all probability, Chamberlayne never knew that the man he called an "imbecile" in 1862 forgave and forgot Chamberlayne's harsh criticisms. It also appears that after 1862 Chamberlayne no longer wrote any criticism of Pendleton.

Lieutenant Colonel William Poague of Lexington, the former commander of the Rockbridge Battery, recalled that Pendleton almost always stopped by at his headquarters on his inspection tours at dinner time knowing he would get a good meal. As Poague noted, "No one enjoyed a good dinner more than he." Pendleton urged that Poague be promoted to full Colonel, but the war ended before any official action was taken. On August 17th he rode along the lines with the recuperated E. Porter Alexander. Together they made recommendations as to the placement of defense to defeat any further mines and to strengthen the front lines. On the 18th Lee ordered Pendleton to ride to Chaffin's Bluff and open a brisk fire on the enemy's ships. A heavy rain fell spoiling any efforts to set Federal shipping ablaze.

On Sundays he attended regular services with either Pendleton or the Reverend William Platt presiding. He preached to the Army headquarters staff as the regular preacher was ill, using text from Numbers 23:10 for the lesson ("Who can count the dust of Jacob, and the number of the fourth part of Israel? Let me die the death of the righteous, and let my last end be like his!"). The congregation was attentive until a dog wandered in and began to rub first Robert E. Lee's leg and then A. P. Hill's leg. Lee continued to live in an old leaky tent, refusing any offers of shelter and giving away any food given him to the soldiers. On one occasion in September while Pendleton presided over services, he was "again protected by God" when a shell exploded nearby.

Pendleton wrote home that he was living "rough," eating only scraps of fatty bacon, fried apples, and corn or wheat bread twice a day. Occasionally the troops were served beef from the recently liberated Shenandoah Valley. The diet made Pendleton ill, on the 22nd forcing him into bed at a house 100 yards from his camp. Despite his illness he still spent that day moving guns from the main line to prevent a Federal attack westwards towards the rail lines. A week later he directed that the Whitworth rifles fire at the Federal wagon trains and told other batteries to slightly vary their angle of fire to strike enemy soldiers. He made other suggestions to the Corps artillery chiefs to improve the effectiveness of their firepower.

Pendleton also passed on to Lee the reports of an elderly Virginia militia Colonel captured by Hunter in the Valley and then manacled and jailed in a tiny cell. Lee ordered that a senior Union officer be given the same treatment until the Federals released their prisoner. At the end of the month Pendleton was told by the Chief of Ordnance that the Federal troops were mining again. Pendleton inspected the area and countermining begun. He reiterated the recommendations he made to Lee with Alexander of installing additional defensive lines behind the areas where mining was suspected.

As the month of September loomed before them Pendleton wrote home to Anzelotte of the beauty and horrors of night shelling:

> You would be interested to witness the mortar shelling sometimes at night. The shells with their fuses burning appear like small stars moving thru the sky, and some of them are thrown to such prodigious height that they seem as if aimed at the very stars. When exploding high in the air the noise of their disruption is deafening. The Yankees throw some as large as 13 inches in diameter, weighing when filled about 250 lbs. These make a report like thunder when they burst. Frequently they strike the ground without bursting, and then the depth to which they penetrate into the hardest soil is astonishing. I had measured day before yesterday several of the enormous cavities they had made and they were 11 feet deep.

On a visit to the heavy guns at Battery Danzler Pendleton found widespread illness among the men. The attending surgeon told him that if he could obtain a sufficient amount of quinine he could control the diseases. Pendleton discovered that this battery was not alone in suffering from this illness, and sought Lee's assistance in procuring more quinine.

He also lodged a complaint to one of the artillery chiefs that the field artillery in a portion of the line lacked any systematic communication between the chief artillery officer and the division commander. He faulted the artillery chief for failing to ensure that officers assuming their duty positions in the lines were not properly briefed on their proper fields of fire, lacked sufficient men to man the guns, and failed to repair broken guns or equipment. Additionally, he encouraged the batteries to be more aggressive in shooting at Federal work parties or enemy batteries when the opportunity arose. Finally, he discouraged the practice of drafting infantrymen to dig the artillery's trenches.

On September 30th Pendleton issued a general order to all the field artillery to protect the gunners in preparation for an enemy attack. Every battery was to provide mantlets and other protection for gunners from enemy sharpshooters. If the Union artillery opened a general bombardment all along the line the Confederate gunners were to hide and not respond absent specific orders to do so. However, should any enemy troops "appear within range at any time every available gun will immediately open upon them." If the bombardment lasted all night the guns were to be prepared for an infantry assault at first light. Finally, "all guns must be habitually kept covered from the enemy's fire and view during the day, and at night moved into position."

*   *   *   *

Following Hunter's rapid retreat to the west of the Shenandoah Valley, Jubal Early led his small Army of 14,000 men north up to the Potomac River accompanied by his chief of staff Sandie Pendleton. On July 6th he entered Maryland near Harpers Ferry and turned down river towards Washington, D.C. On the 9th he routed a small Union force at the Monocacy River just outside Frederick. Two days later he was in the suburbs of Washington. Observing the heavily reinforced garrison around Fort Stevens, Early opted not to risk an attack, and the next day began his retreat back into Virginia. He skirmished with pursuing Federal columns until he rested his men at Martinsburg, Virginia. Nearby was the burned out house of Pendleton's son-in-law Ned Lee. During the withdrawal some of Early's cavalry under John McCausland burned Chambersburg as retribution for the burnings by Federal troops of Lexington and other locations in the Valley.

Grant placed General Phil Sheridan in command of the Union troops in the Valley to destroy the ability of the Valley to feed Lee's Army. He wanted it so that a crow crossing the Valley would need to carry his own provender with him to survive. On the 19th Sheridan advanced up the Valley and attacked Early's positions around Winchester, forcing the outnumbered Confederates to fall back. General Early retreated twenty miles south to positions at Fishers Hill. The line at Fishers Hill was too long to be defended by his small army, now reduced to 8,000 men. Late on the 22nd Sheridan struck the barely defended left of the line and routed the Confederates. They did not stop until they reached Waynesboro eighty miles up the Valley.

Sandie Pendleton tried to stem the retreat. While placing troops in a rear guard near Tom's Brook at dusk he was struck in the abdomen by a musket ball. Henry Kyd Douglas and others carried him to an ambulance, and he was taken to the home of Dr. Murphy at Woodstock. Dr. Hunter McGuire told Sandie that his wound was fatal and offered to stay with him but Sandie insisted he flee to safety. McGuire noted Sandie's delirium and craving for ice as "dangerous symptoms." There the Confederates left him to his fate behind enemy lines. Federal surgeons took over his care but he died on the evening of September 23rd and was buried in the Lutheran Cemetery in Woodstock.

When news of Sandie's wound reached Lexington his sister Susan P. Lee tried to find transport down the Valley to nurse him but got no further than Staunton. Anzelotte was on her way to Petersburg to visit General Pendleton when the news reached her that Sandie was wounded but not fatally. She abandoned her trip to return home where she told Sandie's wife Kate the grievous news. General Pendleton was waiting for his wife at the Peterkins' home in Petersburg when he got word. General Lee gave Pendleton a two weeks leave to return home. The family and all of Lexington fervently prayed that Sandie would recover. The Presbyterian minister Dr. White consoled the family.

For weeks there was uncertainty as to Sandie's fate, and the family refused to give up hope so long as there was any chance Sandie was still alive. Pendleton wrote home to Anzelotte:

It has pleased God to permit a heavy grief to fall upon us. Our dear Sandie so severely wounded, and far away, where we not only cannot minster to his comfort but cannot learn of his actual condition.

The uncertainty and suspense render the trial perhaps even more distressing. From the weight on my own heart I can judge somewhat what you all feel. But what precious mercy we have along with the bitter sorrow! There is a perfectly wise and kind Father watching over and ministering to our beloved in his distant suffering, a sympathizing friend and great Physician attending unceasingly by his bed of pain, and a sustaining Comforter ever with him to soothe his spirit with sweet influence of peace. He is a child of god, a servant of Jesus, a partaker of the Holy Ghost. It cannot be but well with him.

Oh how it extracts the bitterness from affliction to know that it is ordered by our Almighty Father as a part of his boundless plan of righteousness and love!

Shall we not, therefore, submissively bow under His dealings? "Father not my will but thine be done" God may take to Himself our precious boy. Often as we have failed in our duty to that dear child, the merciful and gracious Lord has enabled us to rear him to be under grace an honor to us, a joy to his sisters, a treasure to his wife, an ornament to society, and a Christian hero in his country's service. It may be hard to give him up, should it please the Master to take him to Himself, but shall we murmur?
If it be the Lord's will to take him, never will my heart cease to feel the sorrow that on earth I shall see him no more, but not then for an instant would I

wish him back....Would that I could be with you all for a season now.

Lee's staff had information before Pendleton's departure for home that Sandie was probably dead but could not bear to tell him. On his arrival in Lexington Pendleton was greeted by the good news that Sandie was improving. On October 1st Sandie's enslaved African servant Jim Lewis arrived and reported that the wound was dangerous. Henry Kyd Douglas wrote of a potential recovery. On the 3rd Dr. Hunter McGuire arrived in town and was visited by Pendleton at his hotel. McGuire told Pendleton that he heard Sandie died soon after his wounding, and later that day a letter arrived from Ned Lee confirming it. The next day Pendleton visited McGuire again clinging to hope on the basis that reports of the death were still unconfirmed. Nevertheless, he must have been convinced as he started back to Petersburg on the 11th. On October 12th Early's little army re-entered Woodstock following the pillaging and burning Sheridan back down the Valley. The news of Sandie's death was finally officially confirmed on October 17th when Mrs. Murphy's letter announcing the news arrived in Lexington.

Anzelotte wrote her husband thanking God for the assurance that Sandie was now in heaven. He replied:

> This day has brought our dear child and you all more vividly and constantly before me. Our fallen nature finds it hard to realize how blessed are they whom God prepares and takes to Himself, and how peacefully we may walk with Him even in sorrow while waiting all the days for our appointed time.
> To dwell on the loss of Sandie and on the trying circumstances of his removal, as there is some natural tendency in my mind, would so accumulate grief as to render it painful beyond expression and unfit me for duty. Such indulgence, therefore, I know is not right...It seems to me you may, as I try to realize myself, finding pleasing solaces in many natural scenes. The sweet blue heavens speak of where the beloved of our hearts is now rejoicing; the lovely landscape, with its varied beauties, tells of scenes far more exquisite in which his ransomed

spirit from henceforth delights and where we may hope to join him in sacred joy.

Sandie's body was disinterred and sent to Lexington with a military guard of honor. From Staunton Ned Lee advised General Pendleton that Sandie was on his way home. Anzelotte wrote Pendleton that he should not feel guilty about being back on duty, "You are where Sandie would desire you to be, at your post of duty." She and Susan went to the town cemetery to select a gravesite. The casket arrived on the 24th and was placed in Grace Episcopal Church. Anzelotte wrote Pendleton, "Oh that you were here, but as it cannot be so, I trust the blessed Savior will be with our spirits and comfort and sanctify us in these sorrows." His grieving widow Kate emerged from her room to say farewell to Sandie at the church that evening. The next day he was buried with full military honors.

The loss grieved Pendleton deeply but did not affect his deep religious faith for a moment:

> The satisfaction of having our dear son's remains suitably disposed where they will likely remain undisturbed, and where ourselves and others who valued him can visit his honored grave, is a cause for thankfulness. But the incidents connected with that removal and internment could not but be to you all a reopening of the sources of sorrow, while the denial to myself of this privilege of sharing with you this sad tribute to our beloved has been to me a hard sacrifice of domestic to public duty....

> Our dear Sandie seems as much in my thoughts as the first week of our mourning, and with an inexpressible sense of loss. He comes before me in many scenes; as in his boyhood, student life, and in the Army; when he and I went to Moss Neck; as he stood before me with his beloved bride; as we were at home together last winter. But I must try to think more of him as rejoicing in the Master's likeness and presence, and awaiting us all there.

Later, in reviewing Sandie's life Pendleton found discussed his many fine qualities:

> If this world were all, or chief, what a strange dispensation would be the removal of one like Sandie every way so superior! But in view of the heavenly world in which he is exalted, it is no longer perplexing. That fine disposition, those noble endowments and attainments, and the consecrating grace which rendered him through the Mediator acceptable to God, find freer and happier scope in the blessed sphere to which he is advanced. Sure of this, we can combat the sadness, and find more comfort in the certainty for him and the hope for ourselves.

*   *   *   *

Pendleton was back at headquarters by the 15th of October. Lee asked him to remain responsible as chief of artillery along all of the Petersburg lines, although Lee insisted he continue to consult with him on other matters. The next day he rode with General Long along the lines to examine the status of the artillery and noticed that Grant had extended his forces further west. For the most part Pendleton continued to operate as an inspector general of the artillery corps and organizer but did occasionally advise that certain batteries be re-positioned. On the 16th he preached to a large congregation at Pegram's headquarters and found the men to be devout and attentive. Pendleton noticed in walking through the Army that the men in the trenches were wet and cold and lacked any good shelter as winter approached. They also had to cope with the continuous firing along the lines. The sight pained him because of the suffering, and pleased him by the devotion of the men to their cause. Pendleton observed the engagement at Burgess Mill on October 27th, and hoped that "A. P. Hill might destroy the column thus engaged, but we were too slow or the inclement weather rendered it impossible." The truth was that the Army of Northern Virginia no longer had the capability of launching an effective attack.

On the 17th he rode north of the James to examine the lines there along with General Lee. He was asked to stay to share Lee's simple fare at dinner. Pendleton was so hungry he sat down and began to eat. Lee remained silent. A day or two later Pendleton penned an apology to Lee for failing to say grace. Lee replied:

> I have received your note of the 19th. I had expected you to ask a blessing on our table, and turned to you with that need. It was my fault I think in not making a more pointed request, which I should have done. Finding you apparently preparing to take your seat, I failed to request your office, and as is very frequently the case with me at our informal camp meals, offered a silent petition of thanks.
> I reciprocate in the fullest manner your feelings of friendship which has always been to me a source of pleasure and am deeply obliged to you for your fervent pious prayers in my behalf. No one stands in greater need of them. My feeble petitions I dare hardly hope will be answered.

Other things battled for Pendleton's attention. He acted as pallbearer for General Gregg in a solemn and impressive funeral at the Capitol in Richmond. A nephew implored him to assign to him a position somewhere he could not be hurt as he faced the draft. And he commiserated with Anzelotte on the loss of their son. Anzelotte hoped to write a memoir of Sandie. Pendleton advised her to do whatever she must and was able to do. On November 4th Kate gave birth to Pendleton's only grandson, Alexander Pendleton, Jr. Several weeks later Pendleton packed his bags to go to Lexington to officiate at the child's baptism and was ready to start when word reached him that Lee denied his application for leave on the grounds that mass desertions from the Army needed to be met with greater discipline. Lee, it "seemed to object to my being away. So that I have to make a virtue of necessity and deny myself the happiness of seeing them all at home." The child was not baptized until after the war ended.

Lee summoned Pendleton on December 8th to make adjustments in the artillery necessitated by Federal movements. The work took all day, during which he was under some "pretty severe shelling." Pendleton took the opportunity to go into Richmond and visit daughter Susan Lee, Jefferson Davis, and the Secretary of War Seddon. Davis, though ailing with one of his chronic severe headaches consoled Pendleton on the loss of his son, noting that it was a loss for the country as well as for his family. On the 19th the Federals fired 100 salvoes of artillery in celebration of Sherman's completion of his march to the sea at Savannah, Georgia. The news depressed Pendleton. He blamed Hood's doomed invasion of Tennessee for the disaster. "I take for granted it is so. It is a serious blow to us and will give us much trouble....while I greatly desire the full achievement of our independence, I am willing to leave the issue to supreme wisdom, meanwhile trying to do present duty as far as I can see it."

The Confederacy's remaining time passed too quickly. Pendleton spent Christmas 1864 at the Lynches. On his 55th birthday on the 26th he confessed that God had given so much to him of which he was undeserving. His letters home grew shorter and shorter. News arrived that the Federals had arrested his ailing older brother Walker, only to release him thirty six miles from home. Walker was compelled to walk the whole way home. On the 17th Ned Lee and Susan left Richmond on a secret mission to Canada by sea on a blockade runner where they settled in Montreal.

   *   *   *   *

The number of men assigned to the artillery corps dwindled due to desertion, illness, and casualties. By October 30th only 5,978 were present for duty. The strenuous campaign over the summer rendered certain changes in the command necessary. Colonel Cabell was sidetracked as having been promoted beyond his level of competency in the field, although in early 1865 he served as the I Corps Chief of Artillery when Alexander departed on leave. Much the same thing occurred to Pendleton over the years as he was gradually displaced from tactical command. Promotions were given to younger and more capable tacticians. Walton's Louisiana battalion was ordered to be re-attached to I Corps, prompting Walton to resign. Pendleton opposed the promotion of a Major Moseley to be Beauregard's chief of artillery, but was ignored. Pendleton sought to dissolve the old Virginia 1st Regiment of Artillery but was overruled by Jefferson Davis.

Having some time on his hands Pendleton drafted legislation to "to organize the artillery of the Confederate States," a reiteration of his proposal in May 1864, and forwarded it to Lee for consideration. He wished to create artillery battalions consisting of batteries of between four and six guns. Each battalion would have two field officers. Battalions could be combined, at the discretion of the commanding general, into brigades and divisions of artillery. Lee concurred with the bill inasmuch as it conformed to the organization of artillery in his Army. Lee suggested that commissary officers be included in the planned organization for supply purposes. However, he felt that the use of brigades or divisions of artillery was too cumbersome and disadvantageous. Lee included his recommendations and sent the whole on to the Secretary of War James Seddon. Pendleton forwarded the request with a cover letter noting that the bill would provide for more needed field officer ranks in command. Besides, "the extreme restrictions in the existing law as to rank of artillery officers operate alike unjustly and injuriously. We have a number of most deserving field officer to whom promotion is eminently due, and yet they cannot be justly rewarded as the law now stands."

Seddon did not "recognize the necessity of legislation to the extent you propose." The organizations applicable to one of the large armies in the field would not be appropriate for some of the smaller forces, and therefore, overarching legislation would not be commensurate with the good of the service. It would be better if these goals were accomplished by War Department orders rather than laws, thus providing more flexibility in handling each situation. Furthermore, current laws forbid removing officers from any permanent Army unit, reducing the ability to promote the best officers. Seddon concluded, "The only point on which I think legislation is really needed is in allowing higher rank to the generals of artillery. Major-generals, at least, should be assignable to artillery service, or major-generals of artillery be directly appointed. I would prefer the former [which would exclude Pendleton], but will cheerfully recommend either plan."

Pendleton responded rather archly on November 15th ignoring the offered carrot of a potential major-generalcy for the betterment of his officer corps. The legislation was necessary because, "although we have artillery battalions formed under orders of the commanding general, sanctioned by the Department, and although this organization has proved one of the most efficient instrumentalities in our great struggle, the result is attained at the cost of very serious injustice to a large class of most deserving officers….. In truth, my dear sir, there ought to be more scope for promotion in this arm. Officers painfully feel that they are not fairly estimated, that in spite of noblest service they are often left needlessly far behind their brethren of other arms." The contribution of the field artillery was a critical factor in the Army's successes to date, and the officers know it. These were not matters of "speculation or fancy" but "are realities seriously felt by some of the best men we have in service." Pendleton concluded that if the plan was unacceptable or damaging Lee would have said so.

The dispute found its way to the desk of President Davis. He regretted that the law did not include artillery officers in promotion the way it did infantry or cavalry officers. He suggested that "Authority to confer temporary rank to supply temporary vacancies" would insure the recognition of the services given by competent officers. Otherwise, Davis thought that changing from a battery to a battalion organization promised "no good, but to threaten some evil." The matter was dropped.

Pendleton was proud of his artillery corps and wished to award them. Around this same time he wrote of his officers and men:

> In the whole of the eventful campaign of 1864, the Artillery of the Army of Northern Virginia bore a distinguished part, and in every portion of the widely-extended field of operation rendered signal service. It was everywhere and at all times proved reliable, howsoever great the emergency. In the wildest fury of battle and ceaseless harassment and exposure from sharpshooters and shelling on the lines, on the toilsome march, amid all the hardships of the trenches, through summer, fall, and winter, and when steadily breasting the tide of reverse against friends unnerved or overpowered, and foe flushed with triumph, the brave officers and men of this branch of our army have almost without exception exemplified the very highest virtues of Christian soldiers battling for their faith, their honor, and their homes.

Through the winter Pendleton maintained the artillery corps headquarters near a railroad cut on an extension of Halifax Street southwest of Petersburg. With Pendleton's constant inspections, along with those of his aides, the area was the center of ceaseless activity. Pendleton later commended his staff by writing, "It is but just that I should say they have uniformly discharged their duties with faithful alacrity and to my entire satisfaction." The staff at that time consisted of his nephew Captain Dudley D. Pendleton as Assistant Adjutant-General; Lieutenant George W. Peterkin and Lieutenant Charles Hatcher as aides-de-camp; Captain John Esten Cooke (later a famous historian and novelist) and Lieutenant E. P. Dandridge as Assistant Inspector Generals; Major John C. Barnwell as Ordnance Officer; Dr. John Graham as Surgeon; and Pendleton's cousin Major John Page as Quartermaster.

Overall Pendleton was pleased with what he accomplished through the 1864 campaigns in keeping the field artillery well manned, armed, and supplied. He reported in early 1865 that the condition of the Artillery at the close of the year 1864 was actually better than when it left winter quarters the preceding spring. He concluded that "I am able to report that our artillery remains at the close of this arduous campaign in a condition of most encouraging efficiency, and that with reasonable effort toward supplying it with a few guns to replace some lost in unfortunate affairs that have been described [the losses by Early in the Valley], and with horses to re-establish a number of teams disabled in action or worn down by hard service, it will be in full strength for the campaign of the ensuing spring. It may be confidently relied upon to accomplish, by the Divine blessing during the next season, as it has so well done through the last, its entire share in the defense of our country."

*   *   *   *

He greeted the New Year in his tent during a fierce cold snap. In the distance he could hear the pickets firing at each other in the dark and felt deeply for the "poor fellows meeting death." Some were found frozen to death at their posts, mostly due, Pendleton believed, to poor nutrition. Several days later he was deluged by an "extraordinary rain" lasting a full day and night. He spent portions of the month with former Governor, now General, Henry Wise preaching and lecturing to YMCA meeting where the men sat on logs in the cold wintry weather, and at prayer meetings.

Pendleton received a letter from daughter Susan mailed from Nassau in the Bahamas, to which he replied at length. While he had not feared for her safety it was still a "great comfort to know that you are so far at least safe from Yankee outrage. The perils of the

318

sea are in my estimation as nothing in comparison with even a moderate risk of falling into the hands of that perfidious, canting, cowardly, and cruel race." He cautioned her not to indulge in the loss of Sandie, "because it is too far a selfish condition of thought and feelings." The family knew with certitude that Sandie was in heaven with his Savior. Pendleton was discouraged by the news coming through the lines from Federal sources. For one thing he found "[t]heir systematized falsehoods are so shameless and so notorious that all the world must distrust them." But yet, the reverses reported were true to a large extent, including the news of Sherman and Hood. He found some consolation that Hood "seems to have gotten back safely across the Tennessee, with reduced army and affluence. What he will be able to do, we shall see after a time."

For Pendleton "[t]hese misfortunes have rather darkened our skies for a season and occasioned some despondency in the minds of a portion of the people." Yet while success made the "Yankees more arrogant and offensive than ever, they have not, however, abated one jot of our resolution to resist Yankee domination to the last...." Then much like the Preacher in Ecclesiastes, after many words of discouragement Pendleton concluded that all would turn out well and independence achieved. "[W]e begin this year with sufficient resources and with an unyielding spirit so that by the blessing of that God whom we confidently invoke to judge between us and our enemies, as the God of justice and truth, we shall yet frustrate their iniquitous scheme of plunder [and] subjugation...."

On the 12th he visited General Lee and found him worn out from overwork. He did not ask for leave to go home as "The burden on him is so heavy that those on whom he at leans ought to help him to bear it as well as they can." Instead, he asked that Mrs. Pendleton and Mary come for a visit to Petersburg. Since the canals were frequently frozen or at high flood at that time of year he suggested they travel to Staunton to catch the train. They arrived about a week later and stayed with the Lynch family in a house about 200 yards from Pendleton's tent and over two miles from Petersburg. The road to town was frequently shelled during their stay, the weather freezing, and the roads were fields of mud. Nevertheless the Lynches put on fine dinners for their guests consisting cornbread, black eyed peas, bacon, and occasionally fowl and dried apples. Dessert was made with sorghum molasses.

By mid-January the Army's artillery corps shrunk through illness, death, and desertion to only 4,881 men and 245 officers. With the defeat in the Valley of Early's II Corps portions of his field artillery needed to be re-assigned. Pendleton recommended that two battalions of artillery be returned to the main Army while the II Corps kept the rest. Lee hoped to use the men to man the heavy artillery guns "defending [the] James River from Drewry's Bluff to Howlett's - a noble charge, that will try the best officers and men if the enemy pushes up his monitors, as the general seems to anticipate. Some may also be needed here at Fort Clifton, on the Appomattox." Field artillery was not available to them due to the lack of horses to pull the guns. Some of the men could be offered to the horse artillery. He left it to Early and his chief of artillery to determine which men were sent to Petersburg.

Fort Fisher, the Confederacy's last connection with the outside world, fell on the 18th, but food was still arriving in Richmond through the Carolinas by rail. However, Pendleton complained about the quantity and quality of the food provided to the men. Generally, it was just little portions of coarse cornmeal, small pieces of bacon fat, served with a small amount of coffee. Officers gave up half their rations to their enslaved servants in the line. When Pendleton rode through the lines he distributed whatever coffee he could find.

On Sunday, February 5, 1865, Pendleton accompanied Anzelotte and Mary to church services with General Lee. A note arrived for Lee which he quietly read and put away. The services continued, Lee took communion, and then departed. Grant's men had seized portions of the Confederate defenses at Hatcher's Run. Lee called upon Pendleton to make sure that the defensive lines around Petersburg were on the alert for an attack. Pendleton took his wife and daughter to depart for home on the train to Staunton . On their arrival in Staunton they were unable to proceed any further due to Federal threats following the rout of Early's small Army at nearby Rockfish Gap. Friends in Staunton took them in until the Union troops occupied Staunton. Mrs. Pendleton and Mary were briefly detained and then paroled as prisoners of war. Only then could they head home. On arrival they discovered that all their bacon had been stolen from the smokehouse, and there was little meat available for the ten whites and four blacks in the household. .

The final campaign of the Army of Northern Virginia, one in which Pendleton played an important role, was about to begin.

Gen. W. N. Pendleton 1864

Captured Confederate cannon 1865

15. "THE ARMY MELTED AWAY TO
A MERE HANDFUL"

[APPOMATTOX, 1865]

I cried unto the LORD with my voice, and he heard me out of his holy hill. I laid me down and slept; I awaked; for the LORD sustained me. I will not be afraid of ten thousands of people that have set themselves against me round about.

Psalms 3:4-6, King James Version

Yea, though I walk through the valley of the shadow of death, I will fear no evil: for thou art with me; thy rod and thy staff they comfort me.

Psalms 23:4, King James Version

New Year's Day 1865 brought no fresh hope to the Confederacy. It was obvious that the end was near. No foreign recognition or intervention was coming to save the South. Federal forces occupied most of the South, and the writ of Confederate authority was limited to the eastern seaboard states above Savannah, the unoccupied portions of the South from Florida to the Gulf Coast around Mobile, and the Trans-Mississippi. The two main Confederate armies east of the Mississippi faced overwhelming Federal forces in South Carolina and Virginia. In February there was a glimmer of hope when Confederate commissioners met with Lincoln at Hampton Roads, but any hope of peace with independence was shattered when the commissioners returned with Lincoln's conditions for surrender.

Robert E. Lee was fully aware of the desperate nature of the military situation and knew the longer his Army was saddled with the defense of Richmond the more certain and nearer was its defeat. Pendleton agreed, later writing that "[t]he ill fed and depleted army, daily exposed to sleet, snow, and rain, and almost without food could not continue long." Lee felt that the only hope was to pull his Army out of the lines around Richmond and Petersburg and head for the mountains. In the alternative, he could join Joseph Johnston (once again in command of the Army of Tennessee) in North Carolina and seek to destroy or defeat Sherman's armies before turning back to defeat Grant. It was an audacious and forlorn hope, but in it rested the Confederacy's last chance for success.

Lee called Pendleton to his headquarters and asked him to strip down and streamline the field artillery so that it could move quickly into the field as it was "in such a movement the most difficult of withdrawal...." The problem, Pendleton advised Lee, was in "[t]he question of our horse supply" which was "hardly second to that of supplying men for the army, or food for the men." It was necessary to adopt any measure to keep up the horses and "for having strong teams in sufficient number for our artillery and transportation by the opening of our spring campaign."

Both Lee and Pendleton worked through February to strengthen the artillery arm by securing horses. Reports came in from some of the batteries in the Petersburg lines that their horses were dying from lack of proper forage and clean water. The horse depots Pendleton established were of enormous benefit, rehabilitating large numbers of exhausted horses and mules. But the battlefield losses and strain led to more losses than recovered animals. At the start of the month Pendleton estimated that he needed 6,000 horses and 4,000 mules. However, all he could possibly obtain before spring were 5,000 horses; 3,000 from Mississippi and 2,000 in Virginia. Pendleton approached the Inspector General of Transportation to fulfill the Army's needs. He also, once more, protested against the practice of herding condemned artillery horses only to see them die from neglect when they might be spread out over many farms to be fed and recuperated.

Pendleton felt that in the coming spring campaign the army would face a severe hardship. He re-organized the field batteries, limiting them to only those batteries he could supply with forage, men, and horses. He sent some men to Lynchburg to recover guns left there by General Early. Men from the batteries without horses were sent to help man the heavy artillery in the trenches. The morale of the artillery corps improved as some hope of movement and escape from the trenches inspired them. By mid-February 1865 the artillery corps had recovered from the desertions and illness, reporting 6,113 men present for duty. On March 2, 1865 the insignificant remnants of Jubal Early's Army in the Valley were routed at Waynesboro, opening the road to Lynchburg and the southern railroad network. On March 7th Pendleton sent three batteries to Lynchburg to defend that city from the approach of Sheridan, but a sudden rise of the waters of the James River and the destruction of the bridges over the river forced Sheridan to pass further north.

On March 9th Lee advised the new Secretary of War John C. Breckinridge that his supplies were very low and that "The country within reach of our current position has been nearly or quite exhausted." Other departments had to send supplies to Richmond, and reports indicated they lacked either the supplies or the means to send relief to the capital. Lee concluded that "unless the men and animals can be subsisted the army cannot be kept together, and our present lines must be abandoned." Lee offered a glimmer of hope for the future. The Army needed to break out from Richmond and find military success, "I do not regard the abandonment of our present position as necessarily fatal to our success."

Lee's proposal was passed on to Jefferson Davis who vetoed any proposal to abandon Richmond. As Douglas S. Freeman noted, Davis decided that the fate of the Confederacy would take place at Richmond and not elsewhere. A few days later Pendleton proposed to create three fully efficient batteries in the II Corps by cannibalizing the rest of the batteries, thereby creating an effective, mobile, and efficient military force. In light of Davis' decision Lee disapproved the plan, advising Pendleton instead to try to rehabilitate all of the batteries in the Corps. Lee had to make the best out of the political decision to keep the Army trapped in the Petersburg lines until they broke, and ordered Pendleton to breakfast with him in the morning to review their plans.

324

The next day Pendleton sent additional recommendations to Lee. He felt that with the difficulty in finding healthy horses so as "to render impracticable the full re-equipment of all our batteries. It becomes therefore necessary to assign some of the organizations that have served as field artillery to such other duty as may be most suitable and useful." Pendleton needed to reduce the total number of batteries so that the field artillery was prepared for rapid movement in the spring campaign. Those men left behind should be used to man the guns in the Petersburg lines. Some batteries failed to take good care of their horses and should be left behind as well. Others could be merged. Lee must have agreed because beginning on March 20th Pendleton issued a stream of orders consolidating the efficient batteries and re-organizing the rest. He instructed the "several commanders to direct their energies to the thorough preparation of their respective commands for efficient service in the campaign soon to open and apply your own efforts to the same end. There is no time to be lost." He sent officers out into the countryside as far away as the Blue Ridge to find healthy horses. One of the batteries he kept intact was commanded by his vocal Shepherdstown critic Captain Chamberlayne.

Back in Petersburg Lee began to grasp at whatever straws he could to prolong a war he knew the South could not win. General John Gordon proposed an assault on the eastern end of the Union line where it was the thinnest and seize the enormous Union supply depots on the Appomattox River. The plans were made without any input from Pendleton or the Corps Chiefs of Artillery. Pendleton did not know of the attack until summoned to headquarters at 5:00 a.m. on March 25th just before the assault was launched. Pickett's and Gordon's division were sent, with little artillery support, to storm the advanced Federal Fort Stedman. Initially the attack succeeded, and Fort Stedman was taken, but the advance to break through the rest of the Federal defensive line fell apart in a mass of confusion. Before dawn broke the Union Army fiercely counterattacked and drove the Confederates back into their original lines before 8:00 a.m. A Federal assault on the Confederate main defenses in the area followed but was repulsed. The final effort by the Army of Northern Virginia to seize the initiative failed, and the Army was doomed to another week of starvation and cold in the muddy trenches of Petersburg.

Even in Lexington there were food shortages. For months the area had been drained to feed Early's Army in the Valley, and was now trying to raise food for Lee. Arriving home Anzelotte found that she had over five barrels of flour, 20 bushels of corn, eggs, and a handful of meat. She sought to purchase seeds for peas and snaps from the Staunton lunatic asylum and Lynchburg. Pendleton did what he could to provide food for his family in Lexington. He sent some guineas in gold he received as a gift and ordered some garden seed for Anzelotte. In an ominous vein he asked his friends in town to give his family meat for which he promised to pay in cash in Confederate dollars or the "current currency after the war…"

*   *   *   *

It was now only a matter of time before the paper thin Confederate lines broke. On March 31, 1865 the Army had between 44,000 and 56,000 men left, 5,000 of them in the artillery. They occupied a front thirty-seven miles long, leaving a defense of about 1,300 muskets a mile, or men placed four feet apart. Grant understood this and kept stretching his huge Army westward towards the vital railroads keeping Lee and Richmond fed and supplied. When Sheridan's forces from the Valley joined Grant before Petersburg on March 27th, Grant had all the men he needed to finish the job. He just kept sending more and more troops westward until the Confederate lines stretched beyond their ability to repulse an attack.

On April 1st Sheridan attacked the Confederate forces under Pickett at Five Forks which lay west of the furthest reach of Lee's trenches, and not far from the Southside Railroad. Pickett and his other commanders were enjoying a shad bake when the attack started, and for the longest time ignored the messages of alarm they received until they could see Federal troops coming towards them. Sheridan's rout of Pickett opened up Lee's flank and threatened to cut the lifeline that was the Southside Railroad. Lee removed a division from the lines to reinforce his right wing, stretching the Confederate lines at Petersburg even more. There so few defenders left in the trenches that each infantryman stood paces away from his nearest comrade.

For the next few days Pendleton displayed how good an artillery commander he could be when sufficiently driven and comfortable with his assignments. Perhaps his bitterness and enmity of the "damn Yankees" since Sandie's death contributed to his motivation. Alerted by the news from Five Forks, General Pendleton spent April 1st preparing for an anticipated Union assault. He moved Poague's battalion of artillery to the III Corps front as a reserve, and told Poague to stay long enough, if necessary, and sacrifice the guns but to save the horses and caissons. He also placed a battery to enfilade the Federal troops as they advanced near Battery 45 on the Appomattox. Pendleton also moved other batteries forward to protect the lines behind Lee's headquarters.

Grant ordered a full assault all along the line to begin at 4:00 a.m. Despite the paucity of the resistance most of the Union attacks were beaten back. But in the area guarded by A. P. Hill's III Corps a large hole was opened up in the line by the Federals. Hill rose from his sick bed and rode off into the night to organize resistance but was killed by Union soldiers. Poague's guns proved valuable in slowing the enemy attack. Federal troops punched through the lines near Lee's headquarters and the guns placed by Pendleton "were used to good effect."

Pendleton was everywhere on Sunday, April 2nd. Daybreak found him riding with General Lee back from the III Corps area penetrated by the enemy attacks. In the area of I Corps he directed that a battery take position on the Plank Road to support the infantry brigades being pushed back by overwhelming numbers of Federal troops. He spent some of the day at Battery 45 "and directed its guns against columns of the enemy moving down the valley toward the Weldon railroad. The officers in charge of this part of the line deeming an attack imminent, I ordered two pieces of artillery to strengthen the position." During the day he also made the time to arrange for the withdrawal of all the field artillery for an escape to the west. He decided which batteries would leave with the Army, and which ones would stay. Any guns remaining behind were to be disabled. Only the best equipped batteries remained with the Army.

Lee took charge of the effort to stem the tide but after a valiant effort the lines gave way. The Army of Northern Virginia began to dissolve. Pendleton later commented that "so discouraged [were] the majority of our soldiers in the ranks as to take all the fight out of them. And therefore, when the disaster of a broken line at Petersburg occurred, and we had to evacuate at night…." The sun went down on the 2nd on a scene of mass chaos and confusion in

Petersburg and in Richmond, which had negligently been torched by its defenders.

That evening found Pendleton in the rear of the II Corps. At 8:00 p.m. he received orders from Lee to begin the withdrawal, and ordered the field artillery to carefully withdraw from the lines. They headed down through the cobbled streets of Petersburg and across the Appomattox River bridges, and then west on Hickory Road. He accomplished this task despite the constant barrages from the Federal artillery and in the general chaos and confusion of that night. Only ten disabled pieces were left behind. By 2:00 a.m. on the 3rd the entire field artillery corps was across the river and westward bound. Along with the guns rode a weary General Pendleton. The withdrawal was a complete success, and nearly flawless, a fact remarked upon by even the judgmental Douglas Southall Freeman.

It is believed that approximately 30,000 men escaped the Federal encirclement of Richmond and Petersburg. The column coming out of Petersburg consisted of 13,000 infantry under Longstreet and Gordon, Mahone's 4,000 man division, and 3,000 men of the artillery under Pendleton. The men all marched westward through the dark. The column stopped and started as marching columns do, slowed down by the 200 guns and 1,000 wagons using what few roads were available. A constant rain muddied the roads and made the passage even more miserable and difficult. For Pendleton the march was "fatiguing and very slow, on account of the immense number of [civilian] carriages with the army. At night I bivouacked on the roadside about nine miles from Goode's Bridge." They marched all the next day on Monday, April 3rd, pummeled by heavy rain. As one of Pendleton's aides remarked, "No note [was] taken of day or night; one long confused dreadful day." There was no front or rear, enemy cavalry appeared on both sides or behind the column. For two days there was no food, and the men subsisted on "handfuls of uncooked corn, horse feed, and bits of raw bacon. Men dropped by the road side in exhaustion."

Early on Tuesday April 4th Pendleton arrived at Amelia Courthouse. The fleeing Army stopped for a while expecting trains full of food to appear but the usual incompetence in the commissary officer corps struck for the last time, and no food was delivered. When the food did not appear Pendleton took steps to ease the burden on his men and horses. It was now obvious that the Army would find little food on its retreat. The field artillery Pendleton spent so much effort on improving over the winter now exceeded the number of batteries for the limited size of the remaining Army and he needed to pare it down, making "arrangements for reducing the artillery with the troops to a proportionate quantity, and properly to dispose of the surplus." Surplus guns were sent towards Lynchburg under General Walker. The column of the artillery not needed by the Army moved to the right on a parallel the line of advance from that taken by the main force. Inspecting his artillery at Amelia Courthouse Pendleton found ninety-five mostly loaded artillery caissons sent early in the winter for the anticipated spring campaign. They were no longer needed and were blown up, their explosions sending a flaming column of smoke skyward and alarming the troops.

During the evening of Wednesday, April 5th Pendleton's column took the road towards Danville, but Lee found it blocked by Federal troops. Lee turned northwest towards Lynchburg instead, marching deeper and deeper into the rolling farmlands of the Piedmont. In order to out run the Union troops to their south they marched all day and all night to Farmville in a slow drizzle. The men were exhausted and hope was fading. Hungry after days without food, weary from fighting and marching, many straggled to forage for food, others simply turned towards home.

Pendleton reached Rice's Station at ten in the morning of Thursday April 6th, nineteen miles from Amelia Courthouse and six miles from Farmville. He and Alexander set up a defensive line sweeping the road towards Burkesville and the enemy. Around noon Pendleton held off enemy troops probing their lines. Reports came in that Federal cavalry had attacked the wagon train two miles to the rear. Lee asked Pendleton to take charge of whatever men he could find and seek to recover lost property from the wagon train. Along the way Pendleton encountered "a few wearied men of Harris' brigade, and taking from them some twenty volunteers proceed with them to the road where the train had been attacked." While looking for anything of value to recover Pendleton saw to the side of the road in the distance "a line of the enemy in a thick pine wood, and supposing it to be but a small body I arranged for an attack upon them [with] one of General Cooke's regiments, which had just reported to me in consequence of a message previously sent to the commanding general." The small enemy unit turned out to be quite substantial, and pressed Cooke back towards the main road.

Pendleton fell back a half mile until reinforced by two cavalry regiments. He once again moved forward but when Cooke left with his infantry Pendleton ordered his remaining force to return to the main force. While he captured some prisoners he found the Army's wagons burned and the road blocked by the enemy.

The rear of the Army did not keep up with the vanguard, leaving gaps in the line of march. At 2:00 p.m. the head of Ewell's columns from Richmond found the road between them and the vanguard under Lee blocked by Union soldiers. Ewell turned his wagons north toward Sayler's Creek and away from Lee. It was a fatal decision. Ewell lacked adequate artillery, most of which was up with Pendleton in the vanguard. Now half of the Army under General Ewell was isolated and beyond help. The trapped soldiers were tired and hungry, and unwilling or unable to make the effort necessary to break out. Some Confederates, unwilling to give up, broke through the Federal lines and re-joined Lee, including the eccentric Henry Wise, Pendleton's cohort in YMCA classes that winter. The rest soon surrendered, including Lee's son General Custis Lee. When he heard that Ewell had been cut off Lee took some troops and went to see what he could do but quickly realized that any rescue was hopeless. On his return to the vanguard Lee met Pendleton, remarking that "General, that half of our army is destroyed."

That evening the Federals engaged in "heavy skirmishing" with Pendleton's defensive line but no major attack was made. However, "[n]ot long after the enemy made a sudden rush, and succeeded for a time in running over our small cavalry force, and threatening the unprotected rear of our line; our cavalry regiment, however, speedily rallied and charged in turn, and inflicted merited punishment upon their greatly outnumbering assailants. Shortly after night closed our guns were withdrawn…" The remainder of Lee's once powerful Army withdrew at 8:00 p.m. and headed towards Farmville. As Pendleton recalled they "continued retreating … , mainly at night, while offering battle in the day with a vastly outnumbering force of cavalry, as well as of other arms, literally surrounding us, our men scattered in the woods, etc., until the army melted away to a mere handful…."

The weary Army crossed the bridge over the Appomattox's north bank and entered Farmville as dawn broke on Friday, April 7th. Here for the first time in days food was found and distributed.

On his arrival Pendleton placed several batteries on the north bank to cover the approaches over the river but left intact the bridges for stragglers to cross. The guns were "used to good purpose on the heights north of the river." When the last few stragglers crossed over Alexander burned the bridges. When one of the burning bridges was threatened by Federal troops Pendleton took personal charge of the batteries driving the enemy back. Two miles further down the road Poague's batteries were used to fend off enemy attacks on the wagon trains.

Late that day there was a meeting of senior generals about the Army's prospects. They were slowed by the wagons, weakened by desertion, and attacked on both flanks. The council considered recommendations for Lee including disband the Army and let the troops escape and reform at some other; abandon all the trains, concentrate the troops, and cut through the enemy lines; or surrender at once. It was agreed that the ideal option was to surrender, and by making this recommendation remove from Lee's shoulder the burden of making such a decision. Pendleton attended this meeting on behalf of Longstreet, but when it came to how to present this idea to Lee all the other generals present backed out and asked Pendleton, as a close personal friend of Lee, to make the presentation. First, Pendleton needed to consult with Longstreet as second in command of the Army. However, Pendleton was unable to locate Longstreet before the Army was once again underway, and the presentation of the proposal to Lee was postponed. At midnight the Army moved out on the road towards Buckingham Court-House, once again marching all night. Despite the poor condition of the country roads, they made good time. Appomattox Court House was now only thirty miles away.

Early on the morning of Saturday, April 8th, Pendleton caught up with Longstreet and divulged the recommendations of the council of generals. His timing was poor. The sunny skies and blissful spring weather made the terror of surrender more remote. The army had outmarched their enemies and was no longer under attack, their bellies were not gnawing at their stomachs, and the morale picked up a beat. Hope grew that they could reach Lynchburg and the safety of the Blue Ridge. Longstreet's response to the proposal brought by Pendleton was pert and sharp. After reminding Pendleton that it was a death penalty offense to suggest surrender, Longstreet sagely noted that "If General Lee doesn't know when to surrender until I tell him, he will never know!" Pendleton's later contretemps with Longstreet, well after the war, clouds what happened next. Pendleton reported that Longstreet calmed down and agreed to the plan, while Longstreet later claimed he did not and that Pendleton went to Lee on his own.

Pendleton found Lee resting on the ground at the base of a tree. Unknown to Pendleton, Lee and Grant had already been in touch regarding surrender. As one historian noted, Lee took no one into confidence as to his intentions. As his hand became harder to play he played it more and more alone. Pendleton disclosed the proposal of the council of generals wishing to take responsibility for the decision to surrender. Lee's actual response is unclear due to the many versions offered by history, but according to Pendleton it went something like this:

> Surrender? I have too many good fighting men for that....Oh no, I trust it has not come to that. We have too many bold men to think of laying down our arms... They still fight with great spirit whereas the enemy does not. And besides, if I were to intimate to General Grant that I would listen to terms, he would at once regard it as such an evidence of weakness that he would demand unconditional surrender- and I would never listen to that—a proposal to which I will never listen... I have never believed we could, against the gigantic combination for our subjugation, make good in the long run our independence unless foreign powers should, directly or indirectly, assist us.....But such consideration really made with me no difference. We had, I was satisfied, sacred principles to maintain and rights to defend, for which we were in duty bound to do our best, even if we perished in the endeavor.

Pendleton was taken aback by the coldness of this rebuff. He replied to Lee that "every man would no doubt cheerfully meet with death with Lee in discharge of duty and that we were perfectly willing that he should decide the question." For several hours Pendleton remained shaken and embarrassed by Lee's vehemence and coldness, discussing it at length with Alexander as they rode west.

As evening came on the 8th the Army approached Appomattox Court House. Pendleton was riding in the van of Gordon's II Corps when he heard gunfire from three miles west in the area of Walker's surplus artillery park, which was still on the road towards Lynchburg. Pendleton found sixty guns peacefully parked and ready to march again in the morning. Suddenly, in the gathering darkness Federal cavalry under George Armstrong Custer burst from a nearby wood and rode through the lounging gunners. Two batteries of artillery, using only muskets, held off the Federals while other batteries unlimbered and fired. The cavalry was beaten off, allowing the artillery force to pull back towards the Court House. Pendleton described the fight as "one of the closest artillery fights" in the war with guns opposing each other up to their muzzles. Pendleton left with half of the artillery reserve but the fight was still ongoing when he was approached by a courier with an order from Lee to come to headquarters. His ride to Lee turned out to be harrowing. On the way he found some Federal horsemen confidently trotting down the road towards the Court House. "When I had reached a point a few hundred yards from the court-house, the enemy's cavalry, which had under cover of dusk gained the road, came rushing along, firing upon all in the road, and I only escaped being shot or captured by leaping my horse over the fence and skirting for some distance along the left of that road toward our column…"

At 9:00 p.m., just before arriving at headquarters Pendleton heard a new burst of firing breaking out to the west. He correctly inferred that it could only mean that Walker's entire reserve and some of the food trains had been captured. Towards the west numerous campfires of enemy troops lit the night sky. Pendleton reported to Lee that half of the artillery reserve had been lost. Lee ordered infantry forward to block any more attacks, but it was clear that there was enemy cavalry on the road between him and Lynchburg. Lee held a council of war that evening which Pendleton attended. They sat on logs or stood around a campfire as there were no tents, tables, chairs or camp stools. The generals discussed the possibility of forcing the lines and reaching Tennessee or the Virginia mountains. It was decided to make one more effort to break through to the west. After midnight Pendleton was summoned to Lee. He reached Lee about 1:00 a.m. on Palm Sunday, April 9th and found him "dressed in his neatest style, new uniform, snowy linen, etc." To General Pendleton's expression of surprise, Lee said, "I have probably to be General Grant's prisoner, and thought I must make my best appearance." Lee told Pendleton to get some rest and be governed by circumstances in the morning.

There was little of the Army left to lead. Hunger, hopelessness, desertion, and fatigue shrunk the Army to a shadow of its former self. The returns for the morning of April 9th reflected that present for duty were only 7,892 infantrymen with seventy-five rounds of ammunition each. The field artillery still had sixty-three guns with an average of ninety-three rounds each, two of which would be lost that morning. At dawn Gordon pushed his infantry accompanied by cavalry westward towards the Blue Ridge Mountains now just over twenty miles away. He forced his way past some light cavalry resistance and wheeled left facing south to guard the escape route of the Army to the west. Almost immediately reports came in of Federal infantry to his right on the road to Lynchburg. After three hours of heavy skirmishing and fighting, Gordon reported to Lee that his Corps "was worn to a frazzle." To the east the Confederates were fighting off Federal attacks. The Army of Northern Virginia was trapped. On Lee's orders Gordon sent out a flag of truce.

Alexander was convinced that something needed to be done. He encountered Lee after the flag of truce and proposed that the men fight their way out and rally men across the South. Instead of snapping, as he had at Pendleton, Lee gently disagreed:

> I have not over 15,000 muskets left. Two-thirds of them divided among the States, even if all could be collected, would be too small a force to accomplish anything. All could not be collected. Their homes have been overrun, and many would go to look after their families. Then, General, you and I as Christian men have no right to consider only how this would affect us. We must consider its effect on the country as a whole. Already it is demoralized by the four years of war. If I took your advice, the men would be without rations and under no control of officers. They would be compelled to rob and steal in order

to live. They would become mere bands of marauders, and the enemy's cavalry would pursue them and overrun many wide sections they may never have occasion to visit. We would bring on a state of affairs it would take the country years to recover from. And, as for myself, you young fellows might go to bushwhacking, but the only dignified course for me would be, to go to Gen. Grant and surrender myself and take the consequences of my acts. But I can tell you one thing for your comfort. Grant will not demand an unconditional surrender. He will give us as good terms as this army has the right to demand, and I am going to meet him in the rear at 10 A. M. and surrender the army on the condition of not fighting again until exchanged.

Alexander was speechless. As he later recalled, "He had answered my suggestion from a plane so far above it, that I was ashamed of having made it. With several friends, I had planned to make an escape on seeing a flag of truce, but that idea was at once abandoned by all of them on hearing my report."

Lee determined to meet with Grant, and news of the impending surrender swept the Army like wildfire. Pendleton sent his staff officers to find all of the artillery units and place their guns with caissons with teams hitched in a battery park on the north side of the Appomattox in preparation for their surrender to the enemy. Lee met with Grant at the McLean house in Appomattox Court House and reached agreement on the general terms of surrender. Lee appointed three general officers to negotiate the specifics, Pendleton, Longstreet, and Gordon. Pendleton's staff wanted him to make the best appearance possible for the negotiations, but all they could find was an old uniform from which they brushed off the dust. He borrowed some gloves and rode on fellow townsman Dr. Graham's handsome black horse instead of his older and less impressive "Old Brown." So dressed as finely as possible and accompanied by his aide Lieutenant Peterkin, Pendleton rode over to Federal General John Gibbon's headquarters to meet the enemy's commission for the surrender.

Longstreet and Gordon handled most of the details. The terms were issued to the Army on April 10th. The Confederates were to march their troops to an open field where they were to deposit all their accoutrements of war. Officers were to keep their side arms and the authorized number of private horses. All public horses and property were to be handed over. Transportation was offered as necessary for the private baggage of officers. Couriers and mounted men of the artillery and cavalry, whose horses were their private property, would be allowed to retain them. Those included in the surrender were the forces operating with the Army except such bodies of cavalry as actually made their escape previous to the surrender and except any artillery pieces more than twenty miles from Appomattox Court-House as the time of surrender.

The amount of Confederate casualties in the campaign and the number of men still with Lee at the time of surrender can only be conjectured due to the poor records kept and the heavy rate of desertion and straggling before the actual surrender. It is believed that many men re-joined the Army after the surrender in order to obtain food and a parole allowing them to go home peacefully, so the number of paroles issued is a misleading figure for Lee's strength that morning. After leaving Petersburg the Army lost 19,132 men captured during the campaign and 6,226 killed or wounded. When it came time to issue paroles the Union authorities counted were 22,349 infantrymen, 1,559 cavalrymen, and 2,576 artillerymen.

In Lee's artillery corps each soldier's parole was signed by his battery commander, and attached to a copy of Grant's order validating the parole. After the surrender was completed the Army broke up for the last time. Alexander came by Pendleton's headquarters and had him sign his parole. Alexander described his parole having the words "Paroled Prisoners' Pass" in "some ornamental work between top and bottom lines, the paper being about three inches by eight." His read, "Brig.-Gen. E. P. Alexander, chief of artillery, 1st corps A. N.V. of Va., a paroled prisoner of the Army of Northern Virginia, has permission to go to his home and there remain undisturbed with four private horses. W. N. Pendleton, Brig.-Gen. & Chief of Artillery." Yet Alexander was not ready to go home, instead he planned to head to Brazil and offer his sword to the Emperor there. He asked Pendleton for a letter of recommendation and Pendleton agreed. The letter dated April 12th introduced the Emperor to "Brig. Genl. E.P. Alexander for the last four years an active & efficient officer in the armies of the Confederate States. Owing to events in his own country Genl

Alexander desires to exercise his talents in some other, and he selects your as presenting important advantages." He praised Alexander's "very superior ability and merit. You will find him full of intelligence, scientific culture, & practical skill. He has here commanded with eminent success a large force of artillery, and is capable of directing in the most distinguished manner that branch of service." Pendleton added that Alexander was also a "sagacious and trained engineer….. a man of genius & service worthy of honorable employment + entitled to your fullest confidence." General Alexander never reached Brazil, on arriving home to his wife, family, and his newborn baby he decided to stay.

Within a day of the surrender Pendleton prepared, without reports from his Corps Chiefs of Artillery, a lengthy summary of the events leading to the surrender while it was fresh in his mind and he was still in the field. After saying his farewells to his staff Pendleton boarded an ambulance along with Dr. Graham and set out on the road to Lexington, sixty-one miles away on the other side of the Blue Ridge. Yet in his heart William Nelson Pendleton's war was not over.

Rev. Pendleton after the war

Washington College (now Washington & Lee University)

16. "AN AUTHORITY I CANNOT RESIST TO ANY PURPOSE"

[LEXINGTON, 1865-1870]

Let every soul be subject unto the higher powers. For there is no power but of God: the powers that be are ordained of God. Whoever resisteth the power, resisteth the ordinance of God: and they that resist shall receive to themselves damnation.

Romans 13:1-2, King James Version

Render therefore unto Caesar the things which are Caesar's, and unto God the things that are God's.

Matthew 22:21, King James Version

It must have been bittersweet for Pendleton when his ambulance crested the hills in Rockbridge County and he could see Lexington in the distance. He once described the town as being in a "beautiful situation in the center of plains as level as a carpet, as green as an emerald, and as fertile as the valley of the Egyptian Nile, walled in on one side by the picturesque peaks of the Alleghenies and on the other side by the azure crests of the Blue Ridge." But in 1865 he returned to a land and a family torn by war, and immersed in poverty.

The war was harsh to the white population of Rockbridge County. One third of the adult white population of the County

339

served in the Confederate forces. Of these, almost a third were killed, wounded, or died in the service. Since the County's pre-war economy was based on small-scale farming and local business enterprises, its basic economy revived quickly but was limited. Horses were scarce, and men were harnessed to plows to work the fields. Food was scarce until the autumn harvests. Despite the failure of the local wheat crop there were bountiful harvests of rye, corn, and oats. There was no mail, no conveyances, and no banks. For weeks the detritus of war drifted through Lexington as paroled soldiers made their way home, begging for food as they passed through town. On one occasion one of the Pendleton daughters went into town and saw six one legged soldiers sitting on a pile of planks. They were resting before continuing to hobble home to Tennessee and western North Carolina.

The first news of Lee's surrender, and for Virginians the end of the war, came to the Pendletons when a wounded soldier confirmed the rumors heard on the streets. The news of the surrender was kept from Mrs. Pendleton for two days for fear it would affect her health. Late on the evening of Good Friday, April 14th, the family heard wagon wheels approaching the Rectory during a heavy rain. The door opened and General Pendleton walked in. He was depressed and full of despair at the outcome of the war, and the welcome was made in hushed tones. Pendleton could not accept how the war ended, and he continued to fight it in his own way.

Pendleton's anger and bitterness lingered for months. He complained about the loss of the business capital of the South through the emancipation of the enslaved blacks, the use of foreigners to shoot down "our noblest population," and the invasion of homes in some mad lust for power and plunder. The truth could not be spoken, for "We have no country left, nor hope of one for an indefinite period......Our people are for the most part disarmed and exposed to insult and attack from the Negroes let loose. These are thrown broadcast upon our society, idle, improvident, homeless, helpless, to perish by the thousands. Yankee adventurers are appearing among us with money to cheat out people out of their little remaining coin. Our banks are all said to be ruined....We have no country, no currency, no law. ...." Pendleton still hoped that God would deliver the South and grant it independence "which is our birthright.... [but] we must be content to live without a country" and instead focus on entering heaven. The black servants, now free from anyone's perspective, remained with the family except for one maid who left for Richmond. Pendleton still viewed the blacks as children, commiserating with them for their freedom, "Poor creatures, they little dream of the difficulties freedom will bring them. They cherished the absurd idea that they would exchange places with us – be gentlemen and ladies in our homes and have us for their Negroes. To find themselves still black, with woolly heads, is to them an immense disappointment. Altogether, the case is gloomy enough."

With Appomattox a recent memory former Confederate soldiers still passed through town and the Rectory's porch was full of them seeking food. The Pendletons handed out what they could afford to the men, but food was scarce, and the only meat the family had was some ham for Easter dinner. Generous strangers and friends came to their aid. One lady in Lynchburg sent Anzelotte two uncooked beef tongues and some sardines. One black lady in town was able to buy some old dresses from the Pendletons for three dozen eggs. Colonel Gilham of VMI provided mutton on which the family dined for four days. Otherwise they had bread, milk, a pot of coffee, dried apples, herbs, molasses, and a little winter lettuce. On many evenings the only food available to eat was herbs. Anzelotte was anxious for the future, "Why we are so prostrated I cannot see. I cannot think we are a dead people, and that all that we have done and suffered is for less than naught I cannot believe."

On Easter Sunday, two days after he arrived home, Pendleton was finally able to baptize his grandson Alexander S. Pendleton, Jr. To maintain his family Pendleton fell back on skills he learned managing the plantation in Caroline County in his youth. He planted a vegetable garden, and used his two horses to plough the lot and plant corn, watermelon, cabbage, and muskmelon with the help of his daughters. The family found wild strawberries and picked them to be eaten with some sugar they obtained. He spent his time reading or planning a biography of Sandie. Without any mail service they did not hear from daughter Susan and Ned Lee in Canada for weeks.

The Rector for Grace Episcopal Church, the Reverend Norton, was recalled to his Alexandria pulpit and departed Lexington. Pendleton was asked to step in as the temporary priest for the church. The sextons were reluctant to offer the pulpit to Pendleton as they had no money with which to pay him. Pendleton accepted the offer and remained the Rector of Grace Episcopal the remainder of his life. At first he was paid nothing but was able to remain in the Rectory. Occasional donations contributed to his cash flow. Sandie's widow Kate could not help financially since her trustee invested all of her money in Confederate bonds. A regular salary was commenced only in April 1867 at General Lee's request.

Their troubles grew when a Union garrison of Pennsylvania soldiers arrived to occupy Lexington. In the anger after Lincoln's assassination the North demanded blood, and Federal troops arrested many of those connected with the Confederacy. On May 17, 1865, former Governor John Letcher and his family were awakened by loud knocks on the door. On opening it he was arrested by Union cavalry sent from Winchester. He packed a few things and was taken away to prison only to be released on parole on July 10th at the behest of James D. Davidson. Other Federal troops occupied the meadow opposite VMI searching for former Governor Letcher. There was a growing concern about the formerly enslaved blacks. One maid treated her former owner as an equal and was sent away as a punishment. Another left to visit family and never returned. Some of the formerly enslaved blacks refused to work but wouldn't leave town. An "armed patrol" kept order in the manner of the recently extinguished past. Anzelotte wrote, "We are afraid to look into the future…"

Newspapers arrived in town from Richmond, Lynchburg, and the North but Pendleton could not bring himself to read them. There were rumors that even Robert E, Lee, despite his parole from Grant, would be arrested. When President Andrew Johnson issued his amnesty for most Confederates Pendleton was not included as he was a Confederate general officer and West Point graduate. He was not sure what might happen to him but was confident that Johnson would not disturb the parole status guaranteed by Grant at Appomattox. On that basis, Pendleton did "not believe they will venture to harm [Lee] or any of us."

Pendleton wrote to Union General John Gibbon, one of the Union commissioners at Appomattox, protesting the treatment that former Confederate officers received arguing that "As one of the commissioners for adjusting the terms of surrender at Appomattox Court House, April 10, 1865, … I respectfully remind you of the conditions of surrender – that officers and men thus submitting should, so long as observing their own pledge and obeying the laws prevailing where they reside, remain 'unmolested by the Federal authorities.'" He noted that Judge Underwood in Norfolk was preparing indictments against former Confederate officers and charged a grand jury that it could "disregard this solemn assurance as a mere military arrangement, not binding upon the civil authorities. You will recollect that at the time it was understood to be a solemn compact, rigidly binding on both sides and accepted on the venerable sanctions of truth and honor." He reminded Gibbon that from the Southern perspective they fought for "rights they believed justly theirs and wrongly assailed," and would have kept fighting absent the "pledge of honor" that they would be protected. Pendleton asked Gibbon to use his influence to avert "the inflictions now sought by prejudice, passion, and unopposed power to be visited upon the defenseless men who relied upon your integrity in so critical a transaction."

Pendleton did not stop there, he admitted to Gibbon that he was not able to apply for executive clemency "because wholly conscious of having the most virtuous intentions in my share of the late defensive struggle, on my part, I cannot do or say anything which signifies that I condemn myself therefor." He noted that one of the bases for his exclusion from the amnesty was his graduation from West Point. He reminded Gibbon that he resigned his Federal Army commission more than thirty years before with the full sanction of Federal authorities. After serving as a preacher he was urged to lead a voluntary company in the recent war "and as the cry of Northern passion seemed to become more furious, and as the pressure of power against Virginia increased, I never found myself at liberty to withdraw from a service thus entered upon." His service earned him his promotions which he did not feel could be declined. Pendleton asks Gibbon to consider the true record in providing him some relief from the exclusion from amnesty. Even so, Pendleton confesses that "my convictions remain wholly unchanged respecting the rights of the States, and the great wrongs inflicted on Virginia and her Southern sisters by their Northern partners, in flagrant violation of the compact of union by the latter which compelled the former to seek redress by separation." Since it pleased God Almighty to permit the South to be defeated Pendleton was willing to "submit myself peaceably to an authority which, whatever I think of its justice, I cannot resist to any purpose." There is no record of a response.

In the ordinary Episcopalian service of the time the priest offered a prayer for the President so that the Holy Spirit could operate through him and bring about God's will for the better good of all. After secession the prayer changed to one for the President of the Confederacy. By the time Pendleton resumed his duties in the pulpit in late May 1865 the prayer for Jeff Davis was banned. Pendleton was also disgusted by the occupation of Lexington by Federal troops and the petty insults and indignities to which Confederate veterans were subjected by them. Nor did he consider the military government of Virginia to be lawful and since there was no legal civil government in the state the Federals could not control what the people thought or prayed. Still bitter, and angry, Pendleton refused to include the prayer for the President of the United States in his service. Instead, at that point in the litany he gave a prayer for all rulers and for all in authority in accordance with the Book of Common Prayer. Most of his parish agreed with him.

After two weeks of this omission or revision, word leaked of it to the military occupational authority. On July 9th a Federal lieutenant sat at the rear of the church during the service. Pendleton's sermon was on the prophecy by Jacob of the future prominence of Judith. Pendleton spoke of how the kingdoms of the world punished the Jews for their sins. He also spoke of the blasphemies heard from "those representatives of the Gigantic power which oppresses the land" in using the Lord's name in vain in public. Later that day, one young lady living just outside of town advised Pendleton that his sermon had given great offense to the Union officers governing the town. It was reported to the Federal occupation authorities that his sermon was "very inflammatory" and that if he did not mend his ways he would be arrested and removed from the pulpit. The next day Pendleton wrote to the Union commander Colonel Stuart that on his way from church the day before he was escorting several ladies when two Union soldiers occupied the sidewalk in such a way as to force the ladies into the filthy mud of the street. Similar incidents were occurring on a regular basis. Pendleton assumed that the officer would not tolerate such behavior as improper and offensive. He signed the letter as a Confederate States Brigadier General, Chief of Artillery for the Army of Northern Virginia. The commander replied only that Pendleton should not sign as a Confederate general anymore. Soon thereafter Stuart was replaced by a new commander, a Lieutenant Colonel McLeester.

On Sunday, July 16th an officer and an armed guard "came clattering into the church" and attended the church service. The congregation became antsy at their presence but Pendleton calmly carried on with his service. The sermon was on the text, "Blessed are we poor in spirit." In the course of the sermon Pendleton spoke of poverty such as the South endured and of "the spoliation of iniquitous power and the atrocities of our devastating enemies have spread this experience throughout our beloved South…" At the conclusion of the service Pendleton returned to the vestry where he was accosted by the Union officer. Pendleton asked that the officer observe the proprieties to which the officer responded, "Damn the proprieties!" The officer demanded a copy of the sermon, which had already been given to a deaf parishioner to read. Pendleton refused to surrender the sermon or the sermon from the week before until he had them copied. "It must be made immediately and sent this afternoon," the officer replied.

Pendleton walked home. Later that day a Union sergeant and three armed soldiers walked into the house and asked "Are you the Reverend Mr. Pendleton?" Pendleton replied it was he. In a "very insolent manner" the sergeant replied "I have come to arrest you." Pendleton asked if he could dine first and was told that would be acceptable provided the sergeant came in with him to dinner. Mrs. Pendleton objected, "You shan't go in my house!" In return the sergeant pushed Pendleton who told him to stop. Things calmed down and Pendleton ate dinner on the portico in sight of the Union patrol. After dinner the sergeant attempted to retrieve the sermon but Pendleton refused to give it to anyone but McLeester. The sergeant told him the commanding officer was having dinner with James D. Davidson and could not be disturbed. The soldiers loaded their muskets and arrested Pendleton. He was marched into town and placed in confinement inside "Old Davidson's corn crib." He wrote a letter of complaint to McLeester accusing the Federals of improperly arresting him, and for violation of his "civilized rights." He alleged that some Federal officer took exception to some of his remarks in the service which the officer purportedly wrote down. But when he read them back to Pendleton and his family it was obvious he had made the offensive language up. He was confined without the right to communicate with anyone and appealed to

McLeester's sense of justice and duty to release him, as a paroled officer, on his word of honor that he would not escape. When McLeester returned after 9:00 p.m. Pendleton was released and sent home.

The next morning at 10:00 a.m. Pendleton was taken again by the soldiers. He carried copies of the sermons in his pockets to the courthouse where the commanding officer questioned the Union officers and Pendleton about what had occurred. Pendleton refused to answer any questions orally but said he would do so in writing. He also advised the Union officers that he was going to press charges against the Lieutenant for breach of his parole and his ungentlemanly conduct. For some reason Pendleton felt that his parole from Grant at Appomattox cleared him of any offenses he might have committed after Appomattox. Pendleton asked if General Alfred Torbert, the Union general in charge of the district, would try him. He asked that copies be made of the sermons and he be given a copy. One officer copied out the sermons but they then withheld the copies from Pendleton. He returned home at about 4:00 p.m. The Federals ordered that the church remained closed until a higher authority agreed to re-open it.

The harassment of the Pendletons increased. Pendleton was made to surrender his only pair of gloves as they were from his service days, and the Confederate buttons of his uniform coat, now converted to civilian use, were covered with black cloth. He was forbidden to leave town. When the family visited Sandie's grave in the town cemetery they found it desecrated. The wooden headboard was pulled up and the headboard seriously mutilated by Union soldiers, three of whom were found in the cemetery with one relieving himself in a corner. Pendleton sent another complaint but every complaint he lodged against this treatment was replied to with rude insults. All of the gentlemen in town sympathized with Pendleton but there is no record that they ever stood up for him against the occupying authority. He continued to hold services at the parsonage and administered communion there.

Colonel McLeester told Pendleton that he was referring the question of charges and the church to General Alfred Torbert in Winchester. When Pendleton asked leave to visit Torbert it was denied and he was told to remain in Lexington. When McLeester left town on leave Pendleton re-opened the church but it was very quickly closed again. Pendleton still refused to have prayers for the

United States President read in church. He advised the congregation that as he was not permitted to preach they should dismiss him as their minister. Instead, the congregation attended the Presbyterian Church and heard Dr. White offer a sermon similar to the one that got Pendleton into trouble.

On July 24th Pendleton applied to the acting commander Captain Bunker for leave to journey to Charlottesville to apply for a position at the University of Virginia. Inasmuch as McLeester was absent, he asked that the Captain approve his departure. He signed the request as "paroled at Appomattox Courthouse as Brigadier General & Chief of Arty ANV." Once again, it was refused. Pendleton was required to procure a new parole in addition to the one issued by Grant. He was not permitted to go until either McLeester returned or August 1st, whichever came first.

On July 26th Pendleton received a list of questions from the Union authorities as to two points; his version of what happened on the 16th and his views on the Constitution and the Union government. He replied directly to General Torbert on the 28th. He noted that his sermon on the 9th used outward poverty as an illustration of spiritual destitution and then briefly as to the spoliation of the town and the devastation that their enemies had spread. Some person present took it as an offense and reported it as inflammatory. The local authorities were determined to arrest Pendleton unless he refrained from any objectionable content and prayed for President Andrew Johnson. The next week he once again omitted the prayer and preached on the text of Jacob's prophecy; "The scepter shall not depart from Judah" an old sermon written years ago. He added the comment that "the controlling purpose of heaven is to make Christ's kingdom really prevalent" and added "as it had been with Egyptians, Assyrians, Babylonians, Persians, Greeks and Romans and the Jews and so it will be with us." These civilizations allowed prosperity and adversity to affect their relationship with God, and God punished them. He also noted that "we might rest assured God would not overlook the wrong on the side of power nor fidelity on the part of the unjust but would approve what He discerns to be virtue" and punish the "infidel and presumptuous tyranny" as He has always done.

Pendleton advised Torbert that he had omitted the presidential prayer for two reasons. First, the Church's General Council for the Southern Diocese had abrogated it years ago, presumably at the time of secession. Second, while he was willing to pray to God to give the President guidance he could not pray for prosperity regarding his course of conduct. Pendleton had not taken an oath to the Union as the need for it had never arisen. He still "seriously" objected to the oath in that it binds the oath taker to supporting the Constitution – "which I am willing to do- and to sustaining the proclamation of emancipation, etc., which I cannot feel to be right – and having acted most sincerely from the first owing to the clear dictates of my judgment and conscience," and given all that he endured for the invaded and suffering Virginia, "I have not the slightest idea or feeling of having therein done any wrong, hence I have shrunk at a step which seems at first at least liable to be viewed as a confession of guilt." However, "in terms of the general orderings of Providence and in view of the necessity laid upon all good citizens" to render conscious support for the recognized government "according to the spiritual sanctions," he was willing "to waive all scruples and both take the oath and ask for 'executive clemency.'"

The next day he again asked Captain Bunker to re-open the church justifying the omission of the prayer for the President. The response came from a Major Redmond, "Your quibbling would be impertinent were it not contemptible. When you are prepared to use the prescribed form of prayer- not a garbled quotation from another part of the Prayer Book, I will request the proper authorities to permit your church to be reopened." On the evening of August 1st a Federal orderly came to the door of the rectory and delivered an order releasing Pendleton from his parole for travel provided he agree to certain restrictions. Pendleton replied the next day that the release from parole provided he not make any treasonable comments from the pulpit, yet the Constitution stated that language alone cannot by law be treason. Nor was Pendleton to use language disrespectful of United States officials in any way, to which he queried, "I suppose you mean disrespectful language." To this Pendleton was agreeable, he would never mention Federal officials again in a service. "I am commissioned to proclaim it is my business to preach, "yet in these times it was difficult to teach the great lessons of the Bible" without some "faithless or malevolent" person getting offended. The Constitution said there can be no abridgment of the freedom of speech and if Congress cannot abridge speech then neither can an official.

The parole also required him to pray for the President and United States officials, but there existed no Constitutional power to order this. Pendleton respectfully protested against force or threats. Yet, as the scripture commanded he would pray for those in authority. He had used and intended to use from the Litany the phrase, "we beseech thee, that it may please thee to bless and preserve all Christian rulers and magistrates, giving them grace to execute justice and to maintain truth." However, if the Federals wanted him to use the Prayer for the President from the Book of Common Prayer he could not do so without violating his conscience as the Church Council had banned its use. Since no earthly power can contradict that of the Church in Church affairs they could arrest him or close the church, as he could not stop them.

Finding his usefulness as a minister seriously impaired by his stubbornness, and at the urgent request of his daughters Pendleton finally took the required "amnesty oath" from notary public Charles Davidson on August 3, 1865, declaring that he would "Faithfully support, protect and defend the Constitution of the United States , and the union of states thereunder, and that I will, in like manner, abide by and support all laws and proclamations which have been made during the existing rebellion with reference to the emancipation of slaves…" On August 4th Pendleton penned a draft letter to President Andrew Johnson applying for executive clemency in the hope that he might soon return to "the peaceful duties which are much more congenial" to him. It is not certain he mailed it then but by late summer he made a formal request that his civil rights as a United States citizen be restored. Still, his battles with Federal authority over the Presidential prayer continued. As late as August 28, 1865 he was writing to the district commander in Staunton that the authorities required that he not say anything offensive from the pulpit, so that Pendleton could interpret it as being restricted to all services connected with prayer, but that the order did not apply to other services such as Communion. So, unless he was told he could not do so, he would not be restricted by any orders in using the Litany, Communion, collects, and sermons from an approved volume. The Union commander did so object. Pendleton applied again in December 1865 to re-open the church but was refused. Only when the occupying troops departed Lexington for good in January 1866 did the church re-open its doors.

*   *   *   *

In mid-July while his battles with the government were ongoing Pendleton saw an advertisement in the paper for a position as a professor and chair of mathematics at the University of Virginia, the same post to which had had been accepted in 1854 but turned down as a favor to a friend seeking the same position. He obtained endorsements from several locals, including Matthew F. Maury, inventor John M. Brooke, VMI Professor and University of Virginia Board of Visitors member William Gilliam, and former Governor John Letcher. He sent the request and a copy of his pre-war application and endorsements to Alexander Rives, the brother of Pendleton's childhood friend and politician William C. Rives. He wrote in the application that he was fifty-six years old with a vigorous constitution and had taught mathematics as a master element in human cultivation at Alexandria before the war. He enclosed his biography from 1854 adding that since then he had published a book on religion and science, a copy of which he included. He added additional manuscripts of essays, including one entitled "The Double Prophecy of Human Progress." However, he advised the Board that he was excluded from amnesty and was at present unable to leave Lexington. He asked a University student to hand carry the application and the additional papers and book to Charlottesville. He did not get the position.

Home life improved with the return of Ned and Susan Pendleton Lee from Canada. Cash was still short. A local investigator for R.G. Dun & Co. (predecessor of the familiar modern credit-rating firm, Dun & Bradstreet), assessed Pendleton's status as: "Pays v[er]y badly but occupies high social position…poor & proud….always 'Hard Up.' " Former parishioners in Frederick sent him a package of dry goods, including a complete suit for Pendleton with a black broadcloth suit, hat, gloves, underclothes and handkerchief. Pendleton even tried to collect unpaid student fees from years before. As cadets and students returned in the fall he rented space to some and provided it for free to those unable to pay. One of his daughters returned to teaching to bring in needed cash. Bishop Johns Richmond made a gift of $30.00 from funds raised to help impoverished ministers. All this helped to put food on the table, for which Pendleton was grateful. After a feast of tomato soup seasoned with chicken, potatoes, cucumbers, corn, he pushed back his chair and said "What a good dinner!"

Sandie's baby son Alexander grew like a weed well into the summer. But in late July he came down with diphtheria. The illness slowly took its toll and on September 1, 1865 the baby was gone. Pendleton was grief stricken. He wrote:

> You will deeply grieve to learn that our dear little grandson has been removed from us. It pleased God to subj him to sickness just 6 weeks ago, which continued with increasing severity in spite of the best medical skill & assiduous nursing until day before yesterday, when without a struggle his ransomed spirit passed to the bosom of our Blessed Redeemer.
>
> He was to me very dear, as not less than a new motive in life, as he was to his grandmother and to all the household. We laid his lovely remains by his father's yesterday, there to rest till the summons shall sound for glorified bodies to be reunited with their redeemed spirits....Father & son are in spirit, we believe, now in the presence of the Savior, together satisfied, & sharing the society of the just made perfect.

Kate remained with the Pendletons taking part in the "home employment of our rather busy household." She was all that remained of both Sandie and his son. Pendleton hoped she would help him prepare a memoir of Sandie. Kate left for home but returned the next spring to stay. In 1871 she married a VMI professor and lived in Lexington until her second husband died in 1906. She then moved to New York City to live with a daughter from her second marriage and died there in 1919. She was buried in the Lexington cemetery near to both of her husbands and child. As Pendleton once wrote, Kate had been "called to a bitter experience early in life."

     *   *   *   *

Washington College survived the war operating as a grammar school. When the war ended the trustees sought to restore it to its former position as a college. The college buildings remained in a usable condition but the Federal troops had looted the library and science labs, and there were no books or equipment. The college was also broke, as all of its prior endowments were no longer performing. With a lot of hope and wishful thinking in August 1865 they offered the position of College President to General Robert E. Lee. Local attorney, politician, judge and law school instructor John W. Brockenbrough borrowed a suit and rode to eastern Virginia to personally tender the offer.

Knowing of his friendship with Lee, College Professor James J. White asked Pendleton to write to Lee urging him to accept. White asked that Pendleton stress that the College would make every effort not to be a denominational Presbyterian school as before the war. Pendleton was more than happy to oblige. In his letter he assured Lee that the College would be non-denominational, and that it would offer Lee an opportunity to help Virginia. He told Lee that "Lexington is, as you are aware, a place of no great importance." But it had attractive mountain scenery and the "the house and appliances provided for the President would present many comforts." Then he used the magic words he knew would affect Lee, "My hope is that it might accord with your views of duty and with your tastes to accept this important trust...One great reason why I hope you may judge favorably of this invitation is, that the destiny of our State and country depends so greatly upon the training of our young men. And now our Educational Institutions are so crippled that they need the very best agencies for their restoration and the revival of high aims in the breasts of Virginia and Southern youths.....I have thought Dear General while thus doing an important service to the State and its people you might be presenting to the world in such a position an example of quiet usefulness & gentle patriotism, no less imperative than the illustrative career in the field."

Lee accepted the position. He replied to Pendleton, "If I thought I could have been of any benefit to our noble youth, I should not have hesitated to give my services, but the position is new to me, and I have not seen that I could be of much good. .... I am very glad that you have returned to the exercise of your sacred profession, for there is no labor so beneficent, so elevated and so sublime, as the teaching of salvation to every man. I hope your career on earth may be crowned with success, and ever-lasting peace and happiness your portion in Heaven."

Lee quietly arrived in Lexington on September 18th, riding his warhorse Traveller alone into town. His coming was a great comfort for Pendleton given their very deep and emotional ties from West Point and the war. In Lexington Lee renewed his friendship with Pendleton as well with Maury, Colonel Smith, and became one of Pendleton's parishioners.

Lee and Pendleton quickly renewed their friendship from the war years. It may be mere coincidence but Lee's arrival corresponded with the end of Pendleton's one man war against the Union. One wonders what Lee might have counselled Pendleton on his singularly self-destructive attitude about the outcome of the war. Lee joined Grace Episcopal Church and quickly became its most influential member, and was selected as a vestryman soon after his arrival. Every Sunday he sat in the second pew in front of the chancel where he knelt in prayer and listened attentively to all of Pendleton's sermons. When other parishioners fell asleep and snored Lee did not react but remained focused on the sermon. Occasionally, Lee visited the Rectory and sat with the family near the stove in the family hall. In 1867 the couples attended the county fair together. After all, Lee, his wife and the Pendletons were scions of Old Virginia and all related to another in some manner.

In April 1867 Lee asked another vestryman to move the board for an annual salary for Pendleton of $800, and succeeded in having it passed. Until then Pendleton survived on $50 in gold from Ned Lee, $50 from the sale of Ned and Susan's belongings before they left for Canada late in the war, from $119 contributed by the church, funds from the state diocese, and income from boarding college students. In November 1867 Lee, as the church chair on finances, reported that Pendleton's pay for 1867 and 1868 were in arrears, and urged it be paid to alleviate Pendleton's chronic pecuniary embarrassment and enable him to pursue pastoral duties worry free. From the correspondence it appears that Lee tried to help Pendleton with his burdensome debts. In February 1868 he wrote to Pendleton telling him to pay specific sums to two of his debtors to close his accounts with them. Lee even worked with his cousin Ned Lee to resolve some of the cash flow issues.

In May 1868 Pendleton persuaded Lee to join him for the annual state church council at St. Paul's in Lynchburg. Lee arrived as a laity delegate dressed in a black suit but was instantly recognized. Admirers flooded him, women wept, and Lee was forced to beat a hasty retreat back into the church for safety. During the proceedings Lee listened attentively and knelt for prayer at the altar. There is a curious article from the April 20, 1869 Staunton Spectator that Lee and Pendleton were expected in town for a meeting of the Baltimore & Ohio Railroad the next day. It is unknown and unlikely they attended.

As soon as the mails were restored letters poured in from Lee's veterans and other students seeking admission into "General Lee's College." Lee was inaugurated as College President on October 1, 1865 in a large classroom on the second floor of Payne Hall. One of his first tasks was to lay down rules for the students, "we have no printed rules here, we have but one rule and that is that every student be a gentleman." This one rule was followed until the 21st Century when it succumbed to socially destructive tides. The College trustees asked Pendleton to seek new endowments with which to fund the school and enable them to hire qualified department chairs. Pendleton travelled to Baltimore, Richmond, and New York City to raise the money, establishing himself as a successful fund raiser.

In the spring of 1866 Pendleton was asked to present a course in declamation on Friday afternoons. His students were not impressed, or were eager for the weekend, and for whatever reason they made fun of Pendleton in class. The first time the students pinned papers to the tail of Pendleton's coat as he went up the aisle, applauded him most noisily before he said a word, and then bombarded him with wads of paper. Pendleton lectured them on their poor manners and managed to finish the hour long lesson, but he immediately complained to Lee about their behavior. Lee sat in on the next class the next week and all went well. But on the following Friday students gathered outside the class windows yelling and blowing horns. When Pendleton refused to stop the lecture someone threw a dog with a tin can tied to its tail into the room. The mad flight of the dog caused chaos. Pendleton shortly thereafter resigned his position. Given that many of the students the first year after the war were Lee's veterans, perhaps some of the poor reputation Pendleton from the war with the ranks carried over.

Nevertheless Pendleton remained actively involved in the life of the campus, after all his church sat on the edge of it. He was on good terms with the faculty members at the College and VMI, many of whom were half of his congregation. He attended the commencements of the College and VMI, occasionally offering prayers. During the commencement in 1867 the College campus was illuminated and a band made the atmosphere lively with its music. Pendleton offered the prayer to open the commencement and Lee handed out the certificates. The dinner for the alumni was held that night at the Lexington Hotel attended by Lee. Pendleton offered the prayer, commenting that the famous prayer he made at Falling Waters in 1861 was made privately and not intended for the public. He spoke glowingly of his old friend Thomas J. Jackson and paid tribute to the men of his artillery corps.

The next year commencement services were held in the newly completed Chapel on campus. Once again Pendleton offered the opening prayer and gave a brief address. At the new Chapel Pendleton and other ministers in town took turns in offering services Tuesday and Thursday evening, and offered prayer at the daily morning service. A wide outpouring of faith led to sixty-two confirmations in May 1869. The commencement held the next month was festive. Once again the campus was illuminated filled with "belles and beaux" enjoying a promenade and music. The alumni dinner was held with numerous toasts at the Lexington Hotel and was attended by Lee and Pendleton. In 1870 Pendleton once more offered the "fervent and appropriate" prayers at commencement.

One day Pendleton noticed that his Washington College parishioners no longer came for service to Grace Episcopal but attended services at the Presbyterian Church instead. Pendleton fretted to Lee that they were drawn by the better eloquence of Dr. Pratt. Lee's response was reported to be either "Well, you know that the Presbyterian Church has its Grace" or "I rather think that the attraction is not so much Dr. Pratt's eloquence as it is Dr. Pratt's Grace," referring to the minister's beautiful daughter Grace Pratt.

On September 12, 1870 Lee advised Pendleton and the other ministers in Lexington that the College would open for students on the 15th. He urged that the students acquaint themselves with the churches in town, and that they be invited to attend regular services. Lee invited Pendleton to attend the faculty meeting at the Chapel on the 15th to offer prayer. Lee also asked Pendleton to continue to offer his daily prayers at the morning services. It was Lee's goal to "inculcate in the minds of the students the principles of true piety." On the 15th the students and faculty gathered in the Chapel where Pendleton gave the service. Lee made announcements and then "expressed his earnest hope that both professors and students would attend regularly the daily prayers at the chapel." One observer commented that it was probably the longest speech Lee ever made at the College.

Wednesday morning September 28, 1870 was pleasant but it turned chilly after noon and began to rain steadily as it does in the Valley in the autumn. After his regular nap Lee left his new home on campus for a meeting of the vestry of Grace Church just fifty yards away. On the agenda was the plan to tear down the old structure and build a newer one made of stone, and an item calling for the payment of Pendleton's paltry salary. Lee wore his old military cape into the unheated old church and sat down in one of the wooden pews. Tired, his face flushed, Lee called the meeting to order at 4:00 p.m. Pendleton told the vestry that he needed at least an income of $1,000 a year or he could retire and allow a younger man to take over his ministry. He also repeated the need for cash for the building fund. Lee waited patiently as each vestryman offered some cash towards Pendleton's salary. When they ended up $55.00 short Lee quietly said, "I will give that sum." The meeting ended at 7:00 p.m., a half hour later than Mrs. Lee's planned dinnertime. In the growing evening gloom Lee bid the other vestrymen and Pendleton a good night and walked back home.

Once home, Lee climbed the steps to the porch, entered the house and went into the chamber where he took off his hat and cape. He then passed into the dining room where he was late for dinner. Mrs. Lee expressed concern that he looked chilled but Lee responded that he was warmly clothed. She then teased him about his tardiness but there was no reply. Lee opened his lips for grace but did not speak. Instead, he slowly sank into his chair. They brought a bed into the dining room and laid Lee in it. The rains continued to fall heavily for days while Lee slowly sank. On October 12, 1870, the Confederate chieftain died. The heavy rains continued, eventually washing out the bridges and isolating Lexington from the world.

Pendleton was appointed to the committee handling the details of the funeral. All of the businesses in town closed and badges of mourning were seen everywhere. Lee's casket was taken from his home in a solemn procession to lie in state at the Chapel watched by a student guard of honor. The 15th dawned with sunny skies. The funeral services at the Chapel were simple in keeping with Lee's wishes. The funeral procession consisted of Confederate veterans, Pendleton and the other pallbearers with the casket, Traveller in black behind the hearse, College trustees and faculty, VMI faculty and Board of Visitors, cadets, Masons and Odd Fellows, and then ordinary citizens. They began at 10:00 a.m. on the campus where the columns of the Colonnade were draped in black. The funeral march proceeded through town where residents wept openly from their porches. No Confederate flags were flown. The VMI band played the dirge and the church bells in town tolled.

The procession returned to the Chapel where students and cadets marched past the casket. Pendleton tendered the services, reading the burial service of the Episcopal Church and then read from Psalm 37:8-11 and 28-40. He closed with an application of the teachings of the Bible to Lee's conduct in life, noting that he had known Lee for forty-five years as a student, a comrade in arms, and as a pastor. He could easily make tribute to the "undeviating rectitude, and consistency of Lee's Christian character…. The law of God was in his heart; therefore none of his steps slide….Mark the perfect man and behold the upright, for the end of that man is peace." Dr. White, of the Presbyterian Church also spoke. They lay Lee's casket into a vault in the center of the basement of the Chapel and placed a marble slab over it. Pendleton finished services on the south side of chapel leading the singing of "How Firm a Foundation Ye Saints of the Lord."

For the last time Pendleton was reminded of the similarity of his appearance with that of Lee. The day after the funeral he visited the home of Matthew Maury. A little boy appeared in Maury's doorway, and drew back in astonishment at the sight of Pendleton, and said "Why, I thought you was dead under the roses!" Pendleton was devastated at the loss of his good friend, leader, companion, and mentor. He offered his resignation to the church but it was declined. Instead, Pendleton devoted many of his remaining years zealously serving the memory of Robert E. Lee.

Rev. Pendleton late in life

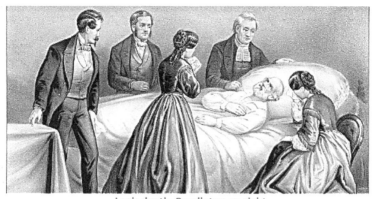
Lee's death, Pendleton on right

17. "UTTERLY CRAMPED AND CRIPPLED FOR WANT OF MEANS"

[LEXINGTON, 1866-1883]

I heard a voice from heaven, saying unto me, Write, From henceforth blessed are the dead who die in the Lord: even so saith the Spirit; for they rest from their labours.

1789 Episcopalian Book of Common Prayer

The Lord bless thee, and keep thee: The Lord make his face shine upon thee, and be gracious unto thee: The Lord lift up his countenance upon thee, and give thee peace.

Numbers 6:24-26, King James Version

The death of Robert E. Lee spawned a number of memorial associations dedicated to preserving his memory with a tomb and a statue. In Lexington a Memorial Association was inaugurated with Pendleton as the President. This local group wanted Lee buried in town with appropriate statuary over the grave. On hearing the news of Lee's death Jubal Early wrote Pendleton from Franklin County, Virginia, that the news was more devastating than that of Appomattox. Even though the attorney Early was precluded by his trial calendar and schedule from attending the funeral, he took an active lead in a statewide memorial association centered in Richmond. The Richmond association wished to place the tomb and statue in the state capital. Thus began the struggle between the establishment powers of Richmond and the local interests of Lexington over the body and name of Robert E. Lee.

Initially there was an intense effort to merge the two associations. Offers were made to the important people in Lexington to join the Hollywood Memorial Association of Richmond, dedicated to locating the tomb in the famous cemetery of the Confederacy. Only twelve days after Lee's death Jubal Early called a meeting of the veterans of the Army of Northern Virginia as it was felt that only proper that the Confederate veterans take guardianship of Lee's remains. However, possession is nine tenths of the law and with Lee already buried in a vault in Lee Chapel Pendleton and his group held the upper hand. Despite heavy pressure from interests in Richmond, the local association succeeded in keeping Lee in Lexington.

Also critical to the success of the Lexington association was the support from Lee's widow. Mrs. Mary Custis Lee asked that the sculptor Edward Valentine be retained to sculpt the statue of her late husband at the College. Valentine agreed to make the statue for $15,000. He came to Lexington and used measurements of Pendleton's torso in his Confederate uniform for the statue. Initial funds for the project came from W. W. Corcoran of Washington, D.C. and W. H. McLellan of Louisiana. Additional funds needed to be raised and Pendleton was called upon to tour the country raising money for the statue. Pendleton offered to resign his pulpit given the expected absences over the next few months, but the Grace Episcopal Church vestry decided to exploit the opportunity. They desperately needed a new church as the old one was falling apart and leaking in heavy rains. So why not combine Pendleton's tour for money for the statue and tomb with an appeal for a new church edifice. After all, Lee's last active hours were spent managing church business. Pendleton was made the chair of the Re-Building Committee. Mrs. Lee, who continued to reside in the President's House, approved of the new church as it was a project close to her husband's heart.

In early 1871 the trustees of Washington College named Lee's eldest son General Custis Lee as the new College President. He was inaugurated in the Chapel during a driving snowstorm. Pendleton presided over the services, offering prayers and a scriptural reading. The trustees then renamed the school Washington & Lee University in honor of its two famous benefactors; George Washington and Robert E. Lee. The trustees asked that Pendleton also tour raising money for the school as well as the tomb, the statue, and the church. He put off his fund raising tour long enough to appear at the memorial soldier's fair in Richmond raising cash for needy veterans where he sat on the podium with Jefferson Davis and Jubal Early, and also asked to judge the flower competition.

By the end of November he was off "wandering about as a beggar." Occasionally he received insulting letters from bitter Northerners but kept up the tour. He raised funds and preached in Louisville, Memphis, New Orleans, and Selma. At Selma he visited with former Confederate General William Hardee at whose home his daughter Rose was a tutor. From there he went on to Augusta and Savannah. His travels took him to Richmond, where he was able to preach at St. Paul's, and to Memphis. Jefferson Davis sent him a valid critique of his Memphis address saying it was not focused as it asked for help on the sarcophagus, college, church, and a monument in Richmond and it needed to be clearer as to where the money was going. Pendleton's efforts paid off very quickly, and from some of the most unexpected sources. Money came in from abolitionist Henry Beecher Ward and New York Democrat politician Samuel Tilden. Republican Radical Thaddeus Stevens and Union General Ben Butler contributed as well. Confederate General Joseph E. Johnston, Pendleton's old mentor and commander, sent $100 from his home in Savannah. In early 1871 Pendleton returned home.

By 1873 the memorial fund was selling engraved images of Lee sold only by subscription and through authorized agents. Mrs. Lee decided that the statue should show Lee lying down as a sarcophagus and a cast of the work was done in plaster. Pendleton noted that "In its very impressive likeness to our beloved commander the figure is admirable, and the entire work, as a specimen of art, is in every way worthy of its great subject." By then the project had only collected $5,000 and still needed $20,000 more. He urged the ladies of the South to hold memorial meetings on Lee's birthday to collect funds. That same year he addressed the Baptist General Convention in Louisville, telling them that considering all of the circumstances Virginia stood foremost in its liberality. He was grateful to be born a Virginian, but was pleased to be in Louisville and wished the convention "a hearty God speed to the body in its future work."

Pendleton then stumbled into yet another controversy, this time with the assistance of Jubal Early. James Longstreet had been Lee's most reliable commander after the death of Stonewall Jackson. He had also been a groomsman at the wedding of Ulysses Grant well before the war. When the war ended Longstreet and Grant resumed their friendship, and Longstreet maintained close contacts with the Grant Administration and the occupying Federal forces in the South. By 1867 his allegiance to the Republicans was becoming clear and the vast bulk of former Confederate officers became critical of Longstreet. This criticism found a new field in January 1872 when Jubal Early criticized Longstreet at the Lee Birthday convocation in Lexington. Early, who had been a division commander with Ewell's II Corps on the left flank at Gettysburg, exonerated Lee of any failure at Gettysburg. Instead, he blamed it all on Longstreet's failure not to attack early on the second day of the battle on the right flank, and for his mismanagement of Pickett's charge on the third day.

The very next year Pendleton addressed Lee's Birthday celebration in Lee Chapel and expanded upon Early's allegations. Pendleton said that he explored the terrain southwest of Gettysburg on the evening of July 1st and reported to Lee that it was a more practical area for attack than the Confederate left. He then said that Lee "informed me that he had ordered Longstreet to attack on that front at sunrise the next morning. And he added to myself 'I want you to be out long before sunrise so as to re-examine and to save time." Pendleton made the early reconnaissance as requested, "No insuperable difficulty appearing, and marching up, far off, the enemy's columns being seen, the extreme desirableness of immediate attack there was at once reported to the commanding general, and according to his wish, a message was also sent to the intrepid but deliberate corps commander whose sunrise attack had been ordered." Pendleton then asserted that Lee "urgently pressed" Longstreet to attack and "manifested extreme displeasure with the tardy corps commander." Pendleton claimed that "All this, as it occurred under my own personal observation, it is nothing short of imperative duty that I should thus fairly state."

It is unclear what Pendleton was thinking when he made these remarks. At dawn on the second day Lee was focused on his left flank trying to persuade Ewell and Early to show some aggressive spirit. Longstreet's Corps had not even yet arrived. It stopped a few miles out of town for the night and still needed to come up to the battlefield once the sun rose. Most of the Corps finally reached the battlefield by 9:00 a.m., but parts did not reach the field until later in the day. It would have been impossible for Longstreet to launch a dawn assault with his Corps. Lee could not have expected an Army Corps to march in the pitch black for six miles only to be routed down unknown roads and deployed in the dark into unknown fields and woods. Pendleton said he heard these things or saw them, but they could not have been true. It should be added that Pendleton's recounting of events was contradicted by his official report written just after the battle.

Longstreet flatly denied the allegations. He was supported by nearly every officer outside of Virginia as well as by most of Lee's staff then living: Taylor, Marshall, and Long. Outside Virginia only Jefferson Davis and General Wilcox thought Pendleton could be correct. On the evening of the 1st Lee's right flank did not extend beyond Fairfield Road and it is believed that Pendleton ventured no further than that. Perhaps it was wishful thinking on his part. Longstreet was quiet at first but in 1875 he demanded evidence from Pendleton of the questioned order. He ultimately wrote articles for publication with the assistance of writers Joel Chandler Harris, and Henry Grady of the Atlanta *Constitution*. In 1877 he attacked Pendleton for interfering with the bombardment before Pickett's charge by removing a few howitzers from the line of fire. He repeated the denial in his 1896 memoirs. Since everyone else involved was dead by then he tossed in a few criticisms of Pendleton's conduct on the third day at Gettysburg and through the war as a matter of revenge.

Jubal Early realized he had gone too far and conceded that Lee only mentioned the possibility of attacking the Round Tops and that if he did so, would do it with Longstreet. But Pendleton could not back down. His aide Lieutenant Peterkin wrote that he did not hear the questioned order only that Pendleton told him later that Longstreet was to attack very early in the morning. Peterkin noted that there was a delay on the second day with Longstreet's deployment after the failure of one guide to Longstreet's column. Peterkin assumed the responsibility to guide the lead division to its jumping off point. Pendleton toured the South making the same allegation on a fundraising tour for the Lee sarcophagus and statue. At a speech in Mobile he wondered whether Longstreet, a relative of Mrs. Grant and the first Confederate to accept Radical largesse, may have turned into a traitor at Gettysburg. Pendleton claimed he had his version of the story straight from Lee's lips. Jefferson Davis echoed the charge in his memoirs of the Confederacy. The allegation became one of the founding tenets of the "Lost Cause" myth. It certainly showed an inexplicable side to Pendleton's character.

By 1875 the Lee statue was ready to be shipped. With Mrs. Lee dead it was up to Custis Lee to decide if the statue should be placed over the grave or over the vault. Custis Lee decided to place it over the vault at the altar end of the Chapel where it was later surrounded by Confederate regimental flags from Lee's Army. The statue arrived by canal boat in Lexington on April 17, 1875 where it was met by the Executive Committee of the association. After a procession from the boat landing to the campus it was housed temporarily in the Paradise dormitory (where Tucker Hall was later built). There it was stored until sufficient funds were raised to complete the memorial. Pendleton wanted a separate mausoleum but was overruled. An annex was built onto the back of the Chapel and a family burial vault was placed there across the hall from Lee's office in the Chapel basement.

The cornerstone for the Chapel annex was laid on November 29, 1878. A large crowd gathered, including General Joseph E. Johnston. Pendleton offered a prayer at the start. It was announced that $22,000 had been raised and $17,000 spent. They still needed another $5,000. Into the cornerstone went papers of the Lee Memorial Association, a copy of the letter from George Washington of his gift to the College, papers showing the election and acceptance by Lee of the College Presidency, a roll call of the Liberty Hall Volunteers, an article on the Lee funeral procession and a copy of Pendleton's controversial address on January 20, 1873 entitled, "Personal Recollections of General Robert E. Lee." Some additional Lee memorabilia and photographs were included as well. Pendleton gave the benediction and the crowd gave three cheers for "Old Joe Johnston." Jefferson Davis sent his regrets from his Gulf Coast home in Mississippi and expressed hope that in a hundred years "it will be more allowable for a Southern man to speak with free breath of the cause which Lee so effectively maintained and so well illustrated." He also referred to the prayers he heard Pendleton offer during the Peninsular campaign when they roomed together and slept on the same narrow cot.

*   *   *   *

As mentioned above, there was a crying need for a new church building for Grace Episcopal Church. It leaked in the rain and was too small to accommodate the growing congregation. Initially, Pendleton sought to raise money for an additional Sunday School room and a lecture room. He sent fundraising appeals to the Northern churches, explaining:

> The church here, of which I am rector, is at once very important and very poor....It was not, like so many other churches in Virginia and farther south, demolished during the war, but it was somewhat defaced and otherwise injured. Our people, however, are, as you doubtless know, crippled in means and unable to do more than struggle for bare subsistence, material, and spiritual. .....much more needs to be done, and the good people cannot do it. The church building requires considerable outlay for its actual protection, and more sittings are needed for the accommodation of the large number of students attending. ... But we are utterly cramped and crippled for want of means. The total ruin which has fallen upon Virginia and her Southern sisters is not imagined by persons at the North....Multitudes can do nothing more than just subsist, many are absolutely starving, and the limited number who, through some special adjustment of Providence, are in a condition rather better, have still to struggle very hard to maintain Christian worship and order, educate their children, etc.

In October 1869 Pendleton travelled North raising funds accompanied by his daughters Rose and Mary. He raised several thousand dollars during the trip. Another tour sent him to White Sulphur Springs where $805 was raised at a benefit concert. When he was finally offered a salary in April 1867 Pendleton preferred that the funds go to repairing the leaking roof, windows, vestibule, fences, and to buy stoves and lamps to promote the comfort and order of the congregation. Additionally, the Rectory was in a "ruinous state," and repairs were made by Pendleton on his own credit. In the summer of 1872 the vestry agreed to start construction on the entirely new church building. The old one was torn down and a stone structure begun on the same spot. The Depression of 1873 stalled work until June 1875 by which time the basement was completed. In the meantime services were held at the Methodist church in town.

*   *   *   *

From the time he returned home until his death money remained a perpetual problem for Pendleton. The need to raise cash for himself or his causes "keep me backward in my own writing." There was "so much to be looked after while means of subsistence are so limited. I must try to economize time." He tried to collect money owed him but ran afoul of issues lingering over from the war. In 1851 he bought a small lot on Chicago which he sold in 1859 taking in partial payment some thirty acres of land near Lexington and notes for the balance. When the balance came due in 1865 the debtor reneged and he was unable to collect. As late as 1870 he fruitlessly dunned his wealthy buyer. Still, he contributed to charity often. Money earned from articles he published were given to the Franklin Society of Lexington, and on one occasion he sent $100 in cash to a struggling church in South Carolina. In 1867 the Pendletons could finally afford to place a marble marker on Sandie's grave, a solid white marble cross six feet high.

Even though his salary increased to $1,200 in 1869 it remained in arrears. He wrote to the church that "You ought not thus to keep me in the dark as to what you might be able to do. My situation is so distressing as to deprive me of sleep. I am sued by different parties in consequence of your disappointing me so entirely. Unless you raise for me at least $500 by the 1st of October I know not what to do. I have no property that can be sold for any purpose. And if I had it ought not to be sacrificed, large and helpless as is my family, advanced is my life, and very small are my resources."

Pendleton sought a better paying situation. Just before Lee died he sent an endorsement for Pendleton for the job of President of St. John's College but by that the time it arrived the place had already been filled. Varina Davis, the former Confederate First Lady, suggested that Pendleton re-open his school for income and he did so. His daughter Susan taught the students with occasional assistance from her father. By 1870 there were ten students, a lawyer, and four servants living at the Rectory with the seven Pendletons. The census for 1870 indicates that Pendleton was a Minister of the Gospel with personal property valued at $1500, and realty valued at $5,000.

The health of Pendleton's son-in-law Ned Lee continued to fail. It was said that Ned took Pendleton as an oracle, except in instances of the use of whiskey and the subject of dinosaurs. Pendleton felt that anyone drinking no more whiskey than he did would be "safe enough." On August 27, 1870 while the Pendletons with Ned Lee and Susan visited Yellow Sulphur Springs for Ned's health. While there he collapsed on a walk and died of a heart attack. Susan remained in the Pendleton household after she was widowed.

Over the years Pendleton was happy to speak on many occasions and subjects. In April 1867 he delivered a series of lectures on science at the Theological Seminary in Alexandria. He promoted the use of textbooks in Virginia schools which were less prejudiced against the South than the Northern books then being used. In December 1867, in the midst of a cold snap so severe that the North River froze he spoke at the Franklin Society. In April 1868 he presided over the funerals of two college students from Maryland who drowned in the North River when their boat overturned. They were from Frederick and he had baptized them there when they were infants. Anzelotte remained busy managing the household. In 1869 her collection of flowers won the first prize at the Rockbridge County Fair. She traveled to see family, care for an ailing daughter, or to socialize. In 1867 she visited White Sulphur Spring with the Lees. On one trip she encountered a man who said he owed the Pendletons $205, sufficient to "pay my debts, enable us to live," and enabled her to send $10 to each member of the family.

     *   *   *   *

Pendleton remained very active in Episcopal Church leadership in Virginia. He wrote articles for the *Southern Churchman* and was an active agent for the Convocation of Southwestern Virginia. Locally he preached all through Rockbridge, Bath, Botetourt, and Monroe Counties. He also was active in the higher councils of the Diocese of Virginia for the Episcopal Church, over the years he was often selected to give the opening and closing prayers at the annual meetings of the Episcopal Council.

The first major issue facing the diocese after the war was whether or not to re-join the national church organization. With the war recently ended emotions were still too raw and bitter to contemplate such a move. When the leaders of the diocese convened in Richmond they initially joined the Council of the Southern Churches. However, the Council adopted the old prayer for the President with a local option for the bishop to determine when it should be reintroduced into the Litany. Bishop Johns had previously requested his clergy to use the old prayer, and Pendleton eventually did.

A year after Appomattox the mood had evolved, and the Bishop promoted a merger with the national church. Pendleton was once again the leader of the opposition to the merger. Yet when asked by the Bishop to be the chair of the committee considering the motion and to advance the merger, Pendleton agreed. As chair he brought the motion to the floor for a vote. He stated that since "the condition that rendered the separate organization of the Southern dioceses no longer exist, and that organization has ceased by the consent and action of the dioceses concerned," and "since the principles of the Diocese of Virginia are unchanged," it was proper, "under existing circumstances, to resume her interrupted relationship to the Protestant Episcopal Church in the United States." Pendleton made a "weighty speech" in favor of the proposal followed by his kin and former military aide John Page. The resolution passed with only nine clergy and eleven laity in opposition. Pendleton later commented that he accepted the reunion as "on the whole under the circumstances was the right thing…"

The next major issue for the Church in Virginia was whether it should divide into more than one diocese, or in the alternative, hire an assistant Bishop to ease the work burden on the Bishop. Pendleton wrote numerous letters opposed to the division of the diocese. He believed that smaller and weaker dioceses led to having smaller and weaker bishops in the leadership. At the May 1866 meeting Pendleton proposed hiring an assistant bishop and was appointed to the committee considering the issue. The committee concluded to hire an assistant bishop and postpone any discussion of division at the next annual meeting at Staunton. Once more in 1876 the Episcopal Council met and discussed the division of the diocese, either with a separate diocese for the new State of West Virginia, or whether the division should be between the north and

368

south. Pendleton opposed either suggestion but in 1877 West Virginia received its own diocese. The next year Pendleton served on a committee that rejected a separate diocese for the Southside of Virginia.

Over the years Pendleton promoted his belief in the Church's duty to pursue missionary activities at home. In 1866 he and his family went to the Hot Springs Bath where he gave a "fine sermon." At the 1868 Council in Petersburg he asked that every minister awaken a lively interest in the Church and make occasions for useful labors, including evangelical missionary work in their parish. He told the session that the ministry had lost much of its power "to do good," and that the laity needed to step in and assist the minister in his work. Laymen should go into "the waste places" and organize Sunday Schools and divine services for the people by reading prayers without violating the conservative principle of order in the Church. Laity could also be used to assist in charitable works. He proposed special collections for any missionary work. In 1869 the application of the all black congregation of St. Stephen's in Petersburg to join the Diocese was considered. Pendleton seconded the motion to give the congregation the support of the diocese and to admit it to the Committee on Colored Congregations.

Pendleton lived his beliefs, and went on the road promoting missionary work. He visited Bristol's new but poor Immanuel Church in late 1868. In May 1869 Pendleton gave the evening sermon in Lynchburg to an attentive audience. At the regional Convocation meeting for Southwest Virginia he was selected to preach the regular Convocation sermon at the next session in Liberty, and was appointed with another minister to preach a series of sermons in Botetourt County. He also served as a delegate to the Board of Missions of the Episcopal Church in Virginia. In May 1869 at the annual meeting of the Episcopal Council in Fredericksburg he gave a lengthy but fascinating report on the works at Grace Church in Lexington, stating that in the past ten weeks alone seventy-five students and cadets had been added to the congregation, many of whom had previously been wild and irreligious. During the address Pendleton spoke with so much emotion he had to occasionally stop to control his emotions.

Beyond this, Pendleton was concerned by the slow infusion into the services of a liturgy similar to that of the Roman Catholic. At the 1871 Episcopal Council in Petersburg, Pendleton offered a resolution instructing the delegates to the national convention to "bear testimony" against the "Romanizing" tendencies in doctrine and worship, and chaired the committee addressing the issue, and was put in charge of the committee on elections. The next year Pendleton spoke in opposition to "ritualistic innovations ministering to perverted doctrines" being used in some of the churches. Such ritual had not been adopted by the House of Bishops and was condemned and forbidden. He also felt that the round dances used in some of the rituals as part of communion were promiscuous.

The next year in Fredericksburg Pendleton opened the Episcopal Council meeting with a prayer defending the old ritual and services. He moved that the original voluntary Convocations not be replaced by Canonical Convocations and to keep the vestry law as it was without change. He prevailed on both counts. He also signed the committee report on ritualism confirming that church wardens and vestry do not set ritual, rites or ceremonies, and cannot introduce ornaments or décor into the worship services. Ministers must obey the Bishop's admonition and re-establish peace and harmony in the Church, and Pendleton defended the authority of the Bishop to issue such a rule. The Bishop ordered that services follow the prescribed ritual without innovations. There would be no change to the color of the table cloth for the altar or flowers. Pendleton loved to place flowers from his garden in his church but announced he would bow to the will of the Bishop and cease the practice.

To ensure that his views on ritual prevailed, in 1874 Pendleton took a "vigorous part" in the various committees working on a revision of the Book of Common Prayer and attended the General Conference in New York that fall. He rode on a "fast train" from Baltimore and went straight to the hotel where he remained a hostage to a heavy rainstorm.

Finally, Pendleton actively participated in proposed changes in the rules governing the vestry of the Church. He served on a committee considering amending the canon so that fewer vestrymen need attend to have a quorum for a meeting, and debated on the question of the right of communicants not contributing to the charges of the parish to vote for vestrymen. On this issue he lost, and the Council allowed anyone twenty-one and older or contributing to vote, not just the pew holders.

Pendleton also remained active as an educator. In July 1866 he declined an invitation to the Convention of the Education Association of Virginia to attend their annual meeting in Charlottesville as he was too busy attending to his pastoral duties. However, in 1869 he attended the meeting in Lexington where he expressed his determined opposition to free schools and his unhappiness with the views advanced in favor of it. He felt that the results of a free education elsewhere were proof that it would not succeed in Virginia. He drew a vivid comparison of the quality of education in Virginia between when it was free or paid. One of Pendleton's primary objections was that a free education must necessarily proscribe religion unless there is a merger of church and state, in which event it would be used towards political ends.

When he returned from New York in 1874 Pendleton gave the opening prayers and address for the "Teacher's Institute" for Rockbridge County trustees and teachers. He lectured on the study of English grammar, the power of the blackboard in communicating, arithmetic, and the defense of public schools at public expense. He was also elected to the Board of Trustees of his old Episcopal High School and Theological Seminary in Alexandria which had re-opened after the war. He kept close ties to the school he first established years before the war. In 1873 he was present for the celebrations of the Fairfax Literary Society at school.

*   *   *   *

In 1873 the old issue of the sectarianism of Washington & Lee University returned to the fore. There was a movement among some trustees and faculty to make the University more Presbyterian in outlook as it had been before the Civil War. Not only was this a danger to the future of the school, it posed a danger to Pendleton's fundraising efforts for the statue, vault, and his church. In a private letter to University President Custis Lee he wrote, "As General Lee's friend, chiefly instrumental in getting him here, by conveying assurances from the Trustees.....I ought never to consent to the appropriateness of his remains, his fame, the wealth he has secured to Washington College & all the influences therewith connected, by the single denomination holding the institution, in direct violation of the agreement that it should be wholly unsectarian, on which alone...he accepted the presidency." In another letter to Custis Lee he asserted that in seeking to make the school sectarian that six or eight of the new trustees had broken their pledge to keep the school non-sectarian, "and some chosen assuredly on that account alone, because other men every way their superiors were rejected and they lugged in." The situation was so serious that he was praying for divine intervention to stop the threat.

In this confrontation Pendleton argued that the Board's course would alienate Lee's friends, and "cause his remains to be removed, and throw the institution back to a mere Secondary College," a danger that did not recur until the 21st Century. He was so pained by the "extremely grave improprieties" that his doctor had "emphatically warned him against dwelling on the distressing subject, and forbade participating in any way publications on questions raised." In the end the Board confirmed that the University would remain non-sectarian which upset the local Presbyterians but pleased both students and alumni. By early 1874 the issue died down although there were occasional flare-ups over the next few years.

*   *   *   *

Pendleton continued to travel, whether on church, college, or other business. He visited with Joseph Johnston at the Rockbridge Alum Springs. During the summer of 1871 Pendleton experienced sudden and alarming "attacks." His physician prescribed absolute rest but Pendleton kept working hard as he believed it to be his Christian duty. Finally, in July 1872 he travelled to Halifax, Nova Scotia, and boarded a ship to Europe, his only visit to the Old World. Pendleton's expenses for the trip were partially paid by the late Matthew Maury's family and others. Pendleton took a "fine steamship" to Liverpool and made a short visit to England and France. He greatly enjoyed the sightseeing. At the age sixty-five he climbed to the highest point in St. Paul's Cathedral in London only to be told "you must be an American, only Americans make such foolish climbs."

He returned three months later on the SS *Peruvian* landing at Norfolk, Virginia. When he disembarked he was asked by a reporter of the Richmond *Dispatch* his opinion on the mass immigration coming from Europe to live in Virginia. Pendleton replied that the recent immigrants lacked a proper knowledge of Virginia and its climate. Nor did they trust land agents, the validity of titles, and the safety of investments. They were ignorant about the impact of blacks on the labor market since they "degraded other workers," or the extent of the business depression. Most of the immigrants with an education first made inquiries of their intended home. It was Pendleton's impression that Englishmen saw Virginia as being very similar "in tone" to Great Britain but without all of its problems. The elite classes in Europe were driving the middle class overseas. If Virginians wanted to bring in the best English immigrants they needed to educate them while they were still in Britain.

*   *   *   *

Pendleton's life slowed down after he turned sixty-five in December 1874. A few months later he asked the vestry of his church to retain an assistant as he was too ill to maintain his duties. He offered half of his salary as compensation. The vestry agreed but after a short while it was obvious that the church could not afford two rectories. In 1877 he once again asked for an assistant, and proposed the church hire an assistant. Pendleton was willing to give him room and board and a third of his salary but the vestry declined the offer. However, from that time Pendleton was limited to officiating only one service and sermon each Sunday, lectures on Wednesday and a communion service at VMI each Thursday. He also held services at Balcony Falls, Goshen, and Glenwood. He was assisted by young volunteers. His daughter Rose taught a black Sunday School class until the funding for it dried up.

As he aged Pendleton's influence in the Church waned as well. In 1881 he offered to substitute Lexington as the host of the next meeting but was called out of order. In 1882 the Council finally agreed to meet in Lexington the next year but later changed its plans.

*   *   *   *

Soon after the war Jefferson Davis and Pendleton commenced a steady stream of correspondence. In August 1867 Pendleton was hand delivered a letter from Davis by Washington & Lee professor William Preston Johnston, the son of General Albert Sidney Johnston, and a former military aide to Jefferson Davis. The letter, from Davis, thanked Pendleton for his visits to Davis' prison cell after the war, "The days you gave to me when I was a prisoner are to me precious and I trust not unfruitful." Davis referred to his "oppressed countrymen," but found comfort that God hated their oppressors. Davis praised the Confederate army as a chivalric and praying army. As to the unhappy ending, "It is true as you say that our consolation is that we have to the best of our ability done our duty…"

373

When Davis embarked on his monumental book "The Rise and Fall of the Confederate Government," in 1880 he asked Pendleton for papers relating to his service. In his work Davis wanted to illustrate events through comments from a group of the most distinguished military officers in the artillery corps. He asked Pendleton for the names of those officers in the Army of Northern Virginia and elsewhere in command of divisions, brigades, or battalions of artillery. Davis wrote that he had not "contemplated a minute account of the campaigns and battles as I knew that could, and hoped, would be better done by those who were actively engaged in them. I wish in general terms to correct some prevailing errors, and to do justice to some from whom it has been withheld, also to show under what great disadvantage we labored from want of the material of war, and some improvident waste of the little we had."

Pendleton sent a list of artillery officers as best as he could re-create, and sent Davis a "sketch" of the artillery corps. In reply Davis expressed his concern that Southerners were "now ready to surrender their birthright for less than a mess of pottage." Davis asked Pendleton to supply a summary "of our losses in heavy guns by the retreat of the Army of the Potomac and that of the Peninsula," a sketch of Gettysburg, and the conditions and possibilities of the "affair at Dalton," to which he meant the offensive plans Davis tried to foist on Joseph Johnston in 1864. Davis needed the material in six weeks, "I have devoted most of my time and attention to the vindication of our cause and conduct." Davis feared that since his writing assistant quit and he not being a writer his case would not be very well presented. He also worried that the government might arrest him all over again once the book was published, "for disturbing the harmony about which they prate."

Davis later returned two manuscripts as Pendleton requested. When the book was published in 1881 Davis sent a copy to Pendleton. Davis used Pendleton's Lee Birthday address excoriating Longstreet but did not use Pendleton's lengthy official reports as there was no room for them in the book of over 1,100 pages, but felt they might be of some use in answering expected allegations by critics. Davis indicated that "It had been my purpose to treat with gentleness any conduct of a Confederate which I could not approve and necessarily regretted." Davis also proposed that

Pendleton turn his archives over to the Bureau of Archives in Washington as they were of value to the military student and especially to any student of artillery. The government should be willing to pay him for the documents. In the alternative, Davis suggested he give them to the Southern Historical Society. Pendleton did neither.

Davis also asked Pendleton to accompany him to Europe to bring home Davis' youngest living child from college in Karlsruhe. The last letters from Davis in the correspondence include a happy anniversary wish in 1881, and acceptance to speak about Robert E. Lee in 1882, but that health forced Davis due to the heat of the season to offer just a written speech. Shortly before his death Pendleton wrote Jefferson Davis that that there could be no enduring good government in America until the dawn of "a far more thorough and prevailing influence of the blessed gospel."

        *   *   *   *

The years were piling up for Pendleton now and he must have felt the icy grip of the grave on his shoulder. In 1873 he buried Lee's widow and daughter Agnes, as well as his good friend Matthew Maury. Hundreds attended the Maury funeral in inclement February weather, complete with honor guards of students and cadets. Two years later his brother Gurdon Pendleton, also a minister, passed away in Wythe County, Virginia, at age sixty-six. John W. Brockenbrough, a parishioner, died that same year. Pendleton presided over the services and there were a large number of friends in attendance. The graveside services were described as the "solemn and impressive" service of the Episcopalian Church. When Professor Alfred Leyburn died, Pendleton helped to preside over his funeral service at the Presbyterian Church, which was described as "deeply interesting and impressive."

He continued serving his community. He gave the benediction at the VMI commencement in 1877 and gave the benediction at the Washington & Lee commencement the next year. Pendleton spent time gardening, tying up raspberries, mulching roses, and watering tomatoes. One day he attended the local court hearings for a murder trial and was overwhelmed by the stench of the country people in the courtroom which he described as being unendurable. He was asked at the last second to replace a debater at the Franklin Society on the question of "Is the division of the Christian church into sects an evil?" Pendleton took the affirmative position. He arose with his watch in his hand and gave a solid and cohesive argument for half an hour.

Pendleton wrote an op-ed article printed in the Richmond *Dispatch* on New Year's Eve 1878 touching on the labor strikes and violence in the North. Responding to an editorial in the *Church Journal* Pendleton stated that labor and capital must find a common ground even in Virginia, "although the truths urged bear more pressingly upon the crowded population elsewhere than people of this favored Commonwealth they are daily becoming more and more applicable to ourselves." He hoped that some legislator would introduce laws for the encouragement and protection of smaller banks where working people could safely deposit their small savings with the larger deposits of those who have more. This would bind together both rich and poor while relieving poverty at the same time. If labor feels invested in the security and growth of money then society could build towards the future without mayhem and riot.

The 1880 Census found both Pendletons at the age of seventy. Their daughters Susan, Rose, Nancy, and Hughella lived with them, as did a niece. There were two student boarders and two servants. When Anzelotte went on a trip that year Pendleton told her to linger and enjoy her company as their next visit would be in Paradise. In July 1881 the Pendletons celebrated their Golden Wedding Anniversary with a large party. Local poetess Margaret Junkin Preston penned a poem in their honor. (Appendix A). Despite arctic weather Pendleton attended diocese meetings in Danville with his daughter Rose. With the river frozen the canal boats were unavailable and they took the train by way of Charlottesville instead.

By the summer of 1882 Pendleton was prostrated by a "long and desperate illness." He suffered nearly total deafness and could no longer follow conversations or help in the pulpit. He complained in January 1883 that his memory was failing. Yet, when criticized that he spent time with "drunks or unbelievers," Pendleton had the wit to reply of his companion, "Poor fellow, he can't hurt me, and I may do him some good." The family acquired another Jonathan Darst home two doors down at 111 Lee Avenue called "The Pines." With Pendleton facing retirement it was finally time to leave their beloved Rectory.

The Pendleton family was still living in the Rectory in January 1883, a month that turned out to be unusually cold and stormy. With the chill there was a marked increase in sickness among the poor. On January 14th Pendleton preached as usual and then took a long walk visiting the ailing poor in town bringing them material for blankets or clothes. The next day he was unusually bright and well, and started working on his next sermon. At 7:00 p.m. he stopped writing and chatted with the family until 10:00 p.m. He led the family prayers and they all retired for the night. About an hour later Anzelotte called out for help as Pendleton was gasping and struggling for breath. He never roused, and died quickly. According to his death certificate he died of "old age." He was seventy-three years old.

His funeral was the first service held in the new stone Robert E. Lee Memorial Episcopal Church building. The vestry praised his service to the church and God by noting that "The last day, and almost the last hour, of his earthly existence found him still employed in the active service of his Divine Master, and he fell, as he desired to do, with his Christian armor on." He was buried in the Lexington cemetery next to his late son Sandie and grandson. Even after he died the undeserved reputation he garnered in the war followed. One of the Army of Northern Virginia's last field grade artillery officers, Colonel David G. McIntosh, wrote of him early in the 20th century, "He and his ponderous staff was regarded in the army as a sort of joke."

    *   *   *   *

The mourning Pendleton family moved into "The Pines" after his death. They built onto the front, added another story and raised the roof in order to house a school. Daughters Susan and Mary ran the "English & Classical School" there for years teaching Latin, Greek, and advanced mathematics with the aid of tutors graduated from Washington & Lee. The home still remains in the family although no direct descendants survive. It was there that Anzelotte Pendleton died in her sleep one day short of a year after her husband. She joined her husband, son, and grandson in the town cemetery.

Other than the widowed daughter Susan only his daughter Hughella Pendleton married. In 1885 she wed Edward Mile Gadsden, a Washington & Lee graduate who served as the Chief Clerk of the Post Office in Washington, D.C. He died there in 1900. Hughella died in Lexington in 1919. They had two daughters, Anzelotte and Ellinor. Anzelotte became an assistant librarian at

VMI and passed away in 1961 in Lexington. Ellinor became an assistant librarian at Washington & Lee and died in 1984 in Lexington. Neither ever married.

Pendleton's daughters Mary, Rose, and Nancy never married, which was not unusual for a young woman in the South after the Civil War with so many young men of their generation dead or maimed. Mary Pendleton decorated the Lee tomb in celebration of the installation of the Stonewall Jackson statue at VMI in 1891, and served on the committee to raise funds to save the Jackson home from destruction. The group agreed to acquire the house for $2,000 in 1905 from Jackson's widow but did so before they had raised any funds for the purchase. When they told Professor Henry St. George Tucker what they had foolishly done he handed them $5 and said, "well, here is a starter." Mary passed away in Lexington in 1918. Rose Pendleton remained active in the church, organizing the first choir, arranging Christmas festivities and decorations, and described as having "A natural music talent and she had a wonderful talent for getting children to do things." She passed away in Lexington in 1910. Nancy Pendleton died in Lexington in 1902.

Susan Pendleton Lee, as befits most Victorians, never remarried. She became a prolific writer of stories and histories, including a biography of her father. She passed away in 1911 in Lexington.

    *   *   *   *

As mentioned at the beginning of this book, William Nelson Pendleton has been maligned by historians in the century and half after the American Civil War. Perfection is impossible, and Pendleton had his flaws and made mistakes as did every other general in the war. His lowest point was his abandonment of the forces under his command after the Battle of Shepherdstown in 1862. At the time he was older, ailing, and had been on his feet or in the saddle for the better part of four days. Perhaps Pendleton should have shown more initiative in the Peninsular Campaign earlier that year, but he was hindered by the poor staff work performed by Lee's Headquarters staff and the novelty of the use of a reserve artillery force for the combat commanders.

However, history has forgotten Pendleton's accomplishments. He created the supply chain for the equipment needed by the field artillery throughout the war, and through proper management of his artillery corps ensured it was supplied as well as possible given the strained circumstances faced by the South. When Lee surrendered at Appomattox the branch of the Army still present and able to fight in large numbers was the field artillery. Any doubts on his accomplishments can be set aside after a comparison of the artillery corps of the two main Confederate armies.

Contrary to many historians, Pendleton could be an effective battlefield tactician. Pendleton's batteries at First Manassas saved the Confederate Army from flight by overcoming the superiority of the Federal artillery on Henry Hill. They also enabled Jackson and others to rout the Federal infantry. At Fredericksburg Pendleton and E. P. Alexander prepared the fields of fire so well that Burnside's assaults against Marye's Heights were hopeless. When Lee realized he needed a road quickly built after the Battle of the Wilderness to provide his Army with a rapid advance to Spotsylvania Court House, Pendleton accomplished the task in one day, building the road miles through thick pine woods and thickets. During the fight at Spotsylvania, Pendleton re-directed the artillery fire on the left flank to suppress the Federal artillery, giving the Confederate infantry an opportunity to repel the Union attack. During the siege at Petersburg he engineered artillery positions that kept Grant's huge Army at bay for several months. Finally, during the Appomattox Campaign Pendleton extricated his field artillery from the collapsing lines around Petersburg and led them in battle to fend off the aggressive Federal attacks until the last day.

Many of the "mistakes" the historians tend to pin on Pendleton are based on ignorance of the command structure, the function of field artillery, or the facts. As an example, it was impossible to deploy an adequate amount of artillery at Malvern Hill in the Peninsular Campaign because of the thick pine woods and swampy grounds. Certainly no one asked Pendleton to do so. Even if Pendleton had deployed all the artillery that day the overwhelming firepower of the Federal field artillery backed by the large guns of the Federal fleet would have rendered success impossible.

Pendleton was faulted at Shepherdstown for failing to hold off the Federals crossing the Potomac, but on the whole he performed well in the battle with the force at his disposal. Lee expected the Federal pursuit to be weak, and the initial probe by Federal cavalry was, in fact, repulsed. No commander in the Army of Northern Virginia could have prevented Porter's V Corps from crossing given his overwhelming superiority in firepower and Pendleton's unexpected lack of infantry support. Had Pendleton remained with his men perhaps history would have been kinder to him. Faced with an identical situation in 1863 Pendleton helped keep the Federals from crossing the Potomac after the loss at Gettysburg. At Chancellorsville Pendleton and Jubal Early followed the orders they were given. Orders are orders, and the fact that Lee's Chief of Staff Colonel Chilton was wrong did not matter. When the Army's chief of staff gives a specific order in the name of the commanding general it must be followed. By the time the correct order was received the heavier field artillery was too far south to recall as the Federals were already across the Rappahannock and advancing in large numbers.

By the time of Gettysburg Pendleton was no longer in tactical command of the artillery. His role was limited to making suggestions as to positioning of the batteries. He was not responsible for moving the ordnance trains on the last day, or for the failure of the commanders to appreciate the limitation of ammunition and capacity of the field artillery. Alexander was in charge of the Army's artillery for Pickett's charge that day, not Pendleton, although he and Colonel Long reviewed the positioning of the batteries. Alexander never requested that Pendleton help with the planning or execution of the attack.

Needless to say, we could spend chapters on the mistakes made by every one of the Confederate generals, many of them quite significant. Pendleton's few mistakes were, on the whole, not determinative of the outcome of battles or the war. While it is true that Pendleton could be pompous and verbose, and that he spent time preaching to the troops, none of this affected his ability to perform his duties as Chief of Artillery. Every Confederate general faced criticism from his comrades, much of it arising out of personal animus. No one, not even Lee, was exempt.

Many officers and men took exception to Pendleton's preaching. In an Army reflecting the very religious nature of its community the religious services provided by Pendleton were of great benefit to many in the Army. Lee, especially, enjoyed the religious teachings and comfort provided by Pendleton, and their friendship and companionship helped Lee to carry the heavy burdens of high command in a losing cause.

The time has come to re-consider Pendleton's contributions to the Confederacy in a new and better light. Maybe he was the easy scapegoat of historians because no one has taken the time to present his viewpoint in light of all the services he rendered. Certainly they made no effort to delve into how field artillery in the war functioned, how the command structure evolved over time, or the effort required to even create and maintain an artillery force in the field when the South lacked either the equipment and guns or the ability to manufacture the equipment and guns when the war began.

      *   *   *   *

Just six months after Pendleton's death, on June 28, 1883, the beautiful Valentine recumbent statue of Lee in Lee Chapel was dedicated. It was a cool but sunny day. Thousands took special trains to come from all over the South to be present, including many former Confederate generals and politicians. Businesses were closed and the town was all aflutter with the impending celebrations. The festivities helped to cement the Myth of the Lost Cause in Southern memory. That morning the proceedings began at Stonewall Jackson's grave in the town cemetery, not far from where Pendleton lay at rest. There was a solemn ceremony with flowers and wreaths placed at the Jackson grave, and a band of veterans provided military honors. The procession headed back to the campus and Lee Chapel where Susan Pendleton Lee chaired the committee of ladies decorating Lee's tomb with evergreens and flowers. In the middle of the decorations stood a Confederate battle flag made of flowers.

In front of the Chapel large stands were placed and seats arranged to try to accommodate the crowd of 8,000 to 10,000 people. General Jubal Early presided over the ceremony filled with prayers and speeches. The moment for the statue of Lee to be revealed came announced by two of VMI's old 6-pounder guns of the Rockbridge Battery which Pendleton commanded at the Battle of Falling Waters in 1861. As the cannons roared the Chapel doors opened and Stonewall Jackson's daughter Julia pulled a cord dropping the cloth covering the statue. That evening festivities were enjoyed by everyone, and the people of Lexington opened their houses to host their visitors.

There should be no doubt that William Nelson Pendleton was there in spirit as well.

Recumbent Statue of R. E. Lee

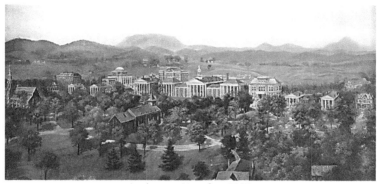

Lexington, Va. after 1881
(R. E. Lee Memorial Church to the left, Lee Chapel in left forefront)

APPENDIX A
POEM FOR THE PENDLETON'S GOLDEN
ANNIVERSARY CELEBRATION

Suppose the grant were given, - that you
Who stand amid the smiles and tears
Of friends who gather here to view
Your wedded path of fifty years.

Might backward turn the tide of time,
And in your youth and beauty bright
Might kneel as in your early prime
A Bride and Bridegroom here tonight,

Would you accept it?
Would you blot
That past with all its joys and pain,
And venture for, you know not what,
Another fifty years again?

Nay, that you would not! All the bliss
Of all your past is fixed secure:
A love troth as supreme as this
Is safe as heaven is, and as sure!

There might be less of cark and care,
There might be less of earth's alloy;
There could not – could not, anywhere,

383

Be more of life's divinest joy!

And what is care, and what is loss,
When the divided burdens fall
Half on each heart? Tis scarce a cross
When both together bear it all.

You have the best life holds in store-
Fair fame, true faith, contentment, love,
Children, and friends, and home, and, more
Than all, the heaven that waits above.

So I can only ask, as one
Who fain would twine my bit of spray
Into your wreath, God's benison
Upon your Golden Wedding Day?

By Margaret Junkin Preston

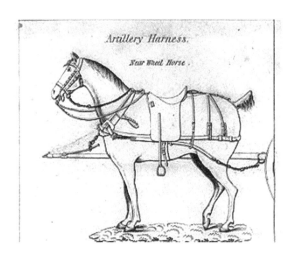

Artillery Harness.
Near Wheel Horse.

NOTES ON SOURCES

This book is intended for a general audience. The use of footnotes would have been burdensome for me and the reader. In the alternative, the sources primarily relied upon will be cited below.

The citations at the start of each chapter come from either the King James Version of the Holy Bible or the 1789 Book of Common Prayer of the American Episcopal Church. Pendleton would have been very familiar with both.

Chapter I: The sources on Pendleton's youth are limited. Primarily, I relied upon Susan Pendleton Lee's *Memoirs of William Nelson Pendleton, D.D.*, (J. B. Lippincott, Philadelphia, Penn., 1893), and on wikipedia articles on the Richmond Theater fire. The best source on West Point for the time period comes from Douglas Southall Freeman's *R. E. Lee*, (4 vols., Charles Scribners Sons , New York, N.Y., 1934, 1935).

Chapter II: I relied heavily once more on Lee's *Memoirs* and on William G. Bean's *Stonewall's Man: Sandie Pendleton*, , (University of North Carolina Press, Chapel Hill, N.C., 1959). The information on his military posts came from Wikipedia articles on the installations. The source for information on the state of the artillery came from Austin Howell's article *Weapons in the War of 1812* from ncpedia.com. My experience as an Army ROTC cadet at Washington & Lee University, and then eight years serving as a commissioned officer, is relied on for some of the commentary on command structure and tactics. The most fun I had in the Army officer basic course at Fort Bragg was directing, targeting, and firing 105 mm howitzers with the 82nd Airborne Division. Various Wikipedia articles were relied on for descriptions of the various schools and towns where Pendleton lived and worked.

Chapter III: I relied heavily once more on Lee's *Memoirs* and on William G. Bean's *Stonewall's Man*. Various Wikipedia articles were relied on for descriptions of the various schools and towns where Pendleton lived and worked. The source for the Pillow hearing is Allan Peskin's *Winfield Scott and the Profession of Arms*, (Kent State University Press, Kent, Ohio, 2003).

Chapter IV: The background on Lexington during this time came from my *Compelled to Fight: The Secession Crisis in Rockbridge County, Virginia*, (Mariner Media, Buena Vista, Va., 2009.) The story of the Blackburn murder trial relies heavily on Daniel Morrow's *Murder in Lexington: VMI, Honor and Justice in Antebellum Virginia*, (Arcadia Publishing Inc., San Francisco, Calif., 2013). Information on Pendleton came from Lee's *Memoirs*, Bean's *Stonewall's Man*, and the Pendleton Papers at University of North Carolina and Washington & Lee University. The source for Pendleton's book is the book, *Science a Witness for the Bible*, (J. B. Lippincott & Co, Philadelphia, Pa., 1860). Roster Lyle and Pamela Hemenway Simpson's is the best work on Lexington's architectural history, *The Architecture of Historic Lexington*, (University of Virginia Press, Charlottesville, Va., 1977.)

Chapter V: The information on the secession crisis comes primarily from my *Compelled to Fight* (Mariner Media, Buena Vista, Va., 2009) and *The Brilliance of a Meteor, The Life and Times of R. M. T. Hunter of Virginia*, (Kindle Press, 2021). Information on Pendleton came from Lee's *Memoirs*, Bean's *Stonewall's Man*, and the Pendleton Papers at University of North Carolina and Washington & Lee University. The information on the early days of the war are from my *Compelled to Fight*, and the Dr. Charles W. Turner series on the correspondence of the participants set out in the Bibliography. The autobiography of William T. Poague entitled *Gunner with Stonewall*, (University of Nebraska Press, Lincoln, Nebr., 1998) provides an excellent description of the early history of the Rockbridge Battery.

Chapter VI: Information on Pendleton came from Lee's *Memoirs*, Bean's *Stonewall's Man*, and the Pendleton Papers at University of North Carolina and Washington & Lee University. I highly recommend three books on the history of the field artillery in the Army of Northern Virginia: Edward P. Alexander's *Military Memoirs of a Confederate: A Critical Narrative (Illustrated)*, (Charles Scribner's Sons, New York, N.Y., 1907) and *Fighting for the Confederacy*, (University of North Carolina Press, Chapel Hill, N.C., 1989), and Jennings Wise's *The Long Arm of Lee; or, The History of the Artillery of the Army of Northern Virginia; with a brief account of the Confederate Bureau of Ordnance*, (J. P. Bell Co., Inc., Lynchburg, Va., 1915.) For the technical data I primarily relied on Jack Coggins' *Arms & Equipment of the Civil War*, (Fairfax Press, New York, N.Y., 1962.) and Wikipedia's *Field Artillery in the American Civil War: Confederate Artillery*.

Chapter VII: Information on Pendleton came from Lee's *Memoirs*, Bean's *Stonewall's Man*, and the Pendleton Papers at University of North Carolina and Washington & Lee University. Much of the military correspondence and orders came from *The War of the Rebellion, A Compilation of Official Records of the Union and Confederate Armies*, (United States Government Printing Office, Washington, D.C., 1880-1901) available on line from the Archives at The Ohio State University. For military campaigns I relied primarily on D. S. Freeman's *Lee's Lieutenants*, (3 vols., Charles Scribners Sons, New York, N.Y., 1943-4) and Shelby Foote's *The Civil War, a Narrative*, (3 vols., Random House, New York, N.Y., 1958). For the Peninsular Campaign the sources also included Stephen Sears' *To the Gates of Richmond: The Peninsula Campaign*, (Ticknor & Fields, New York, N.Y., 1992). For the campaign on the James River I also used the excellent book by Hal Bridges entitled *Lee's Maverick General: Daniel Harvey Hill*, (University of Nebraska Press, Lincoln, Nebr., 1961). D. H. Hill may have been one of the top generals in the Confederacy and a thorough study of his life is warranted. The story of the poisoned milk came from contemporary newspaper articles obtained on line through the Library of Congress archives.

Chapter VIII: The same sources cited above were relied on here for the campaign histories and all correspondence. Additionally, the best book out on the Battle of Shepherdstown is Thomas McGrath's *Shepherdstown: The Last Clash of the Antietam Campaign*, (Schroeder Publ., Lynchburg, Va., 2013) despite its focus on the Federal perspective. The best analysis of what happened before, during and after Shepherdstown is found in Hal Bridges' *Lee's Maverick General*. He has an entire chapter comparing the various versions of events and irons out the most accurate story of the battle. The story on the spy Pendleton caught at Shepherdstown is found in Edwin Fishel's *The Secret War for the Union, the Untold Story of Military Intelligence in the Civil War*, (Houghton, Mifflin Co., New York, N.Y., 1996).

Chapter IX: The same sources cited for Chapter VII were relied on here for the campaign histories and all correspondence. Additionally for Fredericksburg I relied on Jubal Early's *Lieutenant General Jubal A. Early, C.S.A.: Autobiographical Sketch and Narrative of the War Between the States*, (Philadelphia: J.B. Lippincott Company, New York, N.Y., 1912) and Millard Bushong's *Old Jube*, (Carr Publishing Co., Boyce, Va., 1955).

Chapter X: The same sources cited for Chapter VII were relied on here for the campaign histories and all correspondence. For Chancellorsville I also relied on Stephen Sears' *Chancellorsville*, (Houghton Mifflin, New York, N.Y., 1996) and Ernest Furgurson's *Chancellorsville*, (Houghton Mifflin, New York, N.Y., 1996). There are three excellent books on the Army of Northern Virginia's organization, status, strategies, and campaigns. They are Joseph Harsh's *Confederate Tide Rising*, (Kent State University Press, Kent, Ohio, 1998) and *Taken at the Flood*, (Kent State University Press, Kent, Ohio, 1999) as well as Joseph Glathaar's *General Lee's Army, From Victory to Collapse*, (Free Press, New York, N. Y., 2008.) even though their opinions on Pendleton are a bit misinformed.

Chapter XI: The same sources cited for Chapter VII were relied on here for the campaign histories and all correspondence. I also relied on Stephen Sears' *Gettysburg*, (Houghton Mifflin, New York, N.Y., 2003), and Jeffrey Wert's *General James Longstreet, The Confederacy's Most Controversial Soldier*, (Simon & Schuster, New York, N.Y., 1993). In this regard I recommend that you do not read Phillip Tucker's *Pickett's Charge*, (Skyhorse Publ., New York, N.Y., 2016) as the writer lacks any grasp of artillery function, tactics, or supply, and fails to understand the chain of command and the command structure at Gettysburg. Instead, it relies on *ad hominem* attacks without any evidence. For an excellent history and analysis from a participant I recommend E. P. Alexander's *Fighting for the Confederacy*, *supra*.

Chapter XII: The same sources cited for Chapter VII were relied on here for the campaign histories and all correspondence. Pendleton's mission to Georgia, which is not well known, is covered in Stanley Horn's *The Army of Tennessee*, (University of Oklahoma

Press, Norman, Okla., 1941) and Thomas Connelly's *Autumn of Glory*, (Louisiana State University Press, Baton Rouge, La., 1971).

Chapter XIII: The same sources cited for Chapter VII were relied on here for the campaign histories and all correspondence. For the Overland Campaign I also relied on Alexander's *Fighting for the Confederacy*. I returned to Poague's *Gunner with Stonewall* for his description of Spotsylvania. D. S. Freeman's *R. E. Lee* describes the incident at Spotsylvania with the Texas Brigade. The war in the Shenandoah is covered in Jubal Early's *Autobiography* and Bushong's *Old Jube*. I also primarily relied on Richard Duncan's *Lee's Endangered Left*, (Louisiana State University Press Press, Baton Rouge, La., 1998). The Hunter raid is found at my *Compelled to Fight* and in Charles W. Turner's article *General Hunter's Sack of Lexington, Virginia, June 10-14, 1864: An Account by Rose Page Pendleton*, (Virginia Magazine of History and Biography, Vol 83, April 1975 No.2). The Union perspective may be found at David Hunter Strother's *A Virginia Yankee in the Civil War*, (University of North Carolina Press, Chapel Hill, N. C., 1961).

Chapter XIV: The same sources cited for Chapter VII were relied on here for the campaign histories and all correspondence. For the Petersburg campaign I also relied on Alexander's *Fighting for the Confederacy*. Sandie's death is best covered in Lee's *Memoirs* and in Bean's *Stonewall's Man*.

Chapter XV: The same sources cited for Chapter VII were relied on here for the campaign histories and all correspondence. For the retreat from Petersburg I relied on John Gordon's *Reminiscences of the Civil War*, (Charles Scribners Sons, New York, N.Y., 1903) and Wert's *General James Longstreet*. Details regarding the artillery and Alexander are from Alexander's *Fighting for the Confederacy*.

Chapter XVI: Pendleton's one man war against Reconstruction is mostly covered in his Papers and in Lee's *Memoirs*. The retention of Lee as President of Washington College and the end of his life are covered in Freeman's *R. E. Lee,* Charles Bracelen Flood's *Lee, The Last Years*, (Houghton Mifflin Co., New York, N.Y., 1981), Ollinger Crenshaw's *General Lee's College*, (Random House, New York, N.Y., 1969), and A. L. Long's *Memoirs of Robert E. Lee*, (The Blue and Grey Press, Seacaucus, N.J., 1983).

Chapter XVII: Pendleton's fund raising and work at Washington & Lee University is covered in Lee's *Memoirs*, the Pendleton Papers, and Crenshaw's *General Lee's College*. His church service can be tracked through newspaper articles found in the on line archives of the Library of Congress. His last years are covered by Lee's *Memoirs*. The lives of Pendleton's family were traced through searches on Ancestry.com.

The illustrations come from the Library of Congress, in the public domain, or my photographs.

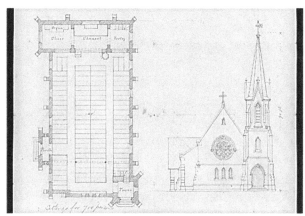
Drawing of R E Lee Memorial Church

BIBLIOGRAPHY

Manuscripts
Alexander, Edward Porter, Papers, University of North Carolina Library, Southern Historical Collection at Louis Round Wilson Collections Library, Chapel Hill, North Carolina.
Lee, Robert E., Papers, Washington & Lee University, Archives, McCormick Library, Lexington, Virginia.
Pendleton, William Nelson, Papers, University of North Carolina Library, Southern Historical Collection at Louis Round Wilson Collections Library, Chapel Hill, North Carolina.
Pendleton, William Nelson, Papers, Washington & Lee University, Archives, McCormick Library, Lexington, Virginia.
Virginia Military Institute Archives

Newspapers
Alexandria *Gazette*
Bristol (Va.) *News*
Central Presbyterian
Lexington *Gazette*
Phenix Gazette
Richmond *Daily Dispatch*
Richmond *Dispatch*
Richmond *Enquirer*
Richmond *State Journal*
Richmond *Whig*
Shenandoah *Herald*

Staunton *Spectator*
Valley *Press*

Official Records
1820 United States Census
1850 United States Census
1860 United States Census
1870 United States Census
1880 United States Census
Annotated Lexington Census 1870, Washington & Lee University Digital Archives, https://dspace.wlu.edu/handle/11021/27330.
United States Military and Naval Academies, Cadet Records and Applications, 1800-1908, ancestry.com, National Archives.
United States War Department, *The War of the Rebellion, A Compilation of Official Records of the Union and Confederate Armies.* United States Government Printing Office, Washington, D.C., 1880-1901, (ehistory.osu.edu/books/official-records)

Secondary Material
Bean, William G., *Stonewall's Man: Sandie Pendleton*, , University of North Carolina Press, Chapel Hill, N.C., 1959.
Boley, Henry, *Lexington in Old Virginia*, Garrett & Massie Publ., Richmond, 1938.
Boney, F. N., *John Letcher of Virginia*, University of Alabama Press, Tuscaloosa, Ala., 1966.
Botkin, B. A., *A Civil War Treasury of Tales, Legends and Folklore*, Random House, NY, 1960.
Bridges, Hal, *Lee's Maverick General: Daniel Harvey Hill*, University of Nebraska Press, Lincoln, Nebr., 1961.
Bushong, Millard K., *Old Jube*, Carr Publishing Co., Boyce, Va., 1955.
Coggins, Jack, *Arms & Equipment of the Civil War*, Fairfax Press, New York, N.Y., 1962.
Connelly, Thomas, *Autumn of Glory*, Louisiana State University Press, Baton Rouge, La., 1971.
Cooke, John Esten. *A Life of Gen. Robert E. Lee*, D. Appleton & Co., New York, N.Y., 1871.
Crenshaw, Ollinger, *General Lee's College*, Random House, New York, N.Y., 1969.

Donald, David & Randall, J. G., *Civil War and Reconstruction*, D.C. Heath & Co, Lexington, Mass., 1969.

Dowdey, Clifford, Ed., *The Wartime Papers of R. E. Lee*, Bramhall House, New York, N.Y., 1961.

Driver, Robert J., Jr., *Lexington and Rockbridge County in the Civil War*, H. E. Howard, Inc., Lynchburg, Va., 1989

Duncan, Richard R., *Lee's Endangered Left*, Louisiana State University Press Press, Baton Rouge, La., 1998.

Early, Jubal. *Lieutenant General Jubal A. Early, C.S.A.: Autobiographical Sketch and Narrative of the War Between the States*. Philadelphia: J.B. Lippincott Company, New York, N.Y., 1912.

Ewell, General Richard S., Official Report on Gettysburg Campaign, civilwarhome.com/ewell.htm.

Fishel, Edwin, *The Secret War for the Union, the Untold Story of Military Intelligence in the Civil War*, Houghton, Mifflin Co., New York, N.Y., 1996.

Flood, Charles Bracelen, *Lee, The Last Years*, Houghton Mifflin Co., New York, N.Y., 1981.

Freeman, Douglas Southall, *Lee's Lieutenants*, 3 vols., Charles Scribners Sons, New York, N.Y., 1943-4.

Freeman, Douglas Southall, *R. E. Lee*, 4 vols., Charles Scribners Sons , New York, N.Y., 1934, 1935.

Freemantle, Arthur, *Three Months in the Southern States, April-June 1863*, S. H. Goetzel, Mobile, Ala., 1864.

Foote, Shelby, *The Civil War, a Narrative*, 3 vols., Random House, New York, N.Y., 1958.

Furgurson, Ernest B., *Chancellorsville 1863: Souls of the Brave*, Knopf, New York, N.Y., 1992.

Glathaar, Joseph, *General Lee's Army, From Victory to Collapse*, Free Press, New York, N. Y., 2008.

Harsh, Joseph, *Confederate Tide Rising*, Kent State University Press, Kent, Ohio, 1998.

Harsh, Joseph, *Taken at the Flood*, Kent State University Press, Kent, Ohio, 1999.

Henderson, GFB, *Stonewall Jackson and the American Civil War*, Konecky & Konecky, 1937.

Holy Bible, King James version, Oxford University Press, Oxford, United Kingdom.

Horn, Stanley, *The Army of Tennessee*, University of Oklahoma Press, Norman, Okla., 1941.

Johnson, Robert & Buel, Clarence, Ed., *Battles and Leaders of the Civil War*, 4 vols., Castle, Seacaucus N.J.,1887.

Lee, Susan Pendleton. *Memoirs of William Nelson Pendleton, D.D.*, J. B. Lippincott, Philadelphia, Penn., 1893.

Long, A. L., *Memoirs of Robert E. Lee*, The Blue and Grey Press, Seacaucus, N.J., 1983.

Lyle, Roster, Jr., & Simpson, Pamela Hemenway, *The Architecture of Historic Lexington*, University of Virginia Press, Charlottesville, Va., 1977.

McGrath, Thomas, Shepherdstown: *The Last Clash of the Antietam Campaign*, Schroeder Publ., Lynchburg, Va., 2013.

Morrow, Daniel, *Murder in Lexington: VMI, Honor and Justice in Antebellum Virginia,* Arcadia Publishing Inc., San Francisco, Calif., 2013.

Morton, Oren F., *A History of Rockbridge County, Virginia*, McClure Co., Staunton, Va., 1920.

Peskin, Allan, *Winfield Scott and the Profession of Arms*, Kent State University Press, Kent, Ohio, 2003.

Rittenburg, Thomas, *The Brilliance of a Meteor: The Life & Times of Robert M. T. Hunter of Virginia*, Kindle Press, 2021.

Rittenburg, Thomas, *Compelled to Fight: The Secession Crisis in Rockbridge County, Virginia*, Mariner Media, Buena Vista, Va., 2009.

Robertson, James I., Jr., *General A. P. Hill, The Story of a Confederate Warrior*, Random House, New York, N.Y., 1987.

Robertson, James I., Jr., *The Stonewall Brigade*, Louisiana State University Press, Baton Rouge, La., 1963, 1991.

Robertson, James I., Jr., *Stonewall Jackson*, Macmillan, New York, N.Y., 1997.

Sears, Stephen W., *Chancellorsville*, Houghton Mifflin, New York, N.Y., 1996.

Sears, Stephen W., *Gettysburg*, Houghton Mifflin, New York, N.Y., 2003.

Sears, Stephen W., *To the Gates of Richmond: The Peninsula Campaign*, Ticknor & Fields, New York, N.Y., 1992.

Tower, R. Lockwood, Ed., *Lee's Adjutant; The Wartime Letters of Colonel Walter Herron Taylor, 1862-1865*, University of South Carolina Press, Columbia, S.C., 1995.

Tucker, Phillip, *Pickett's Charge*, Skyhorse Publ., New York, N.Y., 2016.

Turner, Charles W., *Captain Greenlee Davidson's CSA Diary and Letters 1851-1863*, McClure Press, Verona Va., 1975.

Turner, Charles W., *Letters from the Stonewall Brigade*, Rockbridge Publ. Co., Berryville, VA, 1992.

Turner, Charles W., *Mrs. Eckert's Lexington (1918-1929)*, McClure Press , Verona Va., 1989

Turner, Charles W., *Mrs. McCulloch's Stories of Ole Lexington*, McClure Press, Verona, Va., 1972.

Turner, Charles W., *My Dear Emma*, McClure Press, Verona, Va., 1978.

Turner, Charles W., *Old Zeus*, McClure Press, Verona, Va., 1983.

Wert, Jeffrey, *General James Longstreet, The Confederacy's Most Controversial Soldier*, Simon & Schuster, New York, N.Y., 1993.

Wise, Jennings C., Ed., *The Long Arm of Lee; or, The history of the Artillery of the Army of Northern Virginia; with a brief account of the Confederate Bureau of Ordnance*, J. P. Bell Co., Inc., Lynchburg, Va., 1915.

Primary Material

Alexander, Edward Porter, *Fighting for the Confederacy*, University of North Carolina Press, Chapel Hill, N.C., 1989.

Alexander, Edward Porter, *Military Memoirs of a Confederate: A Critical Narrative (Illustrated)*, Charles Scribner's Sons, New York, N.Y., 1907.

Chamberlayne, J. H., *Ham Chamberlayne- Virginian, Letters and Papers of an Artillery Officer in the War for Southern Independence, 19861-1865*, Dietz Printing Co., Richmond, Virginia, 1932.

Davis, Jefferson, *The Rise and Fall of the Confederate Government*, Da Capo Press, New York, N.Y., 1990. Volumes I & II.

Douglas, Henry Kyd, *I Rode with Stonewall*, University of North Carolina Press, Chapel Hill, N.C., 1940.

Gordon, John, *Reminiscences of the Civil War*, Charles Scribners Sons, New York, N.Y., 1903.

Longstreet, James, *From Manassas to Appomattox*, J. N. Lippincott & Co., New York, N.Y., 1896.

Moore, Edward A., *The Story of a Cannoneer Under Stonewall Jackson*, The Neale Publishing Co., New York, N.Y., 1907.

Pendleton, William N., *Science a Witness for the Bible*, J. B. Lippincott & Co, Philadelphia, Pa., 1860

Pendleton, William N., *The Chronology of Creation*, Quarterly Review of the Methodist Episcopal Church, Vol. 10 (Apr. 1856), p. 178.

Poague, William T., *Gunner with Stonewall*, University of Nebraska Press, Lincoln, Nebr., 1998.

Sorrel, G. Moxley, *Recollections of a Confederate Staff Officer*, Neale Publ., New York, N.Y., 1905.

Articles

Bloomberg, Arnold, *Fire! A Brief History of American Field Artillery*, The National Interest Blog, 2020. nationalinterest.org/blog/reboot/fire-brief-history-american-field-artillery-170756.

Claiborne, John H., *Personal Reminiscences of the 'Last Days of Lee and his Paladins.,* Southern Historical Society Papers, Volume 28., Ed.5.

Howell, Austin Gage, *Weapons in the War of 1812*, North Carolina State University, NCPedia: 2013. ncpedia.org/weapons-war-1812.

Krick, Robert A., '*A Stupid Old Useless Fool*,' Civil War Times, Vol. 47, No. 3, June 2008

McGrath, Thomas, "*Battle of Shepherdstown*," The West Virginia Encyclopedia, September 20, 2016.

Luse, Christopher, *Slavery's Champions Stood at Odds: Polygenesis and the Defense of Slavery*, Civil War History, December 2007.

Norris, David A., *Battle of Shepherdstown*, America's Civil War, September 2005.

Turner, Charles W., *General Hunter's Sack of Lexington, Virginia, June 10-14, 1864: An Account by Rose Page Pendleton*, Virginia Magazine of History and Biography, Vol 83, April 1975 No.2.

References on the Internet

Ancestry.com.

Antietambrigades.blogspot.com/2012/08/alexander-lawtons-brigade-cs.html

Battlefields.org/learn/maps/shepherdstown-september-20-1862

Beyondthecrater.com/resources/ors/vol-xl/part-1-sn-80/or-xl-p1-294-w-n-pendleton-art-anv

Bullrunnings.wordpress.com/

Civilwarhome.com/Pendletongettysburgor.htm

Civilwarhome.com/part3antietam.html

Civilwarintheeast.com/confederate-regiments/virginia/1st-rockbridge-virginia-light-artillery/

Civilwartalk.com/threads/antietam-more-veterans-for-mcclellan.185631/

Civilwartroops.org/1862-09-19-shepherdstown/

Comparing Grant and Lee: A Study In Contrasts" History on the Net, © 2000-2022, Salem Media. March 9, 2022 <https://www.historyonthenet.com/comparing-grant-and-lee-a-study-in-contrasts>

Encyclopediavirginia.org/entries/shepherdstown-battle-of/

EncyclopediaVirginia.org/Pendleton_William_Nelson_1809-1883.

En.wikipedia.org/wiki/Battle_of_Shepherdstown

En.wikipedia.org/wiki/Bristol_College_(Pennsylvania)

En.wikipedia.org/wiki/Caroline_County,_Virginia

En.wikipedia.org/wiki/Field_artillery_in_the_American_Civil_War #Confederate_artillery

En.wikipedia.org/wiki/Fitz_John_Porter

En.wikipedia.org/wiki/Fort_Hamilton

En.wikipedia.org/wiki/Fort_Moultrie

En.wikipedia.org/wiki/Newark,_Delaware\

En.wikipedia.org/wiki/United_States_Military_Academy

Episcopalhighschool.org/news-detail-heads--faculty?pk=901980

Fassbender, Michael, michaeltfassbender.com/nonfiction/other-nonfiction/lewis-armisteads-role-in-the-civil-war/

Headquartersanv.blogspot.com/2008/07/personal-recollections-of-general-lee.html

Jeffersoncountyhlc.org/wp-content/uploads/2017/10/JCHLC_BOS_Brochure_Digital.pdf

Justus.anglican.org/resources/bcp/1789/BCP_1789.htm

Noyalas, J. A., *Battle of Shepherdstown*, (2012, April 30), EncyclopediaVirginia.org/Shepherdstown_Battle_of.

Shepherdstownbattlefield.org/battle-of-shepherdstown/

The Civil War Day by Day: William Nelson Pendleton, web.lib.unc.edu/civilwar/index.php/tag/william-nelson-pendleton/

Valley of the Shadow, https://valley.lib.virginia.edu/papers/A1701

223, 224, 225, 265, 269, 282, 380,

Charleston: 27, 28, 78, 82, 276

Chattanooga: 109, 261, 277, 278

Chickahominy: 121, 122, 125, 126, 128, 129, 130, 145, 292

Chilton, Robert H.: 208, 209, 214, 219, 220, 380

Cincinnati: 53, 64, 65

Coggins Point, 140, 142

Cold Harbor: 292

Corbin, Kate (Pendleton): 197, 231, 264, 265, 293, 294, 301, 309, 312, 314, 342, 351

Crutchfield, Stapleton: 139, 187, 199, 202, 220, 223, 269

Custer, George A.: 254, 333

Darkesville: 175, 186, 230

Davidson, Greenlee: 179, 200

Davidson, James D.: 83, 89, 179, 200, 342, 345, 349

Davis, Andrew J.: 40, 58

Davis, Jefferson: 21, 24, 89, 93, 101, 102, 119, 122, 127, 129, 130, 132, 133, 135, 136, 147, 148, 152, 159, 172, 176, 185, 189, 221, 256, 263, 272, 273, 276, 277, 278, 279, 281, 288, 298, 314, 315, 317, 324, 344, 361, 363, 364, 366, 373, 374, 375

Douglas, Henry Kyd:56, 309, 311

Douglas, Stephen A.: 78, 79, 80

Early, Jubal: 171, 173, 206, 208, 211, 212, 215, 216, 220, 234, 264, 265, 291, 294, 300, 308, 324, 359, 360, 361, 362, 363, 380, 381

Edmundsbury Plantation: 13, 14, 26

Episcopal Church: 10, 15, 23, 31, 34, 35, 39, 40, 41, 42, 44, 45, 46, 47, 48, 50, 51, 53, 54, 59, 61, 62, 64, 73, 74, 75, 77, 114, 146, 185, 204, 266, 270, 302,

405

163, 164, 165, 171,
172, 173, 175, 176,
181, 186, 191, 204,
211, 230, 231, 252,
253, 254, 255, 256,
260, 264, 282, 289,
308, 374, 379

Rappahannock River:
12, 13, 191, 192, 193,
194, 197, 203, 204,
205, 206, 210, 213,
217, 218, 226, 262,
263, 264, 265, 282,
380

Rectory, 60, 79, 82,
83, 270, 281, 296, 300,
340, 341, 342, 353,
366, 367, 376

Reid, Samuel McD.:
60, 83, 296, 297

Richmond: 13, 15, 16,
18, 24, 26, 83, 84, 89,
93, 98, 102, 103, 104,
109, 115, 119, 121,
123, 125, 126, 127,
128, 129, 131, 137,
138, 143, 146, 147,
148, 157, 169, 179,
187, 192, 198, 200,
203, 205, 206, 208,
209, 211, 216, 220,
222, 229, 257, 258,
261, 265, 266, 267,
272, 273, 274, 276,
277, 279, 282, 286,
287, 288, 291, 292,
293, 294, 302, 303,
305, 314, 315, 320,

323, 324, 326, 328,
330, 341, 342, 350,
354, 360, 361, 368,
372, 376, 385, 387,
391, 392, 394, 395

Richmond   Theater
Fire: 16, 17

Rockbridge   Battery:
87, 91, 95, 96, 101,
115, 178, 189, 222,
305, 306, 381

Rockbridge   County:
57, 58, 59, 63, 74, 79,
80, 90, 193, 222, 339,
367, 371

Rugswamp Plantation:
31

Sedgwick, John: 205,
206, 207, 208, 209,
210, 211, 213, 214,
216, 217, 218, 219,
221

Sharpsburg: 9,   153,
155, 156, 158, 164,
172, 191

Shenandoah   Valley:
47, 53, 56, 57, 58, 68,
91, 93, 94, 95, 96, 101,
126, 147, 153, 186,
191, 230, 257, 265,
293, 294, 307, 308,
389, 391

Shepherdstown: 66,
90, 91, 153, 154, 155,
156, 157, 160, 163,
171, 174, 177, 179,
181, 182, 185, 186,